Mobilizing Youth

*Communists and Catholics in Interwar France*

# MOBILIZING

# YOUTH

SUSAN B. WHITNEY

Duke University Press

Durham and London

2009

Designed by Katy Clove
Typeset in Cycles by Achorn International, Inc.
Library of Congress Cataloging-in-Publication
Data appear on the last printed page of this book.

*Duke University Press gratefully acknowledges the support of the Centre for
European Studies and the Office of the Dean of the Faculty of Arts and Sciences at
Carleton University, which provided funds toward the production of this book.*

For Nancy and Bill Whitney

# Contents

## Acknowledgments

This book had its beginnings as a dissertation many years ago, when I was the age of some of the activists described in its pages and communism was a potent force in Europe. The project changed shape as I taught, aged, and thought anew about its problems and protagonists. Throughout the long journey to publication, numerous granting agencies, institutions, and individuals provided crucial assistance, for which I am very pleased to thank them now.

North Americans cannot write French history without financial support, and I am especially grateful to those who made possible the research, writing, and publication of this book. A Pre-Dissertation Fellowship from the Council for European Studies allowed me to investigate French archival and library holdings and reformulate the topic when my original idea proved unworkable. A Bourse Chateaubriand from the French government and a Marion Johnson Fellowship from Rutgers University underwrote eighteen months of research in Paris, while a research assistantship at the Institute for Advanced Study's School of Social Science provided the perfect setting in which to complete the dissertation. After I landed at Carleton University in Ottawa, an SSHRC GR-6 Research Award funded additional research trips to France and two sabbatical leaves totaling eighteen months gave me time to write an entirely new manuscript. This version was in turn refined as it made its way through the publication process at Duke University Press. Valerie Millholland supported the project from the outset, displaying the sympathetic professionalism for which she is rightly celebrated. Fred Kameny was the ideal editor. Miriam Angress provided deft guidance on a range of matters. Thanks go as well to the two anonymous readers whose stimulating comments vastly improved the manuscript. The book is published with financial assistance from the Office of the Dean of the Faculty of Arts and Social Sciences and the Centre for European Studies at Carleton University.

x    I extend special thanks to Dean John Osborne and Joan DeBardeleben, the centre's director.

There is little that is straightforward about doing historical research in France, especially when the subjects include Communists, Catholics, and young women. Documents and printed materials frequently end up in private collections or quasi-private archives whose guardians can be suspicious of young American scholars. I owe a particular debt, therefore, to those historians who helped me navigate my way. Father Jean-Pierre Coco opened doors to former Jocists and passed on private correspondence and then inaccessible archival materials on the strikes of 1936 used in his book on the anniversary congress in 1937 of the Jeunesse Ouvrière Chrétienne. Annie Burger-Roussenac arranged entrée into the world of French communism and shared material on Paul Vaillant-Couturier, the subject of her own doctoral research. François Bédarida, Annie Fourcaut, Patrick Fridenson, and Michelle Perrot helped me track down and gain access to sources, while Sylvie Van de Casteele-Schweitzer explained the politics of French communist historical scholarship. Siân Reynolds pointed me toward the CD-ROM version of the Maitron and generously lent me her apartment in Paris for an important month of research in 2000. During that time Laura Lee Downs offered much-needed enthusiasm for the project and ideas about sources.

Those connected with the youth movements examined in this book facilitated my research in diverse ways. Philippe Guilleman, president of the J.O.C. at the time of my initial research, put at my disposal pamphlets, newspapers, speeches, and reports contained in the Bibliothèque Historique of the Archives Centrales de la J.O.C. when the archives were in transition and partial storage. Reading these materials amid the bustle of J.O.C. life in the suburban mansion that became the J.O.C.F.'s headquarters in the 1930s gave me a sense of life in the youth movement that I would not otherwise have had. After deposit of the J.O.C. *fonds* at the Archives Départementales des Hauts-de-Seine in the 1990s, the movement again granted me access to its papers. Jeanne Aubert, the founding president of the J.O.C.F., shared memories and documents from the early J.O.C.F. and gave me a copy of her own just-published book on the movement in 1990. The photographs in chapter 4 are drawn from this volume, and I am grateful to Éditions de l'Atelier / Éditions Ouvrières for permission to use them here. Marie-Claude Vaillant-Couturier, Yvette Semard, and Juliette Plissonnier welcomed me to their homes and recalled for me communist life in the 1920s, 1930s, and 1940s.

Acknowledgments

Talking to these four women was a highlight of my research, and their stories continue to intrigue and inspire students in my women's history classes.

Librarians and archivists also provided important assistance. Special thanks go to Michèle Rault of the Archives Municipales d'Ivry-sur-Seine; Helen Solanum of the Hoover Institution; Jean Claude Lamezec and Catherine Bensadek of the now defunct Bibliothèque Marxiste de Paris; Elliot Shore and Marcia Tucker of the Institute for Advanced Study; Karen Lynch and Calista Kelly of Carleton's Interlibrary Loan Office; and Isabelle Widloecher of the Musée de la Résistance in Ivry, who graciously allowed me to read and photocopy the issues of *Jeunes filles de France* that had found their way there.

Writing a book in which adult efforts to shape young people figure so prominently has made me particularly mindful of the scholars who influenced me and this project. Philip Nord sparked my interest in French history and Third Republic political culture. While I was a doctoral student at Rutgers, John Gillis introduced me to social and youth history and commented perceptively on my dissertation, urging me to pay greater attention to the social history of youth as I took the project forward. Victoria de Grazia revealed the pleasures of studying interwar Europe and did much to guide my initial research. My indelible debt is to Joan W. Scott, with whom I began graduate school at Brown. During the project's early stages, she patiently taught me how to write a dissertation chapter and provided ideas, encouragement, and resources at critical junctures, most notably when she brought me to the Institute for Advanced Study as her research assistant in 1993–94. In the ensuing years she read and commented on chapters whenever they got written and offered advice at a moment's notice. Her unwavering support and intellectual example have made an enormous difference to this book, to my education as a historian, and to me personally.

Carleton University has been my institutional home since 1994, and I have gained much from colleagues and students. Carter Elwood and Jeff Sahadeo have aided me in my forays into Soviet history here and elsewhere, with Carter reviewing early versions of the Introduction and chapter 1 and Jeff making bibliographic suggestions for the Stalinist era. Chris Faulkner lent me French films of the 1930s and let me pore over his wonderful collection of French magazines, song sheets, and exhibition guides. Katherine Taylor, a former student and now historian with Parks Canada, contributed expert research assistance during the summer of 2005. Richard Bastien brought

xii   his translating expertise to difficult passages and Ian Bell and Marilyn Trew helped with technology. Aviva Freedman, then dean of arts and social sciences, and Pauline Rankin, then director of the Pauline Jewett Institute of Women's Studies, allowed me to take up full-time residence in the history department in 2002. My experiences teaching courses in twentieth-century European history, youth history, and comparative women's history broadened my perspective, as did my students' reactions to the material I was teaching them.

Friends and family have joined in the effort. In Paris, Brenda Clarke was a wonderful friend, even taking me in when I was flat on my back and none too cheerful. In New Jersey, Felipe Agüero, Gretchen Galbraith, Maureen McCarthy, Megan McClintock, Lisa Norling, Tori Smith, and Julie Shapiro did much to make graduate school stimulating and enjoyable. In Ottawa, Alan Cumyn, Joanna Dean, Suzanne Evans, Deborah Gorham, Mark Phillips, Ruth Phillips, and Pamela Walker shared the ups and downs of writing, editing, and academic life and publishing. So too have my brothers Jim and Doug, who read and commented on parts of the manuscript (Jim), shared life in Paris (Doug), and generally enriched my life. Ellen Furlough has suggested sources, talked things through, and done much to sustain me since we became friends in 1985. Rebecca Rogers brightened my early days in Paris and cheered me by e-mail in the later stages. She also read late versions of the Introduction and chapters 3 and 4, offering just the right combination of approbation and astute, yet manageable, suggestions. No one has lived this book more intensely than my husband and colleague Norman Hillmer. From the moment he came into my life in the summer of 2001, he has shared all aspects of this project—bringing his sharp historical and editorial sense to every version of every chapter, puzzling over translations, and joining me in contemplating French politics past and present. This book is a product of our life together. I dedicate the book to my remarkable parents and first teachers, Nancy and Bill Whitney, who supported me in the adventure from beginning to end.

## Introduction

Youth moved to the forefront of European politics in the 1920s and 1930s, but the ways this happened varied across the continent. As historians have demonstrated, Soviet Communists and Italian and German fascists pioneered techniques for mobilizing young people in the service of their political projects. Associating their parties with youthfulness and generational renewal as they built support for their movements, politicians in these countries made transforming the young integral to the establishment of new states and societies.[1] Despite differences in ideology and the roles ascribed to generational struggle, both fascists and Communists created party-controlled youth organizations, eliminated or undermined competing youth organizations, and restructured educational systems. Organizations and schools were used to impart new values, encourage new allegiances, and reconfigure the relationship between young people and the state and family. Youth became an enthusiastic builder of socialism and fascism, taking key positions in ideologically driven campaigns and reporting those, including parents, who failed to comply.[2] They were pivotal to the creation of new worlds.[3]

But what was youth's role in interwar France, where nineteenth-century political structures held on in the face of challenges from twentieth-century parties of the left and right? Here too youth became important to politics, although the process by which this occurred and the shape that youth politics took differed markedly. The most important difference lay in the degree of state involvement. In late Third Republic France the state played a minimal role in youth affairs. For most of the interwar period it did not sponsor or support youth organizations, much less monopolize them. The state involved itself more after the Popular Front government came to power in June 1936, as leaders intensified their attention to youth in an effort to demonstrate that democratic France could mobilize the young as effectively as other states could.[4] The government raised the school-leaving age to fourteen, bringing

France into compliance with the International Labour Convention of 1919 on the minimum age for admission to industrial employment,[5] promoted youth leisure and physical fitness, and created an aviation program to train young men to fly under the Republican banner. Still, the Popular Front government's efforts were minimal when set in an international context.

The nature of French youth politics was on display at the World's Fair of 1937 in Paris. A highly politicized event, the fair became a propaganda battleground where participating nations employed a variety of methods to tout the strength of their ideologies and regimes.[6] French planners hoped to use the exhibition to show that France, "like other nations," had made youth one of its most urgent preoccupations.[7] The final product was unconvincing. The youth rally, which would have brought 100,000 young athletes to Paris in a show of force similar to those found elsewhere in Europe, was canceled, the funds originally dedicated to this purpose redirected toward a popular accommodation center for visitors to the fair.[8] Fair planners built a youth center, which included a model youth hostel, a scouting pavilion, and an arts center, but events held there fell short of expectations. In the end the arts center mounted few spectacles and fair planners consoled themselves by noting that the leader of the Hitler Youth and the youth delegate from the Soviet Union had been impressed by the building's modern architecture.[9]

If the efforts by the Popular Front government to highlight its commitment to youth proved disappointing, other participants were more successful in demonstrating their dynamism. Prominent among them were Communists and Catholics, the principal subjects of this book. Communists, who had been the driving force behind the creation of both the Popular Front coalition and its parallel youth front, held a Rally for French Youth that displayed the Communists' approach to Popular Front youth politics. Combining bicycle and motorcycle races with political oratory and a procession dramatizing episodes from the French and Soviet revolutions, Communists drew an estimated fifty thousand young people to Buffalo Stadium in the southern suburbs of Paris. Thrown on the defensive by the Popular Front's electoral victory and by the massive strike movement of May–June 1936, Catholics similarly used the fair to assert their strength among French youth. Catholics staged the biggest gymnastic demonstration of the summer, the largest held in France since 1923,[10] and they controlled half the space at the scouting and hostelling centers. More strikingly, they attracted an estimated eighty thousand young workers to the Tenth Anniversary Congress of the Young Christian Workers, the Jeunesse Ouvrière Chrétienne (J.O.C.).

In three days of mass meetings and highly choreographed religious pageantry, identically attired young workers of both sexes demonstrated their
allegiance to the movement and to the Catholic Church. The congress was
the most impressive gathering of its kind during the fair, its male and female
delegates filling the accommodation centers built by fair planners after the
youth rally was canceled.

The World's Fair of 1937 highlighted the salient characteristics of youth
politics in France of the late 1930s: attention to youth was by that time intense but fragmented, the most vibrant efforts to mobilize youth originating
outside the state. By this date a large number of youth movements dotted the
fractured French political landscape. Young people, as French scholars have
pointed out since the 1970s, could choose between a variety of political and
religious youth movements, scouting movements, and youth hostel movements.[11] But the young were not simply joining youth movements in unprecedented numbers. They had moved to the center of political life and discourse. As the socialist leader Léon Blum announced in the summer of 1934,
"We live at a time when everyone assumes the right to speak in the name of
youth, when everyone, at the same time, wants to grab hold of youth, when
everyone is fighting over youth."[12] During the municipal election campaign
of the following spring, the eminent Communist Marcel Cachin told Young
Communist leaders, "Today, all eyes are turned towards youth."[13] Attention
to youth intensified during the legislative campaign of 1936, as politicians
shared platforms with youth representatives and published books such as
*Youth, What Kind of France do You Want?*[14] "Never," the Young Communist
secretary general Léonce Granjon declared, "had there been as many appeals
to youth at the beginning of an election campaign."[15]

How had French youth become a prime target of mobilization and a highly
prized political constituency by the mid-1930s? What forms did youth politics take during the two decades after the First World War? These questions
have received little attention from French scholars, who have tended to focus
their investigations on young intellectuals or individual youth movements,
often drawing clear distinctions between those movements that were explicitly political and those that were not.[16] This book contends that Communists
and Catholics played vitally important roles in mobilizing youth during the
1920s and 1930s and that their efforts should be examined in relation to each
other. During these decades both Communists and Catholics demonstrated
an acute appreciation of the possibilities presented by the young, who combined an energy, enthusiasm, and inexperience that could be channeled to

**4**  adult projects. Importing ideas, methods, and movements from elsewhere in Europe, Communists and Catholics created dynamic youth movements and competed intensely, often adjusting their strategies in response to the others' endeavors. By the mid-1930s their approaches to youth converged in important ways, especially in the domain of gender and family.

This book centers on the Jeunesse Communiste (J.C.) and the Jeunesse Ouvrière Chrétienne (J.O.C.) and their female branches, the Union des Jeunes Filles de France (U.J.F.F.) and the Jeunesse Ouvrière Chrétienne Féminine (J.O.C.F.), in order to analyze communist and Catholic efforts to mobilize youth and harness generational aspirations in France between the two world wars. Drawing on a wide range of archival and printed sources and interviews, it analyzes the movements' origins, their ideology and major campaigns, their styles of political and religious engagement, their approaches to male and female youth activism, their ideas about masculinity and femininity, and the impact that their oft-changing efforts had on youth politics. The book does not simply track the initiatives of the mobilizers but examines the responses of the mobilized, the young men and women who joined the movements and became activists.

Since political and religious movements create strategies and construct identities in response to constantly changing conditions, the analysis is set against the social, economic, political, and international developments affecting French young people. Special attention is paid to the context in which these movements operated and young people made choices, as the narrative shifts back and forth between the circumstances of young people's lives and the constantly shifting tactics devised to mobilize them. Thus it traces the impact of the First World War on the children, adolescents, and soldiers who became involved in interwar communist and Catholic youth organizing, and it details the effects of economic crisis on young lives and youth political strategies and discourses in the 1930s. It also travels beyond the borders of France to consider the impact on French youth politics of developments in Germany and the Soviet Union.

Although this book revolves around two youth movements, it is not restricted to their internal workings, however contextualized. It also examines the interaction of ideas about age, gender, and class in interwar French Catholicism and communism. This is possible, as well as necessary, because both movements intersected with adults and their concerns at critical junctures. Young Communists were deeply involved in party politics during

French communism's formative decade in the 1920s, while priests functioned as the J.O.C.'s central animators during the movement's early years. Moreover, both movements were assigned political and symbolic significance by adults, especially during the 1930s. My study uses the youth movements as starting points from which to consider broader questions about the place of age and generation in interwar politics. It illustrates how the generational tremors brought on by the First World War played themselves out in the political life of the new Communist Party and the religious life of the long-established Catholic Church; how Catholics pivoted their postwar overtures to the working class around its youngest members and how Communists assigned to youth an important place in antifascist politics; and how ideas about gender functioned centrally in communist and Catholic thought and practices. By concentrating on Communists and Catholics and analyzing their efforts comparatively and within a broad framework, we begin to understand the emergence of a new politics of youth in interwar France.

French Communists were the driving force behind many of the principal developments in interwar youth politics, and we begin by examining the politics of age and generation within French communist politics during the 1920s. From the foundation of the French Communist Party in December 1920, Communists made youth and generational appeals important to their political strategies in ways that other French political parties did not. In part this reflected the generational upheaval unleashed by the First World War, but it also had much to do with the intense involvement of Soviet Communists, or Bolsheviks, in French communist politics during the 1920s. Bolshevik leaders viewed young people as vital to communism's future. It was they, according to V. I. Lenin, who would build communist society in the Soviet Union.[17] It was they, as the historian Anne Gorsuch puts it, who would be the "guarantor of future social and political hegemony."[18]

Significantly for our story, Soviet leaders also recognized the importance of young people for the establishment and successful operation of an international communist movement. As Soviet Bolsheviks endeavored to mold communist parties in Europe and Asia into revolutionary parties that took their lead from Moscow in matters of strategy and organization during the 1920s, they devoted special attention to the training and promotion of a new generation of party activists and leaders. Young people were valued by Comintern leaders for their lack of allegiance to older forms of socialist politics and their willingness to embrace radical solutions often shunned by adults.

**6**   In France of the 1920s, Young Communists' enthusiastic embrace of hardline positions made them useful to Comintern leaders, who promoted youth leaders when it suited their purposes and demoted them when it did not.

The raison d'être of Young Communist movements was organizational. Starting in 1921 the J.C. was directed to mobilize the masses of young workers and educate them in communist ideas according to interpretations developed in Moscow. (This effort is examined in chapter 2.) Despite the importance of both the Soviet model and Soviet intervention, the context for French communist youth organizing differed dramatically from that found in the Soviet Union. In the Soviet state membership in the Communist Youth League, or Komsomol, conferred status, promised political, educational, and economic mobility, and put young people at the heart of state-sponsored attempts to create a communist culture and society.[19] Engagement in the French Young Communists, by contrast, put members in direct and sometimes violent opposition to dominant political, social, and economic values and structures. Except in communist-controlled municipalities, the first Young Communists were political pariahs who embraced some of the most radical positions in French politics and paid for the courage of their convictions with multiple arrests and frequent prison terms. Organizing communist youth in democratic France followed a distinctive course that has not been explored by historians.

Youth held vital importance for antifascism, the great cause of international communism during the 1930s. Recognizing that fascists had recruited young people successfully across Europe, Comintern leaders worked to do the same as they sought to forge antifascist coalitions in defense of democracy in the mid-1930s. French Communists led the way. Party leaders stepped up their overtures to the young and Young Communists transformed their approach to youth politics and organizing. Dropping their revolutionary posture, redefining their notion of youth, and embracing Republican traditions, commercial culture, and mainstream demands and ideas about gender, French Communists became the driving force behind Popular Front youth politics. By the fall of 1936 the Young Communists claimed 100,000 young male members. Young women, who had been marginalized during the 1920s, took center stage in their own organization, the Union des Jeunes Filles de France, which began at the end of 1935 and boasted twenty thousand members by the close of 1937. These developments constituted an integral yet understudied component in the history of the communist Popular Front (they are explored in chapters 5 and 6).

Catholics similarly put young people at the center of their interwar political strategies, and nowhere was this more apparent than in the struggle to combat communism. Unlike Communists, Catholics had worked to mold and mobilize the young for centuries. Beginning with the Catholic Reformation, clerics emphasized education, relying on primary and secondary schools to spread the faith and combat the church's enemies. The attention to education intensified during the nineteenth century, as Catholics battled Republicans for ideological and political supremacy.[20] After the Ferry Laws of the 1880s established free, secular primary schools and made school attendance compulsory until the age of thirteen, Catholics explored other avenues of influencing the young. They introduced a slew of parish youth groups, established a Catholic sports organization, and created a network of camps for the newly minted summer vacation.[21] Like others in turn-of-the-century France, Catholics paid increasing attention to those young people situated between primary school and military service, *les adolescents.*[22]

Clerics again looked to the young in the mid-1920s. The electoral successes of the antireligious, determinedly revolutionary, and increasingly class-based French Communist Party intensified longstanding concerns over the gulf between the Catholic Church and the working class, which seemed to exist outside the religious and moral influence of the church. Young workers were believed to offer more fertile apostolic terrain than their elders, whose long-established prejudices and irreligious ways made them impervious to Catholic overtures. Young workers were also thought to be well suited for more active roles in spreading the faith. At a moment when clerics realized that workers viewed them with great suspicion, socially minded priests hoped to turn to their advantage what Father Georges Guérin, who founded the French J.O.C.'s first section in 1926, described as young workers' "generous, ardent, and easily enthusiastic" natures. Within the J.O.C. young workers would be transformed into activists, even apostles, who would bring Catholicism to their fellow young workers and subsequently to the working class as a whole. Catholics hoped thus to avert communist revolution, a prospect that seemed all too possible a decade after the Bolshevik Revolution.

The J.O.C., which was the prototype for the era's Catholic Action youth movements, marked a departure from earlier organizational efforts in significant respects. (Its early years are explored in chapter 3.) Unlike pre-war youth offerings, and to the dismay of the many Catholics frightened by even the slightest hint of class struggle, this movement targeted only young workers. Moreover, it assigned to them the central apostolic role in the church's

**8**    mission to the working class. Not that clerics turned over all responsibilities to their young charges—far from it. One of the movement's telling features was the way its clerical initiators created the impression of youth self-governance while retaining important powers for chaplains. These priests, who usually were recently ordained, established and oversaw local sections, chose youth leaders, and developed the J.O.C.'s distinctive Christ-centered popular piety. Most significantly, they directed the effort to remake young workers by educating them in Catholic religious and moral values according to the movement's pedagogical command to "see, judge, act."

The attempt to forge a powerful religious movement of young workers that furthered the political aims of church leaders necessitated careful positioning of the J.O.C. in relation to parties and movements on the Marxist left, the usual political home of French workers. The J.O.C. was instructed to remain outside and above politics, and youth activists known as Jocists were prohibited from engaging in political activity, a prohibition applied most forcefully to political engagement on the left. As economic crisis deepened in the 1930s, the J.O.C. developed its own brand of political activism that focused on representing unemployed youth in the public arena and providing them with concrete assistance. J.O.C. unemployment centers found jobs for unemployed youth, served free meals, provided training and leisure activities, and distributed clothing and footwear. When unemployment peaked in early 1935 the J.O.C. presented its case to government officials and joined forces with Young Christian Worker movements elsewhere in Europe to organize a successful petition drive to the International Labor Office in Geneva. Faced with the élan and appeal of Popular Front politics in 1936, J.O.C. leaders defended the superiority of its youth-focused public activism over adult-controlled party politics to a membership largely excluded from the franchise (then restricted to French males over the age of twenty-one not serving in the military). It also focused energies on the preparation of religious pageantry suitable for an age of mass politics, which was displayed so effectively in July 1937. (These efforts are examined in chapter 7.)

This book draws on and engages with approaches from a number of areas of historical scholarship. The project is situated first within a larger discussion of youth that began in the 1960s. As historians have illustrated, youth is a particular historical subject. The word itself has a number of meanings. Depending on usage, it can refer to an idea or mystique, a group, an individual, a stage of life, or a cultural or political identity. All these meanings are socially constructed and therefore constantly changing.[23] All have a history.

The precise age markers that delimit youth from childhood and adulthood
vary in different historical and cultural contexts, as do the rites of passage
that mark entrance into and exit from this stage of life. Moreover, the group
of young people designated as "youth" changes over time and depending on
who is doing the designating. Finally, the roles and meanings of youth vary
at different historical moments.[24]

Analyzing the meanings attached to youth and the roles assigned to young
people in interwar France requires careful attention to gender. Although the
term gender has been discussed variously since its emergence as a category
of historical analysis in the 1980s, the approach here is to take gender to
mean cultural knowledge about biological, or sexual, difference. As Joan W.
Scott has argued, the creation of this knowledge is neither a static nor an isolated process; instead, meanings assigned to sexual difference are constantly
generated and intimately connected to politics and relationships of power.[25]
Examining gender in a study of youth politics entails demonstrating how the
apparently neutral categories "youth" and "worker youth" were frequently
associated with young men when used politically. It also involves interrogating the production of ideas about masculinity and femininity and delineating
the complicated and often changing ways that ideas about sexual difference
figured in political and religious strategies, practices, and discourses. Gender was vitally important to interwar youth politics, partly because youth
included young men and women for Communists and Catholics and partly
because youth was viewed as a stage of life in which gender identity was not
fixed but could be shaped, even manipulated, for political purposes.

One of the striking features of interwar youth politics was the Communists' willingness and capacity to alter approaches to gender as their strategies and circumstances evolved. During the 1920s both youth and worker
youth were coded as male, and a particular notion of masculinity, which
could be described as revolutionary virility, became woven into the Young
Communists' political identity. Youth activists believed that their toughness and willingness to engage in revolutionary violence distinguished them
from both adult Communists and Young Socialists. This gendering of Young
Communist political practice affected young women, who were viewed as
equals in theory but were assigned a marginalized place in practice. Within
the masculinized political milieu which resulted, the small number of young
women who participated did so on male terms.

When Communists embraced antifascism in the mid-1930s, however,
they dramatically recast their gendered understandings of youth and youth

**10**    organizing. Youth as a political identity was reimagined as mixed-sex and communist youth politics were stripped of their revolutionary thrust and masculine cast. Leisure became increasingly important, and for the first time Communists concentrated on reaching the masses of young women, whom they saw as especially susceptible to fascist and Catholic appeals. Young women were to be politicized along lines radically different from those of the 1920s, with sexual difference functioning as the organizing principle of the all-female U.J.F.F. that began to emerge at the end of 1935. Within this organization (discussed in chapter 6), young women were encouraged to embrace behaviors and forms of political engagement consonant with prevailing notions of young womanhood in France, including those found in Catholic organizations such as the J.O.C.F. The remaking of Young Communist femininity was not incidental but a crucial ingredient in the party's attempt to reposition itself as a more moderate political force.

Gender was no less important to Catholic strategies, although Catholic approaches emerged from distinctive concerns and assumed distinctive shapes. French Catholics had long been sensitive to what historians have referred to as a feminization of religion during the nineteenth century,[26] and interwar Catholics were attuned to the political value of public demonstrations of men in defense of the faith. In these circumstances the establishment of a strong movement of young men was vital in the fight against communism, it-self a masculine movement. But these young working-class men could not be accepted as they were: they needed to be taught new approaches to religion, sexuality, morality, and family. They needed, in short, to be transformed into paragons of young Catholic manhood, ones who honored Catholic teachings about sexual morality and fatherhood and were willing to struggle to spread them throughout the working-class milieu regardless of the ridicule that doing so might inspire. Remaking masculinity became one of the essential goals of the movement. As important as the male Jocists were, clerics recognized the importance of young working women to rechristianizing the working class. Within the all-female J.O.C.F., young working women were instructed in Catholic femininity: they were trained to remain sexually pure, to prepare themselves for motherhood, to resist the lure of dancing and the cinema, and to become religious activists whose efforts complemented those of male Jocists. (This undertaking is explored in chapter 4.)

Examination of the J.O.C.F. allows us to probe the impact of ideas about sexual difference on young women's religious lives and public activism. Any such investigation is indebted to the rich scholarship produced by historians of women and religion in the last twenty-five years. As these scholars have shown, women received clerical messages about devotion and activism different from those received by men, and they in turn carved out gender-specific ways of acting on their faith, in the process often stretching the spheres commonly relegated to women.[27] In the case of France these inquiries have tended to focus on the period before 1914, and to exclude working-class women.[28] An investigation of the J.O.C.F. permits us to explore how clerics faced with the challenges of the mass politics and mass culture of the 1920s and 1930s strove to sculpt female devotional practices and modes of activism that were both similar to and distinctive from those offered to young male workers. It also allows us to suggest how young working women responded. The entire endeavor was more complicated than might be suspected, as the J.O.C.F. offered young working women opportunities that were unusual for the time. Some of the female Jocists who later left the church and gravitated to the Marxist left still credited the J.O.C.F. with teaching them how to think, how to take responsibility, and how to work on behalf of the working class.

Because the history of Communists and Catholics in interwar France unfolds against the backdrop of social, cultural, and economic developments affecting the young, it offers an introduction to the social history of interwar French youth, a subject that has yet to find its historian. Although young people and their lives have not been entirely absent from the history of the period, those who have appeared have usually come from the élites. This is especially true of young male intellectuals, who have been featured in important studies of intellectual and cultural life.[29] These young men could not, however, have been less representative of their age group in a country where only a tiny minority continued their education to university. The number of young people in their teens who worked full-time vastly outnumbered those who continued on to secondary school, let alone university. Indeed, the French census of 1936 found that approximately 1.82 million young people under the age of twenty were part of the working population; this can be contrasted with 204,000 young people who attended secondary school in 1939.[30]

The young workers who constituted the primary constituency for both the Young Communists and the Young Christian Workers lived very different lives from students—lives that for the most part have escaped the notice of historians.[31] Most young workers entered the workforce permanently at thirteen, or twelve if they had received their certificate of primary studies. At

**12**   this point childhood ended and youth began, with an abruptness that could be devastating. Once in the workforce, young workers toiled long hours under difficult and often dangerous conditions. Although the eight-hour day and forty-eight-hour workweek were established in April 1919, they were not always observed, especially for young workers. Even the forty-eight-hour week held special challenges for the youngest workers, whose bodies had not fully matured, and they suffered disproportionately from industrial accidents. Neither young industrial workers nor apprentices benefited from significant age-related protections at the workplace, and they became victims of hazing and harassment. In his classic account of working-class youth in early twentieth-century France, René Michaud described how in one workshop, older workers welcomed young male workers by tackling them, opening their flies, and covering their penises with glue.[32] Harassment was even more explicitly sexual for young women workers, especially in factories. A female factory inspector reported that in one textile factory, male workers overwhelmed female apprentices and touched them inappropriately; elsewhere, she noted, "young women are hung upside down by their feet until they surrender and let themselves be kissed."[33]

Work was the dominant reality in young workers' lives, and Communists and Catholics attempted to mobilize young people around work-related issues. How the movements went about this was neither obvious nor consistent, a fact partly related to the complex relationships that young people had to work during this period. The interwar period witnessed the spread of techniques of organizing work first used during the war, and these practices affected young workers in a range of ways. Some industries, including sectors of the metalworking, chemical, and electrical industries, saw increased rationalization, which generated new classes of semiskilled jobs. Young male and female workers could be used to undercut the wages of adult male workers, complicating the movements' organizing efforts. A further complication was the range in maturity, work experience, skill, and earning power among the large group of young workers between the ages of thirteen and twenty-four. Within this group gradations of maturity and independence were generally recognized, with male workers under sixteen treated quite differently by their employers and parents from those in their late teens and early twenties. The range of jobs performed by young workers was also considerable. For all these reasons, the life of a fourteen-year-old apprentice *boulanger* had little relationship to that of a twenty-three-year-old skilled metalworker, but neither had much in common with an eighteen-year-old female textile worker, whose reality in turn was far removed from that of a thirteen-year-old domestic servant. The exact segment of "worker youth" targeted by the communist and Catholic movements shifted frequently, as did the demands formulated to appeal to them.

Lengthy work weeks did not preclude leisure. With fewer family responsibilities than adults, young workers were avid consumers of leisure. And during the 1920s and 1930s the options available to young people increased as leisure time expanded. Some pastimes were more popular with one sex than the other, as sport, both spectator and participatory, attracted more young men, and novels and romance magazines more young women. The cinema, dancing, and aviation captured the imaginations of both sexes. Young workers flocked to movie palaces to watch the latest French and American films, escaping the prying eyes of adults in the process. They also crowded the dance halls that had begun to emerge in the late nineteenth century, their bodies coming together in ways that scandalized adults. Young workers avidly followed the exploits of daredevil pilots of both sexes who competed to set records across the globe, many yearning for the chance to take to the skies themselves. After the establishment of paid vacations and the forty-hour week in June 1936, young people, including workers, were prominent among those taking advantage of reduced train fares and the cheap lodging provided by hostels to discover the mountains or the ocean.

Communists and Catholics incorporated leisure into efforts to mobilize and mold young people, their positions shifting over the course of the two decades. During the 1920s Communists attacked "bourgeois" sport and commercial culture as instruments of capitalist domination that diverted young workers from their revolutionary tasks. In the communist view, leisure had to advance revolutionary training and goals. Catholics also attempted to subordinate leisure to a higher purpose, although they worried most about the moral dangers of popular after-work activities. Both Communists and Catholics made greater room for enjoyment in their offerings to the young after the mid-1930s, when leisure time and opportunities expanded. The communist turn proved most dramatic: a youth movement that had been centered on workplace-based political and trade union activism became one built around neighborhood clubs aiming to entertain and educate. After the Popular Front reforms of 1936 the two movements strove to provide opportunities for popular tourism, including camping trips and excursions

**14**　to the ocean. Attendance at the youth congresses of 1937 promised visits to Paris and the World's Fair, the movements combining sightseeing with more serious work.

Since both the Communist Party and the Catholic Church occupied crucial places in twentieth-century France and have been the subject of very considerable attention by French historians, interwar communist and Catholic youth politics is not wholly unexplored territory. Beginning with Annie Kriegel's pioneering studies, historians of French communism have been sensitive to the role that generations have played, especially during the party's first decade.[34] Scholars have argued that French Communists are born twice, once biologically and once politically, with membership in a political generation being more important than membership in a biological one. Those belonging to a political generation, it is argued, are forever shaped by the line or strategy in place during their formative years in the party.[35] Historians have also incorporated the Comintern's use of youth radicalism into their accounts of the party's formative years.[36] But if the political meanings and manipulations of age and generation figure in studies of French communism in the 1920s, they are absent from accounts of the 1930s, when the adoption of an antifascist strategy put the spotlight on youth and transformed communist approaches to youth organizing. Communists helped push youth to the forefront of Popular Front politics and developed new strategies for mobilizing the young. (These developments are discussed in chapters 5 and 6.)

Little historical attention had been paid to the precise contours of communist youth politics during the party's first two decades. The one book-length study of the interwar Jeunesse Communiste was written by a journalist and former member of the student branch of the Young Communists.[37] Many of its interpretative schemata reflect long-established and now discredited party interpretations, and the book contains no systematic consideration of the role of young women or the importance of gender to communist youth politics. Making gender a central category of analysis, as English-language historians of German and Soviet communism have begun to do,[38] offers fresh perspectives on French communism, which has had its historiography dominated by French historians for whom gender is not yet an important line of inquiry.

The J.O.C. has been studied more extensively than its communist counterpart. We have a careful study of the movement's origins in France, a suggestive account of the congress of 1937 by two priest-scholars, and a jointly

written history of the movement's first sixty years, *La J.O.C.: regards*
*d'historiens*.[39] These works have much to contribute, especially concerning
the movement's distinctive spirituality, but they should not be taken as the
final word. For one thing, the interwar J.O.C. in *La J.O.C* is examined largely
through the prism of the group's self-presentation as a youth movement
governed and administered by young people. Yet it is important to acknowledge the role of clerics, especially during the movement's early years, when
young postwar priests worked hard to build the movement and transform
their young charges into apostles who could go where they themselves
could not. It is also important to insert the J.O.C. fully into the political
struggles of the 1930s, and to acknowledge more openly the movement's
moral agenda, which was more pronounced than French scholars, perhaps
sensitive about suggesting any ideological links with the Vichy regime, have
acknowledged.

Scant notice too is given in the literature to young women and none to
ideas about masculinity and femininity, even though both were embedded
in Catholic plans and initiatives. The exclusion of young women's specific
experiences from *La J.O.C.*, even after female militants had provided recollections and memorabilia to historians, so displeased the J.O.C.F.'s formidable
interwar leader, Jeanne Aubert, that she produced her own history of the
movement, collecting first-hand accounts from over eight hundred female
Jocists in the process.[40]

In the two decades following the First World War, youth took on and was
assigned importance across Europe, and this involved both constantly redefining youth and politicizing youth in all its meanings. Youth thus became
politically significant as an idea and as a group of individuals who could
be harnessed to adult political initiatives. How this happened in interwar
France is the subject of this book.

# 1

## The Politics of Age
## and Generation in French
## Communism, 1920–1931

Communism was born in France when a majority within the French Socialist Party, formally known as the Section Française de l'Internationale Ouvrière (S.F.I.O.), voted to join the newly established Communist International, or Comintern, at the party congress in Tours in late December 1920. In keeping with number seventeen of the twenty-one conditions for membership in the Communist International, the party took the name Parti Communiste, Section Française de l'Internationale Communiste (S.F.I.C.). Little else was settled about the new party, especially since the nascent communist movement attracted a diverse group of men (and a smattering of women) with a range of political, syndicalist, and socioeconomic backgrounds and divergent ideological outlooks. Remaining to be decided were the party's structure, operations, and relationship both to the Soviet-dominated Comintern and to French socialist and syndicalist traditions.[1] These matters were worked out during the 1920s through political maneuvers and battles involving the leaders of the Comintern, the French party, and the Jeunesse Communiste, which had demonstrated its enthusiasm for communism by joining the Communist International two months before the adult party.

Age and generation were at the core of formative struggles within French communism during the 1920s. The French party, like its Russian counterpart, was a young party.[2] In a political culture dominated by middle-aged and often quite elderly male politicians (especially at the top), most of the founding communist leaders were under forty, while the rank and file were usually in their twenties or thirties.[3] Communism's appeal to the young can be traced in large part to the generational conflict unleashed by the First World War. In the aftermath of this devastating conflict, a broad spectrum of men drew on generational thinking to articulate social and political identities, with some viewing communist revolution as the best way to replace a world forever discredited by war. Embittered veterans attacked older politicians for sacrificing a generation on the battlefields of Europe, while men who had been too young to fight but who had come of age during the upheavals of the war and the immediate postwar years positioned themselves at the forefront of revolutionary activism. Comintern leaders appealed to these generational aspirations and resentments when it suited their purposes, and attempted to defuse them when it did not. Generational politics and youth—as an idea and a group forged in particular circumstances—became embedded in French communism's formative struggles. The manner in which this happened is the subject of this chapter.

For most of the 1920s the politics of generation within French communism pivoted around the relationship between the youth cohort in charge of the Jeunesse Communiste and Comintern leaders in Moscow. Seeing themselves as a virile, revolutionary youth cohort, J.C. leaders claimed for themselves a vanguard role in the construction of French communism. Comintern leaders appreciated the possibilities presented by this self-consciously radical and relatively unformed cohort as they worked to forge a French party in the image of the Russian one. At key moments during the decade Comintern leaders enlisted J.C. support for unpopular positions and approaches. This strategy involved a tacit alliance between Comintern and J.C. leaders, and it resulted in the promotion of J.C. militants within the party and, to a lesser extent, the international communist movement. Although the alliance often benefited individual J.C. activists, it had negative effects on the J.C. as a whole. The organization was required to mute its age-based identity and subordinate itself firmly to Comintern leadership. And although the J.C. was allowed an important role within French communism when it was advantageous to the Comintern for it to have one, the establishment of Comintern control within the party meant that independent youth action was no longer necessary and hence no longer tolerated. By the early 1930s the J.C. existed only as a subgroup of a firmly class-based, bolshevized party, confined to the organization and education of working youth.

**Age, Generation, and the Great War** To understand the politics of age and generation within French communism during the 1920s, it is necessary to begin with the First World War. Four years of war reconfigured the generational landscape in France by altering understandings of youth, creating generational identifications and resentments, and upending the lives of young people. These developments had significant consequences for both communist and Catholic youth politics throughout the interwar period.

The war's impact on issues related to age and generation was far-reaching and complex. Although obligatory military service, which was established in 1889 and divided the male population into military classes according to dates of birth, had already encouraged age-based identification among French young men, the Great War greatly accelerated this process. The French war effort brought together larger, more diverse groups of men than ever before, with France mobilizing a higher proportion of its eligible male population than any belligerent country except Serbia.[4] By war's end 7,800,000 of the 9,697,000 men from the military classes of 1887 to 1919 had been incorporated into the French armed forces.[5]

Between August 1914 and November 1918 teachers, university students, industrial workers, white-collar workers, peasants, priests, and colonial subjects were thrown together in what quickly became a horrific and lengthy ordeal. After initial battles that pushed the French Army to the brink of defeat, the two sides dug themselves into positions that remained relatively unchanged until the war's conclusion. From trenches snaking their way from Belgium through northern and eastern France to the frontier of Switzerland, soldiers experienced a new kind of warfare, one that often approximated hell on earth. During ferocious and seemingly futile battles on the western front, soldiers were met by a deadly array of weapons which assaulted men's bodies in unprecedented ways, resulting in "mass corporeal destruction," agonizing death, and high mortality rates.[6] When the conflict was over, more than 40 percent of the nearly eight million mobilized men had been wounded at least once and 16.8 percent had lost their lives.[7] An additional 1,118,000 men returned home permanently disabled.[8] Those who died came disproportionately from the younger military classes, with the classes of 1911, 1912, and 1913 suffering losses of 25 percent or more and the class of 1915 losing 27.8 percent.[9]

Definitions of youth were among the first to be affected by the conflict. Before the war broke out in August 1914, the group designated by the term "youth" was generally limited to male intellectuals. Other young people fell outside this category, and were described by such terms as young worker, young woman or juvenile delinquent. Thus the much discussed survey "Young People of Today" ("Les Jeunes Gens d'Aujourd'hui," 1912), by "Agathon," provided a portrait of the younger generation based on surveys of male university students between the ages of eighteen and twenty-five.[10]

But after war and seven or eight consecutive years of military service for some young men, previous ideas about the outer age limit of youth no longer seemed relevant. During a debate in April 1919 in the Chamber of Deputies over the conditions under which students who had been mobilized during their studies could return to university, Deputy Bouffandeau noted, "When we say 'youth,' alas, there's a certain irony in our words because, at the present time, we are talking about students who are almost thirty, students who waged war for five years."[11]

It was not only the age parameters of youth that had been disrupted. Another of the war's consequences was to bring ideas of generational identification to a larger segment of males. Between 1912 and 1927, as Robert Wohl argues in his classic study *The Generation of 1914*, distinct groups of French men who were relatively close in age all defined themselves in relation to the war, but they did so differently. There was, as Wohl notes, a piling up of generations.[12] Although Wohl's generations are primarily literary and exclusively male, the process of generational formation that he describes and the age-based cohorts that he identifies have broader significance. Wohl identifies three generations within the larger "generation of 1914." The first included men who had already established themselves or were close to being established before they were called to the front, and its members interpreted the war's effects very differently from those who were younger. Although these older men were profoundly marked by the war, they returned home as survivors who insisted on resuming their pre-war lives.

The war had a transformative impact on the second war generation, whose members were born in the 1890s and whose military classes suffered the highest losses. As the war ground on, these men became increasingly angry at the men and women on the home front, who they believed either profited from their misfortunes or had little understanding of their plight.[13] Having been mobilized while still in their youth, those who returned home did so as angry young-old men alienated both from the society around them and from more established veterans. These men blamed older politicians for sacrificing their generation and for robbing the survivors of their youth. The men's generational despair and resentment crossed national and class boundaries and was expressed with especial vigor in the phenomenally successful novel *All Quiet on the Western Front* (1928), by the German Erich Maria Remarque (born 1898).[14] At the end of the novel Remarque lamented: "men will not understand us—for the generation that grew up before us . . . will return to its old occupation, and the war will be forgotten—and the generation

Age and Generation in French Communism

**20**   that has grown up after us will be strange to us and push us aside. We will be superfluous even to ourselves, we will grow older, a few will adapt themselves, some others will merely submit, and most will be bewildered; the years will pass by and in the end we shall fall into ruin."[15] If some members of this war generation retreated into despair, others were determined to work for change in order to prevent a similar catastrophe from happening again. As the Frenchman François Colt de Wolf wrote from America in the fall of 1919, "The old must no longer send the young to their death. 'Big words' must no longer be used to wipe out a country's youth."[16]

The generational anger of this group of veterans took a range of political forms in Europe. In France some members of this cohort found their way to communism. Paul Vaillant-Couturier and Raymond Lefebvre typify the veterans whose lives and political outlooks were upended by their wartime experiences and who ended up on the revolutionary left. Born in the early 1890s to middle-class, Protestant families, these men were religious, and they became friends during their years at *lycée*.[17] Both were mobilized in August 1914, both served with distinction (with Vaillant-Couturier receiving the Croix de Guerre), and both were wounded. Like other members of their cohort, they were politicized by their experiences at the front. Lefebvre explained in the summer of 1916: "I have no difficulty in saying that it's the war which made me join the Socialist Party. I suffered; I watched others suffer even more. It's our duty to act from now on."[18] These self-described *nés de la guerre* moved from revolt against the war and support for pacifism to a belief in the need for revolution and, more particularly, a revolution along Bolshevik lines. During this journey Vaillant-Couturier and Lefebvre helped found the veterans' organization the Association Républicaine des Anciens Combattants (A.R.A.C.) in November 1917. They were also important to the foundation of the journal *Clarté*, which, as the celebrated war author Henri Barbusse announced in its first editorial, advocated the destruction of the old world and its replacement by a new one.[19]

Once Vaillant-Couturier and Lefebvre became convinced of the need for revolution, they participated actively in the campaign within the s.f.i.o. in favor of membership in the Communist International. During party debates these veterans presented themselves as a younger, sacrificed generation whose support for communist revolution was inextricable from their hostility toward the older politicians responsible for the war, and framed as a desire for generational renewal. Putting themselves forward as spokesmen for their generation, Vaillant-Couturier and Lefebvre accused the older

Socialists of betraying a generation of men by abandoning their interna-
tionalist principles and sending soldiers to fight the most terrible of wars.
Vaillant-Couturier described his fellow Socialists in stinging terms at the
s.f.i.o. party congress in February 1920, "Many of them are old, old as Clem-
enceau. They belonged to the generation that sent us to the trenches . . . and
stayed in Bordeaux. They're still alive and holding the reins. France is ruled
by its old men. That's what we are fighting today, here, at the Chamber, everywhere: the dictatorship of terrible old men [*la dictature des vieillards*]."[20]

For these veterans only a new revolutionary party with a different,
younger leadership would be acceptable, and the Section Française de
l'Internationale Communiste (s.f.i.c.) corresponded to their desire for a
party open to younger men. When the majority within the s.f.i.o. voted to
join the Communist International, older elected officials were more likely
to remain with the old party; of the sixty-eight s.f.i.o. deputies elected in
1920, only a dozen changed their allegiance to the Communist Party.[21] At the
local level, men in their twenties and thirties predominated within the new
party, both in the leadership and in the rank and file.[22] Once part of the
s.f.i.c., this cohort of veterans (minus Lefebvre, who disappeared in the
fall of 1920 while returning from the Soviet Union) assumed a vastly altered
position. No longer removed from the centers of power and authority, its
members were counted among the party's collective leadership. From this
position they worked within the Comintern-backed left to construct a party
consistent with their revolutionary ideals.

With this group of veterans at the center of the new party, the locus of generational conflict within French communism shifted to the Jeunesse Communiste, whose first generation of leaders came from the ranks of young
males who had been too young to fight but had come of age politically during
the war and the immediate postwar years. Young male workers formed the
core of this group, and their experiences will be explored in greater detail.
The lives of young male workers in unoccupied France were marked by a
new wartime organization of labor and the absence of older French-born
male workers from workplaces, neighborhoods, and working-class organizations. Once it became clear that the war would not be a short one, government officials and industrialists faced the task of maximizing production,
especially of war matériel, despite the absence of large numbers of adult
male workers. The government recalled skilled workers (500,000 servicemen were sent back to factories by the end of 1915), and employers recruited
heavily among foreign male workers, French-born male workers too young

for military service, and female workers. The composition of the industrial workforce changed drastically within a short period. Employers also reorganized the production process by remaking the work space, introducing the assembly line, and creating new semiskilled jobs.[23]

Wartime alterations had significant consequences for young male workers. Although the war did not bring working-class adolescent males into the workforce, it allowed them to move into well-paid jobs, skilled or semiskilled, more rapidly than in peacetime. Many of the J.C.'s leading figures between 1920 and 1928, including Maurice Laporte, Henri Barbé, and Jacques Doriot, were skilled metalworkers in wartime munitions factories.[24] There young men were able to assume positions of power and authority at the workplace not normally allowed to adolescent males. In this wartime world turned upside down, they sometimes had the run of factories. Barbé, an adolescent wartime munitions worker in the Paris suburb of Saint-Denis, recalled that a "reign of youth, of adolescence" existed in his factory, where male workers between fifteen and eighteen became little despots whose authority female workers contested.[25] That this adolescent power was exercised over women contributed to the masculine cast of this emerging group.

The unusual authority of male adolescents was not limited to the workplace but extended to the working-class community through the Jeunesse Socialiste (J.S.). Founded in 1912, the J.S. numbered only two thousand members when war began in August 1914. The war years brought an influx of members to the organization, especially among young workers; by early 1920 the J.S. claimed eight thousand members.[26] The J.S. grew not simply in size but also in influence. In the absence of so many men at the front, local Young Socialist groups assumed the functions of depleted socialist organizations. In the socialist stronghold of Saint-Denis, the J.S. became the organization that coordinated aid for soldiers and strikers, and for their families. According to Barbé, it also became the organization through which mounting discontent with the war could be expressed.[27] These young men's wartime status in the factory and working-class community shaped their generational identity.

Involvement in the labor struggles that rocked France between 1917 and 1920 further stimulated their generational consciousness. During this period of often intense industrial conflict, some young male workers began to constitute themselves as a determinedly anti-reformist and pro-revolutionary generation. The economic demands of total war were heavy, and initial support for the *union sacrée* gave way to discontent on the part of many workers as the war continued. Long hours, often dangerous conditions, and shortages of food and coal took their toll on workers' morale. By the unusually cold winter of 1916–17, individual and collective protests became more frequent and involved future Young Communists. Maurice Laporte (born 1901), who was instrumental in founding the J.C. and served as its secretary general from 1921 to 1923, first came to the attention of French police in 1917, when he led a small group of munitions workers in a refusal to work overtime in their factory in a suburb of Paris.[28] These kinds of small protests often evolved into collective protest after prices exploded and purchasing power fell in the spring of 1917.[29] In May and June 1917 strikes broke out in many French cities, often initiated by workers with little experience in trade union activism.[30]

These strikes took place against the backdrop of worker enthusiasm for the first Russian revolution. The February Revolution brought the collapse of the Russian autocracy and the establishment of a democratic provisional government in France's eastern ally. News of the revolution was received with great excitement in France; this was partly because, as Robert Wohl suggests, people often saw what they wanted to see in this revolution.[31] In the heady first days of the revolutionary process in Russia, French Socialists and Republicans often viewed the events in Russia through the lens of French revolutionary history. The Russian Revolution was interpreted as a triumph of democracy, one which had important parallels to the French Revolution.[32] Whatever the precise interpretation—and there were many—the revolution engendered enthusiasm among war-weary French workers, and this affected both strike movements and their perception by government officials and ordinary citizens. Letters opened by postal censors in June–July 1917 reflected widespread concern over the possibility of revolution in France. As one Parisian complained, "Rumour has it that the strikers wanted to blow up the Renault munitions factory last night. We are living in a volcano and everyone is complaining. The example of the Russians bodes no good."[33] Another wrote, "Life in Paris is terrible; people are afraid of a workers' uprising."[34] There can be little doubt that young workers were affected by the enthusiasm for the February Revolution prevalent among French workers. The only young woman to sit on the J.C.'s first national leadership committee, "Rosa Michel," began to attend political meetings after the February Revolution.[35] She joined the J.S. in the following year. For Henri Barbé, the February Revolution constituted one of four principal reasons he joined the J.S. in mid-1917.[36]

Age and Generation in French Communism

The February Revolution was merely the first of two Russian revolutions in 1917. In October the Bolsheviks overthrew the provisional government and began the process of creating a communist state and society. Although the Bolshevik Revolution was initially met with less enthusiasm by French workers,[37] support for it grew as the union sacrée disintegrated by war's end. According to the historian Jean-Louis Robert, striking workers held up the Soviet revolution and Soviet power as examples to emulate in the fall of 1918.[38] Young workers were among those enchanted by the Bolshevik Revolution, especially in retrospect. As René Michaud, who spent his youth in the Jeunesses Anarchistes, recalled, the Russian Revolution, with its promise of land and peace, "exerted a fascination" over him and his "entire generation."[39] For this generation of young workers, the Russian revolutions of 1917 proved a crucial element of the charged period during which they had their formative work and political experiences. Michaud, Barbé, and Michel were not the only young workers whose politicization was shaped, at least in part, by these revolutions.

Labor unrest did not end once the war was over. Strikes exploded again in 1919, when 2,026 strikes occurred involving 1,150,718 workers.[40] The numerous strikes in the metalworking industry in June helped form the cohort of young metalworkers who would play such a pivotal role in the early J.C. During the conflicts strikers lashed out against union leaders, whose age and long tenures became a focal point of criticism. A striker at the Citroën factory argued, "Their ambiguous statements are no longer sufficient; they are too old to take action. They must be replaced."[41] As the strike movement neared its unsuccessful end, attacks on trade union leaders sharpened; not only were they seen as too old, but they were vilified as traitors and sellouts.[42] It was the Bolshevik Revolution that engendered enthusiasm among the strikers, who often placed many of their hopes in it.[43]

According to Barbé, the strikes between 1917 and 1920 shaped a new generation of working-class leaders.[44] As he explained, "It was these great movements which formed us, which provided our social and political educations; it was likewise these movements which oriented us at the time against reformism, conciliation, social collaboration and submission before the repressive violence of public authorities."[45] The workers who later played prominent roles in the J.C.'s first decade bitterly resented what they considered the reformist policies defended by the trade union leadership. According to Barbé, members of his generation were "anti-reformist and violently opposed to Jouhaux, who was considered the *saboteur* of the great strike movements."[46] Indeed, belief in the treachery of both Jouhaux, leader of the Confédération Générale du Travail (c.g.t.), and the Socialist Party became a defining myth for this first generation of Young Communists, one whose importance extended beyond those who had actually taken part in the strikes. Jean Bruhat, who was born in 1905 and attended lycée during the strikes, signaled the myth's importance to his generation when he explained: "social democracy had deserted, nay, betrayed the revolutionary movement, which explained our generation's hatred of it."[47] For Bruhat, Jouhaux was a strikebreaker, and he told him as much during Jouhaux's visit to the École Normale Supérieure in 1927.

Young workers were not the only adolescent males to be politicized during the war and the immediate postwar years. Lycée students and white-collar workers also became radicalized. Like their working-class counterparts, these young men usually joined the Jeunesse Socialiste in the later stages of the war, and they too helped turn the socialist youth organization into a communist youth organization. Gabriel Péri, born in 1902 in Toulon, belonged to the group of wartime secondary school students. The war pushed the young Péri to wider reflection and reading; according to his autobiography, he read to discover an explanation for the war.[48] In 1917, after French soldiers had been executed for their roles in the mutinies and revolution had erupted in Russia, Péri and his classmate Aimé Carlier founded a small, clandestine pacifist newspaper called *Le Diable Bleu*. Péri later explained how the war had altered his intellectual universe and brought him to socialism: "My adherence to socialism was not the result of a revolt inspired in me by the spectacle of social injustices. Nor was it the influence of my friends or of my family upbringing . . . I grew to intellectual maturity in a world that was still at war. War was *the* event; one met it at every turn of the road. It arose every time one began to think; and it molded my reflections, my conception of life."[49] Péri had a more illustrious career than Carlier: he became the J.C.'s national secretary in 1922 and served as a communist deputy from Seine-et-Oise from 1932 to 1940.

The political journey of François Billoux provides another example of the effects that wartime upheavals had on this cohort. Billoux was an office worker whose father was mobilized in 1915. The events of 1917 had a profound effect on both father and son. The father became excited about the February Revolution and his army unit was strongly affected by the mutinies of 1917; Billoux the younger participated in the strikes and demonstrations of 1917 and joined the J.S., either because the father enrolled the son during one of his military leaves or because the son was moved to do so after hearing a pacifist speech by Hélène Brion.[50] Billoux, whose father died of war wounds in 1921, became part of the youth group that was promoted to party leadership in 1928.

Whereas those who were adolescents during the war dominated communist youth politics for much of the 1920s, those who lived the war as children began to take important positions in communist and Catholic youth organizations in the late 1920s and early 1930s. Although Wohl's generational analysis omitted children, both his contemporaries and recent historians have included them. Children of primary school age were subjected to an unprecedented campaign to mobilize them for war. As Stéphane Audoin-Rouzeau has argued, children were encouraged to believe that their thoughts and actions should contribute to the delivery of France.[51] The war was woven into lessons and activities in both Republican and Catholic primary schools: pupils learned about French heroism on the battlefield, celebrated France's allies, designed propaganda posters, and raised money for the war effort. At home, children encountered patriotic messages in games, puzzles, toys, books, and children's magazines. The exact extent of children's psychological mobilization is hard to gauge, but the concrete effects of the war on their educations are not. Across France, schoolchildren lost teachers and schools, while children in rural areas were kept out of school in larger numbers than usual to perform agricultural labor ordinarily performed by men at the front. All of this had long-term effects. Indeed, the Army later found that members of the military class born in 1910 had higher than usual rates of illiteracy.[52]

Wartime conditions for children were especially trying in northern and eastern France, where war came directly to their towns and even homes. In his remarkable diary, Yves Congar, a ten-year-old from Sedan, recorded how his and his sister's play was interrupted during the early days of the war by the realization that French soldiers were digging up the family's property to install machine guns. When Yves brought the soldiers food the following day, planes appeared overhead, prompting the French soldiers to return fire.[53] In areas like Sedan that were directly touched by the war, children witnessed its multiple destructions firsthand. They walked among destroyed buildings and churches, encountered dead and wounded soldiers laid out on stretchers at the train station, witnessed lines of Belgian refugees straggling past, and lay awake at night listening to the roar of nearby canons.

The situation worsened after the Germans became occupiers in areas spanning ten departments in the fall of 1914. Although civilian suffering in the occupied territories was long marginalized in historical narratives, Stéphane Audoin-Rouzeau and Annette Becker argue that it is impossible to grasp the impact of the war without close attention to the realities of occupation.[54] They demonstrate that life under German occupation was extremely difficult, as French citizens of all ages endured the privations and the unrestrained German authority that would become commonplace across Europe during the Second World War.

Children were spared little, as Congar's powerful diary makes clear. The entries are filled with anger at constant food shortages, never-ending German demands for money, frequent requisitions of everything from food to furniture, the pitiful state of prisoners who arrived from the front, German regulations governing all aspects of life, and the merciless deportations of those unable to work. Congar was particularly outraged over German treatment of the weakest and youngest members of the community. He was incensed that the Germans conscripted adolescent males like his two older brothers to perform forced labor, and especially disgusted that the Germans also conscripted adolescent girls and forced them to labor. Along with other members of his family, he agonized after his father was taken hostage and transported by train in early 1918 to German territories captured in the east.

Other children in the occupied departments had similar experiences, and their recollections could later be invested with specific political meanings. Jeannette Thorez-Vermeersch (née Jeannette Vermeersch) was a case in point. Four years old when the war came to her suburb near Lille, she begins her autobiography with the First World War and the arrival of the Germans. She describes the deprivations she endured: Germans lived with her family from the first months of the war, her nursery school was requisitioned for use as a hospital, and food was a constant concern. In her telling, the wartime years had a profound impact on her childhood and her subsequent political commitments: "I was only a little girl, a kid. But I witnessed the daily horror, the occupation, the wounded, the dead, the prisoners, the requisitioned houses, all the horrible suffering of war, and that doubtless marked me forever. I hated war my entire life."[55] In 1932 Vermeersch would be installed, alongside Gaston Coquel, who was conscripted by the Germans as an adolescent, at the top of Young Communist politics.[56]

Even though the capital escaped occupation, the war created severe hardships for Parisians of all ages. When German forces were poised to reach Paris in early September 1914, government officials and French citizens fled.

Age and Generation in French Communism

**28**    According to René Michaud, a young worker at the time, adolescents were among those who initially took refuge in the country, with many fearing a repetition of the horrific siege of Paris during the Franco-Prussian War.[57] As the war ground on, food was in increasingly short supply, and large sections of industry and commerce struggled. Many children, especially those in working-class households, had less to eat during the war, and memories of wartime deprivation remained with them for the rest of their lives.[58] Children and adolescents also suffered the consequences of direct German attacks on the city, which began on 30 August 1914 and became noticeably more intense during the first six months of 1918. On the night of 30–31 January 1918 ninety-three bombs were dropped on the city; on 11 March German bombs killed one hundred and wounded seventy-nine.[59] Children took refuge in shelters with their mothers and lay among the dead and wounded once the attacks were over. Eleven of the Parisians who died after German shells hit the Saint-Gervais Church on Good Friday were under the age of eighteen, and a nursery was destroyed less than two weeks later.[60]

The participation of fathers, uncles, and older brothers in the war had special consequences for children. In the short term these men's departures for the front brought financial hardship in many families. With separation allowances of only 1.25 francs a day, mothers, especially in urban, working-class neighborhoods, struggled to keep families afloat.[61] Some participated in the workforce in new ways, their children leaving school early to earn money or performing odd jobs after school. Children received less supervision than before the war. Both parents and journalists expressed concern over the impact that this might have on juvenile behavior, and rates of juvenile delinquency rose in Paris during the war and the immediate postwar period.[62]

The termination of the conflict did not always bring an end to suffering for huge numbers of young people. Across France, brothers, uncles, and fathers failed to return, leaving an estimated 760,000 orphans and countless others who mourned the loss of siblings or uncles. As Audoin-Rouzeau and Becker have argued, these deaths affected families and children intensely.[63] Among young people the sense of loss was most profound for orphans, the majority of whom were born between 1910 and 1916.[64] These children watched as mothers struggled to carry on, and they dealt with the loss of fathers they had barely known. Some were urged to assume the responsibilities of their dead fathers,[65] while others, like the future Young Communist Léonie Décaster, who lost her father and three maternal uncles during the war, were subsequently raised "in the hatred of war" by their mothers.[66] To make matters worse, war orphans mourned their fathers within the context of glorifying the war and their fathers' memories *and* their own status as props in national commemorative exercises.[67]

The lives of children were also changed by the return of men who had been forever altered physically and psychologically. An estimated 1.1 million soldiers came home permanently disabled, and countless others were affected in less obvious but still profound ways. For some, the war's lingering impact on their fathers led to a deep and lasting hatred of the war. Marthe Gallet (born 1914), who became a Communist, explained, "Among my earliest impressions is hating the war which destroyed my father. He was a good, intelligent man, but the war changed him, making him susceptible to episodes during which he began to drink and, while in a delirious state, he ranted about what he had gone through—his horse killed out from under him, the death of his comrades from Chemin des Dames, the massacres, the slaughter."[68] Even fathers who returned relatively healthy could clash with children who had become accustomed to wartime independence. One mother lamented that her husband, who was no longer as patient as he had been before the war, disciplined her son far too frequently in its aftermath.[69]

Those who were children and adolescents between 1914 and 1918 constituted their own "war generation." Children were less likely to attend school than previous generations, and their bodies bore the scars of wartime shortages. They coped with the absence of fathers, brothers, and male relatives, and with the consequences of death or severe disability. Many experienced German occupation or bombardment, and some developed a hatred of war that affected their subsequent political choices. Of most immediate importance is the way the war years shaped the political consciousness of a group of young male workers and students who came to view themselves as an age-based, revolutionary cohort. Unlike older Socialists, who could only move to communism by repudiating past political practices, this group had little allegiance to long-established forms of working-class politics and trade union activism. As a result, its members could embrace, unproblematically and enthusiastically, the new Communist Party and its ideology.

**A Vanguard within a Vanguard Party** By 1920 the nature of the French left's relationship to revolutionary events in Russia, and more particularly to the newly constituted Communist International, established in 1919, loomed as the major issue to be decided. Debate raged within both

**30**    the Socialist Party and the Jeunesse Socialiste.[70] In the J.S. radicalized male youth such as Maurice Laporte and Gabriel Péri campaigned vigorously for membership in the Communist Youth International (C.Y.I.), founded in the fall of 1919. Support for joining the C.Y.I., and doing so independently of the adult party, grew during 1920,[71] and proponents of membership in the Third International campaigned with a clear notion of youth's role as "the most active and revolutionary segment of the proletariat."[72] In a sign of things to come, this self-conception was nourished by adult Comintern propagandists such as Boris Souvarine, a veteran of the First World War who received subsidies and directions from Moscow.[73] In the lead article of the inaugural issue of *L'Avant-Garde ouvrière et communiste*, the official paper of the Committee for the Communist Youth International, Souvarine told Young Socialists that they were leading the movement toward the Third International and setting an example for adults. They were, he continued, the guardians of the sacred flame of hope lit by the Bolshevik Revolution and the vanguard of the new revolutionary movement.[74]

By the opening of the special Young Socialist national conference on 31 October 1920, those advocating membership in the Communist Youth International had won the majority of delegates to their position. On 1 November, almost two months before the adult party fractured at Tours, Young Socialist conference delegates voted 5,443 to 1,958 to join the Communist Youth International. *L'Avant-Garde* was the newspaper of the new organization, which was known originally as the Fédération Nationale des Jeunesses Socialistes Communistes and became the Fédération Nationale des Jeunesses Communistes in the following year.

The decision to join the Third International involved much more than a simple name change. Those at the helm of the Jeunesse Communiste were determined to create a revolutionary youth organization that would be diametrically opposed to the J.S. in crucial respects. In contrast to the J.S., which had concentrated on educating and organizing youth, the J.C. would take political action as its primary focus. This political action would be based not on parliamentary politics but on "revolutionary intransigence" and would aim to establish a dictatorship of the proletariat to be exercised through workers' councils, or soviets.[75] For the Jeunesse Communiste, the number of members paled before their revolutionary commitment. This, they believed, placed the Young Communists in the forefront of the revolutionary struggle in France.

The young men drew strength from the conviction that they were part of an international youth vanguard which was becoming aware of its revolutionary role in world history. As a member of the Committee for the Communist Youth International explained in *L'Avant-Garde* in October 1920, "In all countries, whether in Europe or in the most backward regions of the world, youth is aware of its historic role and takes its place in the vanguard of the revolutionary movement."[76] The writer's enthusiasm might have led him to exaggerate the global nature of this phenomenon, but there was little doubt that youth was on the move, and convinced of its mission across Europe. As Richard Cornell demonstrated in his history of the formative years of the Communist Youth International, the combination of wartime suffering, labor upheaval, and revolutionary stirrings radicalized young male workers and students throughout western and central Europe.[77] Young Socialist organizations emerged from the war enlarged and emboldened, their leaders determined to play an important and autonomous role in creating an international communist movement. It was in Berlin—and not in Moscow—that self-described revolutionary youth gathered in the fall of 1919 to establish an international communist youth organization. According to Cornell, the notion of youth as the vanguard of a vanguard party was first clearly articulated there. For the delegates in Berlin, Young Communists deserved to be leaders in the revolutionary movement because they were more militant, more dedicated to revolution, and impatient with the old.[78] Young Communist organizations would push tired socialist parties toward communism.

Youth claims to vanguard status conflicted with Bolshevik notions of the young's role in international communism, but this was not immediately obvious because Comintern leaders sought to balance appeals to youth radicalism with attempts to direct and control that radicalism. During the revolutions of 1917 young workers had been important in pushing events forward. When revolution broke out in Russia in February 1917 and leading Bolsheviks were far from the center of revolutionary action, young male workers in the capital, Petrograd, pressured their adult male counterparts to join the female workers who had begun the strike movement.[79] Within days the strike movement became a revolutionary movement that brought about the collapse of the autocracy. As the Bolsheviks prepared for a new revolutionary phase in the summer of 1917, young male workers moved in large numbers to the Red Guards, formed to aid the seizure of power; indeed,

**32**  43 percent of the Moscow Red Guards were under the age of twenty-five.[80] By the fall, skilled urban young male workers predominated among revolutionary activists.[81]

As they worked to establish a communist state and society and an international communist movement after the October Revolution, the Bolsheviks had a clear vision of youth's role. For Lenin and other Bolshevik leaders, radical youth were useful at moments when a drive toward the extreme was necessary. But there was no possibility that youth would be given more than a temporary leadership role within communist parties. For the Bolsheviks, the Communist Party was the undisputed force within the international communist movement; youth organizations were, in the final analysis, auxiliaries which were subordinate to adult leadership and focused on educating and organizing youth.

Since the Bolsheviks' conception of youth's role differed so dramatically from that held by many of the young, the precise place of youth within communism was something to be worked out. The issue first came to a head in Russia, and the outcome of this contest affected the situation across Europe. Because the youth activists of 1917 had been politicized outside Bolshevik youth organizations, the Bolsheviks' first task was to channel youth radicalism into a communist youth organization and ensure that this organization be guided firmly by the adult party. To this end the Komsomol, or Communist Youth League, was established in the fall of 1918 and quickly brought under the control of the Bolshevik party.[82] Bolshevik leaders used the Komsomol to mobilize youth energies for their various campaigns, carefully emphasizing attributes of youth that corresponded most closely to the desired outcome at any one moment. Thus as Anne Gorsuch has demonstrated, Bolshevik messages to and representations of youth often varied dramatically from one revolutionary moment to the next. During the Civil War, when Komsomol members were vital cogs in the Red Army, youth was lauded for its bravery, toughness, and courage. But when the war ended in 1921 and Bolshevik leaders replaced War Communism with the decidedly less revolutionary New Economic Policy (NEP), youth was celebrated for its moderation, discipline, and rationality. In Bolshevik iconography, images of youth as a shock force on the front lines of revolution gave way to images of the young as engineers methodically building the new socialist society.[83]

With the Komsomol established as an auxiliary to the adult party, Bolsheviks turned their attention to the Communist Youth International. Unlike Komsomol leaders, who had little involvement in socialist youth politics before 1917, communist youth leaders from western and central Europe drew strength from a history of socialist youth activism that extended back to the late nineteenth century. Until mid-1921 leaders of the Communist Youth International clung stubbornly to the notion that they should be allowed an independent, political role within the communist movement. The show-down came in the spring of 1921. When Communist Youth International leaders held their congress in Germany, the Russians refused to recognize its legitimacy. Instead the Russians held a second Communist Youth International Congress, closely following on the heels of the Third Comintern Congress in Moscow in July 1921.

The Third Comintern Congress marked the triumph of the Bolshevik position on youth within the international communist movement, which was laid out in a resolution of 12 July, "The Communist International and the Communist Youth Movement." Although socialist youth organizations had "acted as the vanguard in the revolutionary struggle" during the First World War and young workers had been "quicker to show enthusiasm for revolutionary struggle than adult workers," the establishment of the Communist International and individual communist parties had altered the function of revolutionary youth organizations. Now, the resolution declared, "the youth movement relinquishes to the communist parties its vanguard role of organizing independent activity and providing political leadership." The resolution went on to warn against "the further existence of Young Communist organizations as politically independent and leading organizations" which would compete with communist parties. Deprived of their leading role, Young Communist organizations were directed to turn their attention toward organizing the masses of young workers.[84] The Comintern position carried the day within the Communist Youth International. By the close of its congress in Moscow later that month, the Communist Youth International had renounced its earlier claims to be a vanguard and lost any meaningful independence.[85]

The contest over youth's role within French communism was related to the struggles within the international communist movement, but the issue resolved itself differently. Youth claims to vanguard status were made within the context of a nascent French communist movement whose adult leaders often proved reluctant to follow Moscow's lead and transform the party into a revolutionary party along Bolshevik lines. As long as adult Communists resisted Moscow's vision, a radical youth cohort was useful in pushing the party to the Bolshevik-defined left. This possibility was admitted in the

**34**  Comintern's resolution on youth. Young Communists were to do everything possible to "rejuvenate" communist parties; moreover, Comintern leaders had flexibility when enforcing the resolution's guiding principles, depending on the stage of development of the party in question. Because it was in the Comintern's interests, the J.C. was allowed to maintain an independence denied elsewhere during the 1920s. But the J.C.'s independence came only in relation to the party, not to the Comintern itself. Beginning in the summer of 1921, Comintern leaders worked to shape, direct, and control the political action of the J.C. so that it more clearly reflected Comintern approaches and goals.

The efforts to educate the J.C. and channel youth leaders' enthusiasm began at the Third Comintern Congress in July 1921. In the months preceding the congress, J.C. leaders pressed their claims to a vanguard role within French communism. During the winter and spring of 1921, J.C. leaders writing in *L'Avant-Garde* repeatedly criticized the adult party for being insufficiently communist. By contrast, they portrayed youth as wholly devoted to the revolutionary cause. One author spoke loudly about these young men's sense of their revolutionary mission: "we lay our youth and our life on the altar of humanity . . . we devote our energy and our intelligence to the course of truth and justice."[86] The Jeunesses Communistes sent a delegation to the Communist Youth International Congress in Berlin that had run afoul of Bolshevik leaders, and they adopted the congress's policies regarding the need for youth organizational autonomy and political independence. As May ended, *L'Avant-Garde* affirmed, "In the proletarian movement, we will continue to be in the vanguard and to fulfill our historical mission of pushing the party toward action."[87]

When meetings of the Comintern Congress got under way in Moscow in July, the J.C. secretary general, Maurice Laporte, continued the youth organization's criticism of its parent party. At the meeting of the Executive Committee devoted to the situation in France, Laporte claimed that the J.C. "was the only revolutionary group active in France" and demanded full independence for the Jeunesse Communiste.[88] As extreme as these charges were, it was Laporte's discussion of the campaign against the recall of the military class of 1919 that prompted a lesson from assembled Comintern leaders. Laporte criticized the party for not doing enough to organize protest demonstrations and to support the J.C.'s efforts to discourage young men from reporting for service.[89] For him the party's inaction demonstrated its insufficient revolutionary commitment. When queried by Comintern lead-ers about his use of the term "insubordination," Laporte insisted that it was necessary "to go all the way and undertake armed resistance!"[90] In response, Comintern leaders lectured that the revolution would be made not by the military class of 1919 but by the working class.

Comintern leaders did not intend to dampen the Young Communists' revolutionary ardor but rather to shape and discipline it to fit Comintern purposes. As the Comintern leadership's directives to the party made clear, the Executive Committee had high hopes for the Jeunesses Communistes. Explaining that the party included many who were Communists simply because the majority within the Socialist Party had voted to join the Third International, the directive noted that those Communists who still operated "in the old way" were incapable of understanding the character and demands of the new epoch and the new action. For this reason it was necessary to recruit new militants, especially from the Jeunesses Communistes.[91] That Comintern leaders had high hopes for a disciplined J.C. was also evident from Grigorii Zinoviev's comment to Laporte in the closing days of the con-ference. According to Laporte, Zinoviev, the head of the Communist Inter-national, instructed him, "Tell the Young Communists to work in France. We're counting on them. They are our source of hope in the world." Appar-ently half-smiling, he added, "And always move to the left. Make sure that the Fourth (Comintern) Congress takes place in Paris next year."[92] As this encounter suggests, the balancing act of encouraging and disciplining youth radicalism would last longer in France than it had elsewhere in Europe.

But this was not immediately obvious. In the aftermath of the congress, the J.C. struggled to respond. When Laporte first commented publicly on the developments in Moscow in a special issue of *L'Avant-Garde* (26 August), he defended his organization's actions at the congress and reiterated his ear-lier criticism of the party's unrevolutionary conduct. Laporte used a careful analysis of the Komsomol's position vis-à-vis Soviet communism to argue that the Russian youth organization should not be a model for communist youth organizations in other countries.[93] *L'Avant-Garde* then ceased publi-cation until December 1921, when Young Communist leaders reluctantly conceded the movement's subordinate role. Since the party was asserting itself more than ever, Maurice Honel argued, the J.C. had to "on pain of death forswear the political action which had been theirs by force of circumstance but which could no longer be."[94] The J.C. National Federation also disavowed local J.C. sections which had been involved in inappropriate efforts to move the "class of 1919" toward revolutionary action.[95] The J.C. would take its direction from Moscow.

**Forging an Independent Political Role: Antimilitarism** Even as J.C. leaders signaled outward acceptance of Comintern dictates regarding youth, they continued to claim a leading role within French communism during the 1920s. They were aided by the nature of campaigns at the forefront of communist struggle during this decade. Two of the most important, those protesting French occupation of the Ruhr in 1923 and French involvement in the Rif War in Morocco in 1925–26, privileged agitation within the military. This was the special responsibility of the young, and it was a sphere where youth revolutionary fervor was acceptable to and even useful for Comintern leaders.

J.C. leaders made antimilitarism the focal point of their revolutionary struggle against capitalism from the organization's earliest days. That the J.C. should choose this issue as its revolutionary focus was not itself revolutionary. Military service directly affected all French young men, and there was an important tradition of antimilitarist action in France. Groups of young people had begun to protest militarism after universal male military service was established in 1889. By the beginning of the twentieth century, Yolande Cohen argues, the determination to struggle against militarism provided common ground among anti-establishment youth on the left and right.[96] To say that young men agreed on the necessity of fighting militarism does not imply, however, that they subscribed to the same analysis of the problem or the methods required to combat it.

The Young Communists had their own interpretation of antimilitarism, adhering closely (especially after July 1921) to guidelines established by Comintern leaders. Communists distinguished between illegitimate and legitimate war: war was unjust if it served the interests of capitalist regimes but just if it functioned as an instrument of working-class or colonial liberation. According to this analysis, "imperialist" wars waged by capitalist powers were to be vigorously opposed while "revolutionary" wars waged by oppressed peoples were to be vigorously supported. For the Jeunesse Communiste, this meant turning the French military into a revolutionary force, as it had been in 1917, and encouraging resistance to the French Army when it was used to bolster imperialism. These efforts were to take place wherever the military was stationed, be it Europe or the farthest reaches of the French Empire.

Although J.C. leaders did not immediately appreciate the fine points of the Comintern's antimilitarist analysis, there was little question that they embraced the outlines of this militaristic approach to antimilitarism. In so doing, they differentiated themselves from many adults in the party, who supported a broader definition of antimilitarism that condemned war in all its guises. During the first years of French Communism, the J.C. used the party's apparent failure to move beyond "pacifism" as grounds to attack adult Communists for insufficient commitment to revolutionary principles.

The antimilitarist struggle of J.C. leaders and militants confirmed the young men's notion of themselves as forming an explicitly revolutionary organization. Leaders wrote articles explaining the organization's position and appealing to conscripts; these appeared in *L'Avant-Garde* and in *Le Conscrit*, which was published semiannually to coincide with the twice yearly departure of conscripts. Leaders also drew up tracts, stickers (*papillons*), and posters. The stickers and posters were pasted on city walls under cover of night, while the tracts were thrown over barrack walls or deposited surreptitiously on mess hall tables. Young Communists were assigned special responsibilities when they performed their military service: they were expected to use their time in the military to advance the revolutionary cause and make themselves into trained soldiers of revolution. Unlike young anarchists, who were urged to combat militarism by refusing to perform their military service, communist conscripts were instructed to carry out their assigned duties as completely as possible and become "good" soldiers. As such, they were to master the latest weaponry with a view to using this knowledge in the service of revolution.[97] Young Communist militants were further told to advance as far as possible through army or navy ranks, all the while endeavoring to establish communist cells in their units. Each young communist was directed to attain the rank of corporal or noncommissioned officer, and if possible to position himself to become an officer if called up again as a reservist.[98] Those Young Communists who were university students eligible for officer training were expected to advance as far as possible within the military hierarchy. The J.C.'s attempt to produce highly trained soldiers in the name of antimilitarism was contradictory, a fact that did not go unnoticed by some Young Communists. Bruhat's small group of Communists at the École Normale Supérieure in the mid-1920s attempted to resolve this contradiction by studiously applying themselves during the military training course given at the local barracks but staging a sit-down strike on the day of the examination.[99]

**38**     Although Young Communists assumed these kinds of antimilitarist responsibilities throughout the 1920s, specific campaigns brought an intensification of action and new assignments. The campaign against the French
invasion of the Ruhr was the first major antimilitarist effort by the J.C. On
11 January 1923 French and Belgian troops (along with a token Italian troop
presence) entered the Ruhr in an attempt to compel the Germans to meet
reparations obligations mandated by the Treaty of Versailles. Coming after
a period of revolutionary quiescence in Europe, this occupation seemed—at
least to European Communists—to create the possibility of revolution again
in Germany. French Communists moved quickly to undermine the occupation and foment revolution. Less than a week before the invasion, adult party
leaders traveled to Essen to join other European Communists for meetings
and demonstrations designed to encourage the Germans to resist French
invasion. On the day when troops moved in, leading party officials were
arrested for "plotting against the security of the state." As historians of communism have pointed out, this show of state force helped unite a heretofore
fractious party; in the new circumstances, dissenters were cast as traitors
to the party.[100]

Although adult Communists bore the brunt of the state's initial repression, the J.C. soon assumed the leading role in French communist antimilitarist activities in the Ruhr. J.C. activists carried out their missions in the
Ruhr under the direct leadership of Comintern officials, who viewed the
behavior of the French Army as crucial to the outcome of any revolutionary
uprising in Germany.[101] Communist Youth International officials chose the
rising Young Communist Jacques Doriot to oversee French operations in the
Ruhr.[102] Doriot, who had first become prominent within the J.C. in the spring
of 1921 when Laporte and other leaders were in prison, had his own relationship with the Comintern that was independent of the French party.

J.C. militants were instructed to undermine the French occupation in all
possible ways. A focal point was the publication and distribution of propaganda. In the spring, Young Communists affixed stickers and posters and
distributed thousands of tracts in French, German, and Arabic, the last aimed
at the twenty thousand North African troops in the Ruhr.[103] These materials
called on soldiers to fraternize with German workers, especially those in the
coal mines that were vital to the region's industrial output. Young Communists serving in the army were directed to establish cells in their regiments
and do whatever they could to undermine the French occupation and promote revolution in Germany. Henri Barbé, who had initially been posted to

the army in the Rhineland, was sent to the Ruhr in 1923, where he was put in charge of a sensitive railway spot on the border between the occupied and unoccupied zones and given orders to arrest known Communists who tried to pass through. Barbé disobeyed these orders and let Communists slip through undetected, eventually getting caught by authorities.[104]

Although Communists claimed to have created nearly two hundred cells, the Young Communists failed to achieve their goal of winning large numbers of French soldiers over to their cause. Military reports on troop morale in Germany in August 1923 affirm that morale was good among officers and enlisted men alike.[105] According to General Degoutte, commander of the French forces, "Propaganda remains without effect regardless of its origins."[106] But while Young Communist efforts in the Ruhr did not lead to proletarian revolution in Germany, they did allow J.C. militants to assume an independent and significant role on the front lines of revolutionary activity in Europe. This not only proved enormously exciting for the young activists, who were convinced that revolution was again at hand, but it also helped them to earn their revolutionary stripes. Doriot and Barbé emerged from this campaign with enhanced reputations in both the French and international communist movements.

The campaign against the Rif War in Morocco in 1925 and 1926 provided the next showcase for the J.C.'s antimilitarist agitation and the revolutionary fervor of the organization's leaders. The communist campaign was the product of French colonial involvement in Morocco and intensified Comintern interest in the anticolonial struggle. Once the last revolutionary flames had been extinguished in Europe in the fall of 1923, Comintern officials turned their attention to the struggle against imperialism in Africa and Asia. Morocco, which had become a French protectorate in 1912 but included a small area of Spanish control in the northeast, furnished the setting for Communists to challenge French colonial policy. Tensions began in 1921, when rebels from the mountainous Rif region led by Abd el-Krim inaugurated an independence struggle against the Spanish. In 1924 Abd el-Krim declared an independent Rif state, a move interpreted as a threat to French interests. War broke out between the French and Rif rebels in April 1925 after rebels attacked French forces.

Under the leadership of Jacques Doriot, by now the J.C.'s secretary general, the J.C. played a leading role in the campaign against the French presence in Morocco. In this struggle J.C. leaders received money directly from the Comintern, and their actions contrasted with those of party leaders, who had earlier been rebuked by Comintern officials for insufficient commitment to the anticolonial struggle.[107] Doriot's campaign began in September of 1924, when he (representing the J.C.) and Pierre Semard (representing the party) sent a telegram to Abd el-Krim congratulating him on his victory over the Spanish and expressing hope for his continued success in the struggle against imperialists, including the French. Ending "Long live Moroccan independence! Long live the international struggle of colonial peoples and the world-wide proletariat!," the telegram quickly became notorious in a France where Communists were the only major political party to challenge the consensus on empire.[108] The telegram, apparently written by Doriot,[109] was followed later in the month by statements from the J.C. urging French soldiers to fraternize with the Rif people.

The communist campaign against French military involvement built steadily in the spring, summer, and fall of 1925, with Doriot and other J.C. leaders in the forefront. As head of the party's newly created colonial commission and one of its leading parliamentary voices, Doriot delivered what were considered treasonous speeches in the Chamber of Deputies against French colonialism and inveighed against the war in often well-attended public meetings. Doriot also grabbed the spotlight during an ill-fated mission to Morocco to meet the rebel leader. When French police, who had been following the communist delegation since its departure from Paris, informed the Communists that there was no way they would be allowed into Morocco, Doriot separated from the group and attempted to slip into the country illegally. Much to the excitement of *L'Humanité*, he eluded the police for nineteen days before resurfacing in France.[110]

The J.C. focused its energies on protesting the war in Morocco in the summer and fall of 1925. J.C. militants in Paris were instructed to drop all other work and organize protests in neighborhoods and factories and foment unrest among the colonial population in the Paris region.[111] Communists organized meetings and distributed tracts and pamphlets tailored to diverse audiences. Those aimed at women workers presented the war as a conflict on the scale of the Great War which would affect their families in new and pernicious ways. The bourgeoisie, which had taken their husbands during "the great slaughter," was now taking their sons for war in Morocco.[112] The high point of the campaign came with the general strike of 12 October 1925, which erupted in violence between strikers and police. Although the general strike did not succeed, French authorities were alarmed by the intensification of antiwar action during 1925, especially in the Paris region. As noted in the **41** summary police report on communist action, communist work against the war in Morocco had become increasingly pronounced, to the point where it was now "an intensive revolutionary action which aimed at nothing less than undermining the loyalty of our troops and compromising the success of our armies."[113]

Throughout the campaign special attention was directed toward soldiers, who were encouraged to resist the war and show solidarity with the peoples of Morocco. Hundreds of thousands of tracts addressed to conscripts, soldiers, and sailors were printed and distributed throughout France and, when possible, in Morocco. These materials mixed criticism of the French army's treatment of its own soldiers with attacks on the imperialist war in Morocco. They also placed the Rif War within the context of the wars and revolutionary uprisings of the previous decade. One tract equated the war in Morocco with the conflict of 1914–18, accusing bourgeois politicians and socialist leaders of reneging on their promises of peace and again sending soldiers to their slaughter.[114] This piece, like other J.C. propaganda, called on soldiers and sailors to fraternize with Rif rebels and undermine the war in Morocco. It encouraged them to see such action as an extension of the heroic army and navy uprisings of 1917 and 1919, when French sailors mutinied in the Black Sea. To underscore the link between the Morocco campaign and the recent revolutionary past, André Marty, the hero of the Odessa uprisings of 1919, was sometimes brought in to tell his heroic tale and urge soldiers to undertake similar action. Young Communists directed their members to do all that was possible within the army, and they sent special delegates to Algeria and Morocco to establish communist cells.[115]

The Young Communists achieved relatively few concrete successes among the troops stationed in North Africa. Before el-Krim surrendered in May 1926, instances of collective insubordination were restricted to a small number of warships in the Mediterranean. This was partly because French military officials paid careful attention to the composition of forces sent to Morocco, using few conscripts.[116] The experience of André Ferrat highlighted the difficulties that Young Communists faced in trying to infiltrate the army. When Ferrat was called up for military service in November 1925 after a three-year student deferment, he was posted to Algeria and enrolled in a reserve officers training program in Algiers. Ferrat later reported that he undertook an active, clandestine propaganda campaign against the Rif

Age and Generation in French Communism

war.[117] But the Army soon discovered his status as a J.C. leader, expelled him from officer training, and shipped him to the disciplinary section of his unit. There he remained until well after the end of the war.

Even though the J.C. failed in its ultimate goal of halting the war and ensuring Rif independence, its leaders were celebrated by Comintern officials for their energetic leadership of the French campaign. At the end of 1925 Doriot and Barbé were summoned to Moscow to report to Communist Youth International leaders on the J.C.'s campaign. They were congratulated on their efforts.[118] According to Barbé, the Comintern Executive Committee's president Grigorii Zinoviev lauded Doriot and told him, "Finally we have a real Bolshevik in France."[119] The J.C.'s antimilitarist campaigns of 1923 and 1924–26 had allowed the organization to assume a leading role on the front lines of the revolutionary campaigns most valued by Comintern leaders. They had also allowed J.C. leaders to take an increasingly important position within both French and international communism.

The J.C. leaders' increased stature stemmed not merely from their antimilitarist efforts but also from their having waged their antimilitarist struggles in the face of intense state repression. Throughout the 1920s civilian and military authorities saw French national defense as seriously threatened by the Young Communists' efforts to transform the military from an institution that transmitted Republican values (*l'école de la nation*) to a training ground for revolution. As a result, both worked assiduously to thwart Young Communist efforts in this area. French military officials, who were strongly anticommunist and mindful of the mutinies of 1917 and 1919, monitored Communists closely.[120] Communist newspapers were strictly prohibited, and those servicemen discovered to be engaging in antimilitarist activity were disciplined and sometimes removed from the military altogether.[121] For their part, civilian authorities pursued Communists with great vigor. They arrested activists for writing antimilitarist articles, giving antimilitarist speeches, singing antimilitarist songs, and distributing antimilitarist tracts.

Although arrests occurred throughout the decade, they became much more frequent during specific campaigns such as that of 1921 against the remobilization of the class of 1919, the Ruhr campaign of 1923, the Rif War campaign of 1925–26, and the campaign in 1927 to protest the reorganization of the military. The charge of inciting soldiers to insubordination was the most common charge laid against J.C. militants in the 1920s. Many of the J.C. activists whose names appear in the *Dictionnaire biographique du mouvement ouvrier français* were arrested at least once on this charge. Prominent leaders

were arrested many times, and sometimes charged with more serious of-  **43**
fenses involving threats to national security. This was especially true during
campaigns like those in the Ruhr and in Morocco. Significantly for both their
self-conception and their position within the Communist International, J.C.
leaders did not submit meekly but often tried to elude arrest or refused to
serve prison sentences. When Doriot was finally caught for the first time
by the police in late 1923, he faced sentences related to six separate charges
totaling thirty-four months in prison and 600 francs in fines.[122] Barbé racked
up sentences totaling eighteen years in prison and 100,000 francs in fines
between 1926 and 1929.[123] Other leaders had similar records.

Far from dissuading Young Communists, the heavy-handed state response
nourished the J.C.'s self-definition as a revolutionary combat unit that deserved a frontline, independent role in French Communism. The J.C. took
care to represent the arrests of its leading militants as a validation of the ex
plicitly revolutionary nature of its work, as well as the revolutionary mettle
of individual Young Communists. When J.C. leaders were first arrested in
early 1921, *L'Avant-Garde* used the arrests to underline the organization's
claim to being *the* communist organization in France. The author noted
sarcastically, "How nice it is to find amidst all the working-class organizations one organization which puts into practice the resolutions passed in
the congresses and which does so above all without opportunism, boldly,
meeting the stepped up attacks of the bourgeoisie with a wall of fierce and
resolute will."[124] The J.C. continued to refer to the multiple arrests of its
members with considerable pride as the decade proceeded. In January 1923
the opening speaker at the J.C. Congress boasted that the organization's
antimilitarist work had resulted in many trials and the "heroic spectacle" of
Gabriel Péri, one of its leaders, being dragged from his prison cell after an
eight-day hunger strike.[125] Within the J.C. the response to repression functioned as a kind of barometer of revolutionary fortitude. The organization
steadfastly refused to bow before searches and widespread arrests, inform-
ing followers that Young Communists who feared arrest had no place in the
organization.[126] Doriot captured the determination to confront state forces
head on. On the day of the general strike against the Rif War in 1925, he led
Communists in a violent brawl with French police. Doriot ended up badly
wounded and in jail for his efforts. By contrast, party leaders were noticeably
absent from the mêlée.

The J.C.'s brand of revolutionary action was deeply gendered. The ideal
militant of the 1920s was virile, tough, and unafraid of violence or war. He

**44**  was, quite literally, a revolutionary fighter. For the Young Communists the claim to a tough revolutionary virility was as central to their distinction between themselves and adult Communists or Young Socialists as any ideological difference. Maurice Laporte contrasted a virile Jeunesse Communiste with a whining Jeunesse Socialiste by proclaiming, "We do not moan about war and its horrors as those in the Second International do. Down with sniveling and humanitarian pacifism. As we declared recently in *L'Avant-Garde*: war itself does not frighten us at all."[127] The phrase became a kind of J.C. incantation, trotted out again by Laporte during the revolutionary excitement of the Ruhr campaign.[128] Doriot became the exemplar of this revolutionary virility during the mid-1920s, and his violent encounter with French police became legendary. As Drieu La Rochelle wrote ten years after the event, "Those who saw Doriot standing alone, confronting two hundred police men, charging ahead, swinging a café table above his head, lifting people onto his powerful shoulders, stopping only when completely exhausted, *know that there is in France at least one politician who is a real man*."[129] It was as real men and real Bolsheviks that Young Communists set themselves apart from adult Communists throughout the 1920s.

**The J.C. and Party Politics**  The configuration of French Communist Party politics during the 1920s furthered the J.C.'s aspirations to play a leading role within French communism. Throughout the decade party members resisted the imposition of Bolshevik methods, strategies, and control in a range of ways, with relations between the party and Comintern leaders particularly strained in the party's early years. By 1922 clear fractions had developed within the party; by January 1923 a "Committee to Resist the International" had been formed. At pivotal moments between 1922 and 1924 Young Communists could be counted on to support the Comintern's attempts to mold the party into a highly centralized, disciplined revolutionary party, which would take its marching orders from Moscow. They backed the new policy of expelling dissenters from the party in 1922, and worked vigorously on behalf of the campaign begun in 1924 to "bolshevize" the party. Youth support for Comintern positions was significant and young people were rewarded for their loyalty.

The bolshevization campaign involved reorganizing party structures and altering the membership's socioeconomic composition so that the party corresponded more closely to the Russian Bolshevik Party. The factory cell replaced the neighborhood section as the party's basic unit, and workers were assigned prominent roles in the party. The construction of an explicitly proletarian revolutionary party became the goal. To facilitate the promotion of workers, recruiting drives were undertaken and quotas established for communist electoral lists. During the national legislative elections of the spring of 1924, 90 percent of the spots on communist electoral lists were reserved for workers and peasants, who functioned as a sort of rhetorical add-on.[130]

Young Communist leaders proved enthusiastic supporters of the bolshevization campaign. The effort coincided with the young men's desires to transform the party into a new kind of revolutionary formation. As Albert Vassart later explained, "the young people with whom I associated wanted to be part of a real recasting of the party's structure and methods. With the bolshevization campaign, I saw more than anything else the beginnings of this necessary reorganization."[131] The J.C. played a leading role in the campaign to restructure the party around the factory cell. Because the J.C. was so closely aligned with the Communist Youth International, it had begun to address the need to replace neighborhood sections with factory cells in the fall of 1922.[132] By the time the Comintern's bolshevization campaign began in 1924, the J.C. had amassed a certain expertise in this area. Young Communists became the campaign's principal propagandists. Roger Gaillard delivered the key speech on the factory cell at the Third Party Congress in January 1924, and he wrote the major pamphlet on the subject, *Factory Cells*. André Ferrat also assumed prominence in the campaign.

If leading Young Communists had a clear ideological affinity with the bolshevization campaign, they also stood to benefit from its implementation, further cementing their support for the initiative. Comintern efforts to transform the French party involved marginalizing those who demonstrated too much independence and promoting a generation of Communists loyal to Comintern policies.[133] Bolshevization intentionally fostered mobility for younger workers within the party. Efforts to recruit members intensified and young workers, who were often active in both J.C. and party organizing and politics, began to constitute a more important voice within the party. Indeed, young workers accounted for two-thirds of the delegates to the party's Fifth Congress in January 1925.[134] Young workers also figured prominently among those made full-time party employees, or *permanents*, who received training in France or the Soviet Union. Finally, young workers were among those who appeared on communist electoral lists for the first time. It was no coincidence that the J.C. leader and former metalworker Jacques Doriot

**46**   was first elected to the Chamber of Deputies in May 1924, even though he
was in prison during the campaign.[135]

As J.C. leaders threw their support behind the bolshevization campaign,
they paid less rhetorical attention to age and more attention to class as the
source of their revolutionary commitment. That they should have done so
was not surprising, for as French communism was reshaped in the image
of Russian communism, class background became an increasingly important indicator of affinity for and even commitment to the communist cause.
In Soviet Russia those with working-class backgrounds were advantaged
when it came to justice, party membership, and access to higher education,
housing, and food rations, while those from other class backgrounds were
discriminated against and frequently cast as enemies of the state.[136] The J.C.
therefore took pains to emphasize the working-class nature of its membership. In January 1925, for example, J.C. leaders proudly reported that 181 of
203 delegates to the J.C. national congress in December 1924 were union-
ized; of those, 84 were metalworkers.[137] In this atmosphere leading Young
Communists who came from non-working-class backgrounds sometimes
reinvented themselves as workers. Mostly, however, they overcame their
potential liability by becoming full-time Communists and hence professional revolutionaries, often breaking with their families in the process.
Those who had been fortunate enough to continue their education to lycée
or even university put their talents to work as propagandists or journalists
within the J.C. and often, simultaneously, the party. Even though J.C. leaders were less apt to trace their special revolutionary commitment to their
youth than they had been earlier in the decade, they still had a clear sense
of forming a revolutionary youth vanguard that would lead the adult party
toward communism.

Comintern leaders exploited this self-conception one last time in the late
1920s, as they pushed party leaders toward adopting more radical tactics
and carried out the second stage of bolshevization. A central impetus for the
move to the left was the Comintern's analysis of European capitalism. Having passed through periods of revolution (1917–23) and stability (1924–27),
capitalism was now, in the view of Comintern leaders, entering a period of
crisis, which would bring about a radicalization of the masses.[138] To adopt
uncompromising revolutionary tactics appeared a logical necessity. Doing so
involved confronting state authorities with intensified antimilitarist action
and attacking "reformists" on the left with vigor. These "class against class"
tactics, as they became known, cast Socialists as "social fascists" who were

considered little better than fascists of the right and rendered impossible any electoral cooperation with parties on the left.

The uncompromising line reflected new realities in Moscow. By the end of 1927, when the party's central committee formally approved the turn, Stalin had consolidated his hold on power after a bitter struggle and begun to identify enemies bent on destroying the USSR inside and outside the borders of the socialist state.[139] Vigilance against enemies and saboteurs gained new importance within the international communist movement, and defense of the Soviet Union became a priority for European communist movements and their antimilitarist campaigns. This more intransigent approach met with less enthusiasm among adult party leaders than among those associated with the J.C. For the French party, in fact, the "class against class" approach marked an abrupt tactical shift away from a more conciliatory approach adopted in late 1925. During a by-election in 1926, party leaders had signaled a readiness to ally with "reformist" organizations on the left and center-left, and they made tentative overtures to members of the middle classes.[140]

While the party pursued a more moderate course in 1926 and for much of 1927, the J.C. practiced extreme politics. Youth militants stepped up their antimilitarist work, taking aim at proposed laws to reorganize the military and continuing their attempts to sabotage the "imperialist" French Army, whose latest colonial adventure was taking place in China. The J.C.'s big show of revolutionary mettle came during demonstrations in support of the Italian-American anarchists Sacco and Vanzetti on 23 August 1927. On this day Young Communists were in the front ranks of militants who arrived armed and ready to do battle.[141] When police moved in on the demonstrators, Communists fought back, attacking police forces on their flanks and discombobulating police horses by rolling marbles under their hooves. In a pitched battle that lasted for hours, communist militants held their ground.

In the days that followed, J.C. leaders pointed to the events of 23 August as the latest illustration of young workers' unsurpassed revolutionary ardor. *L'Avant-Garde* crowed on its front page that young workers were once again the most combative group among communist protestors and that the J.C. was ready to lead them to revolution. Not only did the organization form young workers politically and defend their demands, but it was ready to fight to train them for the "great battles to come."[142] For J.C. leaders the ultimate revolutionary confrontation must have seemed very close indeed. As *L'Avant-Garde* noted, class struggle was at its highest level since the revolutionary year of 1920.[143] In this atmosphere J.C. leaders (with the exception

Age and Generation in French Communism

of Doriot) greeted the Comintern's new policy with enthusiasm. The J.C. secretary general Henri Barbé later explained: "What seduced us and pulled us in was the newness and intransigence of the position."[144] That position might be novel for the party, but it was, as J.C. leaders pointed out at the end of 1928, consistent with J.C. campaigns of 1920, 1923, 1925, and 1927.[145]

Since the Comintern's "class against class" line conformed to the J.C.'s longstanding approach to revolutionary politics, Comintern leaders turned to youth leaders to help them implement the new line within the party. In 1928 they restructured party leadership around a core of youth leaders led by Barbé and including Pierre Célor, François Billoux, and André Ferrat.[146] These Young Communists, probably contacted by the Comintern representative Dimitry Manuilsky in the fall of 1927, were entrusted with the task of running the party in conjunction with adult leaders such as Maurice Thorez, Pierre Semard, Benoît Frachon, and Gaston Monmousseau. Working collectively, the leaders would implement the Comintern line within the party and continue the promotion of younger elements at all levels. According to Philippe Robrieux, the young men had a special responsibility to keep Comintern officials abreast of developments in France.[147]

Implementation of the new line within the party and its affiliated organizations, including the J.C. and the sports organization la Fédération Sportive du Travail (F.S.T.), involved unsparing methods. Opponents were tarred as "opportunists" and marginalized or expelled from the party. As this occurred in 1928 and 1929, J.C. leaders viewed their organization as leading the struggle to remake the party into "a real Bolshevik party in France" and fight mercilessly against any kind of "rightist" or "opportunist" deviation.[148] On one occasion young militants occupied the offices of *L'Humanité*, expelling seven insufficiently revolutionary subeditors.[149] The Communists' radical tactics brought intensified state repression. Police raided the offices of *L'Humanité* and *L'Avant-Garde* and hunted communist leaders. Leaders went underground, establishing a secret operations center in Brussels. As it had earlier, police repression fueled the young leaders' sense that they were on the front lines of a revolutionary struggle. *L'Avant-Garde* proclaimed excitedly in July 1929, "The battle rages between the bourgeoisie and us."[150]

However exciting this episode was for Young Communists, it proved disastrous for party membership and communist influence in France. Comintern officials stepped in during 1930, summoning Thorez and Barbé to Moscow in the spring. The party, they were told, was now to be vigilant against dangers from both the right and the left,[151] and Thorez was made secretary general.

But the situation in France failed to improve according to Comintern
wishes, and by the spring of 1931 Comintern officials were no happier with
the party and the direction taken by its leaders. To shift gears definitively,
Comintern officials turned against their former youth allies, manufacturing
a crisis that became known as the Barbé-Célor Affair, which made youth
leaders into scapegoats for the Comintern's misguided policy.[152]

The affair began with a devastating critique of the party and its leadership
by the Comintern's Executive Committee in July 1931, one that prompted
Thorez to submit a confidential letter of resignation to Comintern leaders.
In August party leaders met three times in the presence of the Comintern
officials Fried and Manuilsky to discuss the situation. At the first meeting
Ferrat, who had been the party's representative to the Comintern since 1929
(and who Kriegel and Courtois believe was in league with the Comintern's
representative in France, Eugen Fried), initiated a discussion of "groups"
working within the party. Ferrat identified the existence of "groups" from
both the trade union and youth movements. By the second meeting Ferrat
had turned the heat on a single group, the youth group, to which he said he
had belonged since the summer of 1930. But the most damaging accusations
came from Guyot, the secretary general of the J.C. At this meeting he confirmed the existence of a youth group, named its leading members (Henri
Barbé and Pierre Célor, who were conveniently absent from the meeting),
and discussed its workings.[153] The intrigue did not end in Paris but continued
to develop in Moscow, as events in France became enmeshed in the political
battles then raging in the Kremlin. As interrogations proceeded, the French
youth group was accused of being a conspiratorial cohort bent on seizing
power within the party and working at cross-purposes with the Comintern.
Its "fractional" activity was linked to the work of "fractional groups" that
had already been condemned by Stalin and his allies. Barbé himself was
goaded into admitting that the group's effort to "carry out a certain policy"
was "a real crime against the Party."[154]

The Barbé-Célor Affair had significant long-term consequences for both
the party and the J.C. According to historians of French communism, it
marked the triumph of a bolshevized party that would take its direction
from Moscow. For Annie Kriegel and Stéphane Courtois, the episode proved
the party's second major phase of bolshevization, after that initiated in 1924.
For Jean-Paul Brunet, the resulting installation of Thorez as undisputed
party leader (which he would remain until the mid-1960s) signaled the
achievement of full Comintern control over the party and its leadership.[155]

Age and Generation in French Communism

The J.C. was also left with a leader closely linked to Moscow. As the youth movement's secretary general, Guyot would shepherd the J.C. successfully through the Popular Front period, rising to the top of the Communist Youth International in 1935 and a position on the party's central committee, which he held from 1936 until 1985. The Comintern had found the leaders it was looking for in Thorez and Guyot.

The Barbé-Célor Affair also had crucial consequences for the role of youth within French communism. It foreclosed the possibility of a vanguard or even politically independent role for youth. With the denunciation of the youth cohort for ultraleft politics and the establishment of firm Comintern control over the French party, the J.C.'s role as an independent political force within French communism was no longer useful and therefore no longer tolerated. Moreover, since the youth group's vanguardism was held responsible for the excesses of 1928–31, denunciation of all forms of it became de rigueur for the J.C. leadership after Barbé-Célor. The new leaders energetically denounced past manifestations of vanguardism and promised more appropriate future conduct.[156] The J.C.'s role as a subgroup within a class-based party had been firmly established. The Comintern's vision of youth had triumphed: in the future, the J.C. would be an auxiliary organization firmly subordinate to party leadership.

# 2

## Building a Communist

## Youth Organization

As Jeunesse Communiste leaders maneuvered to play a leading role in French communism, they could not avoid the assignment of building a youth organization that reflected principles set forth in the Comintern's resolution on youth of July 1921. According to this declaration, communist youth movements across Europe needed to focus on organizing young workers and educating them in the ideas of communism. No longer, Comintern leaders warned, could youth movements limit themselves to small propaganda circles; instead they had to win over the masses of worker youth by using novel communist strategies.[1] French youth leaders greeted these instructions with apprehension. Jacques Doriot tried to put a brave face on the situation as he outlined the new reality in *L'Avant-Garde*, but his words underscored the leadership's uneasiness. He stated, tellingly, "the mass of young proletarians can no longer frighten us and we must, following the advice of the second congress, move closer to them without fear of being pulled in another direction."[2] Despite their reluctance, J.C. leaders began the work of creating a communist youth organization that corresponded to Comintern directives.

Throughout the 1920s the J.C.'s commitment to youth organizing was never consistent, as it was affected by both its engagement in adult communist politics and the strategic line emanating from Moscow. The intensity of the leaders' focus on mass organizing was often inversely related to their participation in Communist Party politics, and the ebb and flow of their efforts paralleled the chronology laid out in chapter 1. Few steps toward mass organizing were taken during 1921, 1922, or 1923, when the J.C. focused on antimilitarism and battles taking place within the adult party. More intensive focus came in 1924, with the emergence of fascist movements in France and the turn toward bolshevization in French communism. But the new interest was not long sustained. Attention waned during 1925, when the J.C.

**52** campaigned vigorously against the war in Morocco, and especially in the late 1920s, when the movement adopted an increasingly hard-line position. J.C. attempts to reach the masses of young workers thus proceeded in fits and starts throughout the decade, the high point of J.C. membership coming at the beginning of 1927 and the low point early in the next decade.

As the 1930s opened, the J.C. was clearly failing in its assigned task of attracting the majority of young workers and educating them in the ideas of communism. Young Communist efforts were hampered by extensive repression on the part of industrialists and state authorities. But many of the organization's difficulties were of its own making. The leaders' attempts to play a leading role in French communism often relegated youth organizing to a position of secondary importance. Even when the Young Communists turned their attention to organizing, their approach limited the movement's appeal. Both the J.C.'s understanding of the category "worker youth" and its strategies for attracting this group privileged workers who were male, employed in large industrial concerns, and in their late teens and early twenties. Although the J.C. was open to young female workers, the movement did not seek them out or facilitate their participation. As a result, the tiny number who became involved did so on male terms, becoming androgynous revolutionary comrades. Even the J.C.'s offerings to young male industrial workers had limited appeal. J.C. leaders created an organization that differed little from the adult party in orientation, and its efforts to entice young workers through sport were deeply politicized. Perhaps most importantly, the J.C. defended a program that subordinated the needs of young workers to the interests of the communist movement.

The organization's first decade underscored the main challenge faced by J.C. leaders: How to forge a political identity, agenda, and organization that reflected young workers' special mixture of age-related, class-related, and sometimes gender-related interests within an international movement which took class as the ultimate category of identity, exploitation, and mobilization? When it came to workplace organizing, the focal point of Young Communist efforts in the 1920s, youth radicalism again presented a Janus face: useful in sparking larger strike movements, it threatened deviation from the accepted communist course. Youthful radicalism therefore had to be carefully controlled so that the interests of the party and the Communists' principal constituency, adult male workers, predominated. For the Comintern and the Communist Youth International, the preservation of working-class unity trumped the defense of young workers' specific age-related interests, and the J.C.'s rhetoric and action reflected this approach. So although J.C. leaders like Doriot could speak eloquently about the age-related exploitation of France's youngest workers, they refused to privilege young workers' special needs when a choice had to be made. Instead they emphasized the importance of maintaining working-class unity, even if this meant calling on young workers to ignore the most blatant generational inequities. Little wonder that J.C. organizing efforts did not attract the masses of young workers, however defined.

**Organizing Young Workers at the Workplace** The J.C. took its first steps toward mass organizing in early 1922, establishing the general contours of its strategy for the remainder of the decade. The movement centered organizational efforts around the workplace and subscribed to the Communist Youth International's analysis of young workers' position in the capitalist economy and in the international communist movement. According to the C.Y.I., young workers were the most oppressed segment of the working class, one whose situation became more desperate every day. Nevertheless, past failures of independent young workers' movements had demonstrated the futility of fighting capitalism alone; instead, young workers had to join forces with adult workers under communist leadership.[3] This insistence on shared struggle would have important consequences for the J.C. campaign to mobilize young workers.

Many J.C. militants were ambivalent about mass organizing, which seemed an insufficiently revolutionary activity for a vanguard organization. Forced to defend the endeavor, J.C. leaders stressed its revolutionary nature: since the J.C. defended a maximalist set of demands that had no chance of being accepted under capitalism, it radicalized young workers by convincing them that only communist revolution provided the answer to their problems.[4] Despite these assertions of revolutionary significance, J.C. militants preferred direct involvement in party battles in 1922 and 1923. At the J.C. national congress in May 1922, delegates spent so much time debating party politics that discussion of the economic struggle was cut short.[5] For most of 1923 key J.C. militants threw their energies into the antimilitarist campaign in the Ruhr. In an assessment of the situation in mid-1923, *L'Avant-Garde* admitted that the economic struggle had hardly moved beyond the level of theory.[6] J.C. membership rolls remained small.

The establishment of fascist movements in France in 1924 increased J.C. attention to economic organizing. After the Cartel des Gauches won the

**54**   legislative elections of May 1924, it announced plans to reverse policies pursued by the center-right Bloc National government, in power since 1920, including abolishing the French embassy to the Vatican, extending the laic laws of the early twentieth century to Alsace and Lorraine, recognizing the USSR, and granting amnesty to French Communists condemned during the First World War. The measures infuriated conservatives, Catholics, and nationalists and helped lead to the formation of two fascist movements, the Légion and the Jeunesses Patriotes, in 1924. A third, the Faisceau, followed in 1925.[7] Anticommunism was a mainstay of these movements from their inception. Pierre Taittinger, leader of the Jeunessses Patriotes, declared, "Communism calls forth fascism" in an open letter to Prime Minister Édouard Herriot, and vowed that the J.P. was ready to use "any means necessary" to defeat communism.[8] Antoine Rédier, the leading figure in the Légion, lashed out against communism in speeches.[9] These movements sent their uniformed members to disrupt communist meetings and vowed to bar the road to communist revolution.

Because fascists made the regenerative power of youth and "new men" central to their manifestoes and appeals, the emergence of fascist movements in France assumed special significance for Young Communists. Taittinger noted in his *Notebooks of Young France*: "New men are needed to stave off new dangers. The men who have governed since the war have retained the mentality and customs of the pre-war period. They are no longer equal to the situation, which they no longer fully understand. They are old. The young are needed."[10] For Taittinger, as for other European politicians of the 1920s, the appeal to youth was often vague. Although students and the young had a role to play in the defense of a France whose values and imperial identity were under siege, veterans were assigned the key role in the country's reorganization and recovery. According to Taittinger, veterans had a right and a duty to govern France.[11] Rédier similarly believed that veterans were needed to create an entirely new regime,[12] while Georges Valois and Jacques Arthuys of the Faisceau equated youth with the war generation in their rhetoric.[13] Rhetoric aside, police reports indicate that these movements drew supporters from among university students, veterans, and supporters of General de Castelnau, the head of two powerful Catholic defense organizations.[14] By 1926 the Jeunesses Patriotes, the Légion, and the Faisceau grouped an estimated 135,000 active members between them.[15]

As they would again in the 1930s, fascist appeals to youth as a group and a mystique infused J.C. organizing with political significance and urgency.

The J.C.'s national congress in December 1924 paid special attention to the challenge posed by "the fascist offensive" and especially by fascist appeals to young people across the socioeconomic spectrum. Delegates discussed how fascist attempts to profit from youth's enthusiasm, political inexperience, and desire for action meant that the J.C. had to struggle with fascists for influence over French youth, and there was some mention of working to defend the political and economic rights of all French young people.[16] Mostly, however, J.C. leaders vowed to intensify the organization's efforts among young workers. Given the transfigured political context, it was imperative that the J.C. bring in all young workers and become the mass organization of worker youth.[17]

The fascist threat not only sharpened the J.C.'s focus on mass organizing but also allowed Young Communists to flex their muscles as revolutionary fighters. As tensions between fascists and Communists mounted in early 1925 in the run-up to the spring municipal elections, Young Communists played prominent roles in communist efforts to challenge fascists physically in meeting halls and in the streets. The high point of J.C. action came on the night of 23 April, when the Jeunesses Patriotes held an electoral meeting in the working-class eighteenth arrondissement of Paris; this was interpreted by Communists as a provocation, since they viewed the meeting as an incursion into their territory. Revolver in hand, François Chasseigne led the J.C.'s security service into battle outside the meeting hall. In the aftermath three students from the Jeunesses Patriotes lay dead and thirty more were wounded.[18] Chasseigne boasted of a "victory over fascism" on the front page of the next issue of *L'Avant-Garde*.[19]

The campaign to bolshevize French communism provided further stimulus to the J.C.'s organizing efforts and claims to vanguard status. This campaign, which began in earnest in 1924, aimed to restructure the previously fractious French party more closely along the lines of the Russian Bolshevik Party and enhance Comintern control over the party. Attempts were made to increase the proportion of working-class members and thereby turn the party into a genuine workers' party; to forge a cadre of professional revolutionaries loyal to Comintern analysis and directives; and to reorganize the party to make the factory cell, not the neighborhood section, the locus of communist organization and action.

These goals signaled a departure from past practice within the French left, accentuating generational divides within the party. This was especially true when it came to implanting factory cells. Because the new emphasis on factory cells challenged a longstanding division between trade union activism and socialist politics, some experienced trade union activists worried about the consequences for the autonomy of trade unions. The Young Communists had no such qualms. By establishing cells in factories, Young Communists believed that they were transforming the party into one that was communist and not socialist, revolutionary and not reformist. This was yet another demonstration of the organization's vanguard aspirations within the party, some of whose members were accused of failing to comprehend that the move to the factory cell would radically transform communist action.[20]

The J.C. stepped up its efforts to enroll young workers during 1924. Young Communists presented themselves as defenders of young proletarians in the political arena and the workplace. The high point of the political effort came in December 1924, with Jacques Doriot's speech to the Chamber of Deputies. A twenty-six-year-old former metalworker, Doriot addressed the Chamber for nearly two hours as both an elected deputy and the leader of a political organization composed overwhelmingly of young workers. Never before had young workers been represented so directly in the Chamber. The speech itself diverged considerably from Doriot's usual brand of Bolshevik revolutionary rhetoric, which was often greeted by heated interruptions and cries of "nasty Russian."[21]

The speech had multiple aims: it inserted young workers into larger political debates, analyzed and decried their economic exploitation, and outlined the Young Communist program of solutions. Doriot began by attacking the absence of worker youth from parliamentary discussions of issues such as social assistance, childhood protection, the future of the French race, France's demographic depression, and the crisis of the birth rate. These issues had figured prominently in French political anxieties and debates since the late nineteenth century. For Doriot, young workers were vital to the health of the race because they were its most immediate future.[22] Yet no government study of young workers' scandalous exploitation existed. The J.C. had undertaken its own investigation and the movement's findings provided the basis for his report.

Worker youth, which Doriot defined explicitly as workers under eighteen and implicitly as those who were male, constituted the most exploited segment of the working class. Using examples drawn from the J.C.'s investigation, Doriot presented a measured, documented analysis of their exploitation. He described the derisory wages paid to young workers across the country and detailed how apprentices were exploited as a source of cheap labor, especially in small shops. He argued that few young workers received any real training, pointedly using a noncommunist report to show that three-quarters of apprentices received no practical technical training.[23] Nor was there enforcement of labor laws designed to protect the young. Young workers often worked longer hours than adults, performed dangerous tasks prohibited by the Labor Code, and left school well before they were legally eligible to do so. Doriot described the deplorable sanitary conditions in many French workplaces, arguing that these created special problems for young workers whose bodies were still maturing. He also deployed official statistics to demonstrate that workers under eighteen were much more likely than adults to be the victims of industrial accidents.

Doriot's analysis reflected the experiences of many of France's young male workers. Its broad outlines were shared by socially minded priests, but the Young Communists' remedy differed drastically from that put forward by Catholics. The J.C.'s political program offered both a long-term solution—communist revolution—and the immediate defense of young workers' interests. The model was the Soviet Union, where according to Doriot, young workers did not enter the workforce until sixteen, were prohibited from performing night labor, and worked only a six-hour day. Soviet young workers, moreover, had the right to the paid vacations available to all workers and the supplementary vacations available to adolescent workers.[24]

Throughout the decade, Communists of all ages made stories of the Soviet Union a mainstay of their propaganda, with the first socialist state's treatment of children and youth functioning as a symbolic barometer of its superiority. In the years after revolutionary uprisings had been defeated across Europe, the Soviet Union was held out as tangible proof that revolution could be achieved. French Communists depicted the workers' state as a utopia that could be established in the here and now, its leaders mythic figures who would lead workers throughout the world to the promised land.[25] French Communists were encouraged to feel an affinity with the socialist homeland, and be ready to defend it and its people whenever necessary. During the early 1920s French Communists collected money for Soviet famine victims; later in the decade, when Soviet leaders became increasingly concerned about the threat of war, they took to the streets to demonstrate against an "imperialist" invasion of the Soviet Union.

Young Communists represented the Soviet Union as a concrete example of all that socialist revolution offered to youth, relying especially on accounts from those who had traveled to the workers' state and seen it firsthand.

Building a Communist Youth Organization

Leading Young Communists voyaged to Moscow to attend meetings and, by the late 1920s, to attend the International Leninist School. Movement activists and sympathetic young workers also traveled to the Soviet Union as members of workers' delegations. Upon their return these eyewitnesses described what they had seen in *L'Avant-Garde* and at mass meetings across France. At the end of 1925 a speaking tour sponsored by the J.C. sent returning young worker delegates to Sillaumines, Decazeville, L'Isle-sur-Sorgue, Marseille, Toulon, Nice, Bourges, Nevers, Commentry, Saint-Étienne, Brest, Dournenez, Rennes, Nantes, Trignac, Saint-Nazaire, Reims, Nancy, and Revin.[26] On this and other tours, the Young Communists endeavored to gather the largest possible audience to hear accounts of the worker paradise, sometimes supplementing the testimonials with Soviet films to heighten visual immediacy and drama.[27] The speaking tours often generated considerable excitement and attracted large crowds (up to five hundred in some instances); they were among the J.C.'s most successful propaganda endeavors.[28]

The testimonials given at mass meetings and in articles in *L'Avant-Garde* celebrated the Soviet state's responses to young workers' most pressing needs at the workplace and in the realm of leisure. The article "What We Saw in Red Moscow" (December 1925) was typical. According to this report, young people began work only when they reached eighteen, attending apprenticeship schools full-time after leaving primary school. Once they entered industrial labor, young workers earned good wages and participated in all decision-making bodies at the factory. They also had at their disposal a variety of clubs and activities, ranging from choral societies to sports clubs. Even the conditions of military service in the Soviet Union surpassed those in capitalist France. Red Army soldiers were subjected to only four hours of military exercises a day, with the remainder of the day reserved for "cultural and political education."[29]

The Soviet reality was very different. As the historian Anne Gorsuch makes clear, many young workers were desperate in the workers' state.[30] Rates of adolescent unemployment were horrendous. In 1926, for example, more than two-thirds of Russian workers under eighteen were unemployed. The next age group fared only marginally better, with close to half of those between eighteen and twenty-four out of work.[31] Their sizable communist youth organization, the Komsomol, which French Young Communists usually described with a certain awe, did little to defend the rights of young workers.

The gap between Soviet representations and realities in Young Communist accounts was not simply a case of cynical propaganda. The Soviet Union was a source of tremendous hope and possibility for many French workers, especially committed Communists. Travel to it could resemble a pilgrimage, which like other pilgrimages frequently took place under trying conditions. Workers endured many days of travel in train cars outfitted with only wooden benches, traveling on illegal passports and with few provisions. Both the conditions of the journey and the very real repression that Communists faced in France heightened the sense of excitement upon arrival. As Jeannette Vermeersch remembered, reaching the Soviet Union for the first time was "literally like entering into a dream." It was, she continued, "an overwhelming and realistic dream, a fantastic country where there were no more bosses, where the army and the police were our brothers and struggled with us."[32]

Soviet hosts maintained this dreamlike state through careful supervision of visits. Communist delegations were housed in relative luxury and given access to items not available to Soviet citizens. Carefully planned itineraries included visits to select factories and carefully scripted Komsomol meetings whose political pageantry featured songs, banners, ceremonies, and torchlight processions.[33] The enthusiasm and the unity of purpose visible at these meetings impressed Young Communists operating on the margins of French law and society.[34] Henri Barbé reported enthusiastically on a Komsomol youth club meeting in 1924. The club's many rooms, including its "antireligious room," were decorated with large murals painted by young workers. The French youth delegation was greeted by a tremendous ovation from the four to five hundred young workers present. Excitement continued to build with the arrival of a "superb red flag" presented to the French delegation, accompanied by an "indescribable ovation." A thunderous rendition of the International followed. Barbé was moved by the "will and invincible faith in the world revolution" that he described seeing on the faces of those singing the workers' anthem.[35] If Young Communists had doubts—and Barbé himself later described the technical backwardness he saw in Soviet factories on that first visit[36]—they usually kept them to themselves.

For Doriot and the Young Communists, only a socialist revolution would bring real improvement in the condition of working youth. Until this occurred, however, the J.C. intended to fight for improvements in the immediate circumstances of worker youth. The J.C. leader called on the state to enforce existing youth labor laws by increasing the number of inspectors, improving their quality, and giving working-class organizations a role in inspection. But as Doriot told his fellow deputies, he was under no illusion that the government would implement these improvements, especially since such a large portion of the state's budget was devoted to military spending. It was up to young workers to organize a powerful communist youth movement to impose their demands.

The J.C.'s appeal to young workers around workplace issues relied on a number of strategies. On the one hand, the J.C. strove to represent itself as the champion of young workers' economic interests. The movement argued, with a certain justification for much of the 1920s, that it alone defended young workers, and it denounced youth exploitation in the Chamber, in the J.C.'s newspaper, in tracts, and in pamphlets such as *The Labor Code and the Defense of Young Workers*, which used long extracts from the Labor Code to inform young workers of their rights. The J.C. paid special attention to the difficulties that young workers faced in obtaining adequate training, its explanations for this sorry state shifting over the course of the decade. During the early 1920s deficient training was often traced to wartime exigencies. A front-page article in *L'Avant-Garde* explained in 1923: "You belong to the generation forged in the crucible of war. You were brought up on daily communiqués . . . At school, they filled your head with words and numbers distilled with hate but they forgot to teach you a trade."[37] The collapse of apprenticeship, long declining during the nineteenth century,[38] only exacerbated young workers' problems. J.C. literature repeatedly attacked "apprenticeships" that did nothing more than extract cheap, menial labor from young people. When Communists turned their rhetorical attention to the problems created by the rationalization of French factories after 1927, they made it the prime cause of young workers' insufficient training. According to Young Communists, young workers suffered most from rationalization, whose first consequence was "the ever more complete disappearance of the opportunity to learn a skill."[39]

The J.C. compiled programs of demands that it promised to defend at the workplace and vis-à-vis adult unions, which, the J.C. correctly noted, did little to defend youth workers. Although specific demands varied, they tended to be far-reaching and largely unattainable. At a time when paid vacations were barely conceivable to many workers, when unions fought to maintain the eight-hour day, when wages were unregulated, and when the meager unemployment benefits were calculated according to age, the J.C.

demanded four weeks of paid vacation, a six- or eight-hour day encompassing professional training, a youth minimum wage, and full unemployment benefits. Young Communist leaders believed that advocacy of unattainable demands would radicalize young workers by demonstrating the impossibility of winning meaningful reform under the capitalist system. This strategy often put the Young Communists at odds with an older generation of leaders of the Confédération Générale du Travail Unitaire, who were more concerned with defending workers' immediate needs.[40]

In accordance with the bolshevization drive, the J.C. set out in 1924 to establish factory cells throughout French industry. Large workplaces in the metalworking, mining, and textile industries were especially targeted because of their importance to both the French economy and youth employment. The factory cell, whose meetings were held in a nearby café, became the fundamental unit of communist organization, formation, and struggle. Since the effort to create factory cells marked a departure from earlier communist efforts, militants were given precise instructions in pamphlets such as André Ferrat's *Bring Our Cells to Life!* and in the schools begun by the J.C. and the party in the second half of 1924. In keeping with its vanguard status and its close relationship to the Comintern, the J.C. opened the first central communist school in Saint-Denis in the fall of 1924; the party soon followed with its own school in Bobigny. Students attending the J.C. school were attached to factory cells and expected to participate fully as part of their practical training.[41] To help revolutionary trainees hone their speaking skills, the J.C.'s Paris federation organized meetings at important factories in the region.[42]

Communist instructions extended to all aspects of the cell's foundation, recruitment, and action. Young Communists were directed to begin by studying the conditions within a particular factory and to generate interest in the communist cause by talking to young workers, making speeches at factory gates, and writing and distributing propaganda materials such as tracts, stickers, and especially factory newspapers, which usually consisted of three to four typed pages and bore names such as *The Young Bolshevik of Renault*. Young Communists were instructed to move back and forth between denouncing specific injustices, such as low wages or terrible hygienic conditions, and the more general exploitation of the working class by the bourgeoisie.[43] In recruiting members, Young Communists were told to pay special attention to those who were on the verge of departing for military service, for their apprehension could be useful in making them susceptible

**62**   to communist appeals. Militants were also made aware of the importance that concrete, if limited, improvements such as soap for bathrooms or better ventilation for workshops could have in winning young workers to their cause. They were further reminded of the necessity of total obedience. Directives emanating from all levels of the party had to be executed, "even if they did not seem to respond to the needs of factory life."[44] Finally, Young Communists were advised of the importance of generational unity. They had to work closely with adult organizations, down to having an adult present at all J.C. meetings, and be mindful of their mission to fight for the working class in general and not young workers in particular.

As convincing as the communist analysis of the factory cell's operation could be on paper, J.C. factory cells attracted only a small but disciplined minority of mostly male young workers during the 1920s. Employers' repression proved one of the major challenges Young Communists faced as they tried to establish factory cells. In the larger, more modern factories targeted by the J.C., employers proved especially vigilant against attempts to create unions or communist cells, and they had the force of law on their side. Employers hired spies and security agents to monitor workers, with one aircraft manufacturer habitually shouting, "No Soviets! No Soviets!" when he saw groups of two or three workers talking.[45] Workers who were discovered trying to organize were fired and sometimes placed on industry-wide blacklists, while those who spoke at factory gates risked arrest. In 1924 communist deputies were regularly sent to the local police station to rescue students who had not returned to the communist school in the afternoon.[46] In these circumstances workers risked their jobs and professional futures to join a cell. Those who became J.C. militants bounced from factory to factory and could be driven to seek work under false names. Even in communist strongholds like Saint-Denis, this was something that not all communist workers were willing to do, and the drive to implant factory cells suffered.[47] Employer repression also limited the effectiveness of cells that were successfully established. A Young Communist explained his cell's decline by pointing out that its last two secretaries had been fired for communist action.[48]

The communist vision of factory politics was not without appeal, however. In the mid-1920s factory cells drew a small, dedicated cohort, with young, skilled male workers prominent among them. For these young workers the campaign accorded with a desire for radical action and did not clash with earlier notions of trade union activism. And so as 1924 ended at the giant Renault plant, the J.C. cell was two and a half times as large as the adult cell, and more active.[49] In the aircraft industry, Herrick Chapman estimates that the typical communist trade union activist in the late 1920s and early 1930s was young, male, and skilled.[50]

Despite the relative paucity of archival materials, there is little doubt that the J.C.'s effort to draw young workers into factory cells reaped immediate benefits in the mid-1920s, altering the shape of the organization. In 1924 the J.C. witnessed an influx of new members among young workers, and it claimed to have close to ten thousand members by year's end. By early 1925 that number was said to have reached twelve thousand. The J.C.'s national congress in December 1924 demonstrated the organization's success in attracting new, committed working-class members. Of the congress's 203 delegates, the overwhelming majority were workers, with 84 employed in metalworking. Over half the delegates had joined the organization in 1924.[51] At the same time, the J.C. expelled students for what it referred to as intellectual and petty-bourgeois deviations.[52] The J.C. was refashioning itself to become more proletarian and, in its words, "wholly young."

The J.C.'s success contributed to the growing influence of the organization and its leaders within French communism in the mid-1920s. At the party congress of 1925, young workers were believed to make up the overwhelming majority of the roughly 66 percent of delegates who were working-class.[53] For their part, J.C. leaders often became full-time party employees, or *permanents*, with overlapping roles in the J.C., the party, and the adult trade union movement. Barbé is again a good example. By the time he was named to oversee the J.C.'s economic and social action in 1925, he had already been the effective head of the adult party in Saint-Denis and was serving as secretary of the Union des Syndicats de la Seine.[54]

Despite the continued prominence of J.C. leaders, the mid-1920s were less the starting point for future successes than the high point of the J.C.'s organizing efforts during this first decade. By the late 1920s the J.C.'s membership had declined considerably; by the early 1930s the organization was a shell of its former self, counting only 3,500 members in January 1932.[55] The campaign to establish factory cells had stalled. In 1931 J.C. leaders admitted that fifteen of twenty regions did not have a single factory cell, and this included important industrial centers such as Marseille, Bordeaux, and Toulouse.[56]

The reasons for this decline were numerous. Repression by employers and the police restricted the J.C.'s numbers. As the J.C. became ever more oppositional in the late 1920s, police surveillance intensified. Militants were arrested for speaking, for organizing and attending antimilitarist meetings, and for selling *L'Avant-Garde*. Leaders went underground, and police officials found that the arrest of a small number of militants spread fear among others.[57] But the strategies of the Young Communists themselves limited the movement's appeal among the masses of young workers, especially during the late 1920s and early 1930s. At this time of heightened communist intransigence, demands became increasingly divorced from everyday realities. The party and the J.C. emphasized issues and positions that privileged the needs of the communist movement—as defined by the Comintern—over those of ordinary workers. Both gave the highest priority to generational unity and the attempt to forge a united front of young and adult workers, compromising the J.C.'s ability to rally young workers.

The emphasis on generational unity was particularly apparent during strike movements, which were on the rise among young workers during the 1920s. By the end of the decade the J.C. recognized that important strike action was being undertaken by the young in the Paris region and in the Nord. These movements put Young Communists, who usually had no part in their outbreak, in a difficult position, especially since young male workers' age-based demands differed from those of adult male workers. For the Young Communists youth strike movements were a doubled-edged sword: the promise of youthful radicalism and combativeness carried with it the danger of dissension and generational discord. One internal J.C. report admitted in 1929, "If these youth strikes demonstrate a clear commitment to struggle on the part of young people, we should also examine the potential dangers created by these movements."[58] As in the early days of Russian Bolshevism, young workers' radicalism had to be shaped and controlled to advance the aims of the party. The J.C.'s Central Committee was clear about the organization's priorities. Although the Central Committee vowed to help youth strike movements attain their goals, it noted that the organization's "essential role" was to ensure that this more combative segment of the working class could be used to energize the entire working class.[59] When strikes occurred, the J.C. called for generational unity and working-class solidarity in its messages to young workers. During the lengthy strike in the wine-growing region of Rivesaltes in 1928, young *vignerons* were celebrated for remaining united with adult workers even though youth demands had not been taken up by the strikers. *L'Avant-Garde* proclaimed, "It's a good example for all young workers. There is not one scab among the young people of Rivesaltes. All went out, although no special youth demands were made."[60]

Building a Communist Youth Organization

The J.C. thus had little influence over the masses of young workers or their strike movements by the late 1920s. As the Young Communist in charge of union work for the Paris region told fellow members of the J.C. in 1929, "One can say without exaggerating that nothing was accomplished—or even attempted—during the workers' struggles; young workers went out on strike in the factories and demonstrated without any involvement from the J.C."[61] The news from the strike movement of 1930 in the Nord was equally dismal. According to a J.C. report, the organization had been almost completely cut off from young workers, having no presence in factories whatsoever.[62] J.C. leaders were taken by surprise at the outbreak of the strikes and overwhelmed as events unfolded. Attempts by J.C. national leaders to save the situation came to naught, with few workers bothering to attend meetings. In the end the episode resulted in a weakening, not a strengthening, of the J.C.

The J.C. similarly made little headway in rallying conscripts to the communist cause in the late 1920s and early 1930s. Although the J.C. made demands for improving the immediate and often trying conditions facing conscripts an important feature of its propaganda, attempts to promote these demands took second place to the effort to convince conscripts that their actions should support the goals of the international communist movement and its version of antimilitarism. By the late 1920s this meant that conscripts had to struggle to prevent the army's use against liberation movements in Asia and the Middle East and, more importantly, against the Soviet Union. By 1928, in fact, the "struggle for the defense of the USSR" had become the axis of the J.C.'s antimilitarist work.[63] J.C. cells that focused too closely on the immediate demands of conscripts were criticized,[64] and the movement opposed the reorganization of the army in 1927, which reduced the term of military service to one year.

**Organizing Young Workers at Play** Despite the J.C.'s attention to the workplace and the military, it did not ignore the realm of leisure in the effort to build a mass organization. In France of the 1920s the question of leisure had become salient for organizations seeking to enroll young workers, who had more leisure time than ever before. Although the eight-hour day and forty-eight-hour week voted by parliament in April 1919 were contested and unevenly applied by the early 1920s, they were widely applied in the large industrial workplaces targeted by the Young Communists.[65]

**66** Moreover, the young male proletarians who dominated the Young Communist movement had fewer domestic constraints on their after-work time than adults or young women. They were prime consumers of leisure, and any effort to mobilize them had to address their lives outside work. During the 1920s the J.C. fashioned a politics of leisure that drew heavily on analyses and organizational structures conceived in Moscow and was geared primarily toward young men. At its core was a belief in leisure's fundamentally political nature. Leisure could never be politically neutral, as its bourgeois purveyors claimed, but was always invested with political significance; it always served the interests of either capitalists or the Communists struggling to overthrow them. Following from this analysis, the J.C. endeavored to wean young workers from leisure offerings controlled by the bourgeoisie and attract them to communist-sponsored ones. Neither effort was terribly successful.

Sport provided the focal point of the J.C.'s leisure-oriented rhetorical and organizational efforts, which followed the general chronology evident in workplace organizing. When the J.C. stepped up its organizing in 1924, it identified sport as young workers' favorite after-work activity. In nice weather, *L'Avant-Garde* reported, young Parisian workers used their Sundays to head to the countryside to canoe or swim in the Seine and Marne, play soccer, jog, or cycle.[66] In the paper's telling, young workers, again assumed to be male, took great pleasure from these unorganized sporting activities, which had the added benefit of taking them away from unhealthy workplaces and neighborhoods. However, as Young Communists well knew, young workers' attachment to sport went beyond these healthy, restorative diversions. Young workers were also keen participants in the numerous sporting clubs and associations sponsored by the Communists' principal opponents, and avid fans of increasingly commercialized, increasingly popular professional sport.

By the postwar decade the effort to appeal to and shape young men through sport was well under way in France. As historians have demonstrated, sport had been harnessed to a range of political projects since the late nineteenth century. In the aftermath of France's humiliating defeat in the Franco-Prussian War of 1870–71, nationalists viewed sport, especially gymnastics, as a means of regeneration amid mounting concerns over national decline, racial degeneration, and a crisis of masculinity.[67] Gymnastic clubs allowed nationalists an opportunity to strengthen male bodies and instill values in an appealing setting, and their numbers grew. Catholics similarly recognized the possibilities presented by sport as they sought to win over adolescent males in Republican France. Sports clubs were added to parish youth groups and connected by a national association, the Fédération Gymnastique et Sportive des Patronages de France (F.G.S.P.F.). Catholic sport received a boost after the separation of church and state in 1905; by the eve of the First World War the F.G.S.P.F. counted 180,000 active members.[68]

The effort to reach youth through sport expanded further in the postwar decade. Large employers, especially those in the automobile and aircraft industries, provided sports clubs and recreational facilities, including pools and playing fields, for their workers. These offerings were designed to prepare workers physically and psychologically for the demands of the modern, rationalized workplace and to encourage company loyalty.[69] The state intensified its efforts, in 1928 establishing a state agency to oversee sport, le Sous-secrétariat National aux Sports. The F.G.S.P.F., meanwhile, continued to flourish. For Catholics concerned about perceptions of the church as a feminized institution, public exhibitions of muscular, male Catholic gymnasts asserted the strength and virility of the church's followers. Membership in all sporting associations rose sharply in the 1920s,[70] with sports clubs especially popular among young workers. According to the J.C., the various sporting associations counted four million members by the late 1920s, the majority believed to be young workers or young peasants.[71]

The high rate of participation by young workers in bourgeois-controlled sport had to be combated because Young Communists viewed it as "an instrument of capitalist domination."[72] Through participation in employer-sponsored sports clubs, young workers were pulled away from unions, tethered to the factory, and transformed into stronger, more productive workers for their capitalist masters, into "better human production machines."[73] Sports clubs robbed young workers of any sense of class identity and any "spirit of rebellion."[74] Communists also linked the practice of bourgeois-controlled sport to preparation for capitalist war, pointing, as historians subsequently would, to the period before 1914 as proof. According to L'Avant-Garde, the bourgeoisie recognized the military uses of athletic discipline and created competitions and certificates, brevets militaires sportifs, which endowed sport with specific military applications.[75] Communists understood the value of sport in forging a masculinity that served nationalist and militarist goals.

Young Communists believed as well that spectatorship distracted young workers from the revolutionary cause. Young male workers were avid consumers of the professional sports that were so popular in France of the

1920s. *L'Avant-Garde* took care to depict the exploitative side of sports in its tiny sports section, a feature increasingly present in the postwar French press. The paper devoted special attention to professional cycling, which held particular allure for young working men who enjoyed riding their own bicycles and cheered the often dizzying successes of the numerous working-class racers.[76] Many of these racers were young themselves, with some combining racing and apprenticing.[77] To dampen enthusiasm, *L'Avant-Garde* depicted professional cycling as a capitalist enterprise in which athletes were controlled and exploited by disciplines analogous to those experienced by young workers in the industrial workplace. These critiques were leveled with particular vigor against the Tour de France and its chief Henri Desgrange, whose attempts to wring maximum profit out of his "pedal workers" were frequently assailed by the adult communist daily *L'Humanité*.[78] In the context of growing communist condemnation of the rationalized workplace in 1927, *L'Avant-Garde* emphasized that Tour racers were nothing more than expendable workers whose performance was measured against the clock. *L'Avant-Garde* explained, "As the factory owner requires his workers to produce ever greater amounts, so too does the Tour's boss seek to require his workers to do sport. As if sport could be done on command!"[79]

But sport was not to be discounted. The Communists' goal was to harness sport to their own revolutionary purposes. While the bourgeoisie had used sport to domesticate the proletariat, the Communists intended to make it an instrument of working-class liberation.[80] Proletarian sport served the revolutionary movement by developing a cadre of strong, physically fit revolutionaries who could prepare and defend the revolution.[81] Proletarian sport also served young workers' needs by fortifying them through the development of their bodies, which were constantly under siege by unhealthy working conditions.

To persuade French young workers of the glories of proletarian sport, the J.C. again enlisted Soviet examples. The exploits of Soviet athletes competing at home and in France were chronicled prominently in *L'Avant-Garde*. By championing the male Soviet athlete and praising him for his physique and discipline, the J.C. celebrated a Soviet sports system accessible to millions of workers. The Soviet athlete was integrated into J.C. iconography, becoming a tangible symbol of the success of the Soviet revolution and the benefits it brought to the working class. During a visit of Soviet athletes to France in the winter of 1925–26, *L'Avant-Garde* challenged readers: "We ask skeptics who persist in thinking that the Revolution has brought nothing to the proletariat to come see for themselves."[82] For Young Communists the healthy, sculpted, **69** and visibly strong male bodies made manifest the Revolution's ability to create a new society and a new socialist young man.

Whereas Soviet sport was the pinnacle of proletarian sport, the French communist version offered to young workers proved only a pale imitation. French communist sport occurred within clubs affiliated with the Fédération Sportive du Travail (F.S.T.), which had emerged in 1919 and aligned itself formally to the Red Sports International in 1923. The F.S.T. functioned as the J.C.'s principal auxiliary organization during the 1920s and served two major purposes. It offered a network of communist sports clubs, the number of which police estimated at 129 in Paris and the provinces in November 1925.[83] It also sponsored proletarian competitions and sports festivals designed to offer an alternative to the "bourgeois" Olympic movement, in which the Soviet Union refused to participate.[84]

Extreme politicization was the most striking feature of the F.S.T. in the 1920s and early 1930s, with the practice of sport subordinated to revolutionary aims. As the Red Sports International explained, "sports and gymnastics are not the goal to be pursued, but merely a means of carrying out the proletarian class struggle."[85] The F.S.T. demanded full participation from its athletes in the J.C.'s major political campaigns. When the bolshevization campaign began in earnest in 1924, F.S.T. athletes were instructed to work among conscripts, attend J.C. conferences and meetings, and work alongside Young Communists in factories.[86] As communist tactics became more intransigent later in the decade, F.S.T. efforts were expected to evolve in a similar fashion. At the end of 1926 the Comintern's Executive Committee voted a secret resolution aimed at reorganizing and arming communist sports organizations in Europe.[87] During the "class against class" period, the F.S.T. was expected to orient its activities around "the development of revolutionary action and propaganda."[88] Similarly, the red camping groups, introduced by the J.C. in 1929 to counter bourgeois scouting associations, had as their goal "the revolutionary physical training" of participants through a program of gymnastics, wrestling, shooting, sporting competitions, and self-defense exercises.[89]

Sport as revolution did not attract the masses of French young workers. By the end of the 1920s the F.S.T. could claim only fifteen thousand member athletes.[90] The Spartakaid athletic competition in Lyon in 1932 illustrated the F.S.T.'s failures. With this event French organizers attempted to mount a sports competition and festival after the Soviet model to counter enthusiasm for that year's Olympics in Los Angeles. Spartakaid was designed to draw athletes from across Europe and France, and plans were made to film the arrival of athletes from Paris in Lyon. F.S.T. members were directed to sell sixteen thousand copies of *L'Avant-Garde*. According to police agents, however, nothing matched organizers' hopes. Crowds were sparse and indifferent, and the contingent of participating athletes was small. In the end organizers were left wondering how they would pay their bills.[91]

The situation of proletarian sport was not uniformly dismal in France. There is evidence that local J.C. organizations could be less dogmatic and more flexible in their approach to communist sport than national directives and analyses might suggest. The situation in Vénisseux, a suburb of Saint-Étienne, is an example. Under the leadership of the spirited Lise London, the local J.C. acceded to the demands of athletes and allowed the existence of two competing F.S.T. clubs. It also founded an F.S.T. club specifically for young women.[92] A photograph of these female athletes posing proudly with clenched fists suggests that support for revolutionary politics could coexist with the excitement of athletic competition.[93] In this section, no doubt as in other locales, the gap between directives and implementation could be huge, especially when J.C. cells were usually tiny and overseen by militants with little experience and even less theoretical training. All this created the possibility of multiple local realities.

So too did communism's differing status in localities across France. Both the F.S.T. and the J.C. thrived most in municipalities controlled by Communists. Although the Communists controlled only a small number of seats at the national level, they won control of several municipalities in 1925, including eight in the belt of suburbs ringing Paris. In these "red suburbs" Communists enacted ideology at the local level. Communist governments renamed streets to honor their heroes; built public housing; initiated welfare measures, including a range of programs for proletarian children; created alternative celebrations for rites of passage, including baptism; and directed money to communist organizations.[94] Government and party functions sometimes so overlapped that it could be hard to distinguish communist sections and associations from the municipal government itself.[95] In this thriving political culture, Communists were not a persecuted minority but a powerful majority, and their organizations were not pursued by state authorities but nourished by official sanction and support.

Because proletarian sport provided French Communists with powerful images of a strong, disciplined working class, it played an important part in municipal communism. In Halluin in the Nord, the communist government made the construction of a sports stadium rivaling that of its adversaries one of its first capital projects.[96] Other communist municipal governments followed suit, and the stadia that became prominent in Parisian suburbs during the 1920s provided settings for F.S.T. athletic competitions, as well as for communist political pageantry. The privileged position of proletarian sport in communist municipalities contrasted sharply with the situation elsewhere in France, where the absence of municipal support was coupled with state repression, including the cancellation of athletic competitions. This was especially true in the late 1920s.

The J.C. did not totally neglect the other great interwar youth pastime, the cinema, to which the Bolsheviks assigned much importance in revolutionary propaganda and education. According to *L'Avant-Garde*, the cinema was "the best means of propaganda for socialism and the dictatorship of the proletariat."[97] Given the J.C.'s minority status in France, the organization adopted a two-pronged strategy which mirrored its strategy with sport. The J.C. attacked "bourgeois" movies as decadent and corrupt and promised a specifically proletarian, revolutionary alternative. But although Soviet films were clearly shown at some communist gatherings, they seem to have played only a small role in J.C. activities during the 1920s. French Communists did not produce their own movies, and police reports only rarely mention the showing of films at J.C. meetings or events. On those occasions when entertainment was provided, it was most likely in the form of revolutionary plays, skits, songs, and poems. A J.C. young workers' festival in Paris in 1930, for example, featured a program with revolutionary songs and poems, skits by factory workers, an antireligious play performed by a local group of Pioneers (the communist children's organization), and rhythmic dances and gymnastic displays by F.S.T. athletes.[98]

The determinedly revolutionary approach that characterized J.C. organizing and leisure did not go unchallenged within the movement in the late 1920s and early 1930s. The first serious effort to redefine the J.C.'s approach came in 1928 in response to the emergence of the Jeunesse Ouvrière Chrétienne. This Catholic overture to working-class youth made immediate inroads into working-class, even communist strongholds, and Young Communists soon identified Jocists as their "most dangerous adversaries."[99] Faced with J.O.C. successes, especially among apprentices and young workers in their teens, the J.C. attempted to adopt a more "youthful" approach, beginning with *L'Avant-Garde*. Arguing that the paper should no longer be pitched toward young workers returning from military service, the editors tilted toward young workers between the ages of fourteen and twenty.[100] A writing style more closely geared toward this younger segment of worker youth was introduced, and games, puzzles, and amusing stories were added to the newspaper's back pages.

A less politicized approach to young workers' leisure accompanied these changes to *L'Avant-Garde*. The F.S.T. announced that it was taking steps to become a mass organization, and the J.C. sponsored new activities. Sunday cycling trips through the French countryside, recently scorned for distracting young workers from more important revolutionary work, were held up as an example of ways to attract young workers to the J.C.[101] Festive gatherings, from outdoor festivals in the tradition of that sponsored by *L'Humanité* to parties and dances, were similarly employed to reach a broader spectrum of young workers. *L'Avant-Garde* singled out a gathering that featured "un jazz" organized by the J.C. of Roubaix, a J.O.C. stronghold, as a particularly fine example of this new approach.[102] As the newspaper pointed out, these overtures would allow the organization to reach beyond its base of young native-born males and attract young women and immigrants.

The new strategy conflicted with the J.C.'s promotion of the "class against class" revolutionary line, however, and soon disappeared. In an atmosphere of heightened revolutionary fervor and increased state repression, bicycle outings and dances gave way to armed combat in the streets and renewed concentration on implanting factory cells. By June 1929 the organization was castigating itself for not being "a Bolshevik-style organization based in the factory" and for relying on "social democratic organizational methods."[103] A new approach to leisure and youth politics would have to await the adoption of a Popular Front strategy.

**Organizing Young Women** Any analysis of the J.C.'s organizing efforts would be incomplete without a discussion of the movement's relationship to young working women. Women constituted close to 40 percent of the French working population under the age of twenty-four in the mid-1920s and became a special target of Catholic organizing efforts. Yet young women represented only a tiny share of the small number of Young Communists during the 1920s and early 1930s. Although membership records do not exist and police reports on cell membership are few, available evidence indicates that young women's participation in the organization was extremely limited at all levels. One young woman, the Polish-

born "Rosa Michel," sat on the J.C.'s first leadership committee, but she did  **73**
not play a prominent role and quickly moved on to other tasks within the
international communist movement.[104] It was only in the early 1930s that
two young women, Jeannette Vermeersch and Danielle Casanova, reached
the J.C.'s governing body. The situation was similar at the local and regional
levels. One young woman appeared on the list of forty-three J.C. militants
seized by the police in Caen in 1927, and another figured among the twenty
students at the J.C.'s school in Bordeaux in 1932.[105] The J.C. was overwhelmingly male in its first decade and a half.

That young women should have been so rare within the organization during the 1920s was neither obvious nor foreordained. The postwar decade
witnessed new attention to women on the part of the Soviet government
and the Soviet youth organization, the Komsomol. Laws mandating equality
in marriage, civil society, and the economy were passed in the first months
of Bolshevik rule, and a government bureau devoted to women's issues was
created in 1919. The Bolshevik government endeavored to rally women of
all ages behind the Bolshevik revolutionary program and the government's
military campaigns during the Civil War, paying special attention to young
women.[106] In the fall of 1920 the government established compulsory pre-
military training in sports and gymnastics for large groups of young women
between the ages of sixteen and eighteen.[107] Young women also made up a
larger proportion of Komsomol membership in the 1920s than did adult
women within the party. Although a range of factors denied young women
equal participation in the Soviet Communist Youth organization,[108] young
Soviet women were active in much larger numbers than in France.

This fact was not lost on the Young Communist leader François Billoux.
Describing his visit to a factory in Moscow in 1924, Billoux reported being struck by the number of women and young women participating in
party and Komsomol meetings. The French delegation was "strongly embar-
rassed" when asked to discuss the role of women in the French party and
youth organization.[109] Billoux did not indicate how the French Communists
answered this question, but it is clear that young women were pushed to
the periphery by the J.C.'s deeply gendered approach to politics. The J.C.'s
brand of youth activism emphasized political struggle and revolutionary
action, often within the all-male institution of the military. This was a revolutionary politics in which toughness and virility were prized, and a willingness to wage war and battle police and fascist forces was embedded in the
movement's self-conception as the communist vanguard.

**74**     The marginalization of young women and their concerns is clear from early debates and publications. The first article in *L'Avant-Garde* devoted explicitly to young women appeared only in January 1922. And when it did, the piece portrayed the young woman as the polar opposite of the young man in language more reminiscent of Jean-Jacques Rousseau than Vladimir Lenin or Alexandra Kollontai. She was more passive and timid, more susceptible to parental control, and more apt to be guided by feeling than by reason.[110] According to the author, such female attributes called for distinct methods of organizing and education, especially since girls had to be made to feel the communist ideal more strongly than their male counterparts. This call for gender-specific overtures met with little response. Only the Paris region appears to have created a short-lived women's secretariat in 1923,[111] and it is doubtful that this body undertook any serious work.

As the J.C. expanded its efforts to reach the masses of young workers and conscripts, young women continued to be sidelined. Since young women did not perform military service, they were by virtue of their sex excluded from appeals to conscripts and from most antimilitarist action. The J.C.'s understanding of "worker youth" and "young worker" as male categories contributed greatly to young women's marginalization. When Doriot spoke about the plight of worker youth for close to two hours in the Chamber of Deputies, he had nothing to say about the specific conditions facing those workers who were young *and* female. Moreover, the pamphlet *The Labor Code and the Defense of Young Workers*, a mainstay of the campaign to rally young workers, was silent when it came to young female workers, *les jeunes ouvrières*. Analyses of young workers' leisure similarly neglected pastimes favored by young women.

Although young women workers were cast as others who could be ignored in the first half of the 1920s, they became more troublesome figures as the decade progressed. Female workers, who were always paid less than male workers, had long been perceived as threats to male employment prospects and wages, and they had long been the object of male efforts to exclude them from workplaces and trade unions.[112] Yet concern over the threat posed by female labor intensified within French communism after 1927, when communist trade union leaders devoted more attention to the challenges posed by rationalization in French industrial workplaces. In communist analysis, the reorganization of work led to greater use of young male and female labor; male trade unionists worried that if they were not careful, youth and female workers could be used as a reserve army of labor to undercut male

wages.[113] Young Communist leaders adopted this notion of the potential
threat posed by both groups. *L'Avant-Garde* explained the danger posed by
young female workers in 1928 in an article which ironically celebrated International Women's Week. According to the newspaper, young women's low
wages allowed them to be pitted against adult workers as well as young male
workers, resulting in the dismissal of male workers and their replacement
by young women.[114] Young women workers were at best tangential and at
worst dangerous.

Given this vision of young working women, it is not surprising that
Young Communists made few sustained efforts to organize young women
workers at the workplace, or elsewhere, in the 1920s. There were occasional mentions in *L'Avant-Garde* of the specific exploitation faced by young
female workers as the 1920s advanced, and the party's far-reaching platform regarding women's rights was sometimes published as International
Women's Day, celebrated on 8 March, approached.[115] But this did not trans-
late into serious work to mobilize young women. The J.C. did not establish
a national body for young women's issues as the party did, and it rarely appealed directly to the relatively small number of young women workers who
labored in the large factories targeted by the Young Communists.[116] When
young women workers were singled out, it was to equate their exploitation
with that of young male workers and to urge them to see that their real
interests lay in common struggle with young male workers and the working class more generally.[117] Young Communists made little effort to attract
young women workers where they predominated, including in the fashion
industry, domestic service, and white-collar work.

Young working women who wanted to take part in communist activities
had to seek out the youth organization or auxiliary organizations like theater troupes and sports clubs.[118] Those young women workers who became
members of the J.C. and wanted to pursue trade union activism sometimes
had to do so in organizations at a certain remove from the J.C.'s own activities. That Yvette Semard, a fashion industry worker and active Young
Communist militant who was the daughter of the communist and C.G.T.U.
leader Pierre Semard, was forced to organize within a union associated with
the rival labor federation the C.G.T. in the 1920s highlights this problem.[119]
Only one young woman worker, Jeannette Vermeersch, made a name for
herself in both trade union organizing and J.C. action in the late 1920s and
early 1930s, and she was exceptional in most respects. A textile worker from
Lille, she participated in her first strike at seventeen, joined the C.G.T.U. and

then the J.C., and organized a J.C. group in her factory with the help of one of the most noted communist women trade union organizers of the time, Martha Desrumeaux.[120]

Young women who were intrepid enough to join the J.C. in the late 1920s were expected to comport themselves as their male counterparts did. Within the J.C., a model of revolutionary androgyny prevailed. Young women were thought to require no special measures to encourage or facilitate their involvement; they were expected to participate in the full range of J.C. activities, regardless of the violence or police repression that might result. Thus Vermeersch was dispatched to oversee J.C. efforts during important strikes, while she and other young women distributed antimilitarist literature or helped disrupt political meetings of rival parties and groups. Yvette Semard joined male Young Communists in brawls with fascists in the early 1930s.[121] Such actions could lead to trouble with police and blacklisting at the workplace. Young women also traveled to the Soviet Union as part of worker delegations or to attend communist training schools.

Like their male colleagues, young women were expected to subordinate their private lives to the larger revolutionary struggle. Many of the key Young Communist women of the late 1920s and early 1930s embraced a companionate revolutionary heterosexuality, which saw them pair up with leading Young Communist men and devote their coupled lives to the communist struggle. When Vermeersch reached the highest levels of Young Communist politics, she was romantically involved with Maurice Thorez, the party's secretary general. Danielle Casanova, who was named leader of the Union des Jeunes Filles de France in the mid-1930s, shared her Young Communist activism with her husband, Laurent Casanova. Gabriel Péri's front-page obituary of the communist militant Juliette Nédelec expressed the quintessence of Young Communist femininity at this time. After lovingly detailing Juliette's run-ins with police, which apparently included arrests and beatings, Péri recounted her last moments: "a few minutes before her death, Juliette called her companion, her father and her mother into her little room. She asked them for news of the metalworkers' strike. She listened. Then, as life was slipping away from her, she asked that they join together to sing the International."[122]

This model of gender-neutral political activism in an avowedly revolutionary, mixed-sex organization challenged ideas about acceptable behavior for young women in France. Although the 1920s have often been viewed as a time when young women enjoyed a wide range of new freedoms, young women's behavior was vigorously contested and their movements and activities considerably more restricted than those of young men.[123] This was especially true for young female workers in their teens and early twenties, who usually lived at home under the watchful eyes of parents and older brothers. Venturing out alone at night to attend meetings was problematic.[124] One female militant could only attend J.C. meetings after her cell moved its assemblies from weeknights to Sunday afternoons to accommodate its one female member.[125] A trip to the police station was seen as a disgrace.[126] Simply joining a mixed-sex youth organization challenged social norms in a society where students overwhelmingly attended single-sex primary and secondary schools.[127] As a result, young working women who became Young Communists had to flout convention and brave family resistance. For Vermeersch, being the only girl in a J.C. group created all sorts of trouble within her family, especially with her older brothers, who were convinced that her participation in the overwhelmingly male group dishonored the family.[128] Lise London encountered a similar attitude from her older brother, who was himself a J.C. militant and son of a longtime communist activist. She was forced to begin her association with the J.C. as a shadow member, later taking advantage of her brother's absence from the region to join the organization officially.[129]

Young women also encountered resistance from male members once they joined the organization. In 1923 Gilberte Lesage, the head of the Paris region's women's secretariat, complained, "Too often our male comrades spread the little bourgeois idea that women can not and must not be active in politics."[130] Years later Vermeersch recalled how young women were relegated to secondary positions within the J.C.: "girls were useful as treasurers; they typed, made copies, and eventually did housework."[131] Juliette Plissonnier agreed with this assessment. As she explained, young men wanted women as treasurers because they were used to overseeing household budgets, because men hesitated to give young women the same responsibilities, and because someone had to do the cleaning.[132]

Vermeersch's assessment exposes a striking characteristic of young women's relationship to the J.C.: at a moment when the J.C. strove to become an organization of the industrial working class and when "young worker" was an overwhelmingly male category, many of the small number of young women who became active in the J.C. during this period were white-collar

**78**    workers, especially typists and stenographers.[133] Those who fit this profile included "Rosa Michel," the only young woman in the leadership in 1920, as well as the prominent female members Lise London, Josette Cothias, Claudine Chomat, and Henriette Schmidt. Charlotte Delbo, later celebrated for her accounts of her incarceration in Auschwitz, was a "sténo-dactylo" (stenographer-typist) active in the J.C. in the 1930s. Jeannette Vermeersch's status as a textile worker made her unusual among this group of prominent Young Communist women. Young female white-collar workers generally had more formal education than their male blue-collar counterparts, and they possessed skills that were useful to the J.C. and other communist organizations. From the J.C.'s early days right through its involvement in the Resistance, these women typed the minutes, reports, pamphlets, tracts, newspapers, and other written materials that were crucial to the organization and activities of the J.C. and other communist movements.

So while young women were expected to embrace a model of gender-neutral political activism, their relationship to communist political activism looked quite different indeed. Some fashioned alternative approaches to militancy. After joining the local J.C. group in her brother's absence, Lise London quickly became its leader. As the unit's head in the early 1930s she worked to expand its membership by addressing issues of direct interest to young people. She organized a literacy course for children of immigrants with little or no schooling, and was proud to watch it grow quickly to fifteen children, but she was rebuked by the party for pursuing a "reformist politics not in keeping with the organization's revolutionary nature."[134] Undeterred, she organized a girls' sports club. London also served the party in her working life. She worked first as a secretary to the regional communist leader, doing her fair share of editing tracts and correspondence, and was later sent to Moscow as a secretary in the French section of the Comintern.

Young women like London and Vermeersch were exceptional. Mostly, young women remained a marginal presence in this decidedly masculine, decidedly revolutionary organization. Few gender-specific efforts were made to recruit young women into the organization, and those who joined faced a variety of obstacles. In these circumstances only the toughest and most committed young women remained, and very few advanced to leadership positions. For the intrepid, though, the J.C. offered the possibility of serious political action in a culture that continued to deny women of all ages the right to vote. But the opportunity for political action did not come easily or entice many. During the Popular Front the party would adopt a radically

different approach to young women and femininity, putting in charge the
young women forged in the masculinized J.C. of the late 1920s and early
1930s.

During the 1920s the J.C. was a determinedly revolutionary organization
whose campaign to organize the masses of young proletarians offered young
male industrial workers in their late teens and early twenties the possibility of revolutionary action on behalf of communist goals. The movement's
approach subordinated the age-related economic interests of young male
workers to those of adult male workers, and paid scant attention to young
women workers and their gender-specific needs. The J.C.'s organizing efforts
also demonstrated little recognition that young workers were an age-specific
constituency to be appealed to, educated, and mobilized using methods different from those used for adults. Although the J.C. recognized that young
workers were passionate about their leisure activities, the organization's
offerings were deeply politicized and oriented toward serving larger revolutionary goals. Even those designed to attract large numbers of young people
offered little that could be considered even remotely youthful. In 1927 the
Young Communists of St-Étienne celebrated International Youth Week with
a four-hour evening meeting featuring five lengthy speeches, three of which
were delivered by adults and devoted to topics of general communist interest.[135] Police agents spying on such gatherings reported that they elicited
little in the way of positive response from young workers. In Lorient "the
speakers were so unenthralling that those present, who numbered around
thirty, left the room one after another, or lost interest well before the end
of the meeting."[136] A self-proclaimed revolutionary vanguard, the J.C. of the
1920s was a junior party for those too young to join the adult party, one
compelled to be more revolutionary, more purely communist than its adult
counterpart. The J.C. would only become a true youth organization during
the Popular Front period.

**3**

## Age, Generation,

## and Catholic Anticommunism

The Emergence of the J.O.C.

No one took communist advances more seriously than French Catholics in the second half of the 1920s. Alarmed that Communists were making significant electoral inroads, especially in the Paris suburbs, Catholic writers traveled to working-class neighborhoods to document the party's presence and lament the church's absence. To implant the church in these "dechristianized" areas, Catholics multiplied calls for initiatives to win over children and adolescents, who were generally lumped under the rubric "youth." For clerics such as the Jesuit Father Lhande, author of the bestselling *Christ in the Suburbs*, young people were the most promising target of countermobilization because they were less rooted in prejudice and ignorance than adults.[1]

As Catholics set out to reach young workers in the 1920s, they married strategies that predated the war to fresh approaches. The Jeunesse Ouvrière Chrétienne (J.O.C.), or Young Christian Workers, proved the most novel postwar initiative in youth and lay organizing. Begun in Belgium by Canon Cardijn in 1924, blessed by Pope Pius XI in 1925, and brought to France in 1926, the J.O.C. departed from earlier models of Catholic organizing in important respects. First, it was restricted to young workers, and did not aim to draw young people from a range of class backgrounds. Second, the J.O.C. assigned to young workers the central apostolic role in the Catholic mission to the working class. Once they had been shaped into Catholic militants, Jocists, as they were called, were dispatched into workplaces and working-class neighborhoods to evangelize their fellow young workers and remake them according to Catholic teachings. The J.O.C.'s founders hoped that the youth apostles would ultimately transform the church's relationship to the working class and keep the threat of communism at bay.

The movement that began to take shape in France in 1926, the high point of Young Communist strength in the 1920s, was directly opposed to its communist counterpart. Instead of using youthful energies to prepare violent, class-based revolution, the J.O.C. aimed to mobilize young people to lead a peaceful revolution of the spirit. The youth apostles, who were drawn from a younger segment of worker youth than Young Communists, were taught that their problems stemmed not from economic exploitation but from spiritual and moral distress. The Jocists' salvation lay not in overturning existing political or economic structures but rather in altering their operations through the infusion of Christian values. Education was at the core of the movement. Using the pedagogical method of "see, judge, act" devised by Canon Cardijn, chaplains taught Catholic values to Jocists; in the process, they endeavored to remake them from head to toe. Special attention was paid to refashioning young men's perceptions of morality, masculinity, and family.

Evaluations of the interwar J.O.C. have tended to view the J.O.C. through the prism of its self-presentation as a youth movement whose motto was "amongst them, through them, for them." Although French historians who have examined the movement's beginnings acknowledge the part played by clerics,[2] the major analysis of the J.O.C. from 1926 to 1939 emphasized the role played by the young in the movement's functioning and governance. As Michel Launay asserted, "The J.O.C. is a government of young people by young people."[3] In fact the movement's ideology, structure, and management owed less to the efforts of young workers than to those of a cohort of recently ordained, relatively young priests searching to bridge the gulf between the church and the working class in France after the First World War. The J.O.C.'s first section was founded not by a young worker, as J.O.C. materials claimed,[4] but by Father Georges Guérin, a veteran of the war ordained in 1925. Other newly ordained priests who shared Guérin's preoccupation with the working class soon established sections elsewhere in the Paris region. Working from Belgian materials and in consultation with Jesuits from Action Populaire, these priests laid the groundwork for the movement. They defined their audience, wrote pamphlets and small books, often anonymously, and devised a spirituality revolving around "the Worker Christ." The priests always put young workers front and center, while leaving for themselves the role of overseer and spiritual guide. The history of the J.O.C.'s early years is therefore a narrative that functions on two levels. It is at once the story of a postwar generation of priests determined to revitalize apostolic approaches to the working class and the story of the young workers enlisted in the endeavor. In the movement's earliest years, however, priests were in the lead.

**Setting the Stage for the J.O.C.** Communists became French Catholics' greatest ideological enemy in the aftermath of the Bolshevik Revolution. The establishment of a party dedicated to violent, class-based revolution aimed at religion, the family, and private property alarmed French Catholics. It also intensified concern over the church's relationship to the Communists' principal constituency, the working class, and injected urgency into what Catholics had long referred to as the "social question." Since the late nineteenth century many Catholics had been worried that the French working class was forming itself outside and in opposition to the church and embracing political solutions hostile to Catholic teachings and interests. To counter this, Pope Leo XIII instructed French clerics to concern themselves with workers, and social Catholics established organizations to reach them, including circles, charitable organizations, training programs, and the first Catholic trade unions.[5]

The establishment of the French Communist Party in 1920 brought a more serious threat. Catholic fears deepened after the first elections contested by the party, the legislative elections of 1924 and the municipal elections of 1925. Both testified to communist strength in and around the capital: in 1924 the party won 26 percent of the votes in the Paris region;[6] in 1925 it captured control of eight municipal governments in the belt of suburbs ringing Paris. In the aftermath of the elections Catholics feared that Communists would use control of these "red suburbs" as a springboard to national revolution. How easy it would be, they warned, for Communists to shut down communications, take control of transportation, and transform the suburbs' huge metalworking plants into armaments factories. In the mid-1920s Catholics stepped up their investigations into the Paris suburbs, homing in on dechristianization and what the Catholic writer Édouard Blanc referred to as "the Communist peril."[7] They also redoubled their efforts to counter communist successes through new organizational offerings or, at the very least, the establishment of a minimal presence in these forsaken areas.

Young people were integral to Catholic analyses and organizational efforts. The best-selling *Christ in the Suburbs: Investigation into Working-Class Religious Life in the Paris Suburbs*, by the Jesuit Father Lhande, said much about the state of Catholic attitudes and initiatives in the mid-1920s. A pioneer in religious radio broadcasting, Father Lhande began his investigations of the Paris suburbs in 1925, under the guidance of Father Crozier of Action Populaire, a Jesuit organization which had promoted Catholic social action since its foundation in 1903.[8] Lhande's dispatches, published first as articles in

*Études* in 1925 and then in book form in 1927, were widely read and discussed by French Catholics. By 1931 the book was in its 135th printing.[9]

Armed with a Kodak and ferried by the chauffeur of a wealthy widow from Paris, Lhande explored the suburban areas unknown to the overwhelming majority of Parisian Catholics. He began with "the zone," the area immediately beyond the old military fortifications where permanent construction was prohibited. Like other visitors before him, Lhande discovered a sinister no-man's-land where social and gender disorder reigned. Here bandits mixed with rag pickers, children became tattooed delinquents, and young women took on masculine attributes.[10] Lhande found even worse in the adjacent suburbs. The "red belt," as he called it, with "clubs, committees and Jeunesses Communistes," encircled the capital, extending almost uninterrupted across the departments of the Seine, Seine-et-Oise, and Seine-et-Marne. As Lhande moved through these suburbs he was particularly struck by the suburbanites' immoral ways, their wild, unattended children, and their lack of allegiance to France. According to Lhande, these people lived in "the most complete amorality," with adults coming together haphazardly in free unions and neglected children growing up "schooled in all the vices."[11] Lhande also assessed the Communists' suburban presence and surveyed the disparate, isolated efforts to bring Catholicism to these areas. There was no question that the Paris suburbs posed the greatest threat to Catholic France.

Lhande urged Catholics to mobilize. For Lhande, as for other Catholic commentators, the young had to be the primary target of any counter-mobilization. Comparing the church's mission in these benighted suburbs to that "in barbarian lands," he warned that here too "it was necessary above all to take charge of youth."[12] Adults' ignorance and long-established prejudices made them impervious to any real christianization: that adults might be baptized, married, and buried in religious ceremonies was the best one could hope for. Children, on the other hand, could be made into genuine Christians if they were taken early and enrolled in Catholic youth organizations. What was more, young people were there for the taking. Besides a few timid Protestant efforts and an embryonic Jeunesse Communiste, no organization had yet tried to capture these "wild little rabbits."[13] As to approach, Lhande favored multiplying existing organizations, although he implored Catholics to do more to separate the different age groups within the younger population.

By 1925, in fact, a vast array of organizations was already in place, as Catholics had long made the young vital to their political and evangelical initiatives. During the Old Regime and for much of the nineteenth century, Catholics relied primarily on schools to transmit their beliefs and values to successive generations of young people.[14] After the Ferry Laws of the 1880s established free, secular primary schools and made primary school attendance compulsory, Catholics were compelled to look beyond school walls in their attempts to educate and influence the children of the popular classes. So Catholics refashioned their strategy to focus on times and spaces outside the reach of the Republican school. They reinvigorated their youth fellowships (*patronages*), which offered imaginative leisure offerings and religious training on the Thursday afternoons and Sundays when children were not in school.[15] By 1900 Catholics claimed to be operating 2,351 patronages for boys and 1,817 for girls.[16] Catholics also adapted the pedagogical techniques honed in the patronages to the newly created summer vacation, and worked assiduously to build a network of *colonies de vacances*. These summer camps had the advantage of immersing working-class children in an entirely Catholic educational environment for weeks at a time.[17] Accompanying the youth fellowships and camps were numerous parish-based devotional groups. The intensified anticlericalism of the first decade of the twentieth century, which brought the expulsion of religious orders, the closure of many Catholic primary schools, and the separation of church and state in 1905, only confirmed Catholics in their determination to reach the young outside of school.

As the twentieth century began, Catholic overtures to "youth" were varied and ever-expanding, but those aimed at the working class tended to concentrate on children. Still, young workers were not entirely overlooked. At a time of increasing medical, political, legal, and religious attention to the stage of life becoming known as adolescence, Catholics became more attuned to the fate of those making the transition from primary school to the workplace.[18] Entrance into the workforce was believed to be a moment of religious and moral peril, when any religious faith possessed by the child was likely to be lost.[19] To influence the youngest workers, Catholics offered study circles, the occasional occupational training course, and the opportunity to participate in organized sport and gymnastics in the Fédération Gymnastique et Sportive des Patronages de France (F.G.S.P.F.), which boasted 300,000 members by the mid-1920s.[20] Yet as Father Leurent candidly admitted in 1926, all these organizations reached relatively few young workers.[21] The successes of Communists at the polls and the huge number of workers living outside the church's influence argued for fresh initiatives.

Age, Generation, and Catholic Anticommunism

A new generation of priests, one which emerged from the seminary fired with a mission to evangelize the working class and whose first priestly duties included overseeing parish youth organizations, searched for apostolic answers. To understand these men's embrace of the J.O.C. and their role in its birth, we need to return to the Great War, for the war's powers of generational formation extended to the church. As Annette Becker has shown, Europe's first total war brought an explosion of religious devotions at home and at the front. The unprecedented suffering at the front helped many French soldiers discover religious faith while deepening the faith of others. War became, in Becker's analysis, an immense collective imitation of Christ and his suffering.[22] It is not surprising that some soldiers returned home determined to devote their lives to God.

The war also altered the institutional church's place in the nation. After decades of state-sponsored anticlericalism, the French church's enthusiastic support for the war effort elevated its position within the national community. Central to this outcome was the military engagement of priests, monks, and seminarians. In keeping with the law of 1889 extending age-based compulsory military service to clerics and seminarians, France was the only belligerent nation to assign military responsibilities to clerics during the conflict.[23] Between 1914 and 1918, 32,699 priests, monks, and seminarians were mobilized. Of those, around half were assigned medical duties, an estimated fifteen hundred served as military chaplains, and the rest saw active duty, as either simple soldiers or officers.[24] These clerics-turned-soldiers struggled to survive the war's horrors alongside men of vastly different class backgrounds, political views, and religious practices. For their part, military chaplains shared the day-to-day challenges of life in the trenches, and they risked their lives to minister to the wounded in the no-man's land between the trenches and to assist medics in collecting the dead.[25] The future Cardinal Achille Liénart was wounded twice and decorated six times as a result of his stint as a military chaplain; his citations included the Croix de Guerre and the Légion d'Honneur.[26]

The intense contact that priests and seminarians had with ordinary soldiers led to new relationships with their fellow French citizens. Liénart wrote that he left the war with a "more intimate knowledge of the popular soul"; after the war was over he maintained close ties with the men of his unit, often joining them in the bar in Lille where they gathered as a group.[27] For the Jesuit Father Doncoeur, the war became a mythic moment of social

**86** communion, in which priests and ordinary soldiers marched, ate, suffered, and often died together. Such was the exceptional nature of wartime experience that Doncoeur regretted the passing of "this marvelous fusion of lives." After the armistice, he wrote, "we all felt that it was over: a gulf would be created between the people and the priest shut away in his sacristy."[28]

Wartime fellowship, whether exaggerated retrospectively or not, often translated into a redefinition of attitudes toward the working class and its relationship to the church. Georges Béjot, who was mobilized in 1917 and entered the seminary at Issy in 1920, summarized the war's effects in an interview in the late 1970s: "During the war, there was a mixing of social classes. We saw ourselves as having the same destiny! Mutually held prejudices disappeared. Seminarians and priests found themselves close to the working-class world . . . After the war, they no longer tolerated being seen to be in another camp . . . or that the working-class world would always be distant from the Church."[29]

Wartime experiences also altered French seminaries in ways that marked the first postwar generation of clerics and affected the J.O.C. The war led to a number of late vocations, especially at the Saint-Sulpician seminary at Issy-les-Moulineaux, where so many of the first J.O.C. chaplains studied. These men entered seminary with a much wider range of experiences and occupations than seminarians had had before the war.[30] Many began their postwar studies determined to undertake an apostolic mission to the working class. This intention was in turn nourished by professors whose own interest in social issues and working-class evangelizing had been deepened by the conflict. Liénart, for example, took up duties at the seminary in Lille alongside others who were also passionately interested in social issues.[31] At the seminary in Issy-les-Moulineaux, Father Callon wrote of being haunted by "the terrible, ever widening gulf between the Church and the masses."[32] He pushed his students to engage with these questions and organized talks by speakers at the forefront of social Catholicism. These included Father Desbuquois, director of Action Populaire, and Jules Zirnheld, one of the leaders of the Catholic trade union confederation the Confédération Française des Travailleurs Chrétiens (C.F.T.C.), established in 1919 partly as a response to the threat of communism.[33] Seminarians such as Georges Guérin, the J.O.C.'s founder, arranged their own speakers on social issues and eagerly followed talk of new apostolic approaches to the working class. Once the J.O.C. got under way in Belgium, seminarians greeted it with excitement. Charles Véret, who entered Issy in 1922, remembered that he and his col-

leagues were much more interested in discussing the J.O.C. than in studying church history as required by their theology course.[34]

Guérin exemplified the new generation of postwar priests that began to emerge from seminaries in the mid-1920s. Like Canon Cardijn, Guérin was sensitized by his experiences to the need for new approaches to the working class and to the challenges faced by young workers.[35] Having arrived in Paris from a small village at a young age, he and his family lived in a modest building in a modest neighborhood in the 11th arrondissement, whose inhabitants included artisans, white-collar workers, and street sellers. The son of a white-collar employee, Guérin attended the local Catholic primary school. As a child he witnessed the stratification of parish life according to social class. He saw, for example, how the kinds of weddings or funerals that priests performed depended entirely on what parishioners could pay. According to Guérin's biographer, the historian Pierre Pierrard, this appalled the young Guérin and nourished in him the determination to be a different kind of priest. Guérin's educational path resembled that of many working-class adolescents, as he left school after primary school and entered the workforce at the age of fourteen. Once in it he performed a number of relatively low-skilled, usually white-collar jobs until the start of his military service, all the while participating in two Catholic groups, a club for graduates of his primary school and the Association of Saint-Labre. There he met Charles Bordet, who would become his trusted associate in the J.O.C.

A member of the military class of 1912, Guérin's military service was lengthy. He remained under arms from the fall of 1912 until August 1919 and was wounded twice, the second time so seriously as to require a year's hospitalization. Having decided to become a priest early in his military service, Guérin used his time in the hospital to read, write letters, and improve his Latin. The war broadened his contacts among Catholic clerics. It was his unit's military chaplain, the Jesuit Father Danset, who later introduced him to the Belgian J.O.C. and its literature. After his return to civilian life in 1919, Guérin became one of the many "late vocations" who entered the seminary at Issy-les-Moulineaux in the fall of 1920. While there he took Father Callon as his spiritual advisor and moved to the forefront of those preparing for a new social apostolate.

Ordained in the summer of 1925, Guérin was assigned to the parish of St. Vincent de Paul in Clichy, a suburb of Paris captured by Communists in the municipal elections of 1925. In his parish Guérin took up the kinds of low-level duties usually reserved for recently ordained priests, among

them direction of the Eucharistic Crusade, the parish sports and theatrical groups, and the *patronage*. He also performed the 6 a.m. Mass and presided over the most modest weddings and funerals. Guérin did all this under the supervision of a fifty-seven-year-old parish priest from the old school, who according to Pierrard did not realize that Clichy was no longer the village it had been under Louis XIII.[36]

Guérin's main concern was reaching the dechristianized working class. As he explained later, "As a young priest I was naturally preoccupied by its evangelization."[37] Guérin's search for effective methods to bring Catholicism to the young workers in his parish led him to his former military chaplain, Father Danset. Danset, who had attended the Belgian J.O.C.'s first national congress, sent Guérin away with copies of the movement's newspaper, *La Jeunesse Ouvrière*, and its newsletter for Jocist leaders.[38] Here, Guérin came to believe, was the solution and the vehicle.[39] In the months that followed, Guérin subscribed to the J.O.C.'s newspaper and carried on animated discussions with one of the young workers in his parish, Georges Quiclet. In the fall of 1926 Guérin and Quiclet launched France's first J.O.C. section in the Clichy parish.[40]

The section's initial public meeting went well, and word of the J.O.C.'s arrival in France spread among young priests. Other sections were established in the Paris region in the spring of 1927 by seventeen young vicars from the Groupe du Rayonnement d'Entraide (G.E.S.), a sacerdotal support group to help novice priests sustain the enthusiasms of the seminary and discover and implement effective apostolic methods, especially regarding social issues.[41] This group played a crucial role in the J.O.C.'s early years: its meetings provided a place where chaplains could share their aspirations and disappointments, and its monthly bulletin promoted the J.O.C. and its publications.[42]

The spring of 1927 also witnessed the beginning of the J.O.C. in the Lille region, an area with a history of both vigorous support for the church and its organizations and strong cross-border ties with Belgian Catholicism. In the 1920s the J.O.C.'s Belgian founder Canon Cardijn traveled often to Lille, where the Association Catholique de la Jeunesse Française (A.C.J.F.), founded in 1886, was well established. By the mid-1920s this organization, whose members were mainly lycée and university students, was directing increased attention to young workers.[43] Since Catholic associational life flourished around Lille and the first J.O.C. sections usually emerged out of existing par-

ish organizations, it is not surprising that a regional group, the Federation of Lille and its eastern suburbs, was founded in May 1927.[44] Both the Paris and Lille regions became strongholds of the interwar French J.O.C.

The movement was restricted to young male workers. Segregation of the sexes was a bedrock principle of Catholic organizational life, and there was no question of a mixed-sex organization. However, the initial focus on a male movement also reflected interwar Catholics' sensitivity to the gendered nature of their organizing efforts. Although historians have begun to analyze the place of masculinity and fatherhood in the era's extreme-right politics, they have had much less to say about masculinity and its display in Catholic initiatives.[45] Yet Catholics understood that in the world of postwar mass politics, large demonstrations of men conveyed an aura of political strength that was especially important for an institution so often associated with women and children in the popular imagination. French clerics delighted in their ability to return males to church pews after the war,[46] and they mounted powerful, masculine demonstrations in French streets and stadia. In the summer of 1923 Catholics sent 28,000 uniformed male gymnasts onto the Champs de Mars for an exhibition, the largest athletic exhibition in postwar France before the World's Fair of 1937 in Paris.[47]

Catholics also mobilized veterans of the First World War to protest the anticlerical measures announced by the Cartel des Gauches government, elected in May 1924. Catholic men reacted vigorously after Premier Herriot declared in June that he would close France's embassy to the Vatican, expel members of religious orders who had returned to France, and extend the Law of Separation to Alsace-Lorraine, which had been recovered from Germany in the postwar settlement at Versailles.[48] The Jesuit Father Doncoeur helped found the movement Défense des Religieux Anciens Combattants (D.R.A.C.) and devised its simple, effective slogan, "We will not leave!"[49] In October the Assembly of Cardinals and Archbishops turned to the decorated war hero General de Castelnau to create a national movement of Catholic men, the Fédération Nationale Catholique (F.N.C.).[50] During the fall and winter of 1924–25 this organization staged impressive protest demonstrations of men, many of them veterans, in cities across France. Some drew as many as eighty thousand into the streets. This male organizing, and the Jeunesses Communistes' own decidedly masculine ethos, were crucial contexts for the establishment of the J.O.C. as a movement of male workers that sought to refigure Catholic working-class masculinity.

Age, Generation, and Catholic Anticommunism

**Constructing a Movement**  With the J.O.C. young priests set out to build a youth movement that could challenge Communists in the streets and workplaces of France. The clerics drew on the expertise of Jesuits from Action Populaire and took the Belgian J.O.C. as their starting point. The young priests heeded the advice of Canon Cardijn, who addressed Jocist chaplains and militants on numerous occasions in the 1920s and early 1930s, and they studied—and sometimes reproduced—Belgian materials. The pamphlet *J.O.C. Statutes and Organization* (1928) was nothing more than a reprinted version of part 3 of the Belgian *J.O.C. Manual*. Nonetheless, the movement that emerged in France generated its own literature and emphases, which flowed from the French clerics' analysis of "worker youth" and its religious, moral, and psychological state.

The young priests' understanding of working-class youth was heavily skewed toward adolescence. At the beginning the J.O.C. architects concentrated almost exclusively on the youngest workers, those making the transition from school to the workplace, and "worker youth" was often used synonymously with "wage-earning adolescence" in early J.O.C. literature.[51] For these Catholic writers, as for their pre-war predecessors, adolescence was a stage of life replete with danger and opportunity.

This was abundantly clear from the most extended Catholic discussion of the psychology of young workers, Guérin's article "The Protection of Youth from Communism and Other Errors" (1928). In Guérin's analysis adolescent workers were "generous, ardent, and easily enthusiastic," a fact that he conceded was readily understood by Communists like Doriot.[52] Because of these qualities the adolescent worker had a "profound need to give himself over to something great," a noble cause or ideal.[53] This generosity of spirit and need to serve something grand melded with the adolescent worker's inexperience and naïveté to make him more susceptible to the communist appeal than adult workers were. The mature worker was little affected by communist propaganda, while the inexperienced and ardent apprentice could not resist. "His heart pounds," Guérin wrote, "rebellion seizes him by the throat."[54] Given the adolescent worker's nature, Catholics had to create a movement that could similarly capture him.

Like turn-of-the-century Catholic writers, the J.O.C.'s architects identified adolescence as a period of pronounced religious peril. When the twelve- or thirteen-year-old left primary school for the workplace he was thought to enter a world characterized by extreme hostility to religion, which disposed him toward discarding any traces of faith that he might once have possessed.

According to Father Leurent, workers viewed priests as agents of the rich, defenders of capitalism, and representatives of the political right. With these attitudes, going to church had "become a profession of political and social faith, a kind of support for fascism, a betrayal of the working class."[55] It followed that priests could not convert the masses of workers on their own but needed the assistance of youth apostles. Canon Cardijn articulated this idea chillingly when he explained, "The priest reaches out to the masses only through core groups of militants willing to die in the effort to bring their brothers to Christ."[56]

To those constructing the J.O.C., a young worker's adolescence was not simply a time of religious danger but one of moral corruption as well. In J.O.C. literature concern over "impiety and immorality" went hand in hand;[57] often concern over immorality took precedence in both the analysis of threats facing young workers and the proposed solutions. The pamphlet *Essentials for Starting the J.O.C.* began, "The J.O.C. is born out of observation of the moral distress of young workers at the moment when physically as well as morally they are undergoing the biggest transformation of their life."[58] Catholic clerics interpreted morality broadly to include matters of conscience and ethics, but those writing J.O.C. materials were most concerned about sexual conduct and relations between the sexes. Young workers were learning all the wrong values and mimicking all the wrong behavior at this crucial stage of life.

The wrong moral lessons could be gleaned practically anywhere in the working-class milieu. In the overcrowded, run-down apartments that housed the working class in the postwar decade, Catholic writers saw adults thumbing their noses at church teachings on marriage and exposing young workers to promiscuity at every turn. For Father Leurent, it was difficult for young workers to remain moral "when one had to live in filth."[59] Things were no better in the factory, a particular site of moral corruption for J.O.C. writers. There young male workers encountered both brutal initiations at the hands of older male workers and countless provocations by female workers of all ages. Although adult working women loomed particularly large in the Catholic imagination, adolescent girls also preyed on male adolescent workers. As Leurent explained in his assessment of "worker youth," boys and girls often worked together, and "if *patronage* directors are to be believed, female provocations present a constant danger: the attack does not always come. . . from the direction one expects."[60]

Catholics similarly viewed the realm of leisure as a source of pronounced moral danger. Although clerics had long been vigilant toward the corrupting

Age, Generation, and Catholic Anticommunism

**92**  possibilities presented by leisure, the 1920s brought new concerns. The eight-hour day and forty-eight-hour week gave young workers more leisure time, which was filled in an increasing number of ways in the fast-paced postwar decade. Like subsequent historians, Catholics understood that leisure provided spaces in which young people could escape the supervision of adults and experiment with different behavior and identities.[61]

Dancing, a rage in the 1920s, was particularly worrisome to Catholic moralists.[62] For one observer of Parisian life, "Nobody wanted to do anything but dance, dance, and keep on dancing."[63] Young workers were particular fans, frequenting neighborhood balls, cafés, and the dance halls which had begun to emerge in the late nineteenth century. As the J.O.C.'s newspaper *La Jeunesse Ouvrière* conceded in 1931, many young people lived for Sunday, when they could dance until the early hours of the next day.[64] In a society where both classroom and workspace were highly segregated according to gender and where few opportunities for mixed-sex youth sociability existed, dancing allowed young men and women to come together in exciting, frenetic, and sexualized ways. This was especially true of popular dances like the tango, which the archbishop of Paris condemned as immoral in 1920.[65] And Catholics believed that like other forms of commercialized leisure, dancing encouraged young workers to spend their hard-earned wages foolishly, instead of saving them in preparation for marriage and family.

The cinema was, if anything, more troubling. Invented before the war, the cinema's popularity soared in the 1920s, especially among young workers. As the Catholic writer Jacques Valdour discovered in visits to working-class neighborhoods in the immediate postwar period, young people often dominated in the large crowds turning out on Saturday nights and Sundays.[66] At the movies young workers enjoyed a relatively cheap source of entertainment which had the power to transport them outside their often dreary daily lives. But moral dangers lurked. Catholics judged many popular films to have content unsuited to young people at such an impressionable stage of life. Although cinematic immorality affected young workers in many ways, Catholics worried particularly that movies exposed young workers to the latest styles, trends, and manners from across Europe and the United States, which young workers were quick to mimic. *La Jeunesse Ouvrière* lamented that young workers adopted the mannerisms of Rudolph Valentino and Maurice Chevalier in an effort to be up to date.[67] For Cardijn, this mimicking of movie scenes meant that children nine, ten, and eleven years old were committing "sexual acts" (by which he most likely meant kissing and handholding) in the streets of large urban centers.[68] The cinema's dangers extended beyond the films themselves. With their dim lighting and unchaperoned seats, movie halls were viewed as breeding-grounds of immorality.

The movement that the young priests worked to create emerged from this analysis of the young worker's nature and the myriad temptations facing him at this crucial stage of life. Consistent with earlier clerical overtures to the young, the challenge facing Catholics was perceived as an educational one, "a problem of post–primary school education," as one cleric put it.[69] The response was conceived in similarly educational terms. The j.o.c. would be an educational movement that would seize the young worker at this moment of maximum enthusiasm and susceptibility. The aims were ambitious: priests did not attempt merely to teach new religious practices but aimed at a complete transformation of every aspect of young workers' lives and values. Father Ranson explained to industrialists in northern France in 1929 that "the Jocist school remakes its man from head to toe; it dismantles, examines, reassembles, and readjusts every hour of the day; it offers him precise, understandable formulas for every difficulty he encounters."[70]

The effort to instill ideas about work and industrial relations counteracting those promoted by Communists was an essential part of the educational project. Clerics encouraged the young to become exemplary workers, Christian counterparts to the Soviet worker hero Stakhanov. Jocists were to take pride in their work, to safeguard machinery and materials, to quit only with very good reason if they had received training, and not to reject on principle the introduction of new work methods.[71] In contrast to the confrontational stance adopted so enthusiastically by the Jeunesses Communistes, Jocists were urged to reject strikes and to work closely and respectfully with industrialists. The goal, Jocists were taught at study sessions, was a collaboration between Jocist and employer that preserved the employer's authority and the worker's rights.[72] All this, Father Ranson explained, made the j.o.c. useful to industrialists: the organization could introduce measures, especially in key areas like surveillance and morality, that would never have been acceptable had they been proposed by employers.[73]

Devising a movement that could achieve the clerics' ambitious educational goals and still appeal to large numbers of young workers proved a challenge. An important step was designing a role for youth militants that corresponded to the adolescent worker's ardent nature. j.o.c. priests assigned young workers a heroic role in the salvation of the working class and created a religious universe that spoke directly to the circumstances of their lives. Jocist spirituality, which prefigured liturgical changes that would be institutionalized after the Second Vatican Council of the 1960s, pivoted around the figure of the Worker Christ (le Christ Ouvrier).[74] Le Christ Ouvrier was an eminently human Christ whose most important identifying characteristic was his status as a worker. In study materials Jocists were instructed never to forget that Jesus was both a worker and the adopted son of a worker.[75] Born poor, they were told, Jesus earned his living by his labor as a carpenter, living among the objects he had made. Jocists were encouraged to enter into a personal relationship with Jesus and pattern their lives on his.

More important to the movement's missionary goals was that J.O.C. creators entrusted young workers with the primary role in the church's mission to the working class. Cardijn and other clerics repeatedly told Jocists that they were twentieth-century incarnations of Christ's apostles and true missionaries of labor in the vast pagan territories that only they could penetrate as witnesses of Christ's love and Gospel.[76] When Jocists met resistance from Communists and Socialists, who challenged them in the streets and shouted them down at J.O.C. meetings, they were encouraged to see it as akin to the resistance that Jesus' apostles had faced from Roman pagans.[77] They were saviors of the working class.

Communicated in meditations, study sessions, songs, and retreats, this notion of youth's apostolic role was illustrated vividly during the J.O.C.'s pilgrimage to Rome in 1931. The itinerary was carefully planned to allow the twelve hundred identically attired Jocists (accompanied by a hundred chaplains) to retrace the early Christians' steps and receive the pope's blessing. The J.O.C. contingent toured the historical sites of early Christianity, with special emphasis on those of persecution and eventual triumph. At each stop Jocist pilgrims listened to speeches by clerics eager to fuel young workers' faith through direct comparisons of the Jocists' twentieth-century struggles with those of the first Christians. In Saint Peter's cathedral Monsignor Herbigny encouraged Jocists to take heart from the apostle Peter's success, which had seemed all but impossible upon his arrival in Rome. After discussing Peter's initial doubts and eventual triumph, Herbigny challenged the Jocists: "Have confidence in the fruitfulness of your example, in the fruitfulness of silent, Christian work, in the fruitfulness of the Word

you sow in the hearts of your mates, who are hostile today but who may **95**
be, like Saul, tomorrow transformed."[78]

An even more stirring call to battle came at the Coliseum, identified as one of the two most potent symbols of opposition to Christianity and its eventual triumph. Here abbé Bordet, recognized as a spellbinding orator by his peers, gave a dramatic account of Christianity's triumph over Rome, uniting changes in the meaning of work with the revolution wrought by Christianity.[79] Although manual labor had been considered unworthy of free men during the Roman Empire, Christ had rehabilitated work. But modern paganism threatened Christian achievement. Bordet asked Jocists to combat paganism with body and soul, as had the first Christians, even urging them to aspire to martyrdom. Near the end of his speech he demanded that his listeners heed the example of Saint Theresa of Lisieux, telling them, "We must leave here with the resolve and desire to be martyrs."[80]

Although it is difficult to measure young people's responses to these exhortations, some Jocists embraced the powerful apostolic role and drew strength from comparisons to the challenges faced by the apostles—who, as was constantly pointed out, were themselves of modest social origins. In the early days of the J.O.C. in Roubaix, the president of one J.O.C. federation proudly presented the Jocists of his federation to Cardinal Liénart's envoy Monsignor Bouchendomme in the following way: "Yes, Monsignor, we number more than two hundred. We will conquer the working class. There were twelve apostles and they conquered the world, and we're no crazier than they were!"[81]

Only the truly committed, however, saw themselves as apostles, and the clerics were careful to take account of different levels of commitment in the structure of the movement. From the start they created two categories of membership, militants and members, each with very different relationships to the movement. Militants were expected to devote themselves completely to the movement and its mission. They would be forged into a working-class apostolic élite in study circles and religious retreats; they would take Christ's message into workplaces and working-class neighborhoods; and they would be expected to make the ultimate sacrifice to influence and convert their working-class brothers. Members, on the other hand, had fewer responsibilities. They were expected to pay dues, read *La Jeunesse Ouvrière*, attend monthly section meetings, and generally comport themselves according to J.O.C. guidelines.[82] In light of the founders' concerns about morality,

J.O.C. guidelines made "good behavior," which included abstention from any romantic or sexual interactions with young women, more important than religious observance for members.[83]

With the responsibilities of militants and members mapped out, striking a workable balance between clerical authority and youth self-management became critical. Because J.O.C. architects were aware, as Cardijn put it, that young workers "don't want to be instruments, they want to play an active role,"[84] they constructed day-to-day roles predicated on action by the militants and formation behind the scenes by the priests. Thus militants were given responsibility for much of the daily work necessary for the movement's successful operation. They controlled all matters regarding finances and collecting dues, and they produced and distributed *La Jeunesse Ouvrière*. The newspaper was a crucial instrument of movement cohesion: it informed militants and members of the J.O.C.'s goals, positions, and national campaigns, and it strove to create community through reports of section work across the country. The act of selling *La Jeunesse Ouvrière*, which sometimes led to altercations with Young Communists and Young Socialists and perhaps a trip to the police station, heightened Jocist commitment. Militants also took primary responsibility for local recruiting efforts. They organized and ran national congresses and the carefully scripted public meetings designed to interest the unconvinced and unconverted, and they oversaw the network of services that soon began to emerge. Finally, militants governed themselves through committees and councils established at the local, federal, and national levels.

Youth activists did all this under the supervision of chaplains, who held ultimate authority within the movement. Following from their analysis of working-class anticlericalism and the psychology of young workers, the J.O.C.'s architects downplayed the chaplains' authority by designing a role for them that was powerful yet subtle. The young Jesuit abbé Boulier, who wrote the movement's first major pamphlet, *Call of the J.O.C.*, explained that one of the major challenges facing the nascent movement was to convince chaplains of their particular role in the movement: "they must be *everything*—and be the only ones to realize it."[85] Chaplains were instructed to adopt a light touch in their dealings with young workers and to minimize their public presence. At retreats for movement chaplains and in newsletters designed only for their eyes, chaplains were reminded to spend more time listening than talking, and to stay out of view at recruiting meetings aimed at a broad cross-section of young workers.

Age, Generation, and Catholic Anticommunism

Priests had considerable power within the movement, especially during its early days. At the national level they wrote the J.O.C.'s foundational literature, which elaborated the movement's ideology, educational methods, and distinctive spirituality, not to mention its rules and regulations, and they acted as final arbiters of material appearing in *La Jeunesse Ouvrière*.[86] They also presided over religious retreats, which provided intensive training for militants, and meetings of the J.O.C.'s various governing bodies, not hesitating to step in and provide corrections or advice when necessary. At the local level their power was, if anything, more extensive. They founded J.O.C. sections, either by reshaping existing parish youth groups into J.O.C. sections or by starting sections from scratch. The latter approach involved identifying suitable local young workers and working closely with them to get the section up and running. Once sections were established and organs of self-government were in place, priests exercised authority through their power to approve candidates for the section's executive, their supervisory roles, and their educational functions. They were further expected to model disciplined behavior for their young charges; this responsibility included implementing national directives, even when the chaplain knew them to be unsuitable for his section.[87]

In a movement that claimed to be run by and for young workers, this not inconsiderable clerical power had to be explained. *Call of the J.O.C.* admitted that it was sometimes difficult to clarify the precise nature of the relationship between the section's leader and its chaplain. To simplify matters, the pamphlet employed a sports analogy: the section president should be viewed as a team captain, who plotted strategy and directed his players, while the chaplain should be seen as a team doctor, who watched over the players to prevent them from injury. Within J.O.C. sections the youth president directed J.O.C. action in the factory, street, and working-class neighborhood, while the priest supervised the Jocists' moral health, which involved advising, warning, and if necessary forbidding actions in the name of a higher principle.[88] Jocists were informed that it was their duty to accept their chaplain as he was. That was, after all, how God accepted him.[89]

But if *Call of the J.O.C.* likened the chaplain to a team doctor, a more apt comparison would have been to a coach, because the training, education, and formation of J.O.C. militants were the chaplains' most important responsibilities. Without a cadre of militants who had been taught to alter their lives and values according to Catholic teachings and assume an apostolic role, the J.O.C. could not hope to meet even its most elementary missionary goals. The

**98** education of militants occurred primarily in study circles directed by chaplains and run according to what J.O.C. architects considered their innovative pedagogical approach: the "see, judge, act" method. This method replaced the more passive approach found in catechism classes and patronages, which relied on heavy memorization and the transmission of knowledge from the priest to the young person. Instead the J.O.C. sought to educate young workers through active study and evaluation of conditions around them.

The *enquête* was central to this process. J.O.C. militants investigated key issues or problems by working together to complete a lengthy questionnaire. As they answered questions, Jocists learned to see the world around them differently. This meant not only noticing new things but viewing their surroundings through a social Catholic lens. This lens was acquired primarily by having a small number of militants (three or four was considered optimal in the movement's early days) gather with their chaplain in study circles to discuss and ultimately judge their findings. That done, the group decided on ways to act to alter conditions and bring them into conformity with Catholic teachings and values.

The "see, judge, act" method and investigative questionnaire were adapted to a range of purposes. For example, the completion of questionnaires helped to initiate new sections into the life of the movement and prepare them for official affiliation. The enquête also became the centerpiece of national campaigns on young worker issues. For months on end, Jocists worked their way through lengthy questionnaires on workplace safety (1930), working women's relationship to the home (1931), or young workers' relationship to leisure (1933). The goal of the exercise was always twofold: to educate young workers about specific problems and provide data from which the movement could devise action plans, including the establishment of public education campaigns and of services designed to remedy the problem. J.O.C. services were crucially important to the movement's recruiting efforts during the economic crisis of the 1930s.[90]

The J.O.C.'s architects prided themselves on their educational method and took it as evidence of their superiority to their communist adversaries. The prime benefit of the J.O.C.'s method, according to the movement's founders, was that it allowed a program of demands to emerge out of "the facts" of young worker life and not be imposed in conformity with a particular dogma.[91] This contrasted with the communist approach, which involved stuffing young workers' heads full of abstract theses and ultimately creating "a kind of catechism, an ABC of Communism that one had to accept

and recite with eyes closed."[92] Catholics admitted that the J.O.C. had its own
social doctrine, but they argued that Jocists could verify the suitability of the
program as they began and judge results as they progressed.

The "see, judge, act" method was a central tool of individual transformation. Through a guided investigation of diverse issues, militants could be
brought to a Jocist evaluation of their own conduct and a determination to
make it conform with Jocist models. In *How to Begin a J.O.C. Study Circle*, the
questionnaire on morality was three times longer than the one examining
religious life. The questionnaire instructed militants to begin by contemplating conversations around them in a way that left little doubt as to the goal
of the exercise. It began:

—Around us at work and in the neighborhood, what are people saying about young
people and chastity? Is it seen as necessary? Possible? Impossible?

—What are people saying about young men and women dating? Must this be avoided,
why? Sought after, why?

—What are people saying about marriage? Is it seen to be useful? Or, by contrast,
pointless? What is considered the age at which one normally marries?[93]

After these initial probes Jocists were to proceed to "the reality" of the situation. Young workers were asked to comb their surroundings for instances of
immorality, and then to respond to concluding questions such as: "Do we
now understand better why we must have a healthy moral life? Do we now
understand better why we must endeavor to spread it (i.e. morality) around
us?"[94] The exercise ended with recommendations on how to foster Catholic
morality in neighborhoods and workplaces.

Vigilance against public and private displays of "immorality" became
particularly important during the 1920s and early 1930s. In study sessions
and retreats, as well as in the pages of their press, Jocists were exhorted to
refrain from casual dating, to respect young women, and to remain chaste
at all times. Within the J.O.C. chastity was held out as the ultimate mark of
strength and Jocist masculinity. Cardijn told Jocists in 1932: "We must prove,
we must demonstrate that it's only by being chaste that we will develop ourselves fully, that we will be aces, that we will be people who influence others,
who are stronger than others, who are afraid of nothing, who triumph over
difficulty."[95] Chastity marked off militants from those outside the movement and brought Jocists closer to their Christian forebears. Local sections
analyzed the dating practices of young people in diverse industries, solemnly

**100**   discussed the dangers of inappropriate books, and protested against the-aters showing immoral films. When the future J.O.C. secretary general Fernand Bouxom arrived in Paris for the first time, he approached a police officer and demanded the removal of what he regarded as obscene posters from kiosks near the Gare du Nord, the likes of which he had never seen in Lille.[96] Those who refused to comply with the J.O.C.'s strict moral codes were marginalized within the movement. Abbé Godin later regretted that Jocists who flirted with the opposite sex were excluded from study sessions while others who refrained from flirting but never attended mass, even at Easter, were accepted.[97]

The J.O.C. also demanded new behavior from clerics. Priests received con-siderable instruction in their mission, and movement luminaries such as Canon Cardijn counseled chaplains to move slowly, to make religion relevant to young workers, and to allow them an active role in their own education. Clerics were reminded to balance their own desire to instruct with the young worker's need for self-formation and self-discovery, even if that sometimes came at the expense of doctrinal accuracy.[98] It was less important to ensure that young workers learn to perform accepted devotions at accepted times than it was to help them live their lives in a Christian manner.[99]

In this spirit J.O.C. chaplains bent rules and departed from past Catho-lic practice. Young priests were prominent among those adopting a new priestly style in the 1920s and 1930s, with some sporting leather jackets or berets and visiting parishioners on bicycles or motorcycles.[100] It is not surprising that members of this generation exhibited a flexible approach to doctrinal matters. Georges Béjot, an early J.O.C. chaplain, recalled how one of his section presidents, who had come to the J.O.C. from the parish patronage, rushed to him one Sunday after Mass to report a sacrilege: one of the section's apprentices had taken communion without having completed his First Communion or gone to confession.[101] Béjot investigated the matter but did nothing, noting that this happened often and that receiving com-munion for the first time in this way "already implies a much more profound understanding of the mystery of the sacraments and of salvation."[102] Older priests, accustomed to greater doctrinal rigidity, were apt to look askance at these efforts to reach young workers. Monsignor Jean Calvet, who worried that the J.O.C. promoted a superficial religiosity, recorded with distaste how one J.O.C. chaplain explained his approach to religious education: "I'm only concerned about one thing—being with them for as long as I can. They get used to having a priest with them. The rest matters little . . . Of course the

religious instruction is superficial; but they develop a Christian conscience. **101**
Dogma matters little; moral life is the only thing that counts."[103]

The J.O.C.'s educational method was more flexible than the heavy-handed enquêtes suggest and its results more varied than might first appear. Much depended on the individual chaplain, who was asked to minister to young workers in radical, not to mention labor-intensive, ways. Militants' recollections make clear that young chaplains embraced innovation more than their elders did. A chaplain ordained in 1930, for example, held J.O.C. meetings in taverns and installed the section headquarters in a garage. Priests who engaged fully in this apostolic adventure could make a huge difference in the success of local sections and in the lives of individual Jocists. One Jocist from Pas-de-Calais recalled the difference made by abbé Quéval, who was fond of telling him, "If I were not a Christian, if I were not a priest, I would be a Communist!" Quéval played a central role in the young man's development by encouraging him to continue his education and attend conferences.[104]

The J.O.C.'s attempt to provide an integral education to young workers extended far beyond the transmission of Catholic beliefs to include instruction in skills, such as note-taking and composition, which had applications in other settings.[105] Militants wrote later about all they had learned from the study of Catholic texts, the writing of reports, and the planning of meetings under their chaplains' supervision. These activities allowed the activists to practice certain skills and develop others, and this proved advantageous in their adult lives. The J.O.C.'s educational function had considerable appeal for those young workers who viewed their inability to continue their education past primary school as a great disappointment and sometimes a profound social injustice.[106] The J.O.C. became a place where young workers could supplement the rudimentary education they received in primary school.

But the J.O.C. had to offer more than instruction, however broadly conceived, if it was to reach a broad cross-section of worker youth. Focusing initially on the youngest adolescent workers, clerics crafted an appeal designed to resonate with experiences of marginalization and alienation. Those writing J.O.C. materials appreciated the difficulties faced by adolescents making the abrupt transition from primary school to full-time work at the age of thirteen, or twelve if they had received their certificate of primary studies. Adolescent workers had little in the way of placement assistance, and trade unions paid no special attention to the youngest workers, except when it was thought that the young might be used to undercut the wages of older workers. Many twelve- and thirteen-year-olds gravitated toward unskilled, low-paying jobs with little promise of advancement, and they were left to cope on their own with dislocation and harassment. In his classic account of growing up working-class in the early twentieth century, René Michaud described how older workers in one workshop welcomed their younger colleagues by tackling them, opening their flies, and painting their penises with glue.[107] Those who went on to engage politically remembered feeling disoriented and depressed during their first days of full-time work. What had seemed an exciting step out of childhood quickly became the death of youth and the beginning of a life of unremitting toil. E. Stocki (b. 1915) recalled how proud he had been to descend into the mines for the first time at thirteen. But when he finished his first day of work, he told himself, "Tomorrow, I have to start all over again and I have to continue doing this horrible job for years and years," and he began to cry.[108]

J.O.C. architects recruited adolescent workers by evoking their difficulties, disappointments, and loneliness and offering the J.O.C. as an age-specific solution. The recruiting pamphlet *Call of the J.O.C.* began by cataloguing in simple language the frustrations that mounted so quickly after a young worker's first day at work.[109] Didn't the reader realize that his job was not a real trade, that there was no one to help him at the workplace, that his friends were only good for a laugh, and that he was killing what was best in himself by drinking, dancing, and spending too many nights at the movies? And what good was religion? Going to Mass, the booklet conceded, was good for the middle class and for those who had the time, but standing in the back of a crowded church to watch a distant ceremony was of little value. The parish patronage was no better. With its emphasis on sport, it failed to take seriously young workers' interest in ideas and politics. This depiction of young worker life resonated especially well with one early Jocist, who remembered: "[the booklet] conveyed so well what we thought, but didn't know how to express."[110] The overall message was clear: the young worker was alone at sea and only the J.O.C. offered a lifeline. The J.O.C. would help the young worker find a good job, educate himself, and make real friends.

In this and other propaganda, the J.O.C. was presented as an organization that responded to the multiple needs and desires of adolescent workers. Although ministering to the spiritual and moral lives of adolescent workers was the J.O.C.'s preeminent concern, it was not the most heavily advertised. Canon Cardijn was adamant that the J.O.C. should not lead with moral and religious instruction but win the trust of young workers by providing con-

crete assistance.[111] So the J.O.C. set out to establish services designed to aid
the young worker—and, simultaneously, teach him. The first two such services, the job placement program and the savings bank, steered the young
worker toward an acceptable job and taught him to save money, thereby
preparing him for his future role as a father. J.O.C. services, which buttressed
the movement's claim that concrete achievements were more important
than theoretical pronouncements, started slowly and expanded during the
1930s.

The J.O.C. promised to defend young workers' interests at the workplace
and in the public sphere, but its approach contrasted sharply with that of
the Young Communists. The nascent J.O.C. did not protest economic exploitation in the workplace or demand higher wages, considering these areas
the purview of trade unions; meaningful cooperation between Jocists and
Catholic trade unionists would not occur until the mid-1930s. Instead J.O.C.
militants endeavored to improve spiritual and moral working conditions.
They sought to make Christ present at the workplace, through such actions
as stopping work at 3:00 p.m. on Good Friday. They countered "dirty"
songs with pure ones, removed inappropriate magazines from factories and
workshops, and attempted to defend young women's purity by demanding
sex-segregated changing rooms. Jocists also educated young workers about
industrial accidents, whose frequency was highest among the young. Un-
derlying all these actions was the belief that young workers had an essential
dignity as children of God and the right to be treated with respect. Argu-
ably the most effective recruitment techniques were modest interventions
undertaken on behalf of individual young workers. By showing novices the
ropes at work, defending them against abuse from other workers, or simply
befriending them, the J.O.C. militant brought new recruits to the movement
and increased his own stature in the process.

The J.O.C. further appealed to young workers through the provision of
leisure activities and spaces geared specifically to adolescent workers. As we
saw in chapter 2, young male workers were passionate about cycling. Not
only did cycling allow the young to move quickly through their neighborhoods, but it gave them the freedom to explore nearby regions.[112] Eugène
Descamps, who joined the J.O.C. in the 1930s, liked nothing better than
riding his bicycle, especially when it took him through the countryside of
nearby Flanders; by the age of sixteen he estimated that he sometimes covered fifty to two hundred kilometers in a single outing.[113] J.O.C. sections
organized Sunday cycling outings, and they made the section headquarters

a place that young workers viewed as their own. At a moment when working-class housing afforded little privacy, when the working-class community offered few spaces dedicated to adolescent leisure, and when the church had no locales restricted to workers, a section's headquarters could assume a crucial role in the success of the J.O.C. at the local level. There young workers could relax, play pool, smoke cigarettes, put on plays, and even entertain neighborhood friends. This provision of an age and gender-specific sociability and leisure proved popular. Maurice Cliquet, who assumed a leadership position in the late 1930s, remembered waiting impatiently for meetings, play rehearsals, and, in nice weather, Sunday bike rides. That was what mattered most to him about the movement in the late 1920s and early 1930s,[114] and that was what was imitated by the Jeunesses Communistes for a brief period in 1928.

**Measuring the Movement in the Early 1930s** How do we measure the J.O.C.'s successes by the early 1930s, when the membership and influence of the J.C. among young workers had plummeted to new lows? Had clerics created a movement that would ultimately transform the church's relationship to the working class? Initial indicators seemed promising. In Lille, an area of J.O.C. strength, police reported that J.O.C. public meetings attracted up to eight or nine hundred young workers, a number that included Young Communist and Young Socialist speakers allowed to mount the podium and put forward their organizations' point of view.[115] On the national stage J.O.C. congresses drew increasing numbers of young workers. In September 1930 five thousand Jocists gathered at Trocadéro for a congress that *La Jeunesse Ouvrière* pronounced a historic event.[116] The newspaper's banner headline proclaimed: "Everything is possible for him who believes," while the accompanying coverage drew parallels to the heroic deeds of the first Christians. Buoyed by these successes, *La Jeunesse Ouvrière* announced the following month that it would turn more attention to recruiting young workers from seventeen to twenty-one years old, thus challenging the J.C. more directly. The J.O.C.'s successes did not go unnoticed by the Young Communists, who identified the J.O.C. as their "most dangerous adversary" in 1929 and conceded that the organization was particularly adept at recruiting apprentices between the ages of twelve and sixteen.[117] Two years later a J.C. leader admitted that four hundred working youth were enrolled in the J.O.C. in Saint-Denis, "the red city par excellence."[118]

But J.O.C. successes were more limited than the triumphalism of J.O.C. publications and the nervousness of J.C. leaders suggest. For one thing, the movement had yet to win the support of the majority of clerics or lay Catholics. Although the J.O.C. had the strong backing of Pope Pius XI and of important French clerics such as Cardinal Liénart, it met strong resistance too. Many long-serving priests and influential lay people believed that the J.O.C. would encourage, not minimize, revolutionary sentiments among workers. In Besançon, one of Georges Béjot's superiors asked, "Should we long tolerate the fact that abbé Béjot brings revolution to our parishes and gives our vicars bad ideas?"[119] Local parish priests resisted the J.O.C. by refusing to sanction the establishment of sections or acceding to their establishment in name only. Some simply transformed existing parish youth groups into J.O.C. sections.[120]

Both chaplains sympathetic to the J.O.C. and movement militants perceived the clerical opposition in generational terms. Georges Béjot, the future bishop of Reims, recalled how after Father Guérin spoke about the J.O.C. to a few hundred young workers in Belfort in 1928, the local curé responded by assuring him and the overflow crowd that his parish had been doing everything Guérin had talked about for the past twenty-five years. This response caused great consternation among the young vicars "who had studied together in Paris and who had been nurtured on the same preoccupations."[121] For his part, abbé Godin, who was sent to Clichy after his ordination in 1933, complained in his notebook that all but two of the parish priests were clearly rooted in old ways of doing things and opposed to new methods.[122] Jocists evaluated the generational divide in similar ways. A young miner and former militant from Pas-de-Calais recalled an incident that was echoed by others: when Father Guérin asked Jocists during a study retreat to talk about the obstacles facing the J.O.C., the miner shouted out, "Old parish priests"; his answer was met with a spirited concurrence by one of the priests in attendance.[123] Looking back, Fernand Bouxom offered this analysis of clerical attitudes toward the movement: "On the whole, vicars supported us, parish priests a lot less."[124] Awareness of the generational opposition to the movement facilitated the formation of intergenerational bonds between youth activists and their chaplains that no doubt rendered clerical influence within the movement more palatable.

As the 1930s opened, the J.O.C. was far from achieving the lofty missionary goals set by clerics. Instead of bringing Catholic teachings to the masses of dechristianized young workers, the J.O.C. was more apt to give those young

Age, Generation, and Catholic Anticommunism

male workers who were at least nominally Christian the possibility of reconciling two identities that previously had been so difficult to reconcile, especially for male workers. Within the J.O.C. young workers could be Christian and working-class, and they could be so proudly. But this dual identity was not yet a public one. Only with the developments of the mid-1930s—the nadir of the Depression in France, a transformed communist youth politics, and the massive strike movement of May–June 1936—did the J.O.C. emerge as an organization able to defend in the public arena workers who were young and Christian. It was at this point that young workers became the most important part of the J.O.C. story.

# 4

## Rereading the J.O.C.

## through the Lens of Gender

Young Women and the J.O.C.F.

As Catholics labored to refashion young working men, they made the transmission of ideas about marriage and family crucial parts of their educational program. J.O.C. chaplains taught militants that the recovery of the working class was impossible without the recovery of the working-class family, and they drilled young men in Catholic teachings on marriage and family.[1] The resurrection of the working-class family could not be accomplished without young women, however. In Catholic analyses women played pivotal roles as those most responsible for the crisis and those best able to bring about its resolution. As present and future mothers, they had enormous powers: they could sustain the family or destroy it; they could raise the next generation of Catholics or contribute to the church's demise. The construction of a new working class required the creation of a Catholic young working woman who would complement the male Jocist by defending Catholic values in both the public and private spheres. A female branch of the J.O.C. was a logical necessity.

Plans for such a movement began soon after the first J.O.C. sections were established in France. After a cautious start the first female section was officially affiliated in Clichy in February 1928, and others quickly followed in parishes in the Paris region and in the Nord. As the only movement targeted specifically to young working women in France, the Jeunesse Ouvrière Chrétienne Féminine (J.O.C.F.) grew steadily in the 1930s, demonstrating particular strength in the Paris region, eastern France, and Brittany; by 1939 its newspaper enjoyed print runs of over 178,000 copies.[2] The female branch operated separately from the J.O.C., even as it shared the male movement's structure, methods, and overall goals. Thus the J.O.C.F. had its own national chaplain, its own enquêtes, and its own headquarters, which became considerably more comfortable when a female supporter donated a suburban mansion to the organization. It also had its own slate of leaders. Foremost among them was Jeanne Aubert, the formidable founding female Jocist and national president from 1928 until 1939.

How should we evaluate this movement? Historians of the J.O.C. have seen the J.O.C.F. as a subset of the male branch: the authors of *La J.O.C.: regards d'historiens* devoted only three pages to the interwar J.O.C.F. as a distinct movement with specific challenges and accomplishments. The history of the J.O.C.F., the book implied, could be gleaned from that of its male counterpart.[3] But historians of women and religion have outlined the many and profound ways the gender of the faithful has affected religious dogma, practice, and activism. They have analyzed how male religious figures created gender-specific appeals and spiritual practices, and detailed the complicated manner in which women interpreted and acted on these overtures. They have also documented how women used religion to carve out activist roles at moments when their access to public and political life was markedly more restricted than men's.[4] In short, gender matters profoundly as a category of analysis when the object of study is religion.

Reading the history of the J.O.C.F.'s early years through the lens of gender yields a story that is both familiar and strikingly different. Although the female branch employed J.O.C. methods of education and activism, their application to young women caused anxiety and necessitated modification. Chaplains and youth leaders desired a movement of militants who were at once independent activists and complements to male Jocists. Chaplains created modes of activism that reflected long-established patterns of female social action and a spirituality anchored firmly in traditions of female devotional practices, and they were uncertain whether young women could be considered apostles. The J.O.C.F. further taught young working women that they had a complex relationship to work. Even though young women were to take pride in their status as workers, they were to refuse work that was deemed inappropriate for women and prepare for maternal life in the home.

For all its traditional rhetoric and ideology, the J.O.C.F. offered young working women possibilities that were unusual for the time. Even as the J.O.C.F. leadership fretted over the impact of "male" jobs on women and prepared Jocists tirelessly for their vocations as nonworking Christian mothers, it promoted ideas of gender equality and encouraged a spirited public activism that was all the more striking in its historical context. During the 1920s and 1930s, when French women were so clearly viewed as the subordinate sex, the mundane chores of movement life assumed added significance when

performed by militants who were both young and female. Young women
selling newspapers in the streets, addressing large audiences, or visiting
members by bicycle at night elicited different reactions from participants
and observers. So too did young women challenging clerics for control,
which female militants sometimes did with the support of their leaders.
Female Jocists were not passive recipients of movement messages. Instead
they chose what they wanted to hear and act upon, and they turned meetings
and gatherings to their own purposes. That they were young women doing
so made their actions all the more significant.

**The J.O.C.F.'s Origins** Catholic attitudes toward worker youth
in the 1920s were deeply gendered. As clerics outlined the need for a fresh approach to young workers, they wrote little that discussed young women specifically. Guérin, the J.O.C.'s founder, did not include young female workers
in his analysis of communism's appeal to working youth. "Worker youth"
was understood by both Communists and Catholics to be a male category.
And after the J.O.C.F. had been started, clerical supporters did not concoct
pamphlets to justify the initiative to industrialists as they had with the
J.O.C.

These silences reflected assumptions about young working women's relationship to politics and religion. Working-class young women were generally
assumed to be outside politics, especially working-class politics. They did
not have the right to vote and, unlike their male counterparts in the J.O.C.,
could not attain this right once they reached the age of twenty-one. Nor
were they directly targeted by left political parties. Despite the rhetorical affirmation of women's equality by the socialist and communist parties, there
were few sustained efforts to reach out to young working women. Socialists
mobilized few women of any age, and Communists attracted only a handful
of young women to their male-dominated youth organization. Working-
class politics was a male world, and Catholics did not feel challenged by
Communists for female affections. Young working women, like women of
other classes, were further seen as less alienated from religion than their
male counterparts were. As the first male Jocist in France, Georges Quiclet,
explained, male workers considered religion the province of women and
children.[5]

The J.O.C.F. started with little fanfare, and the circumstances surrounding
its birth are only thinly documented. According to the two available sources,
an unsigned account of the J.O.C.F.'s beginnings written in the late 1930s and

the recollections of Jeanne Aubert, the J.O.C.F. began when Father Guérin summoned Aubert, a seventeen-year-old office worker from a neighboring parish in Clichy. Guérin explained the need for a female branch and instructed her to see the vicar in charge of girls' organizations in her parish, abbé Pluyette.[6] In the meantime Guérin would contact her parish priest.[7] Concerned about unleashing the wrath of parish women's organizations, Pluyette determined that the effort should proceed cautiously. Instead of forming a J.O.C.F. section immediately, he counseled Aubert to start a small group that would be called the Daisies.

Abbé Pluyette's caution underscores how parish life took on a different hue when viewed through the prism of sexual difference. In the 1920s bourgeois and aristocratic lay women were an imposing and long-established presence in French parishes. As scholars have demonstrated, the church had undergone a process of feminization during the nineteenth century. When the church stood steadfast against science, reason, and rationality, women predominated among the faithful. As men increasingly left the church or participated only nominally in its rituals and activities, women were more likely to attend Mass, join religious orders, and devote themselves to charitable works.[8] To be sure, Republican attacks on the church in the late nineteenth century and the early twentieth energized Catholic men, transforming some into militant defenders of the faith. But women remained prominent Catholic soldiers in battles over the church's presence in French public life.[9] Heeding the call by Pope Pius X in 1904 to move beyond the confines of charity work, women stormed into the public realm to defend church liberties and promote Catholic models of social action and popular education. When church and state were separated in 1905, Catholic lay women's organizations dwarfed other women's organizations, with remarkably diverse activities.[10] Groups such as the Ligue Patriotique des Françaises, founded in 1902, raised money for Catholic political initiatives, established libraries, encouraged all-female trade unions, ran domestic science schools, oversaw girls' fellowships, and aided poor mothers.[11] Women provided the unpaid infrastructure for much of the church's social work and religious activity, and their actions provided outlets for their prodigious energies.

By the mid-1920s Catholic women's organizations were stronger than ever, and they met the challenges of the postwar decade with fresh initiatives. At a moment of intensified attention to youth, Catholic women's groups sought to extend their influence to the next generation through organizations for girls and young women. Powerful Catholic lay women introduced a Catholic version of the Girl Guide movement to France in 1923.[12] The Ligue Patriotique des Françaises, which boasted 1.1 million members, oversaw a thriving youth league, the Ligue des Jeunes. Both the Ligue des Jeunes and the Guides reached out to young women of all social classes, with Guide leaders pointing to the existence in the Paris region of eleven troops for young working women by early 1927.[13] Women leaders were adamant that any organization for young working women not operate outside their control.

Opposition to an independent J.O.C.F. was particularly strong on the part of Mme Duhamel, the head of both the *patronage* movement and the Guides, and Mlle du Rostu, the leader of the Ligue des Jeunes.[14] Looking back, Jeanne Aubert noted that it took all of Guérin's tenacity to overcome this resistance and obtain approval from Canon Gerlier, the church's *directeur des oeuvres*.[15] With plans to create the J.O.C.F. allowed to proceed, the first section was affiliated in Clichy in February 1928. Its members included four factory workers, an office worker, a salesclerk, an upholsterer, a drawer, a dressmaker, and a milliner. But the nascent movement continued to encounter resistance. News that the J.O.C.F. planned to publish a newspaper led to further protests from women leaders, and Catholic officials bowed temporarily to the pressure. Canon Gerlier informed the J.O.C.F. that it could not publish a newspaper and would have to content itself for the time being with a handwritten bulletin.[16] Pressure continued to be felt in certain parishes in years following. In one town in the Nord, those attempting to begin a J.O.C.F. section at the end of 1930 had to promise that militants would also join the local Ligue des Jeunes in order to obtain the stamp of approval from church officials.[17]

As the female branch got under way, chaplains retained the J.O.C.'s structure, activities, and methods, but used them to fashion activists who would complement and support the young men. The J.O.C.F. took a similar approach to youth activism, and its members were expected to do what their male counterparts did. Dues-paying local members were expected to attend general assemblies and comport themselves as Jocists, while militants were to attend study sessions and take the lead in neighborhood activism. Working with chaplains, militants recruited members, studied movement materials, planned outreach, and sold their newspaper, *La Jeunesse Ouvrière Féminine*, in a range of public spaces. Leaders had more extensive responsibilities. Local ones prepared general assemblies, visited members on bicycle, ran study sessions, and made their way through the often dense social

**Figure 1** Selling movement literature was at the core of Jocist activism, but this activity was often viewed with suspicion when undertaken by young women. Here J.O.C.F. militants pose proudly with their paper *La Jeunesse Ouvrière Féminine*. Used with permission from Jeanne Aubert, J.O.C., *qu'as-tu fait de nos vies? la Jeunesse Ouvrière Chrétienne Féminine: sa vie, son action, 1928–1945* (Ivry-sur-Seine: Éditions de l'Atelier / Éditions Ouvrières, 1990).

Catholic literature. National leaders produced the movement's publications and oversaw its affairs, working closely with local chaplains and the national chaplain, Jesuit Father Guichard.

That young women would do these things was shocking to some, for their performance violated the expectations of many parents and clerics about young working women. Although a small number of female adolescent workers lived independently during the 1920s, most remained with their parents. Daughters were expected to help mothers with housework and childcare, and their attitudes and actions were monitored closely. This was especially true in the Catholic households that provided so many of the J.O.C.F.'s first members. Attending night meetings, selling newspapers in the streets or outside church after Mass, and public speaking were considered suspicious, unacceptable activities for young women. As a result, parents sometimes opposed their daughters' participation in the J.O.C.F. One Jocist admitted that it was her father's opposition to the "new ideas" of the J.O.C.F. that drew her to the movement.[18]

Rereading the J.O.C.

Clerics too were uncertain about the J.O.C.F.'s suitability for young women, who they believed were already well served by parish organizations. In the sex-segregated world of French Catholicism, the close contact between young women and young priests envisioned by the J.O.C.F. hinted at impropriety, especially to older priests. One Jocist remembered, "My old parish priest thought that the J.O.C. would lead me to ruin."[19] Yet even the younger clerics most likely to be movement chaplains had little in their training that prepared them to work closely with young women. Having spent their formative years in the resolutely male settings of the Catholic school, seminary, and military, these men had imbibed lessons about women sure to put them on their guard. According to the historian Pierre Pierrard, Guérin and his clerical cohort had been schooled in the almost obsessional cult of Holy Virtue and purity; this left Guérin "frightened of women and horrified by sex."[20] Indeed, it took time for Guérin to be able to shake the hands of female Jocists firmly.[21] To allay such fears, early J.O.C.F. sections were often run by lay women or nuns, both of whom had long experience animating girls' groups.[22] Many priests apparently accepted the formation of a J.O.C.F. section only on the condition that it have a female advisor.[23] Concerns over the J.O.C.F.'s suitability for young women continued in some quarters throughout the movement's first decade, mirroring fears of revolutionary potential that plagued the J.O.C.

The J.O.C.F. styled itself an organization for young women of the working class. Although the movement was open to all young women who worked for wages, chaplains and youth leaders concentrated rhetorical attention on factory workers, who were deemed the most downtrodden and forsaken.[24] The office worker Jeanne Aubert accepted the position of national president on the condition that she undertake three stints as a factory worker to familiarize herself with the milieu, and Father Guérin stipulated that the J.O.C.F. must be very careful about including white-collar workers; in his opinion, the organization should only accept white-collar workers who did not act as if they were superior to manual laborers.[25]

Reality did not always match intention. As in the male branch, J.O.C.F. sections often emerged out of existing parish youth organizations, in which factory workers or manual laborers were few. The J.O.C.F. struggled to move beyond traditional Catholic constituencies, with the second and third J.O.C.F. sections having to be disbanded and reconstituted with young women drawn more from "the masses."[26] Only in the summer of 1931 was the J.O.C.F. ready to prepare for serious recruitment among the masses of young female workers.[27] As part of this effort, militants were instructed to create parish maps indicating the workplaces of local young women and Jocists.[28]

There is little evidence that the effort to implant the J.O.C.F. firmly among the working masses succeeded. Leaders were primarily white-collar workers, and both leaders and militants articulated the distance they felt between themselves and Jocists who were factory workers or who came from the "working masses." One militant went so far as to say that the J.O.C.F. had appeared to her as a providential answer to the question she had been asking: "What can be done for all these often scorned young female workers who don't have a place in the movements that already exist, religious or otherwise?"[29] Some discussed "discovering" the working class in language reminiscent of nineteenth-century middle- and upper-class reformers, and others described going into poor areas as if they were on a journey into a different, darker world.[30] Perhaps the most striking testimony of the gap between many J.O.C.F. militants and poorer workers was the account provided by a militant who joined the J.O.C.F. at the end of the 1930s. Describing her clandestine visit to a communist meeting, she recalled: "It was really the 'working masses' . . . we looked a little too 'middle class' in their midst."[31] Still, the J.O.C.F. should not be dismissed as a lower-middle-class organization. Although national membership records do not exist, local records suggest that J.O.C.F. sections drew young women employed in a range of jobs and industries, with the precise makeup of sections depending in part on the economic profile of each particular area.[32]

**Making New Women** The J.O.C.F. undertook to train its members in Catholic values and conduct, but lessons were always gender-specific. Using enquêtes, the movement press, and meetings, the J.O.C.F.'s creators pushed movement members to reconsider their lives and social relationships through the lens of social Catholic ideas about women and femininity. Young working women's relationship to the family provided the starting point. Because Catholics considered the family both the basic cell of society and a privileged site of education and generational renewal, they invested its well-being with tremendous significance. Catholic activists vigorously promoted measures to strengthen the family, such as family allowances, and they monitored the health of the family without cease, paying particular attention to the working-class family.[33] In Father Lhande's account of his journey into the Parisian suburbs, random couplings, free unions, civil marriages, abandoned children, and masculinized young women demonstrated the breakdown of the family, and this was both cause and symptom of larger moral decay.[34]

As much as Catholic observers attempted to provide multicausal explanations for this sorry state of affairs, they assigned the primary blame to women. It was women's responsibility to nurture the family and its members. Once married, women had an obligation to leave the workforce and, as Catholics put it, "return to the home." There they would watch over children and extend limitless love and patience. Mothers were highly idealized figures in the Catholic imagination. "A mother!," *La Jeunesse Ouvrière* exulted, "What a magnificent and providential role! Children learn to love by her side. While the father works, she watches over the home with tenderness and . . . weaves a happy web of family intimacy that is so propitious to the education of children."[35] As this excerpt suggests, a mother's power lay partly in her educational role. During nineteenth-century struggles between Republicans and Catholics, both sides had looked to mothers to transmit ideas and values within the home. As Catholics sought to counter revolution in the late 1920s, they again hoped to enlist mothers as teachers.

Catholics worried that the young working women of the 1920s showed few signs of preparing for this maternal role. As Mary Louise Roberts has demonstrated, France in the 1920s witnessed tremendous anxiety about the modern woman, who more often than not was young.[36] Across the country, and especially in urban centers, young women behaved in new ways and adopted new attitudes. They cut their hair, donned more revealing clothes, and embraced the pleasures of the postwar age. They continued to work in jobs that had been the province of men before 1914, and they appeared hesitant about settling down and having the numerous children believed necessary for France's reconstruction. Catholic commentators bemoaned the new fashions and Pope Pius XI banned a bestselling novel about the modern woman, *La Garçonne*.[37] Although the *jeune fille moderne* generated the most anxiety when she hailed from the bourgeoisie or the aristocracy, the young working woman, or *jeune travailleuse*, presented special dangers. According to Canon Cardijn, young working women corrupted innocent male apprentices and threatened the familial and social orders by usurping men's jobs and blurring gender distinctions. He warned that if women continued to compete with men in the workplace, crisis and unemployment would ensue and morality would be adversely affected. Catholics, he concluded, needed a positive program to move young women away from this masculine role.[38]

The J.O.C.F. made the transmission of Catholic ideas about femininity its primary goal, and most of its analyses, activities, and initiatives were related to this undertaking. From the movement's beginnings it taught militants that "woman's inability to fulfill her role as housewife and educator destroys the family,"[39] and it brought in clerics to lecture militants about the disorder that reigned among les jeunes filles modernes. According to Canon Courbe, female Jocists faced a stark choice: they could be angels or demons.[40] The modern woman's antithesis was the Mother, and it was as mothers that young working women would best serve the campaign to rechristianize the working class. Cardinal Verdier explained to J.O.C.F. militants in 1930 that society was estranged from God because "mothers did not know the proper way to teach religion to children and husbands." Having studied these questions, however, Jocists would have no trouble convincing *their* husbands and *their* children.[41] For Verdier the female Jocists were a source of great hope and great joy; they were the vanguard in the working class's return to the church.

It was not enough to lecture young working women. The J.O.C.F. relied heavily on the more active pedagogical approach offered by the enquête. The J.O.C.F.'s first national enquête in 1928 investigated young working women's relationship to the family. Since young women related to families as daughters and future mothers, the questions the militants set out to answer had them reflect on their behavior toward parents and their preparation for future roles as mothers and wives. The militants' bulletin, *L'équipe ouvrière féminine*, left no doubt as to a young woman's responsibilities: the young female worker had to "love her family and her home and fulfill her domestic duties." She also had to prepare to create a Christian household and assume her future role as mother and wife.[42] Purity was a key component, and both this investigation and subsequent ones pushed the Jocists to contemplate the importance of moral rectitude. They were always to be pure in thought, word, and deed: they were not to flirt or go out with young men, they were never to use foul language, and they were to be extremely careful how they spent their leisure time.

Subsequent enquêtes by the J.O.C.F. returned relentlessly to these themes, regardless of political developments. The training of young Catholic women was something that happened outside of political time, and the J.O.C.F.'s activities and campaigns intersected rarely with significant national developments. During 1936–37, when France was convulsed by the Popular Front experiment, the J.O.C.F.'s national enquête examined young women's preparation for marriage. As trade unionists and employers struggled for supremacy in the workplace, female Jocists worked their way diligently through the investigation's questionnaire. They began by exploring young women's inadequate financial and spiritual preparation for marriage and continued by studying the virtues necessary for a successful Christian union. First on the list was the spirit of submission. Wives had to subordinate themselves to their familial duties and to their husbands. As with all enquêtes, the questions that followed developed these themes. Respondents analyzed the character faults evident in broken families in their neighborhood, especially those exhibited by women, and their analysis would help them to achieve the wifely virtues that kept families together, including purity of heart and a sense of charity.[43]

The J.O.C.F. did not rely simply on clerical lectures and enquêtes to alter attitudes toward marriage and motherhood. Following the example of social Catholic women, the J.O.C.F. organized evening gatherings where Jocists learned to mend, cook, and crochet. By the early 1930s some sections offered more formal courses in sewing, embroidery, infant care, cooking, and hygiene, and a select few enlisted doctors and nurses to give informal lectures. At a moment when group singing was a hugely popular activity, the J.O.C.F. also used song to transmit the movement's domestic message, creating its own songs, sometimes by writing Jocist lyrics for contemporary tunes. By singing "Mothers" and discussing its main themes, Jocists learned that maternal love was forged in sacrifice and total devotion to children.[44] These imperatives were reinforced in the J.O.C.F. press. In the movement's newspaper *La Jeunesse Ouvrière Féminine*, "Paula" dispensed advice on the proper way to choose a husband, while Jocist marriages were celebrated in a special column.

J.O.C.F. investigations and actions inevitably found their way to labor, which dominated members' waking hours. During the interwar period young women worked in higher numbers than adult women, with those in their twenties having the highest rates of labor force participation.[45] Work experiences of young French women in the 1920s were incredibly diverse, particularly in the dynamic Paris region, the scene of the J.O.C.F.'s most serious recruiting campaigns.[46] There some young women worked in huge factories in the metalworking, electrical, chemical, and food processing industries, where modern techniques of production, including assembly lines, were most likely to exist and young women occupied new jobs. Other young women held jobs in smaller workshops, especially in trades long dominated

**118**  by women, including fashion, clothing, and leather goods. Although in decline during the 1920s, these trades continued to employ many young female workers and were apt to offer the greatest opportunities for occupational identification. Increasing numbers of white-collar jobs were also available in offices, shops, and discount and department stores, reflecting a trend begun earlier in the twentieth century. By 1931 there was one white-collar worker for every two female industrial workers in France.[47] As unemployment rose in the early 1930s, more young women resorted to domestic work, especially in their first years in the workforce.[48] And some young women performed home-based work. The exact professional map of women's work in a particular city or region depended on its economic strengths and focus. In the Nord, for instance, textile work employed a large number of young women workers.

The conditions faced by young female workers were grim. The youngest among them struggled most, getting little help in the transition from school to the workplace. So abrupt was this transition that some began work on their thirteenth birthday, or the day after receiving their certificate of primary studies at twelve.[49] Working women recalled how bewildering and upsetting this move was, and how depressed they had been after their first days of work. One Jocist who went from shepherding cows in a mountainous region to toiling in a canning factory at twelve and a half remembered that she found it "very, very difficult" to be suddenly locked inside an overheated, airless room for ten hours a day.[50] For some, the most depressing characteristic of their new reality was the work's unremitting nature: workweeks of fifty to sixty hours or more were common, and paid vacations were extremely rare before 1936. A young working woman recalled sobbing to her mother after her first work day at thirteen—not because she had to work, but because she would no longer have any vacations.[51] Regardless of age, female wages were lower than male wages, with few possibilities for training. Apprenticeship programs were most likely to exist in trades long dominated by women, like fashion.[52] But those employed in fashion struggled with the financial hardships of seasonal employment. The more modern industries, by contrast, had no formal apprenticeships for young women, and the 1920s witnessed the elimination of older categories of skilled work for women.[53] Partly because so little training was provided, occupational instability was high among young female workers.

When Catholics involved with the J.O.C.F. analyzed women's work and attempted to shape attitudes toward work, they did not concern themselves with low wages or insufficient occupational training. Instead they condemned the harmful impact that work had on women's moral and reproductive lives. Although the earliest J.O.C.F. writings, which drew heavily on J.O.C. pamphlets, described the dignity and beauty of manual labor, subsequent publications tended to emphasize the problematic nature of work for women. For interwar Catholics, as for legions of nineteenth-century writers and reformers, women's work had an abundance of deleterious consequences;[54] these were underlined ever more sharply during the early 1930s, when Catholics became increasingly worried about rising male unemployment. In the J.O.C.F.'s telling, work by women ran counter to the values and practices that the movement was trying to promote. Work was the principal obstacle to a woman's formation as a mother and housewife; it led, in addition, to a drop in the birth rate and a rise in infant mortality.[55] All industrial work was suspect, but factory work was identified as the most serious problem. According to the J.O.C.F., women's compromised health, broken homes, abandoned children, and immorality could all be traced to that single source.[56] Like social Catholic women, however, the J.O.C.F. stopped short of calling for legislation removing women from the workforce.

Since work was believed to present an amalgam of physical dangers, young women were advised to choose their employment carefully. But there was no emphasis, as there was in the J.O.C., on acquiring skills. Young women were urged to take up jobs that corresponded to Catholic understandings of their roles as women and future mothers. They were instructed to stay away from "men's work," and indeed any work that involved abrupt or violent motions, heavy lifting, or nervous tension; these would damage their health and reproductive capabilities.[57] Instead young women were encouraged to perform work that required attributes deemed feminine, such as patience, taste, artistic sense, and manual dexterity; such work not only would correspond with women's strengths but would develop other skills thought to be "natural" to women.[58] Once they became mothers, young women had to abandon paid work and return to the home. "Women in the home" became a rallying cry for the J.O.C.F., as it did for social Catholic women in the 1930s; in late 1932 the movement's newspaper defined the J.O.C.F.'s mission as making "everyone see that a woman's true place is in the home."[59]

Like their male counterparts, J.O.C.F. writers placed considerable emphasis on the moral dangers posed by entrance into the workforce. The beginning of full-time work, especially factory work, was represented as a brutal initiation into immoral practices and conversations, with profound

**120** consequences for a young woman's moral and spiritual health. Adult male workers were identified as major culprits for their sexual aggressiveness toward female initiates. *La Jeunesse Ouvrière Féminine* complained often about the problem, noting that "too often, under the pretense of being polite, men devote themselves to seducing and corrupting the new female apprentices."[60] Adult working women also figured prominently in J.O.C.F. literature and memories. In Catholic analyses women had long been depicted in dichotomous ways, as angels or demons, mothers or modern women, virgins or sexual temptresses. In J.O.C.F. materials, adult working women became agents of moral corruption who preyed on innocent young women and gleefully initiated them into an adult world of foul language and sexual promiscuity. "Out of sight of their supervisor," *La Jeunesse Ouvrière Féminine* complained in 1932, "older women pass around filth to see how it will affect the newest young female worker."[61] In the fashion industry the J.O.C.F. newspaper reported that "adult women workers sometimes become worse than the men."[62] The image of moral corruption by older female workers remained sharply etched in some Jocists' minds. One remembered over fifty years later, "All the young women who worked in factories were more afraid of married women than of men. They were afraid of 'ces sales bonnes femmes,' as they were called, who wanted to teach the young women a thing or two about life."[63]

The J.O.C.F. attempted to alter objectionable conditions at the workplace and defend young female workers. Like the J.O.C., the female branch did not take aim at economic exploitation or call for structural change. Rather it attempted to bring Catholic values to the workplace and improve the health, safety, and moral environment of young working women. The enquête, which pushed militants to careful observation, again provided the starting point. The national enquête of 1934–35 into young working women's health documented the challenges that young women faced in a range of workplaces; these findings provided the basis for the book *Révélations sur la santé des jeunes travailleuses*, by the social Catholic activists Céline Lhotte and Elisabeth Dupeyrat.[64] Consistent with the J.O.C.F.'s emphasis on the special perils of the factory, enquête militants subjected women's factory work to close scrutiny, finding that approximately a quarter of female factory workers performed shift work, whose irregularity, Lhotte and Dupeyrat pointed out, was especially harmful to female bodies. J.O.C.F. militants identified widespread instances of illegal overtime and generally poor work conditions. Air quality was a particular problem, as Jocists recorded temperatures that were either too hot or too cold, dust, and poor air circulation. Dirty, foul-smelling bathrooms monopolized by young men appalled the J.O.C.F. Significantly, Jocists found that conditions in settings seen as more appropriate for women were often little better. In small shops, Jocists discovered that laws regulating working conditions were routinely ignored and that young women were often assigned heavy lifting and given few chances to use the washroom. In workshops in female-dominated trades like sewing and fashion, Jocists condemned the practice of forcing young workers to work unpaid supplementary hours, especially during the high season, in tiny, stuffy rooms with no windows.

The Jocist agenda was concrete change. Jocists demanded separate toilets for young women or insisted that inspectors stop men from commandeering the women's toilets. They demanded sinks in which young women could wash their hands, lunchrooms where their food would not be covered in dust or other debris, and proper changing rooms. They also challenged suggestive language and men who made advances to young women. Like their male counterparts, they took aim at issues involving workplace safety. Having established that young workers were particularly vulnerable to industrial accidents, they encouraged the use of first aid kits and workplace awareness. Theirs was not an especially critical stance, and even Lhotte and Dupeyrat conceded that the Jocists were much more likely to record their failings than those of their employers.[65] How much was actually accomplished is unclear. Presumably only the well-established and most assertive even attempted these kinds of changes. And although the J.O.C.F. signed an agreement with Catholic women's trade unions in 1931, cooperative efforts seem to have been few before the strikes of 1936.

The J.O.C.F. also sought to shape attitudes toward leisure. Clerics were convinced that leisure pursuits had a range of unfortunate consequences for young women's moral life, health, and preparation for marriage and motherhood. Depending on the activity, a young woman might engage in immoral conduct, imbibe inappropriate messages, weaken her body, or waste money that could be better spent on her current or future family. Given the consequences of misspent leisure time, Jocists investigated all manner of young women's leisure activities and behavior, and J.O.C.F. materials commented regularly on young working women's pastimes. The J.O.C.F.'s enquête into young working women's health in 1934–35 provides an unusual glimpse into their leisure practices. J.O.C.F. investigators found that young working men and women shared some passions but parted company in many others. Few young working women seemed particularly interested in sport or cycling,

**Figure 2** The poor health of young working women was a prime concern of the J.O.C.F., which was active in the sanatoria where some young workers went to regain their health. Used with permission from Jeanne Aubert, *J.O.C., qu'as-tu fait de nos vies? La Jeunesse Ouvrière Chrétienne Féminine: sa vie, son action, 1928–1945* (Ivry-sur-Seine: Éditions de l'Atelier / Éditions Ouvrières, 1990).

but they were as enthusiastic about dance as young men. Young women dreamed of dancing and happily spent money dancing or buying clothes in which to dance; some danced until six in the morning, while others arrived at work on Monday boasting that they had not changed clothes since going out on Saturday.[66] For social Catholics like Lhotte and Dupeyrat, the atmosphere of dance venues was as corrupt as could be imagined, while the late nights and money spent undermined young working women's already fragile health.[67] Dancing, they asserted, was one of the biggest causes of tuberculosis.

The promotion of good health was crucial in the J.O.C.F., for ill health affected individual women and compromised the strength of the French population and the integrity of the race. The movement's focus on health was in part a function of Catholics' emphasis on population politics, but it also reflected concern over adolescents who toiled long hours in unhealthy workplaces, had few forms of healthy leisure, and went home to run-down apartments. As the Jocists documented in their enquête on health and in their publications, serious illness, especially tuberculosis, was a constant threat. Many young working women developed health problems which made working difficult, thousands were sent to recover in sanatoria, and some died young. Obituaries appeared frequently in the Jocist press, and one member reported that her small section was following four patients, each in a different sanatorium, and seven more in the neighborhood.[68] In this context money diverted from food to the movies or dancing could contribute to health problems that had serious consequences for young women's lives.

By the Jocists' own estimation, 35 percent of young working women in the Paris region were undernourished.[69]

The sedentary pastime of reading, which occupied a special place in the lives of young working women, was also problematic. Very worrisome for the J.O.C.F. were cheap popular novels, which young working women seemed to devour on their way to work, on their breaks, and in their off hours. As one Jocist recalled, she read three to four novels a day before she became a committed Jocist.[70] Novels were a threat on a number of levels. They diverted precious resources from domestic expenditures, including food, and from premarital savings. They also carried the wrong messages about love, and encouraged young women, in the J.O.C.F.'s formulation, to "dream of a luxurious existence and of pleasures unworthy" of them.[71] The movement press promoted more appropriate reading materials, including religious texts ranging from papal encyclicals to Marian tracts and biographies. Jocists were to consult their chaplains should they have any questions about an item's suitability.

Reading was further linked to young working women's love affair with the cinema. Although going to the movies was a popular activity for young workers of both sexes, the cinema, with its attendant press and celebrity culture, occupied a particularly significant place in the lives of young working women. The J.O.C.F.'s enquête on health of 1934–35 found that in cities well served by movie theaters, more than 50 percent of young women between the ages of thirteen and twenty employed in factories or workshops went to the movies at least four times a week.[72] In smaller urban settings, the frequency was thought to be once or twice a week. To afford these outings, young working women deprived themselves of the necessities of life or allowed young men to pay for their ticket, practices which were unacceptable to Catholics. Young women also followed avidly the lives and loves of film stars in the era's movie magazines, thus exposing themselves to inappropriate models of femininity and sexuality. *La Jeunesse Ouvrière Féminine* strongly opposed the artifice of the star system, taking special aim at the enormous gap between the stars' public personas and their real personalities.[73] Throughout its commentary on the cinema, the J.O.C.F. focused unremittingly on the home as the source of all happiness. As *La Jeunesse Ouvrière Féminine* reminded readers, "it is much easier for a woman to be happy as a housewife than a movie star."[74]

The J.O.C.F. framed the cinema, not communism, as its most important rival in the battle to capture the allegiance of young working women. *La*

*Jeunesse Ouvrière Féminine* recounted the story of a girl who committed suicide after her father forbade her to pursue a career in the movies. And who could blame her? "Everywhere people are talking about the cinema, in newspapers, books, photographs . . . only the cinema matters . . . at school, everyone discusses the cinema . . . at the workshop, workers make mistakes as they tell themselves over and over 'I can't wait until evening comes so we can go to the movies.'" This girl, "who could have sacrificed everything to an ideal," had not known about the existence of an ideal worthy of her sacrifice.[75] It was up to the J.O.C.F. to provide one.

**Making Female Religious Activists**  The J.O.C.F.'s central aim was to manufacture religious activists who could bring the church's message to working-class neighborhoods, workplaces, and homes. Although the J.O.C.F. relied on the same educational methods as the J.O.C., the exercise was carefully tailored to young women. Both branches of the movement sought to create a spirituality centered on a human Christ who spoke directly to young workers, but his representation and relationship to young workers differed considerably from one branch to the next. For male Jocists, Christ was portrayed as a hardy worker who had performed manual labor and chosen the laboring life; the Worker Christ functioned as the model. Within J.O.C.F. printed materials, however, the depiction of Christ as a worker who ennobled Jocist lives and work was rare, reflecting the movement's ambivalent position on women's work.

The religious meditations appearing in the militants' bulletin, *L'équipe ouvrière féminine*, featured a Christ often referred to as "Our Friend Jesus." This Christ had relationships with young female workers characterized by friendship, emotional intimacy, and sometimes longing. One meditation described the profound sense of loss that Christ's resurrection had caused young female workers, portraying the moment of his greatest glory as a time of discomfort and sadness because of the disappearance of the human, embodied Christ. As *L'équipe ouvrière féminine* noted, "Christ is risen! This explains your discomfort. In the evening, He appeared to you grander, more majestic, but also more distant."[76] The meditation continued: "You have a human heart which needs to love, and you are not ashamed. But you know that love demands the presence of the friend. Now, if yesterday Christ was less handsome to look at, at least he was more human. His smile rested on your soul like a tenderness, His words gave rise to an unspeakable calm in your heart. You felt understood and you were won over."[77] Deprived of

Christ's physical presence, female Jocists were assured of his continuing presence in their hearts. The voice they heard inside their heads was his, they were told, and this voice fulfilled the roles of master, husband, friend, and father.

The intimate relationship between Christ and the young female worker depicted in J.O.C.F. literature could take the form of a mystical union. In another meditation militants read, "I am nothing by myself but everything through Christ. I am attached to Christ, no what's more: I am an extension of Him."[78] The union between Christ and the female Jocist was illustrated through the metaphor of a tree, with Christ the trunk and the female Jocist the branches. Within this metaphor the gift of grace became the Jocist's physical, spiritual, and even sexual nourishment, one which she desired ardently: "As the trunk sends all the sap into its branches, He spills his fertile grace into me. He wants it, He strives for it, He pushes me. And if He wants it so much, what should I long for in turn? Only one thing: His sap, His liquid flesh, His presence, His continuous, rich penetration which spreads through my entire being."[79]

By portraying Christ as a husband, friend, father, and lover, and by encouraging young women to forge intimate relationships with him, the authors of J.O.C.F. materials echoed themes and depictions of Christ that had been prevalent in mid- to late-nineteenth-century French female piety.[80] The messages directed at the young working women of the 1920s and 1930s resembled those found on nineteenth-century religious playing cards for schoolgirls, which bore titles such as The Lover, The Conquest, The Ideal Companion, and The Wife and messages such as "My loved one is all mine and I am all His" or "The imperious need of love is to yearn for union with the object of love, to search for it and procure it by every means."[81] As they had in an earlier time, the themes contained in J.O.C.F. meditations buttressed clerical messages to young working women: by channeling women's desires toward an unattainable Jesus, chaplains furthered the campaign for sexual purity and virginity.

J.O.C.F. authors similarly looked to Mary as they endeavored to provide otherworldly exemplars for youth and to create an intense spiritual world. During the nineteenth century Mary became a centrally important figure in French Catholicism and female piety. Sightings of her were reported with some frequency in rural France, and these apparitions occasioned much popular interest. The church encouraged the adoration of Mary, creating the first modern pilgrimage movement around her appearance at Lourdes in 1858.[82] Clerics also used her to symbolize some of the key messages and virtues that the church was trying to communicate. Mary became a critical vehicle for teaching femininity because she incarnated the most important ideals of nineteenth-century Catholic womanhood: purity, virginity, and maternity.

Jocists were encouraged to read the biographies of Mary that remained so popular, and they pondered the example of her life in study sessions and private meditations. The message was clear: they were to take Mary as their model and emulate her at every turn.[83] The one human being conceived without original sin, Mary symbolized perfection, and militants pored over meditations exhorting them to do all they could to attain her pure state. By forming a partnership with Mary, they would be able to crush the head of the serpent and safeguard their own purity.[84] Mary also symbolized virginity and total devotion to God. Militants learned how Mary loved God more than any other human being, and that her all-encompassing love led to her embrace of virginity. Jocists must love God as fully as Mary had, and concentrate only on him and his reign.[85] Since virginity was to be only a temporary state, J.O.C.F. materials celebrated Mary's role as Jesus's mother, noting that her baptism of Jesus had originated all the graces that the Jocists now received. Female militants pondered this most magnificent and perfect mother, whose centrality to Christianity was everlasting.

As clerics sought to fashion lay missionaries who would bring the church's teachings to young female workers, they were unsure exactly how much apostolic importance to assign to the female Jocists. This dilemma was apparent in the terms used to describe the female militants. Although Cardinal Suhard of Paris referred to them as "apostles" in 1931, others were less willing to confer this exalted status on young women, preferring to call them "witnesses."[86] The safest route was to liken them to the first Christians, so many of whom were women.

Such comparisons were abundant during the J.O.C.F.'s pilgrimage in 1934 to Italy, designed to help shape militants into religious activists and generate excitement for the movement. Meticulously planned, it took twelve hundred female Jocists to Turin, Rappallo, Assisi, Pisa, and most especially Rome, where they retraced the steps of male Jocists. The young women toured the historical sites of Christianity, listening to speeches that drew direct parallels between their challenges and those of early Christians and exhorted them to follow the heroic example set by their heroic Christian forebears, especially those who were women. At the Coliseum abbé Bordet

**Figure 3** Female Jocists visit the Coliseum during their pilgrimage to Rome in 1934. Used with permission from Jeanne Aubert, *J.O.C., qu'as-tu fait de nos vies? La Jeunesse Ouvrière Chrétienne Féminine: sa vie, son action, 1928–1945* (Ivry-sur-Seine: Éditions de l'Atelier / Éditions Ouvrières, 1990).

**Figure 4** J.O.C.F. pilgrims attend Mass in the Catacombs. Used with permission from Jeanne Aubert, *J.O.C., qu'as-tu fait de nos vies? La Jeunesse Ouvrière Chrétienne Féminine: sa vie, son action, 1928–1945* (Ivry-sur-Seine: Éditions de l'Atelier / Éditions Ouvrières, 1990).

extolled Christians who had been willing to die rather than renounce their love for Christ or betray their ideal, highlighting the "humble virgins" and girls of twelve and even younger who had faced lions, tigers, and furious bulls with superhuman courage.[87] In the Catacombs Monsignor Fontenelle again evoked the Christian virgins who "swore to take Christ as their fiancé and sealed their engagement in blood." He had every confidence that Jocists would make the same sacrifices that the virgins had made.[88]

Fittingly for a movement steeped in Marian piety, the final important address was given at Our Lady of Montallegro. There Monsignor Feltin reminded pilgrims of the important example set by Mary, mother of Jesus, faithful servant of the Lord, and most holy Virgin. He urged them to have special affection for Mary and to emulate her example; like her they could give a son to the church.[89] The high point of the trip came when the Jocists were received by the pope. He blessed their effort and explained how they shared in the apostles' glory; in return, the Jocists pledged not to stop or rest until they had returned all French young working women to Christ. To reinforce the lessons they had been taught, Jocists were provided with meditations encouraging them to evaluate their commitment and willingness to sacrifice in light of the example set by the early Christians. "How cowardly I feel," one meditation read, in front of the martyrs who "did not hesitate to accept death," when "I cannot resolve to make the small sacrifices required by daily observance."[90]

While transporting the young female workers back almost two thousand years, the pilgrimage's organizers employed modern technology to heighten the impact of the pilgrimage on those who attended and extend its excitement to those who had remained at home.[91] Capitalizing on cinema's popularity among young working women, the organizers surprised and delighted the pilgrims one evening with a film of them in front of St. Peter's that morning.[92] After the young women returned to France, the J.O.C.F. used a longer film of the event to maintain enthusiasm and generate further excitement. In January 1935 the J.O.C.F. leadership reported that intense demand for the film had prompted the production of another copy, which had already been booked by local sections for months to come.

Besides tapping into young working women's enthusiasm for film, organizers exploited the possibilities of religious mass tourism. At a time when young women workers rarely had much opportunity to travel, the pilgrimage offered visits to renowned Italian cities. Jocists were exposed to the celebrated sites of Pisa and Rome and driven along winding seaside roads to Montallegro. Both religious and secular souvenirs were sold at a nominal price on the pilgrims' special trains to Rome, while commemorative albums, magazines, and photographs were available for purchase once the Jocists returned home. The pilgrimage was packaged as a special event, one that transported young working women outside their ordinary lives and heightened their dedication to the movement.

The pilgrimage seems to have had the desired effect. One Jocist wrote after her return that she had been enchanted by the experience. After listing her most wonderful memories, which included the visits to the Coliseum and the Catacombs, the trips to Assisi and the beautiful seaside town of Rappallo, and especially the warm welcome from the Holy Father, she exulted, "And after all that, how could I not always want to do better for Christ?"[93]

The varied initiatives of J.O.C.F. chaplains and associated clerics generated a piety whose intensity distinguished the movement from the male branch and often troubled those guiding it. Throughout the pages of J.O.C.F. publications there are glimpses of clerics and youth leaders attempting to tone down female religious fervor, to shape the organization into one that was religious to be sure, but more quietly so. Youth leaders chided members for naming sections after religious figures, for relying too heavily on religious motifs when decorating section headquarters, or for letting the study of the Gospels detract from their study of enquêtes.[94] Both clerics and youth leaders cautioned female militants against exhibiting excessive religious fervor.[95] Cardinal Liénart, one of the movement's strongest supporters, let militants know that his admiration for the manner in which they had thrown themselves wholeheartedly into their work was tempered by concern that they might be required to moderate their religious ardor in the future.[96] Monsignor Feltin began his Roman celebration of Mary with the caveat that Jocists should not go too far in their devotion. Youth leaders similarly pointed out that while religious zeal was important, it had to be "reasonable, discreet, modest, and interior."[97] These appeals for moderation were not always heeded. After repeated warnings in 1932 about the place of religion in movement life, leaders conceded that they were bowing to militants' demands for more intensive religious formation. Study sessions for federal leaders would henceforth devote half their time to religious study.[98]

**Complicating the Story** As we have seen, in attempting to shape young working women into female activists in the struggle against communism, the J.O.C.F. had as its overriding goal the forging of militants who would lead morally pure, religiously engaged lives in the present, all the while preparing themselves for futures as Catholic mothers. The J.O.C.F.'s actions proceeded from this goal, with the piety offered in the movement's devotional literature underscoring these emphases and reflecting Catholic ideas about women's work. The J.O.C.F. was in many respects a deeply conservative organization with an outdated ideology. Even the J.O.C.F.'s youth leaders had to remind its militants that the movement was not a traditionalist moral preservation society aimed at rescuing young women from the evils of dancing and the cinema.[99] Such an organization would have held little appeal for many young working women. As one of them responded when asked to join: "Oh no, I have no desire to become a nun! All those who join the J.O.C. end up old maids."[100]

To end the analysis here would be to miss much that made the movement interesting, innovative, and important to the young working women who became its devoted members during the 1920s and 1930s. The J.O.C.F.'s ideology was more complex than a simple paean to purity, virginity, and maternity. Perhaps the most appealing part of the organization's message was its uncompromising assertion of spiritual dignity and equality. Female Jocists learned that Christ had died for them, and that they possessed an essential dignity and worth as children of God. Canon Cardijn transformed this tenet into an effective message of spiritual equality, which he illustrated with the phrase "the soul of a young working woman is worth all the gold in the world." As benign as these words may seem, they had a powerful effect on young women who were repeatedly reminded of their triply subordinate status in French society. Many female Jocists remembered being profoundly affected and empowered by Jocist ideas of spiritual equality and working-class dignity. "It was terrific!," one recalled. "For us, who were called 'factory girls,' having our dignity as young workers, as daughters of God recognized was fabulous!"[101] Another explained, "I was a daughter of the poor. I was ashamed of it sometimes. I sometimes envied girls with well-off parents. The J.O.C. revealed to me the value, dignity, and importance of each person. So I was no longer ashamed. I was proud to be a worker and the daughter of workers."[102] A third Jocist spoke in similar terms: "One felt disparaged belonging to the working class, which some took to be 'inferior.' It's because of the J.O.C. that I'm proud of the working-class milieu."[103] The quietly subversive power of these ideas, especially in conservative areas of France where Catholicism was firmly implanted, is suggested by the experience of a Jocist who was upbraided by her Catholic employer for claiming at a public J.O.C.F. meeting that young female workers were as good as the daughters of their employers.[104]

Jocists used the notion of spiritual dignity to protect young female workers from unwanted sexual overtures by male workers. During the interwar period actions that would be labeled sexual harassment by later generations were widely acknowledged, although little resisted. Young women reported being cornered or subjected to advances by supervisors and other workers; those who did not acquiesce could be fired or assigned undesirable work. An interwar factory inspectress painted a graphic picture of conditions in one textile factory in Lille: "Male workers impose themselves on young female apprentices in the bins by touching them inappropriately. Elsewhere, young women are hung upside down by their feet until they let themselves be kissed."[105]

Framing their efforts as a defense of young women's dignity as Christians, Jocists attempted to protect themselves and others from these kinds of aggression. Jocists turned their backs on suggestive language, whether from men or women, and challenged men who made advances to young working women. One remembered getting into serious arguments with "those foremen who abused young women in their group."[106] As she made clear, the female Jocists' defense of young women workers could extend to helping young workers who had got pregnant as a result; this included those who had had abortions.[107] Significantly, the defense of young women endowed the Jocist morality campaign with gender-specific benefits for female militants. Indeed, if young men's defense of rigid codes of sexual morality usually invited only derision from male co-workers, Jocist efforts could make young women's work lives easier. Although young women too were mocked, their actions helped give them a reputation that could shield them from unwanted advances. Many Jocists commented on this later, with one remembering typically, "I heard my bosses making bets about who would get his way with the young female worker first. But they knew whom to target, because Jocists were considered untouchable."[108]

The J.O.C.F. also took positions on women's roles and femininity that were progressive for the time. Its leaders applauded women who asserted themselves in public settings. The female militant was told: "Be someone, be outstanding. Have character, that's it. Have enough substance to make an impact."[109] Within the movement press, young women demonstrating audacity and tenacity were lauded, and J.O.C.F. femininity incorporated those traits. After Amelia Earhart's successful solo flight across the Atlantic,

*La Jeunesse Ouvrière Féminine* remarked on her energy, self-possession, and boldness, noting that the "foresight, boldness and energy necessary for her flight are in keeping with femininity."[110] In 1933 the movement came out strongly in favor of women's suffrage. Rejecting oft-asserted arguments about women's intellectual and moral inferiority, J.O.C.F. writers framed their defense of women's rights within the context of their familial roles. The militants' newspaper depicted women of the "popular classes" as having more important familial roles than their bourgeois counterparts, functioning in a sense as heads of households. In the civic sphere, the paper further argued, a woman's role as a mother was a duty at least equivalent to a man's role as a soldier.[111]

Female assertiveness was encouraged within the movement even when it touched on sensitive matters. The J.O.C.F. made control of the enquêtes into an issue of female autonomy. By the early 1930s the J.O.C.F. secretariat was adamant that section presidents—not chaplains—should oversee study of the questionnaires. In cases where the chaplain usurped this function, the national leadership instructed leaders of regional federations to step in and raise the matter with their federal chaplain.[112] One militant active later in the decade explained how she had taken these messages to heart: she had tolerated the chaplain if he agreed with her ideas, but resisted him if he insisted on preaching old ideas that she strongly opposed.[113]

The promotion of independent female activism was similarly apparent when it came to the J.O.C.F.'s newspaper. Besides contributing articles, female militants were expected to venture into the streets and public spaces to sell *La Jeunesse Ouvrière Féminine*. This could bring them into contact with young men of rival organizations; in more extreme cases it could result in a trip to the police station. Selling newspapers publicly was viewed as a transgressive activity when performed by young women, and female activists recalled the disapproval that often greeted their efforts. Some met with raised eyebrows, while others were pelted with rotting vegetables or spat upon.[114] At least one woman dealt with irate male relatives convinced that the entire endeavor brought shame on the family.[115] Yet the J.O.C.F. never wavered from sending its militants into the streets. A J.O.C.F. song told the story of a Jocist who gave up her disapproving fiancé rather than abandon her commitment to being a "little newspaper seller."[116] The J.O.C.F.'s position on this issue distinguished the Catholic organization from the Popular Front Communists, who discouraged young women from selling their youth newspaper in the streets after 1935.[117]

Rereading the J.O.C.

The J.O.C.F.'s message of dignity and its support for female activism and assertiveness could have profound consequences for militants. Perhaps the most striking testament to the power of the J.O.C.F.'s ideas about women comes from Yvonne Ruffet, who joined the J.O.C.F. in 1937 but became increasingly disenchanted with the church hierarchy. After the Second World War she left the church, voted for parties on the Marxist left, and became active in the Communist-dominated C.G.T. With such a trajectory, Ruffet had little political motivation for exaggerating the J.O.C.F.'s liberating impulses. Yet this is how she remembered the impact of the J.O.C.F. on her life: "The campaign around women's liberation made me smile sometimes because thanks to the J.O.C. I never felt inferior to men and through my actions after 1937 I'm very aware of having acted and acting on behalf of this liberation. I really have the impression of being free thanks to the dignity I discovered in the J.O.C."[118]

Most young working women, sometimes to their great dismay, had little access to formal education beyond sex-segregated primary schools, and they appreciated the J.O.C.F.'s efforts in this realm. Chaplains and youth leaders took seriously the movement's role as an *école de formation*. The most dedicated chaplains worked closely with female militants as they prepared for meetings and struggled with Catholic texts, instructing them in subjects with little direct relevance to Catholic teachings. Abbé Bordet steered young women toward practical exercises in reading, writing, and speaking, while Father Guichard taught French composition and English. Youth leaders highlighted the educational value of movement activities. Preparing written agendas for meetings, they informed militants, not only ensured that meetings ran smoothly but helped Jocists to retain the habit of writing after they left school.[119] The elaborate preparation for recruiting meetings in the early 1930s suggests that a range of skills could be enhanced or acquired by conscientious militants. Reports had to be ready fifteen days in advance and were submitted first to section committees. After being discussed by local leaders, they were sent on to the next level—the federation—where they might be further corrected by federal leaders. Finally, a leader worked with the speaker on her delivery, often insisting that she practice eight, ten, or twelve times.[120] Expectations were also high when it came to completing enquêtes. Armed with their questionnaires, the Jocists were dispatched into neighborhoods and workplaces to study the young women around them. Each militant carefully recorded her answers to all the questions, which the leaders summarized in report form and sent on to the next level. As

**134**  they did this, the Jocists were transformed into junior social investigators, whose findings twice became the basis for books by prominent social Catholic women.

Many militants wrote later about how much they owed the J.O.C.F. for teaching them skills that would remain important throughout their lives, regardless of their jobs or subsequent role in political and trade union activism. One remembered, "I received a real education in the study circle. I learned to speak publicly and to write reports and tracts."[121] Another explained with pride how indebted she was to the J.O.C.F. and her chaplain: "I only had my certificate of primary studies but my chaplain wanted to give me as complete a formation as possible. Once I became a leader and full-time organizer, I often gave speeches. After these meetings I was asked many times about the education I'd received. I answered proudly! I only have my certificate of primary studies, but the J.O.C. trained me."[122] Others recounted that the J.O.C.F. expanded their horizons. One Jocist put it succinctly: "The J.O.C. replaced the education I would have had. It was my university."[123]

The Jocists' testimonials underscore that the J.O.C.F.'s overtures and activities could have multiple meanings for the young women involved, especially since section life was diverse. Both the quality of the chaplains and their level of engagement varied considerably, and this variability influenced movement life at the local level. There was often, moreover, a gap between the founders' goals and the realities they encountered. Jeanne Bajeux-Labbé recalled that she began a J.O.C.F. section in a small town in the Nord at the end of 1930 by inviting all local young female workers to large meetings and presenting the movement primarily as a friendship society. She had not yet learned the other parts of the J.O.C. message or its approach to education and formation.[124]

Even when they had spent more time in the movement, militants and members were not passive recipients of the J.O.C.F.'s ideology or its efforts to shape them as women and religious activists. They made constant choices about what they heard, and what they acted upon. Young women's complicated responses were evident in one small J.O.C.F. section's experience with an enquête into family life in the late 1930s, which uncovered a widespread lack of respect toward parents on the part of young working women, including Jocists. Parents were treated rudely, with the young calling their fathers and mothers "old people" or "old woman" or "B.I.," for "bagages inutiles" (useless baggage).[125] Many young workers refused to help their mothers, socialize with other family members, or turn over enough money to their parents. When the section respondent arrived at the conclusion of her report, which described plans to improve family life, she had to admit that the topic was a thorny one, as no one was willing to admit her misdeeds publicly. All the respondent could do was leave it to each Jocist to consider how she could reform her own behavior.

Young working women resisted the J.O.C.F.'s efforts in other ways as well. To their consternation, movement leaders found that militants were not studying their manual as commanded.[126] To make matters worse, many Jocists, including militants, refused to attend the evening, domestic-themed gatherings.[127] Three years later the J.O.C.F.'s newspaper conceded that it was difficult to get young women workers interested in courses on housekeeping and housewifery.[128] Those who attended J.O.C.F. gatherings might either fail to pay attention or turn sessions to their own purposes. In a milieu where few opportunities for organized sociability existed among young working women, they sometimes transformed evening gatherings into an opportunity to discuss men, dating, and marriage, and to do so on their terms. Their nighttime conversations were often broader than was intended by chaplains or the J.O.C.F.'s more serious leaders, extending to matters of sexuality, about which they spoke with frankness albeit a certain delicacy,[129] and matters of the heart. As one former Jocist admitted after she became a serious, highly committed militant, at J.O.C.F. gatherings during her early days in the movement she only wanted to talk about romance and love.[130] Another remembered how even when she was the secretary of her local section, she continued to flirt and hang around with young men.[131] And a third described the J.O.C.F. as a place to find a husband, since a section meeting would be followed by a rendez-vous with male Jocists.[132] There were other indications that Jocists made their own judgments about the J.O.C.F.'s message on purity, marriage, and maternity. Six of the twenty-one J.O.C.F. leaders prominent enough to rate entries in the Maitron biographical dictionary of the French working class never married.[133]

So young working women picked and chose, and there was much in the J.O.C.F. that might appeal to young women of the 1920s and 1930s. Many liked being part of a movement of young women with its own insignia, rituals, songs, and ceremonies. The affiliation ceremony, which followed months of preparation, was experienced as a keenly exciting event, especially if the group had faced clerical resistance. For Bajeux-Labbé it was one of the best days of her life.[134] Such was the excitement of belonging to the movement that many clamored for uniforms. Others appreciated the opportunities for fun and relaxation that J.O.C.F. gatherings provided. Jocists put on plays, sang songs, celebrated the festival of Saint Catherine by parading through the streets, and watched movies. One militant remembered being particularly proud that her section owned a small movie projector.[135] As the 1930s advanced, the J.O.C.F. provided ever more elaborate leisure activities, including trips to summer camps and camp outings. In a society where leisure options were more circumscribed for young women than for young men, these opportunities were significant. For many, however, it was the promise of female camaraderie that proved most alluring. A typical reminiscence noted how "the friendship between girl friends was tremendous," while a Jocist militant admitted candidly that the promise of friendship was absolutely crucial in attracting young women to the movement.[136]

The J.O.C.F. differed profoundly from the J.O.C., and its relationship to young women was complicated. The movement combined a traditionally Catholic approach to morality, motherhood, and women's work with a strong dose of spiritual equality and powerful encouragement of female assertiveness and independent action. The very fact that the J.O.C.F. asked young working women to value themselves and make an impact on the world around them made the movement unusual in a country so highly stratified according to class and gender. Many young women active in the J.O.C.F. gained confidence, skills, and a sense that what they did mattered. Many became lifelong activists. To be sure, most interwar Jocists went on to use their newfound skills and confidence on behalf of other Catholic organizations, as had been intended by the movement's founders. What is interesting and significant, however, is that some who went on to make very different ideological and political choices still credited the J.O.C.F. with shaping them as activists. Yvonne Ruffet, who as we saw voted communist and became active in the C.G.T. after the Second World War, credited the J.O.C.F. with making her who she was by teaching her to think, take responsibility, and work always on behalf of the working class.[137] Lucienne Champion, a textile worker who also later joined the Communist Party, admitted, "All that I learned from the J.O.C. remained the basis of my subsequent commitment. It was central to my development as an activist and it prepared me to take responsibility as an adult."[138] That women who went on to embrace communism could credit the J.O.C.F. in this way testifies to the movement's complicated approach and legacy.

Rereading the J.O.C.

# 5

## Youth and the

## Emergence of Communist

## Antifascist Politics

The 1930s saw the emergence of antifascism as the great cause of international communism, and this strategy implicated youth as a political constituency and idea in ways not recognized by historians. The Comintern secretary general Dimitrov explained the need for intensified attention to youth at the Seventh Comintern Congress in 1935, which marked the official triumph of antifascism. Because fascism recruited its shock troops principally from the ranks of the young, Dimitrov informed delegates, Communists active in capitalist countries had to assign them an "extremely important" role in the struggle against fascism.[1] By the time Dimitrov delivered these words, French Communists had already distinguished themselves in the effort to forge new methods of rallying young people against fascism. In recognition of these successes, the J.C. leader Raymond Guyot had been named to the Comintern's presidium and would soon assume the position of secretary general of the Communist Youth International. How French Communists traveled from the dark days of 1931 to a vibrant youth-focused antifascist politics is the subject of this chapter.

The strategy took shape over time and the path was not always straight. Starting in 1932 French Communists moved tentatively in new directions as they sought to rebuild the party and its youth wing after the electorally disastrous hard-line tactics of previous years. Of most importance was the Comintern-sponsored World Committee against War and Fascism, founded in Amsterdam in 1932. Within this movement youth gradually emerged as an age-based, gender-inclusive political constituency, and youth leaders experimented with methods of appealing to the young. As antifascism grew in priority in 1933, 1934, and 1935, party leaders concentrated increased attention on youth, offering the young, industrializing Soviet Union as an antidote to an old France mired in economic crisis.

Yet the primary responsibility for bringing French young people to communism lay with the J.C. Between 1932 and 1935 the J.C. remained a highly masculinized organization, and communist youth leaders clashed with adult leaders over strategy and the place of youth in communist politics, even reasserting claims to a vanguard revolutionary role in the spring of 1934. But after adult leaders in Moscow and Paris came down firmly in favor of a less revolutionary approach to antifascism, J.C. militants showed themselves to be skilled practitioners of the new line. Under the leadership of Raymond Guyot and in conjunction with the National Youth Committee against War and Fascism, the J.C. moved toward a different stance, eventually transforming the political meanings of youth within communism and helping set the tone for the entire Popular Front era.

**Moving Forward after the Barbé-Célor Affair**  The broad contours of the French Communist Party's move to antifascist politics have been delineated by Julian Jackson, who illustrates how tactical alterations adopted in the second half of 1931, and especially in 1932, prefigured more important shifts in tactics.[2] To reverse startling losses at the polls and in party membership in the wake of three years of uncompromising "class against class" tactics, the party after Barbé-Célor took hesitant steps to broaden its appeal under the Comintern's firm guidance.[3] Most notably, it concentrated attention on defending workers' limited, concrete economic demands, *les petites revendications*, and attempted to reach beyond its traditional constituency through the organization initially known as the World Committee against Imperialist War, launched in 1932. Intimately connected to these developments was the rebuilding of the J.C. This effort, which falls outside Jackson's scope, helped lay the groundwork for an altered communist appeal to youth.

By 1932 the situation was bleak for the party and its youth organization. The national legislative elections of May 1932 produced the worst showing of the party's brief history. Its vote totals were 270,000 fewer than in the election of 1928, and its parliamentary group was reduced to ten deputies.[4] By contrast, the Socialists returned 131 deputies to the Chamber. Things were even worse for the J.C. After the hard-line tactics of the late 1920s and the promotion and removal of key youth leaders, the J.C.'s fortunes had reached their nadir. Membership rolls slipped to 3,500 in early 1932, a drop of more than two-thirds since 1925.[5] Declines in party and J.C. membership contributed to a financial crisis that threatened the organization's very existence.

By August 1932 the situation had become so dire, the J.C. leaders informed the organization's central committee and regional secretaries, that it was unable to print any propaganda materials. Simply paying for postage to mail J.C. correspondence and directives was proving a financial hardship.[6] More seriously, the future of *L'Avant-Garde* was in doubt.[7]

For Comintern officials and party leaders, the mission to rebuild the J.C. went beyond shoring up its evaporating membership rolls. It meant destroying any vestiges of the "vanguardist" tendencies that had been so evident during the late 1920s and creating a different youth organization. The rebuilt J.C. would reach out more successfully to young workers while remaining firmly subordinate to the party. The party outlined its plans for the J.C. at the youth organization's Seventh Congress in June 1932, sending the thirty-two-year-old party leader Maurice Thorez to open the congress and lecture J.C. members on their duties and responsibilities. Breaking with past vanguardism, Thorez explained, was imperative.[8] The J.C. had to transform itself into a true youth organization that defended the concrete needs of young workers in a manner consonant with the party's emphasis on *petites revendications*. The desired transformation also meant revamping *L'Avant-Garde*, which one party leader criticized later in the summer as badly conceived, poorly presented, and uninteresting to the young.[9] There was, he continued, nothing youthful about the paper; "les bourgeois," he was forced to admit, could teach them a thing or two.

In the months to come, the J.C. attempted to refashion itself under the leadership of Georges Charrière, a metalworker who had taken over the reins of the organization after Raymond Guyot was again arrested for antimilitarist work. In a speech to the J.C.'s central committee in November 1932, Charrière explained that the organization should not be a carbon copy of the party but should instead respond to young people's needs and desires. The young worker wanted first to eat and live, and then to amuse and educate himself; finally, he wanted to be free.[10] Making revolution, Charrière implied, was not at the top of the list. The J.C. had to fight for things that truly mattered to working youth. It had to be, as the J.C. took to saying, "ever younger."[11] J.C. leaders were not uniformly enthusiastic about the shift. Police informants reported that some of those attending a J.C. central committee meeting at the beginning of November failed to hide their disdain for the strategies of their seniors.[12]

With membership numbers continuing to fall in the key regions of the Nord and Paris, and the J.C. on the verge of complete collapse in Alsace and Lorraine,[13] the J.C. moved hesitantly in directions that anticipated later changes. Young Communist leaders changed the face of their newspaper, introducing crosswords, puzzles, games, and film reviews. But the emphasis remained on political education. "Lenin" was the correct answer to the first crossword clue, and the paper's film reviews worked to expose bourgeois deception. Detective movies were criticized for their positive depiction of the police, while films such as *Rasputin* were blamed for glossing over the suffering of the Russian masses.[14] There was also talk, however halting at first, of changing the form and function of the J.C. cell. The Federation of the Nord, the strongest J.C. federation at the time, discussed having the cell remain a place where young workers formed themselves.[15] The J.C. suggested fleetingly in a pamphlet that it should develop a cultural side to its work and cooperate with other communist groups to organize visits to museums and the theater.[16]

The J.C. turned toward unemployed youth in 1932 as part of its emphasis on youthfulness and the immediate needs of young workers. By then the Depression had arrived in France, and its effects were particularly pronounced for young workers. Both the J.C. and the J.O.C. integrated this reality into their organizing strategies, formulating diverse responses to the crisis and eventually competing directly with each other in the process.

To understand the effects of economic crisis on a generation of young people and the movements seeking to rally them, it is necessary to consider the contours and impact of the Depression in France. France was the last major country to be hit by the Depression and the last to recover. As industrial production fell and unemployment rose in 1930 in Britain, Germany and the United States, many in France believed that the country would be spared serious unemployment.[17] But the global crisis reached France by the end of 1930 and the beginning of 1931. By March 1931 the total number of unemployed had climbed to 452,800; by May of the following year industrial production had fallen 20 percent below the levels of 1928.[18] The economic situation worsened in 1933 and 1934, with unemployment peaking in February 1935. Although national unemployment figures remained considerably lower than in other affected countries, some regions and industries suffered disproportionately. Unemployment was particularly pronounced in the Paris region, with the department of the Seine accounting for over half of France's unemployment before 1934; the metals industry, so important to the region, saw the largest downturn in production.[19] Both the Paris region and the metals industry were key areas of remaining Young Communist strength. Partial

unemployment also proved a serious problem. In November 1931 fully 40 **141**
percent of workers employed in industrial concerns with over one hundred
workers labored less than full-time.[20]

Like most other capitalist countries, France entered the economic crisis
with no national, obligatory system of unemployment insurance. When the
crisis hit, unemployment assistance was available through either government-
subsidized union funds, set up in 1905, or government-subsidized local
unemployment funds, set up in the fall of 1914 in response to the surge in
unemployment caused by the outbreak of war.[21] The vast majority of those
receiving assistance drew on municipal funds, whose operation was regu-
lated by the government through a series of laws passed after 1914.[22] This
dual system was neither comprehensive nor uniform: municipalities were
not required to create unemployment funds, and the funds that existed often
established their own rules.[23] As unemployment increased in 1931 and 1932,
the government responded by encouraging municipalities to provide more
assistance, largely by increasing the amount it contributed to local funds.[24]
The government also increased the maximum days of assistance twice in
1931 before abolishing the ceiling entirely in the summer of 1932, and began
to aid the partially unemployed.[25]

This approach to unemployment assistance created multiple hardships
for the unemployed, especially those from the younger age groups. Many
workers received no assistance whatsoever. In March 1931, for example, only
50,800 of the 452,800 listed in official statistics received aid.[26] This gap in
coverage resulted in part from strict eligibility requirements, which could be
particularly difficult for young workers. According to a law enacted in 1926,
eligibility for assistance depended on the unemployed worker's continuous
residence in the commune for the three months previous to unemployment
and continuous employment for the previous six months.[27] These requirements excluded young workers who had not been able to break into the
bleak job market or, as was so often the case, who were employed in a series
of short-term, casual jobs. Young workers were also disadvantaged by the
way benefits were calculated. For the many still residing with their parents,
benefits were determined by age, gender, and position in the household. According to the 1926 law, those young workers who were older than sixteen
but still residing at home received a fixed sum which was considerably less
than that received by the male head of household; dependents under sixteen
received even less.[28] The household itself was limited to a certain sum, which
could not exceed half the family's previous wages. Moreover, in instances

Youth and Communist Antifascist Politics

where municipalities required the unemployed to work for their benefits, male heads of households were given priority.[29] Young workers and their families struggled to weather the effects of unemployment, frequently relying on vegetables from their gardens and domestic animals to survive.[30]

The J.C. targeted unemployed youth as it sought to remake itself in the second half of 1932. Young Communists denounced the age-based inequities in relief and demanded that all unemployed youth, or *jeunes chômeurs*, be paid the seven francs a day sometimes given to unemployed youth no longer living with their parents. *L'Avant-Garde* highlighted the effects of the economic crisis on the young, introducing a front-page column entitled "I'm Unemployed" in December 1932. The inaugural article was a first-person account by a twenty-three-year-old jeune chômeur representative of the cohort of young workers moving to the fore of communist youth politics in the early 1930s: children or adolescents during the Great War, their youth was now being robbed by economic crisis. For this never-named narrator, the constant illness and eventual death of his father, gassed during the Great War, cast a shadow over his childhood. After the father died the family was forced to sell its small farm and move to Paris. There the young man found work as an apprentice woodworker and then as a metalworker in Saint-Denis, experiencing long hours, low wages, and abuse. Just as he was finding his way and finally able to contribute to the upkeep of his family, he was called to perform his military service. Problems began anew after his release from the army. At that point he was unable to find work and had difficulty becoming eligible for unemployment benefits when the disappearance of a former boss prevented him from obtaining a certificate attesting to his previous employment. After finally sorting that out, his unemployment benefits were limited to four and a half francs a day because his mother and a brother were employed.[31] Other first-person accounts traced the frustrations of adolescents unable to break into the job market, with one fourteen-year-old admitting, "There are times when I think I've lost my head and am tempted to commit a crime."[32]

Contrasting conditions facing worker youth in crisis-ridden France and in the rapidly industrializing USSR lay at the heart of the J.C.'s propaganda and appeal. In the summer and fall of 1932, when the Soviet Union was winding up the First Five-Year Plan and preparing to celebrate the fifteenth anniversary of the Bolshevik Revolution, *L'Avant-Garde* gave prominence to the stunning achievements of the past four years and the pivotal role of the young in building the socialist economy. Readers followed the exploits of Young

Communist shock brigades and the heroic young worker Dmitrousenko **143**
at Dneiprostroi, the world's largest hydroelectric station: the shock brigades
broke world records for production while young Dmitrousenko performed
near magical feats to help bring the project to a close.[33] The heroic tale was
similar in Soviet metalworking plants in Ukraine.[34] The message was clear:
with the advent of the Five-Year Plan, young people and their organization were once again at the forefront of revolutionary change in the Soviet
Union.[35]

Soviet Young Communists were further portrayed as benefiting in ways
that went beyond the satisfaction, however considerable, gained from helping to build socialism. They were upwardly mobile in the new Soviet state,
as many young workers pursued their education in a manner unheard of in
the old Russian Empire.[36] The coverage in *L'Avant-Garde* reflected the Stalinist imperative to integrate women into production, and the steady advance
of young workers portrayed in its pages featured females as well as males.[37]
Making this all the more inspirational was the marked difference between
Soviet progress and French stagnation. The J.C. drew the contrast repeatedly,
nowhere more forcefully than in the issue of 5 November 1932 celebrating
the fifteenth anniversary of the October Revolution. The front-page banner
headline trumpeted: "Three cheers for fifteen years of the country of free
and happy youth! Here it's unemployment and destitution; there it's work
and joy."

Although exaggeration permeated the culture of the First Five-Year Plan,
J.C. claims about worker youth's position in the USSR in the early 1930s may
have been "truer" than they had been in the 1920s, when the portrait of the
Soviet Union as a paradise for worker youth under NEP diverged sharply
from the realities of young people's lives. Youth unemployment had disappeared and Komsomol members had assumed a frontline role in the battle
for production and the struggle to build socialism.[38] Working long hours
under often horrific conditions, Komsomol shock workers—those who con-
sistently exceeded production quotas—competed to produce ever more, ever
faster.[39] By 1931 the Komsomol announced that fully 62 percent of its growing
number of members were shock workers.[40] Komsomol members also heeded
party calls to master the skills and technology necessary for the industrialized economy in the making. In so doing they ensured their own promotion
in the rapidly expanding Soviet economy.

Youth's enthusiastic embrace of the challenges put before them is evident from autobiographical accounts by former Komsomol members. W. I.

Hryshko, a Komsomol member and worker in the industrial city of Kharkov, later recalled the youthful engagement he witnessed all around him: "The atmosphere of undaunted struggle in a common cause—the completion of the factory—engaged our imagination, roused our enthusiasm, and drew us into a sort of front-line world where difficulties were overlooked or forgotten." Underlining the age-specific nature of this commitment, he continued, "Of course, it was only we, the younger generation, who accepted reality in this way."[41]

The tales of youth's heroic labors on behalf of socialist construction were told at a moment when the Soviet Union had a new stature among westerners, the French included. By the time of the First Five-Year Plan, traveling from France to the Soviet Union had become fashionable, and even anticommunist engineers were won over by the Soviet mystique of production.[42] The Soviet government attempted to capitalize on—and manage—this new interest, creating organizations such as the Proletarian Society of Tourism and Excursions to help tourists "see and study the five-year plan in action."[43] Some who did this not only noticed but identified with the youthful commitment and investment of energy. The American John Scott, who arrived in the new industrial city of Magnitogorsk in the fall of 1932 at the age of twenty, contrasted the situation in the capitalist West with that in the Soviet Union. For Scott, the America he left behind offered "few opportunities for young energy and enthusiasm,"[44] while the Soviet Union offered these opportunities in abundance, even if the conditions of life could be extremely trying, not to mention downright dangerous. One of the early scenes in Scott's *Behind the Urals: An American Worker in Russia's City of Steel* depicts a young rigger falling through the sky, only to land on the main platform in a pool of blood.[45]

We can only glimpse the impact that the new Soviet mystique had on French young workers. Léo Figuères later recounted how as an adolescent in rural France he read with rapt attention Paul Vaillant-Couturier's articles in *L'Humanité* on the huge industrial plants going up in the Urals and in Central Asia; they were, he remembered, as "absorbing as a serialized novel."[46] Suzanne Cage, a J.C. member who toured French cities in the summer of 1933 to talk about her recently completed trip to the USSR, reported that young workers told her over and over again, "I would like to go to the Soviet Union too."[47] None of this enthusiasm, however, yet translated into significant support for the J.C.

French Young Communists of 1932 did not simply dream about going to the Soviet Union but also defended it. For Soviet leaders of the time, enemies lurked inside the socialist homeland and outside its borders;[48] defense of the USSR was the primordial duty of Communists in capitalist countries. This had special significance for French Young Communists, since "imperialist" France was identified by Comintern Youth leaders as the biggest threat to the USSR.[49] The J.C., with a glorious antimilitarist past, had to intensify its action in defense of the Soviet Union and against imperialist war.[50]

With both party and Comintern "encouragement," the J.C. plunged back into antimilitarist work, approaching it much as it had done in the 1920s. Young Communists mixed criticism of conditions facing conscripts with efforts to transform the army into an instrument of revolution and revolutionary defense. During the fall of 1932, as the second contingent of the class of 1932 prepared to depart, *L'Avant-Garde* railed against the poor conditions facing conscripts, publishing prominently the number of conscripts injured (631), killed (126), or gravely ill (1,474) as a result of military service.[51] It also demanded that the term of service be reduced. As dangerous as military service was, the J.C. continued to insist that avoiding service was not an option. Young Communists were encouraged to emulate their leader Guyot, whose trial was given extensive, enthusiastic coverage in *L'Avant-Garde* in October 1932. Guyot defiantly told members of the military tribunal that he did not refuse to complete his reserve duty. Yet he served as a soldier of the proletarian revolution, not as a soldier of the bourgeois homeland.[52]

The events of 11 November 1932 suggested that antimilitarism differently defined had the potential to rally young men from a range of organizations and backgrounds. This day witnessed the first important, unplanned incident of cooperation between individual Young Communists and Young Socialists, their rivals on the working-class left.[53] During demonstrations in Paris to mark the end of the Great War, Young Communists and Young Socialists marched side by side under signs identifying their organizations, belting out revolutionary songs as they went. After the demonstration, *L'Avant-Garde* reported, militants from the two organizations mingled in the area near the Panthéon, joining forces to repel members of the far-right Camelots du Roi who challenged them.[54] This demonstration of united action diverged sharply from the longstanding "class-against-class" approach that the J.C. took toward the J.S., which involved deriding Young Socialists as "social fascists," breaking up their meetings, and ridiculing their leaders.

That the first glimmer of youth unity on the left came within the context of an antiwar march is not surprising given that young people of the early 1930s, especially young men eligible for military service, were particularly well positioned to be affected by antiwar messages. As we saw in chapter 1, those in their early twenties had lived through the Great War as children, seeing firsthand its impact on fathers, brothers, and uncles; some had been raised by their mothers to hate war. Those slightly younger had been taught by an increasingly pacifist corps of primary schoolteachers who relied on ever more strongly antiwar textbooks as the 1920s advanced.[55] According to Roland Alix, a graduate student who in 1930 updated Agathon's famous pre-war investigation into the state of French youth, there was unanimous agreement among young men from across the political spectrum about the pointlessness of war. He asked: "Why waste so many lives, so much money, so many years for such a poor outcome?"[56] Young men had to work to "make peace," even if Alix conceded that there were competing strategies for doing so. The broad support for peace observed by Alix made itself felt in the military. In reports on troop morale from the early 1930s, military officials noted with alarm that conscripts demonstrated little enthusiasm for military life or training.[57] By 1932 officials were detecting an increase in incidents of conscientious objection among conscripts and reservists.[58]

After individual members of the J.S. and J.C. joined forces on Armistice Day 1932, the competing movements attempted to institutionalize their cooperation. *L'Avant-Garde* editorialized enthusiastically about the unity on display on 11 November, stating that "the first steps toward joint action against war have been taken by all young workers."[59] The paper urged young workers and even young functionaries to ally with Young Communists in local committees. Further overtures to the J.S. followed. At the end of December, J.C. groups in the Seine and Seine-et-Oise sent proposals for joint action to their J.S. counterparts, who had long been the most radical in the Young Socialist federation. Although J.S. leaders refused to respond directly to J.C. proposals, Charrière continued to pursue the possibility of joint action. In January 1933 he agreed to participate in a public meeting initiated by young Trotskyists and dissident Young Socialists. The J.C. thus radically reinterpreted communist united front strategy, which involved drawing individual workers away from competing left organizations while mercilessly attacking those organizations and their leaders. United action as practiced by the Comintern occurred among the rank and file, not among leaders.

Even though Charrière had party leaders approve his appearance with Trotskyists and dissident Young Socialists, the J.C.'s reinterpretation of united front strategy proved too much for communist officials. In March 1933 the party moved to correct the situation, replacing Charrière with the metalworker Gaston Coquel and attaching the party stalwart Jacques Duclos to the youth organization. Duclos visited the J.C.'s central committee to lay down the law. Conceding that young people were easy prey for fascism and militarism in a time of war and revolution, and that Communists needed to engage with young people's immediate concerns, Duclos reminded Young Communists that the J.C. had to follow the lead of the Communist International and the party as it formulated its united front strategy.[60] For the Comintern, joint action was acceptable only if it took place under the auspices of the World Committee against Imperialist War or the Amsterdam movement. Jeannette Vermeersch, who was chosen as Coquel's lieutenant and was already Thorez's companion, explained the tactic in a front-page article in *L'Avant-Garde*. In the future the J.C. would tone down its references to leisure so as not to ignore the economic struggle and "liquidate the revolutionary character" of communist youth; it would also participate enthusiastically in the World Committee movement.[61]

**New Overtures to Youth: The World Committee** The World Committee against Imperialist War proved the most important precursor to communist Popular Front strategies, especially regarding youth. Initiated by the Comintern, headed by the leading French intellectuals Henri Barbusse and Romain Rolland, and launched formally in Amsterdam at the end of August 1932, the committee sought to forge a mass movement against war that would attract new constituencies to communism by capitalizing on an already widespread anxiety about another war.[62] Committee leaders initially targeted writers and intellectuals, who were prominent among those speaking out against war, whether individually or in the numerous pacifist organizations dotting the political landscape of France after the First World War.[63] The goal, as the founding manifesto announced in its first line, was to bring together "manual and intellectual workers."[64] Although the committee claimed independence from the Third International, the manifesto that emerged from the Amsterdam Congress reflected the Comintern's analysis of the threat of imperialist war, the leading part played by "imperialist France" in preparations for war, and the primordial importance of defending the Soviet Union. It further identified unacceptable forms of antiwar activism, dismissing conscientious objectors, the League of Nations, and what it referred to derisively as "verbal pacifism."[65]

Even though the manifesto made no explicit mention of young people or their unique relationship to war, committee leaders began to cast their eyes toward youth by the end of 1932. In so doing they initiated a process that ultimately resulted in the creation of an age-based constituency within French communist politics. The first step came on 21 December 1932, when the committee's leadership in Paris decided to establish a youth movement that would parallel the adult Amsterdam movement and hold its own international youth antiwar congress the next summer. As 1933 began, adult national committees were instructed to pay close attention to the youth movement's activities and to involve themselves as much as possible.[66] There was no question that the adult committee expected to guide the youth branch: adult leaders created the movement, decided when and where the youth congress would be held, and wrote and disseminated important propaganda. In the spring of 1933 local adult committees in France were instructed to distribute a "Letter to French Youth" among students and within the J.C. and the J.S., whose members had been prohibited by socialist leaders from participating in the committee movement.[67]

The "Letter to French Youth" signaled an appeal to young people different from those previously attempted by Communists and their affiliated organizations. The letter began, conventionally enough, by addressing itself to young workers and singling them out as the first to be sacrificed in international conflicts, but it soon broadened its reach. Declaring that "war does not choose," the authors announced that they were calling on those young people who worked on the land and in factories, lived in the countryside or in cities, and were workers or intellectuals to join the struggle against war. Within the youth movement the group designated by the term "intellectual" was especially large, since it was used to designate teachers and students of all ages. The breadth of the committee's appeal was reflected in the use of such terms as "world youth," "young people," and "youth."[68] The burgeoning antiwar movement was carving out an age-based political constituency within communism.

By the time the adult committee turned to youth in earnest, events in Germany had intervened to alter the shape and focus of the movement. Appointed chancellor on 30 January 1933, Adolf Hitler moved quickly to dismantle the Weimar Republic and consolidate his rule. He struck at opposition parties, and the German Communist Party (KPD) was the first hit.

A fire in the Reichstag building on 28 February provided justification for the suspension of civil liberties and the arrest of four thousand Communists, including virtually all the party's leaders.[69] Arrests continued, and by the end of March twenty thousand Communists were incarcerated in concentration camps in Prussia.[70] Hitler also moved against German Jews, whom he had long ago identified as special enemies of the Reich. Increasing numbers of refugees made their way to France,[71] and concern over events in neighboring Germany grew, especially on the left.

These developments affected the committee movement. In April 1933 police in Paris reported an increase in local committee activity, which they linked to recent events in Germany.[72] These events also focused new attention on the threat posed by fascism. At the beginning of June the committee movement convened an antifascist conference in the Salle Pleyel in Paris. German delegates described life under Hitler, and the congress hammered out a resolution protesting the arrests of comrades Torgler, Dimitrov, Popov, and Tanef.[73] The Communists' status as early victims of the National Socialist state helped form them into early antifascist fighters.

The June antifascist conference signaled the importance of youth to emergent communist antifascist politics. Organizers included a special youth antifascist conference, which drew an estimated 350 young people to Paris to discuss the dangers that fascism posed to youth and to debate appropriate responses. After the youth meeting concluded, leaders issued a manifesto laying out the parameters of their antifascist struggle. Fascism was "the most brutal form of class struggle," employed by the wealthy to safeguard their power and property.[74] Not unique to Germany and Italy, it had special consequences for youth. The manifesto warned, "You are tortured by the hundreds of thousands in army barracks and labor camps; militarized, you are made into cannon fodder for the imperialist war planned by fascism."[75] In this analysis fascism led ineluctably to war, and the Soviet Union was the first country threatened. Yet democratic governments could not be considered an adequate defense against fascism; after all, they had joined fascists in serving youth's mortal enemies. Youth would have to combat fascism with its own antifascist united front. Throughout, emphasis was placed on fighting fascism, often quite literally, whether in strikes, mass demonstrations, or "defensive struggles against fascist provocations."

Coverage of the conference in *L'Humanité* reflected the burgeoning communist awareness of youth's increased importance to European politics. One

Youth and Communist Antifascist Politics

of its writers explained that although the bourgeoisie had always sought to attract young people, recent events had made doing so all the more crucial. "Fascists and the bourgeoisie of all countries speak only of 'youth.' 'Make way for the young' has become the watchword—and for good reason!"[76] In the aftermath of the first antifascist conference, the committee movement, known henceforth as the Amsterdam-Pleyel movement, coupled war with fascism and pledged to work harder than ever to mobilize youth.

The Amsterdam-Pleyel movement provided the acceptable locale for J.C. united front youth politics, and the movement was directed to participate "most actively" in the committee's work.[77] The aim was twofold: to recruit new members to the J.C. and to help build a successful youth movement by enticing young people from rival organizations to join the battle against imperialist war and fascism. Since the French Socialist Party had forbidden Young Socialists to join the movement, committee tactics conformed nicely to the "united front" strategy then in force. J.C. leaders sustained their barrage of verbal attacks on J.S. and Socialist Party leaders, all the while celebrating the local sections and individual Young Socialists who risked expulsion to join the movement. At the June antifascist conference much was made of the decision by the J.S. section from Ajaccio to formally join the committee movement.[78]

Activity within the youth committee movement intensified during the summer and fall of 1933 as it prepared for the inaugural World Youth Congress in Paris in late September. Meetings were held in cities across France, prefiguring the Popular Front era in their tone and the type of participating organization. Police reported from Bordeaux in May that the executives of the local youth committee included representatives from the J.C., the F.S.T., the Young Pacifists, and the Students' Committee.[79] In Paris a youth committee meeting in the twentieth arrondissement in September drew speakers from the J.C., the J.S., the local Committee of the Unemployed, and the Young Israelites.[80] The gatherings sometimes featured generous doses of entertainment, although many approximated more conventional political meetings. The speeches touched on a range of issues affecting youth: the situation of youth in fascist Germany, the desperate conditions facing young workers and students in capitalist countries, and the unique challenges that war posed for youth.

Both the youth committee and the J.C. focused attention on the perils of war for the young. The message was clear: youth would be sacrificed immediately in any conflict; it was in young people's interests to combat war.

A youth committee poster from Reims put the issue directly and forcefully: **151**
"Youth will be the first victims of the impending carnage. We will not allow
ourselves to be sacrificed in vain, as was the case in the First World War."[81]
The Great War became the point of reference, one to which materials returned again and again. Since many potential members had been children
during the war, the J.C. reminded young people of the war's horrific impact
on their male relatives and underscored the pointlessness of their suffering. *L'Avant-Garde* proclaimed: "Although we did not experience the odious
slaughter, we saw our fathers and brothers return (those who made it back!)
having been gassed, suffering from tuberculosis, missing limbs or, worse,
so injured and horrifying that they have to hide themselves from view, *les
gueules cassées*! And why? For whom?"[82] Another article recounted the tale of
a child from Reims who had sought refuge from German attacks in a dank,
rat-infested basement before being evacuated from the city.[83]

Aided by its antiwar message, the youth committee connected with a
wider spectrum of youth opinion. By the beginning of July 1933 the youth
committee claimed twenty thousand members, including 975 from the Jeunesses Laïques et Républicaines (J.L.R.), or Young Secular Republicans, the
largest and most important youth organization within the Radical orbit, 812
from the Young Republicans of Arles, 607 from the Jeunesse Socialiste, 561
from the Jeunesse Communiste, 300 from the youth wing of the League of
the Rights of Man, 300 from a youth hostel organization, 90 Young Pacifists,
1,910 students, and 1,851 teachers.[84] The summer brought further defections
to the committee from the J.S. and the J.O.C. At the end of June *L'Avant-Garde*
reported that the Seine federation of the J.S. had dissolved its central group
because of united action with the J.C.; on 1 August the paper reported that
the J.S. of the Aisne had been excluded for its activities with the Amsterdam
movement.[85] Even the J.O.C. was not immune. *L'Avant-Garde* stated in August
that a small number of Jocists, primarily from the Paris region, had left the
J.O.C. to join the committee movement.[86]

The World Youth Congress held in Paris from 22 to 24 September 1933
marked the high point of the year's youth committee activism. For three days
an estimated 1,098 delegates from thirty-three countries and seven political
tendencies listened to speeches, sang revolutionary songs, and swore an oath
to struggle against war. Antimilitarism had not been stripped completely
of its militaristic qualities. Henri Barbusse initiated the proceedings. He
saluted youth, attacked capitalism as the cause of both war and fascism, and
reminded the delegates of the French revolutionary hymn that proclaimed

**152** "The sons will be greater than the fathers."[87] Raymond Guyot followed with tales of the struggles of antifascist youth in Germany and antimilitarist youth in key factories in France and Czechoslovakia; he also trumpeted Soviet youth's role in the construction of socialism. Next came a representative from the World Committee, who attacked the Versailles Treaty and the League of Nations and set forth alternative strategies for combating war. He exhorted delegates to take the struggle against war and fascism to defense industry factories, youth organizations, army barracks and naval warships, and the villages of France. Pride of place at the Congress was reserved for the Soviet youth delegation, a mixed-sex group of seven advertised as the first contingent of Soviet youth to visit a capitalist country, and its leader Kosarev, the Komsomol's head. The Soviet Union continued to function as the promised land where young people of both sexes knew full employment, lived without fear of war, and played a leading role in the construction of socialism. Soviet youth were, as communist writers were to repeat endlessly in the years to come, "the happiest young people in the world."

The most memorable event of the congress came after the official proceedings were over. Early on the morning of 25 September, *L'Avant-Garde* reported, one hundred taxis carrying five hundred delegates left Paris for an unknown destination. Retracing the route used by the French Army to rush troops to the front during the Battle of the Marne on 5 September 1914, the taxis wound their way to the war memorial in Rethondes, five kilometers from Compiègne. The delegates joined voices and languages with the leaders of six national delegations to swear a solemn oath to confront war. The oath's final lines rang out: "We will no longer spill our blood to profit the rich! We announce the rallying of young people throughout the world! We will avenge the dead! We summon the living!"[88]

Communist coverage of the World Youth Congress was enthusiastic, even ecstatic, signaling intensified party interest in youth. Both *L'Humanité* and *L'Avant-Garde* claimed that the congress was the largest such gathering of youth in history, and they celebrated the diversity of those attending. For its part, *L'Humanité* devoted unprecedented column-inches to youth in the lead-up to the congress and then followed its proceedings closely. The paper carried lengthy, front-page articles on youth by its editor, Marcel Cachin, and shorter articles about the lives of young people, whom Cachin described as "more directly affected by the upcoming slaughter, by the misery of present unemployment, by the anguish and complete insecurity of the future."[89] As Cachin explained, fascist regimes were only built with the support of youth,

and imperialist warmongers counted on docile youth to wage their wars.[90]
The party could no longer remain so far removed from the young masses.

Cachin and his writers stressed age, not class background. He spoke repeatedly of "youth," not "young workers," even stipulating in another front-page editorial that the international congress represented "millions of adolescents in revolt" against a society that did not respond to their "young and legitimate desire to live."[91] Coming from a French communist leader, this language was unprecedented. Equally telling were the vignettes of young lives, which placed young peasants, students, and female white-collar workers alongside the J.C.'s more traditional constituency of young male workers. The Young Communist leader Raymond Guyot similarly employed the new communist language of youth and evoked young people's unfulfilled desires: "We want to live. We want to eat, we want to enjoy all the literary, scientific and artistic riches that life has to offer, and that should be the common property of all mankind."[92] Guyot would develop these themes as communist antifascist strategy evolved.

As excited as French communist leaders of all ages professed to be by the World Youth Congress, Communist Youth International leaders were considerably less impressed with the J.C.'s work. At the extraordinary congress held in the Paris suburb of Ivry from 3 to 7 February 1934, the C.Y.I. pushed the J.C. to bring its actions more closely in line with Comintern directives. The conveners' main concern was the persistence of "opportunistic" approaches begun under Charrière and denounced the previous spring, notably the excessive focus on "distractions" at the expense of revolutionary struggle and the overtures to J.S. leaders for joint action. The J.C. had underestimated young workers' combativeness and was concentrating inadequate attention on organizing protest actions at the workplace and among the unemployed.[93] It had, moreover, fallen behind in the effort to create J.C. factory cells. This insufficiently revolutionary emphasis spilled over into J.C. work in the committee movement, which French police reported had lost momentum in the months following the World Youth Congress.[94] More dangerously, the J.C. demonstrated signs of deviating from the revolutionary struggle against imperialist war and straying dangerously toward pacifism.[95] The attempt to connect with young men's fears of another European war had to be replaced by action to sabotage French imperialist adventures in such places as Morocco and the Far East.[96]

The congress set out to liquidate these dangerous tendencies and eliminate from the leadership anyone who harbored doubts about "the application

**154**    of the Comintern's line and consequently that of the C.Y.I. and the party."[97] The party assumed control over all aspects of the congress,[98] which opened under the aegis of an honorary presidium chosen by Thorez. Marcel Cachin, who had editorialized more vehemently than ever on *L'Humanité*'s front page the previous day about the importance of youth to the future of both the party and the working class, began the proceedings.[99] Guyot was next, laying out the appropriate future course and identifying as principal tasks the campaign against a policy associated with socialist youth and the construction of a united front.[100] In succeeding days those who had strayed from the correct line, including Delaune, the head of the sports organization the F.S.T., and Jeannette Vermeersch, mounted the podium to recant their mistakes. The C.Y.I. representative brought the proceedings to a close by judging some apologies (including Vermeersch's) inadequate and reiterating the International's hard-line position.[101]

During the very days when the C.Y.I. was imposing its conceived-in-Moscow revolutionary strategy on the J.C., events occurred in Paris that eventually shifted the World Committee's focus more strongly toward antifascism. After weeks of intense political violence in Parisian streets, far-right forces massed at the Place de la Concorde on 6 February, unleashing a night of violence that resulted in fifteen deaths and the resignation of the just-installed Daladier government the following day.[102] Communists also participated in the violence at the Place de la Concorde, battling the police of the despised Republic from the opposite end of the political spectrum. J.C. militants were in the streets, although peripheral to the main event as a youth organization firmly subordinate to the adult party. Assigned by the party to protect the headquarters of *L'Humanité* from fascist attack, hundreds of Young Communists made their way from Ivry to the Montmartre intersection in central Paris.[103] There the contingent fashioned torches from newspapers, sang the "International" and the "Young Guard" at the top of their lungs, and shouted their determination to stop the fascists and bring down the government. After receiving word of the events taking place at the Place de la Concorde, they set off arm in arm to reinforce their communist comrades. Before getting far, they were set upon by armed police, who arrived by police van and began to club those at the rear of the demonstration, unresponsive to J.C. cries that they were attacking the wrong people. By the time the Young Communists reached their destination, things were apparently winding down.

In the days that followed, the party maintained its opposition to fascism, the Republic, and socialist leaders, and the J.C. enthusiastically followed its lead. The organization participated in the communist protest against fascists and government leaders on 9 February, and called its troops into the streets for other actions. A J.C. handbill left little doubt as to the Young Communists' position on the Republic, or their combativeness: "Given the choice between fascist plague and democratic cholera, the only solution is to fight! Brought to power on the backs of 30,000 Parisian Communards, the 'democratic' bourgeoisie relies on bayonets and machine guns to stay in power. No, young workers, who are heirs to the Commune, fight not to defend the Republic but to defend their class."[104] Socialist and Young Socialist leaders fared little better than the Republic at the hands of the J.C. Even after a general strike initiated by the C.G.T. on 12 February unexpectedly brought socialist and communist marchers together, J.C. leaders continued to execute faithfully the Comintern's longstanding united front strategy. Guyot and his circle applauded instances of cooperation among individual Young Socialists and Young Communists, while attacking J.S. and Socialist Party leaders mercilessly. The Young Socialists' biggest sin was held to be their defense of the Republic.[105] In the short term the events of February 1934 did nothing to change the J.C.'s united front strategy or its determination to bring about a revolution in France along Soviet lines.

Young Communists played a front-line role in the political violence which plagued Paris during the spring of 1934. According to Paris police, many of the street altercations involved young people recruited to sell political newspapers by parties of the left and far right.[106] Circulating in groups and frequently armed with canes, clubs, and "even revolvers," they picked fights with their opponents that frequently degenerated into full-scale brawls requiring the intervention of security forces.[107] In these "antifascist actions" Young Socialists often joined forces with their Young Communist comrades,[108] political violence providing a basis for joint action among young men. Young Communists furthered the revolutionary cause by trying to break up or prevent demonstrations and meetings by far-right organizations such as the Jeunesses Patriotes, especially those called for areas traditionally controlled by working-class organizations. But right-wing organizations were not the Young Communists' only adversaries. By June, communist street action was of such intensity, the Paris police were reporting, that since 6 February "the Communist Party has shown itself to be particularly aggressive and has demonstrated much more pronounced combativeness. Clashes with police have been much more frequent and the Communist Party has engaged in real attempts at insurrection."[109] Heightened combativeness was

**156**  similarly evident in the J.C.'s antimilitarist action during the spring. In May, Minister of War Philippe Pétain forwarded to the army commander of the Paris region secret reports warning of stepped-up communist efforts to disseminate antimilitarist propaganda among the soon-to-be-inducted conscripts and workers in crucial defense industries.[110]

Young Communists viewed themselves as the revolutionary vanguard. In mid-March, Guyot spoke excitedly about the J.C. leading youth with "ardor, spirit, and heroism" in the drive to defeat fascism and install soviets in France.[111] These attitudes proved too much for party leaders, and in April the J.C.'s central committee was called upon to renounce such deviations and once affirm again its loyalty—and subordination—to the party. On 19 April J.C. central committee members resolved to "liquidate the vanguardist tendencies which have appeared with new vigor in the recent period."[112] They swore fealty to the Comintern's united front strategy, which entailed intensifying its struggle against the J.S., redoubling its efforts within the committee movement, and denouncing the former J.C. leader Jacques Doriot, who was causing trouble within the party by publicly challenging the Comintern's ban on cooperation between Communists and Socialists in his stronghold of Saint-Denis.[113]

The Youth Committee against War and Fascism gathered momentum in the spring of 1934. At a time when young workers from various organizations were taking to the streets to unite against fascist incursions large and small, the desire grew for organized joint antifascist action. The enthusiasm for joint action appears to have been particularly pronounced among young men, whose memories of the bitter divisions on the postwar left were considerably shorter than those of adult militants and who had already attempted to join forces eighteen months earlier on Armistice Day. One witness to both these moments later recounted that when conscripts received newspapers describing how Socialists and Communists had united at the demonstration on 12 February, the barracks exploded to the sounds of the "International" and the "Young Guard."[114]

Moving into the streets, whether to face off against political opponents or publicly affirm political choices in large demonstrations, attracted young men. It was they who pummeled each other in the streets. It was they who were most likely to turn out in large numbers for the demonstrations of 1934, which carried a risk of violence that the later, more choreographed mixed-sex demonstrations of the Popular Front era did not. Marching had varied meanings for young men. Looking back on his own teenage participation in the last legal communist antifascist demonstration in Berlin before the Nazi takeover, the historian Eric Hobsbawm remarked that participation in a mass demonstration "at a time of great public exaltation" combined bodily experience and emotion in a way surpassed only by sex.[115] Through singing, marching, and chanting slogans, he recounts, he merged into the collectivity, experiencing what he later called "mass ecstasy."[116] Marching could also be fun, an exercise in youthful nose thumbing. Such was the experience of the twenty-four-year-old lycée teacher Claude Jamet during the demonstration of 12 February in the small city of Bourges. He recorded in his diary how much he had enjoyed marching behind the red flag and the sign of the Parti Communiste Français (P.C.F.), shouting "Long Live the Soviets!" and singing French and Soviet revolutionary songs, shocking the shopkeepers and local bourgeoisie with every note and every step.[117]

The committee's status as the premier site of youth antifascist action created dilemmas for Young Socialists who yearned for organized joint action but were constantly admonished to stay away from the Amsterdam-Pleyel movement and avoid communist maneuvers.[118] By the time the youth committee's first national congress opened in Paris on 20 May 1934, an increasing number of young people risked sanction, even expulsion, to join the committee movement. It included by then eleven sections (and three federations) from the Jeunesses Laïques et Républicaines, twenty-five sections from the J.S., and a handful of Jocists from the eleventh arrondissement in Paris.[119] Delegates from these noncommunist youth organizations supported the youth committee's revolutionary stance and approach, what leading Young Socialists referred to as "united action against war and fascism *on a revolutionary basis*."[120] Such a program, one J.L.R. delegate admitted, remained a difficult sell to the vast majority of Radical youth, who were still imbued with "a democratic and reformist spirit." But he urged them to realize that they had to go further than the Republicans of 1848 to be loyal to their democratic ancestors.[121]

As the Comintern hoped, the youth committee's successes bolstered the J.C.'s strength. In the days following the May congress, the J.C. announced that it had distributed 2,618 new membership cards since 6 February; the J.S. had lost 2,000 members during the same period,[122] contributing to the pressure on socialist leaders to accept committee overtures for joint action. Two days after the youth congress concluded, the Socialist Party announced that it would work with the Amsterdam-Pleyel movement on well-defined actions.[123] A new era in working-class politics was close at hand.

**From United Front to Popular Front** The possibilities for
united youth action against fascism in France altered dramatically after the
Comintern leadership endorsed joint action with socialist parties in June
1934. Once Thorez made the turn at the party congress at the end of the
month, the Young Communist leadership quickly followed suit.[124] It spoke
strongly in favor of united youth antifascist struggle, pledging to refrain
from criticizing any organization that participated in "common action."[125]
The J.C. made overtures to the J.S. for joint action at the national level and
in cities across France. Success came quickly in Paris. On 8 July J.C. and J.S.
groups from the Paris region, represented by the national leaders Guyot
and Dumon, signed an agreement laying out the parameters of joint action
against fascism, war, and the impoverishment brought on by the still worsening economic crisis. The Paris branches of the two movements pledged to
fight side by side to disarm and dissolve fascist leagues; prevent reinstatement of the two-year term of military service and the institution of any
system of obligatory military training for children; and protest the decree
laws which had cut public spending. Their reform platform also included
unemployment assistance for all adolescents as soon as they left school and
occupational training overseen by trade unions for *jeunes chômeurs*.[126] A similar unity pact at the national level was concluded the following spring.

The rapid achievement of a unity pact in Paris highlights the particular
nature of both youth political activism and the antifascist struggle in the
capital. The area had long been home to some of the most left-leaning Young
Socialists, and Paris had experienced the most important and sustained political violence anywhere in the country during 1934. Young Socialists and
Young Communists had often joined forces, with one J.S. leader telling a
meeting of antifascist youth that the united antifascist front cemented in
the pact had already been realized in the streets.[127] The agreement spoke
to the radical nature of the youth project: it contained no mention of the
defense of democratic liberties that would appear in the unity pact signed
by adult socialist and communist leaders on 27 July. The J.S. leader Fred
Zeller explained: "What youth want is a revolutionary united front. Up until
now, we have always made too many concessions to the bourgeoisie."[128] The
radical tint of Parisian youth politics was further illustrated by the decision
during the summer of the Jeunesses Laïques et Républicaines of the capital
region to join forces with the committee in the effort to obtain the release
of Thälmann from Nazi incarceration and to participate in all antifascist

undertakings.[129] As if to underscore the point, the J.L.R. congress in Paris in 1934 concluded by singing the "Internationale."

Antifascist momentum continued to build in July. That month, agreements similar to the one reached in Paris were signed by J.S. and J.C. leaders in cities across France. Late in July the National Youth Committee and its socialist counterpart, the Antifascist Alliance, agreed to join forces against war and fascism.[130] Of prime importance was the agreement signed on 27 July by socialist and communist party leaders. The two parties pledged to work together to mobilize the working masses against fascist organizations, war preparations, the decree laws, and fascist terror in Germany and Austria, using meetings, mass demonstrations, and strikes. They also agreed to defend democratic liberties, achieve proportional representation, and dissolve the Chamber.[131] The left had officially joined forces to fight fascism, and it set out to demonstrate its force and resolve two days later in the first collaborative demonstration of the new era, a march to the Panthéon to honor the great socialist leader Jean Jaurès.

Both *L'Humanité* and the socialist daily *Le Populaire* exulted over the antifascist unity on display during the demonstration, although they did so in ways that illustrated the different place assigned to youth by the two parties. Building on their earlier recognition of youth's importance to antifascism, Communists made the presence of an "ardent, disciplined, enthusiastic" youth cohort the focal point of their prominent front-page coverage. Indeed the article's subtitle, which was printed in capital letters ("YOUNG WORKERS WHO PREDOMINATED AMONG THE CROWDS ASSERTED THEIR INTENTION TO STRUGGLE AGAINST FASCIST AND IMPERIALIST LEAGUES FORCEFULLY AND ENTHUSIASTICALLY"), the accompanying photo and caption ("Ardent, enthusiastic, disciplined—Communist and Socialist worker youth predominated yesterday among the many thousands of demonstrators"), and the text itself all spotlighted youth participation and its significance for the antifascist struggle. Abandoning the term "worker youth" used in the subtitle and photo caption in favor of the much more inclusive and symbolically important "youth," the article's second paragraph shouted: "Nothing gives a better sense of the day than the youth procession. Young people! They made up the vast majority of the demonstrators. Youth is with us, with the new world, with the only cause that deserves the devotion of young hearts."[132]

In sharp contrast, *Le Populaire* had little to say about the demonstration's young workers or youth. Instead the paper emphasized workers' ability to dominate for four hours an area of Paris that the fascist Croix de Feu and Jeunesses Patriotes believed they controlled.[133] The youth contingent was only described toward the end of the story, in order to place it in the context of the long proletarian struggle, which the paper believed was perfectly symbolized by the contingent of older ex-communards marching in front of the young.

During the fall of 1934 Young Communist leaders worked to enlarge their antifascist coalition and push it in new directions. The J.C. worked in tandem with the committee movement, which was usually the source of the freshest initiatives. Particularly striking was the Young Communists' innovative approach to the J.O.C. After years of slashing attacks on the organization and its leaders, the J.C. began to sketch a more sympathetic and respectful portrait of their Catholic rivals in the pages of *L'Avant-Garde*. In early September the paper unveiled a front-page column, "To You Jocist, Fellow Sufferer," which emphasized the commonalities between J.C. and J.O.C. militants and their goals. The paper allowed J.O.C. militants to speak about their analysis and beliefs uninterruptedly and without snide editorial commentary. *L'Avant-Garde* took pains to stress J.C. support for J.O.C. demands, noting only that J.O.C. strategies for achieving the organization's aims required work. The Jocists could not rely on the good will of government leaders and industrialists; rather, they had to join forces with their fellow young workers to *force* change.[134] To this end the committee sent a delegation to the J.O.C. National Congress of 14–16 September to propose cooperative action. Although forbidden to speak, the delegation succeeded in distributing twelve hundred tracts and used *L'Avant-Garde* to announce its willingness to work with the Jocists in defending the demands of young workers."[135]

The committee had more success at the J.L.R. National Congress the same weekend. Gathering in Perpignan, J.L.R. leaders decided that the organization would collaborate officially with the committee movement. The Young Communists had succeeded in enlisting the cooperation of radical youth in their antifascist coalition considerably earlier than the party would. As Pierre Cot observed ten months later, the young Radicals brought their elders to the Popular Front.[136]

The audacious "Declaration of Rights of the Young Generations," issued by the committee in late October, attracted further supporters. Released four months before unemployment peaked in Depression-era France, the inclusive declaration gave voice to the despair and defiance of young people whose lives were being upended by economic crisis.[137] Never before had

Young Communists reached so broadly. The sad lives of jeunes chômeurs **161** and badly treated young workers were evoked, but so too were the woes of young peasants who watched their parents, "crushed by debt and taxes," contend with bailiffs and police agents, and the problems of students who finished their studies only to find themselves shut out of the job market.

The document's inclusion of students in its analysis prefigured a turn toward university students in communist antifascist strategy. Communists believed, correctly as it turned out, that student populations were especially fertile recruiting grounds for fascist movements across Europe. In France university students figured prominently among the estimated fifty thousand members of the Volontaires Nationaux (v.n.), the Croix de Feu's youth auxiliary, in the spring of 1934.[138] The v.n. constituted the more radical branch of the powerful fascist movement and its members were more than willing to provide the shock troops for a fascist revolution.[139] The declaration marked the first communist effort to reach the critical student constituency, with further overtures following in the months and years to come. The World Committee convened an inaugural International Student Congress in Brussels at the end of December 1934, which received lavish attention from Comintern leaders and from *L'Humanité*.[140]

The rights identified by the declaration of 1934 were as expansive as the committee's young generations were inclusive. So were the committee's demands: for students, jobs that corresponded to levels of study and degrees earned, the abrogation of the decree laws that had cut funding for education, and the reinstatement of cuts to scholarships; for jeunes chômeurs, a public works program, putting an end to the J.C.'s long-standing criticism of any kind of "forced labor"; for young peasants, crisis subsidies and the cancellation of farm mortgage debt; for young women, ruthless punishment of sexual harassment, a central concern of the J.O.C. and the J.O.C.F. As elaborated by the declaration, youth rights extended beyond the economic to the cultural. Young people had the right to be educated and the right to be healthy. They deserved paid vacations and free medical care for the illnesses they contracted in factories and in substandard housing. They needed access to libraries, clubs, game rooms, and sports facilities. Nowhere did the document call for revolution, or even mention it. The foundations of the J.C.'s approach to Popular Front youth politics had been laid.

The declaration proved a master stroke, immediately receiving the endorsement of groups outside the committee movement, including Jeunes Équipes Unies pour une Nouvelle Économie Sociale (J.E.U.N.E.S.) and the

162     Jeunes Équipes de la Jeune République. By enlisting J.E.U.N.E.S., the committee brought in a prominent organization of young intellectuals which advocated economic planning to ensure social justice and, more specifically, a fairer distribution of goods.[141] Emboldened by this success, Guyot in early November called for the creation of a generational front on the front page of *L'Avant-Garde*.[142] Employing language usually associated with Thorez, Guyot announced: "We extend a fraternal hand to all people and all organizations who sincerely want to save youth from distress." He declared the J.C.'s willingness to go wherever youth was gathered to rally young people to the antifascist cause.

The declaration's audaciousness was not initially welcomed by Comintern officials, who were not yet decided on the precise outlines of the new strategy.[143] At year's end the C.Y.I. secretariat sent a letter to the J.C. rebuking the organization for its enthusiastic promotion of the declaration and a generational bloc. The J.C. was reminded that its principal task was the defense of worker youth. Young Communists were demonstrating "dangerous right opportunist tendencies" that distorted the Comintern's united front strategy. The organization had to stop its agitation in favor of a generational bloc and stop using a term borrowed from fascists.[144] Guyot traveled to Moscow and successfully defended the idea of a generational front. During the municipal election campaign the following spring, an internal party report admitted that the J.C.'s recruiting efforts were most successful where the organization used the declaration to get young people involved.[145]

The first months of 1935 saw further development of communist overtures to youth as the party prepared to contest the May municipal elections. The party directed unprecedented attention to youth during its vigorous campaign effort. In February, Marcel Cachin announced that Communists would hold at least one hundred meetings for young people across the country that month to "wrest them from fascist influence."[146] February also brought expanded coverage of youth-related issues in *L'Humanité*. Day after day, the paper devoted part of its front page to an investigation of the difficulties facing young people. Entitled "Le malheur d'être jeune" (The curse of being young), the series was written by Paul Vaillant-Couturier, soon to be reinstalled as the paper's editor in chief. Readers were introduced to "the crisis generation" through an analysis of the miserable conditions faced by young white-collar workers, young civil servants, immigrant youth, students, young peasants, and young female workers. In a sign of the Communists' burgeoning interest in creating a mixed-sex antifascist youth coalition, Vaillant-

Couturier pointed out that young working women were actually more exploited than their male counterparts; indeed, they were also "menaced by a permanent blackmail" which was connected to their gender and to the behavior of men.[147] The series of articles formed the basis of a book of the same name, which was to be distributed during the campaign "everywhere youth gathers"—including at youth meetings, sporting events, and dances.[148]

Vaillant-Couturier created a multidimensional portrait of youth suffering. Young men and women from across the social spectrum and throughout France were encouraged to write in about their challenges. They did so, *L'Humanité* reported, in unprecedented numbers. Vaillant-Couturier published long extracts from their accounts, which provided eloquent testimony to the "the curse of being young" at the moment when Depression-era unemployment reached its highest levels. Students of both sexes spoke of the bitterness and resignation they felt when forced to take positions that had little relation to their diplomas, and young women described their anger over the special difficulties they faced. As they explained, attractive, well-turned-out young women were favored in the tight job market—only to be plagued by sexual advances from foremen, bosses, and bosses' sons once on the job. Young people of both sexes reported feeling disappointed, alone, and old beyond their years. These are the poignant words of a twenty-year-old young man who had lost his mother and left home after his father remarried: "My sorrow at being alone in this impoverished life knows no bounds. Always working to have just enough to live on . . . I'm suffering . . . I've become a grumpy old man. I'm twenty years old. The only leisure I have is cycling, which seems tough after a hard week at work. That's my life at twenty."[149]

Establishing youth's suffering in capitalist France was only part of the equation. Vaillant-Couturier strove mightily to convince the young that communism offered the solution to their problems, associating it with all that was positive and new and young in the world.[150] His analysis repeatedly drew the contrast between the failures of old parties and old states and the successes of the new Soviet Union. French Communists were likewise fresh of leadership, right down to their newspaper, whose writers were considerably younger than those at other papers. In a world of mandatory military service, even Red Army generals were distinguished by their youth. Communism represented the future, and the socialist state the "dawn of the world" (la jeunesse du monde), a breathless Vaillant-Couturier explained at the close of the series. Here young people could conquer the future, master their destinies, and live, love, and construct. Here too the state would spend lavishly on youth and work would go from being a chore to a glorious sport.[151] Vaillant-Couturier hardly innovated. Bolshevik leaders sought to rally the young through similar appeals in the regime's early days, sometimes unleashing generational conflict in the process.[152] Soviet leaders also made images of the new Soviet youth—photographs of athletes, students, young workers, and Red Army soldiers—central to their multi-pronged and ultimately successful campaign to create a positive image of the Soviet Union in France in the late 1920s and 1930s.[153]

As Vaillant-Couturier reached out to French youth, he took great care not to encourage generational conflict that might challenge the party's emphasis on class struggle. He repeatedly described the links and similarities between two generations so important to French communism in the mid-1930s: Vaillant-Couturier's own war generation and the crisis generation that came after.[154] Both were generations of sacrificed youth. Both had their fates decided by adults. Both had been lied to by adults. And both had been victims of technological revolutions, in the shape of machines that replaced people and technology that destroyed human beings. The current conflict was not between young and old but between young men and old ideas, between young realities and old forms, between the new world and the old world.[155] The solution to young people's problems could only be found through cooperation between these two benighted generations. This denial of generational conflict would be affirmed almost ritualistically by young people associated with communism in the months to come.[156]

As Vaillant-Couturier was concluding his investigation into youth distress, Cachin addressed the J.C.'s central committee to lay out the party's electoral youth strategy and explain the J.C.'s role in its implementation. Proclaiming that "all eyes are turned toward youth," Cachin said that Vaillant-Couturier's investigation had given the party a better sense of youth's anguished state of mind.[157] The Communists' inattention to youth had left the field "wide open" for their "innumerable class enemies," but now the party was no longer absorbed in its own construction and had become a major actor in national politics. Its "primary duty" was "to focus its best efforts on the recruitment, education and development of youth under the communist banner."[158] To rally his audience, Cachin outlined the vital role that youth had played in the Bolshevik Revolution, although he was careful to emphasize that its involvement always and necessarily came "under the control and direction of the old Bolsheviks."

Youth and Communist Antifascist Politics

This oldest of French communist leaders proceeded to give the youth leadership directions for the campaign. They were to study the essential works of Marxist doctrine to make it accessible to young people. Catholicism was a particular threat, a fierce enemy of communism and the working class, a crucial supporter of fascism, and a movement on the rise in France. Yet Young Communists had to proceed with tact and diplomacy; crude attacks would only alienate believers. Young Communists should stress the shared nature of young workers' material interests and the need to defend them, much as *L'Avant-Garde* had done the previous fall. They must abandon the doctrinaire and intransigent approaches which had long been essential characteristics of the J.C. To achieve a "common apostolate," it was necessary "to know the workings of their minds and hearts."

J.C. militants thus entered the electoral fray under the direction of a party leadership seeking to balance participation in democratic politics with its longstanding advocacy of revolution. *L'Avant-Garde* ran lengthy articles detailing the improvements made by communist municipal governments in the lives of the young. As the paper reminded readers, communist governments had created subsidized sports clubs, built athletic stadiums and other facilities, sponsored summer camps, bought movie projectors, and sometimes, as in Sevran, paid jeunes chômeurs living independently of their parents the same unemployment benefits received by adult males. There was no better proof of Communists' ability to provide concrete solutions to concrete problems. Young Communist militants also put up posters and distributed campaign literature, arriving with a flourish at markets and fairs, as the party directed, in small groups of motorcycles or bicycles.[159] They used the Declaration of the Rights of the Young Generations to especially good effect, distributed 641,000 copies of the pamphlet *Jeunes!*, and affixed countless stickers to local walls. The stickers briefly and bluntly hammered the main themes of the committee movement. Capitalism and fascism were equated with war and slavery, while communism brought emancipation and peace. This communist vigor led to spectacular successes at the polls. The party increased the number of municipalities under its control from 150 to 297, including twenty-six in the crucial Seine region.

As important as the elections were to party leaders, the months of March, April, and May witnessed developments even more significant to youth leaders. In the spring of 1935 French demography came together with German rearmament to push conscripts to the front of both national and J.C. politics.

**166**   By March 1935 longstanding military concerns over the smaller military classes born during the wartime years of low birth rates, known as *les classes creuses*, collided with stepped-up German militarization to create a sense of urgency among government officials. At the very moment when les classes creuses were poised to begin moving through the French armed forces, Germany was becoming a greater concern on the international stage. Three days after the Nazi government announced the reconstitution of the German air force in defiance of the Versailles Treaty and one day before obligatory military service was reinstated in Germany, Prime Minister Pierre-Étienne Flandin took to the floor of the Chamber to announce that the French government was temporarily extending the term of military service by a year, as Communists had been warning for months that it would do. Repeatedly affirming his government's peaceful intentions, Flandin defended the measure as one necessitated by demographic realities made more dangerous by German aggression.[160]

This was not the extent of government measures toward conscripts that spring. A mere eight days before the first contingent of the class of 1934 was due to be released, the government announced that conscripts would be kept under arms for an additional three months. To further boost the number of soldiers, the minister of war planned to implement the policy contained in circular 3084, which stipulated that soldiers who refused to reenlist would be ineligible for unemployment assistance upon their return to civilian life. As these measures were coming into effect, the government prepared to try Raymond Guyot on charges that he had attempted to "turn conscripts away from their military duty and from the obedience owed their leaders" through his role in the publication of the pamphlet *Death in Peacetime*, printed in April 1934 by the Youth Committee against War and Fascism.[161]

These moves prompted outrage on the left. In the Chamber and in the columns of their newspapers, socialist and communist leaders denounced the extension of military service to two years, drawing repeated parallels between 1935 and 1913, when an increase to three years had been followed quickly by war. Thorez vowed to lead Communists in organizing mass action against imperialist war. The party would not, he warned, allow the working class to be dragged into a war purportedly defending democracy against fascism.[162]

The central responsibility for mass antimilitarist action lay with the J.C. Throughout the spring it worked to fuel protests against the extension of military service, attempting to push them in revolutionary directions. The

J.C. cooperated with other youth organizations affiliated with the committee to organize demonstrations, and *L'Avant-Garde* carefully and excitedly recorded the multiple instances of protests among soldiers, which consisted mainly of refusing to eat, loudly denouncing the extension, and singing revolutionary songs.[163] *L'Avant-Garde* also devoted extensive coverage to the government's prosecution of Guyot, publishing a special edition to coincide with his scheduled court date. For the J.C., the state's pursuit of Guyot and no one else confirmed the organization's lead role in antimilitarism. For Guyot, there was little doubt that the J.C. was at the forefront of a potentially revolutionary antimilitarist uprising. As he ended one editorial, "French youth is rising up as a powerful cohort of red soldiers and fighting for the establishment of a Soviet Republic in France."[164] The J.C. also delighted in the fact that the entire episode further cemented the united youth front, as the leaders of other organizations affiliated to the youth committee rallied to Guyot's defense, sometimes appearing in court on his behalf. Antimilitarism had again mobilized a range of young men and the J.C. was again in its element, challenging authorities and drawing sustenance from the ensuing repression. The writers at *L'Avant-Garde* thought the affair among the most beautiful in J.C. history.[165] By April the J.C. reported that its membership had reached twelve thousand; the J.C. had regained its peak strength of the mid-1920s.

The euphoria did not last. On 2 May the Soviet and French governments signed a mutual assistance pact. When this did little to quell protests against the two-year law, the French government asked Stalin to intervene.[166] On 15 May Stalin released a joint communiqué at the conclusion of his talks with Foreign Minister Laval which declared his full support for French national defense policy. In so doing Stalin nullified the revolutionary nature of French communist antimilitarism and undermined the committee's antiwar efforts. He also stripped the J.C. of its last remaining sphere of truly revolutionary activity and, according to the Young Socialist Fred Zeller, betrayed and abandoned those who had paid for their commitment with time in military prisons.[167]

The about-face on such a critical issue stunned communist militants of all ages. According to Léo Figuères, a seventeen-year-old who had been pouring much of his youthful energy into protesting the new military measures in southwest France, many of his fellow Young Communists were troubled by the seeming contradiction between their efforts and Stalin's pronouncement.[168] Others were more than troubled. Such was the upheaval that the party felt compelled to plaster France with posters declaring "Stalin Is Right" and sent Thorez in front of Parisian party leaders to explain and defend the shift.[169] The J.C. had little choice but to modify its antimilitarism, a move which was strongly criticized by the J.S. federation of the Seine.[170] Coverage of protests against the two-year law virtually disappeared from *L'Avant-Garde*, and army officials noted a decrease in communist antimilitarist propaganda.[171] In the new climate the J.C. limited itself to complaints about the deplorable conditions in the army. By the following July, the J.C. was praising the Republican Army.

If Stalin's about-face closed an era of J.C. activism, it opened the possibility of a tighter communist embrace of French revolutionary traditions and the French nation itself. Both were abundantly evident during the meetings and mass demonstrations initiated by the committee on 14 July 1935, which brought Communists, Socialists, and Radicals together for the first time in the campaign against fascism and for the defense of democratic liberties. After leading figures swore allegiance to the antifascist cause in a crowded Buffalo Stadium in the morning, mammoth crowds made their way from the Place de la Bastille to the Place de la Nation in the afternoon. The day's tone differed markedly from those of previous antifascist demonstrations. The approved slogans stayed well within Republican bounds, and Communists inserted themselves carefully but enthusiastically into the course of French revolutionary history. Communist publications from *Regards* to *L'Avant-Garde* were awash in the symbols of 1789, and the communist speaker Jacques Duclos linked Soviet and French revolutionary symbols and songs as he explained how the still revolutionary Communists had become "defenders of liberties against fascists."[172] For Duclos, the tricolor symbolized past struggles and the red flag future victories. *La Marseillaise* and the "International," Duclos continued, were revolutionary anthems, the first celebrating the liberty the Communists now pledged to defend. The antifascist coalition that the Communists had been nourishing for the past year officially came into being that day as the Popular Front.

Young people were assigned an important place in the day's proceedings, the circumstances of their participation reflecting youth subordination to adults. A representative of the youth movements affiliated with the National Youth Committee against War and Fascism was prominent among those swearing allegiance to the Popular Front, while *L'Humanité* and *Le Populaire* celebrated youth's enthusiastic embrace of the cause. Reviewing the order for the carefully organized afternoon demonstration, *Le Populaire* declared:

"The youth group will be the most ardent, the most enthusiastic, and the most disciplined." Disciplined obedience to the latest *mots d'ordre* was emphasized. Young people were warned not to deviate from the approved slogans and to leave their uniforms at home,[173] but five hundred militants for the radical Seine federation of the J.S. insisted on marching in uniform and chanting their own revolutionary slogans.[174] The youth speaker, the J.C. militant Léo Figuères, was selected at the last minute after J.C. leaders decided that no leader was sufficiently young to represent youth on this important occasion.[175] The youth oath was delivered to Figuères the night of 13 July by the adult secretary of the demonstration's organizing committee.[176]

Figuères's speech applied the day's themes to youth. It began with a ringing rejection of fascism's claim to represent the aspirations of youth.[177] The communist emphasis on generational unity was so great that the version of the speech reproduced in *L'Avant-Garde* omitted this beginning, moving straight to youth's refusal (à la Vaillant-Couturier) to hold the older generation responsible for its difficulties. The speech then laid out youth demands, which resembled a slightly updated version of the Declaration of the Rights of the Young Generation of October 1934. Youths demanded the right to learn a trade, to use their diplomas, and to have access to healthy leisure. The young contingent vowed to fight against the militarization of youth and sport and against forced labor, promising allegiance to the heroic traditions of youth action in 1789, in 1848, and during the Commune. The youth antifascist front that Communists had been building in France since 1933 had arrived.

The successes of French Communists young and old on display in Paris on 14 July in leading the antifascist coalition were celebrated in Moscow soon after during the Seventh Comintern Congress in July and the Sixth Communist Youth International Congress in September. These gatherings marked the official triumph of the antifascist strategy so vigorously promoted by Dimitrov and put into practice in France, one that emphasized the provisional defense of democracy and the formation of alliances with Socialists and other democratic forces.[178] The Seventh Comintern Congress also cemented the importance of youth as a constituency and a symbol in the larger strategy. The Comintern secretary general Dimitrov lectured delegates about the "extremely important" role of youth to the new strategy, and Comintern officials put young people front and center in the carefully orchestrated opening ceremonies. As Cachin recorded in his notebook, young people dominated during the congress's first night.[179] Later in the congress, Cachin sat with ninety thousand others to watch "splendid" male and female athletes march and exhibit their athletic skills and to hear the Komsomol secretary avow that it was youth's role to organize the victory of international socialism.[180]

The Comintern assemblies also highlighted the leading role of the French J.C. in elaborating a communist antifascist youth politics. Now a member of the Comintern's presidium and soon to be elected secretary general of the C.Y.I., Guyot was given the honor of delivering the opening speech at the youth congress in September, the first such gathering since 1928. The Comintern secretary general Dimitrov spoke next. The Comintern congress, he assured his young audience, had devoted special attention to the youth movement in its deliberations. Fascism "attempts by every means to adapt its rotten demagoguery to the state of mind of the vast masses of young people and to use youth's growing combativeness for its reactionary aims, making it a support for a dying capitalism."[181] The only response was the union of all antifascist forces and, in the first instance, the union of all members of the "young generation of workers." This was the thrust and preoccupation of the youth congress. Communists' understanding of youth's role in politics had evolved considerably in the previous four years. As Dimitrov and Guyot made clear, however, there were further changes to come as the Communists moved to adapt their message to youth's "state of mind."

# 6

## Embracing the Status Quo

Communists, Young People,

and Popular Front Politics

With Guyot's exalted status at the Sixth Communist Youth International Congress in 1935 came the honor of laying out the Communists' Popular Front strategy for youth organizing. After reviewing past successes and failures, Guyot explained the path chosen by Comintern leaders. Young Communist organizations were to be transformed into mass youth movements with radically different structures and goals. Young Communists were to leave behind the austere, excessively political cells of the past decade and a half and reconstitute their movements along the lines of groups, clubs, centers, and "all other organizational forms popular among youth."[1] The primary mission of these reconstituted cells was not political but educational, and they were open to all young people who opposed the twin evils of fascism and war and backed the noble but intentionally vague causes of progress, liberty, and peace. Support for the dictatorship of the proletariat was no longer expected upon admission but would be nurtured within the youth groups.

As Guyot and, following him, Dimitrov insisted, communist aims extended beyond refiguring and enlarging youth movements. Communists sought to make them the nuclei of broad antifascist youth blocs that would undergird the adult Popular Front coalitions now being promoted by Comintern leaders. In France and elsewhere, Communists endeavored to rally the young generation under the antifascist banner. To attract the masses of young people to their cause, Comintern officials called for the establishment of separate organizations for young women, students, and young peasants alongside Young Communist groups, and the adoption of a decidedly more youthful approach. Always Young Communists were to take up the vital interests of youth and speak "the lively and fresh language of youth."[2]

Although the course outlined in Moscow in September 1935 represented a logical extension of approaches developed by the Jeunesse Communiste,

**172**  its implementation brought further changes in the understanding of youth as a constituency and actor in French communist politics. The latest plan recast the target audience to make it younger, less proletarian, and resolutely mixed-sex. Strategies for mobilizing this diverse group and models of political activism also mutated. Gone were the promise of front-line revolutionary activism and the appeal to violence, and even the primacy of political action. In their place were educational, cultural, and leisure activities; overtures to Catholics and sometimes fascists; and attention to the hopes of a Depression-era generation of young men and women.

Most striking of all were the organization's new mainstream positions on the charged issues of family politics, youth sport and physical fitness, and gender roles. The J.C. defended young families and promoted youth physical fitness and racial health, while the young women's movement, the Union des Jeunes Filles de France (U.J.F.F.), offered a radically altered vision of female political activism and communist femininity. Although U.J.F.F. leaders continued to speak in favor of gender equality in speeches and articles, they built a movement anchored in gender difference. The U.J.F.F. embraced the form and often the content of the commercial women's press in their newspaper *Jeunes filles de France*, promoted a gendered vision of leisure, and encouraged political behavior consonant with prevailing notions of femininity. In the process Communists sometimes staked out positions more conservative than those of the rival J.O.C.F.

The Communists' Popular Front youth strategy had important consequences for youth's position in communist politics and French politics more generally. Communist tactics helped push youth to the front of electoral politics in 1936 and pointed the way toward state approaches to youth undertaken by Léon Blum's first Popular Front government, in office from June 1936 to June 1937. Blum's government spotlighted youth in the struggle to regenerate France and French democracy, promoting youth sport, fitness, and tourism under the leadership of Léo Lagrange, the country's first undersecretary of state for the organization of sport and leisure. Communists, who refused to join the government officially but prodded it from the outside, expanded their own leisure offerings and assigned to youth an important symbolic role in the communist press and in the era's mass demonstrations. The happy young vacationers featured in communist publications reminded readers of the opportunities created by the party's more centrist approach, while the reassuringly feminine *jeunes filles communistes* symbolized the

extent to which the party had forsworn revolution and embraced the
status quo.

**Transforming the J.C.**  The J.C. set out to implement the new
approach in the fall of 1935, buoyed by the knowledge that its earlier efforts
had helped shape strategy within the Communist International and that
its leader headed its youth branch. The first task, the party leader Maurice
Thorez explained to two thousand communist youths on 15 November, was
to engineer a merger with the Jeunesse Socialiste,[3] creating a large left youth
organization that the Communists were confident they could control. On
27 November members of the J.C.'s central committee asked J.S. leaders to
reunite the organization that had been ripped asunder in 1920.[4] This overture was rebuffed, as were subsequent ones.

The J.C. reached out to the masses of French youth by refining and expanding the generational front introduced the previous fall. In mid-December the
J.C. announced the birth of the Union of French Youth with a manifesto that
quickly appeared on walls across the country.[5] Although many of the demands—for peace, bread, work, liberty, progress, and access to culture—had
been present during the ceremonies of 14 July the previous summer, the
emphasis now fell squarely on the reconciliation and union of French youth
regardless of religious or political affiliation. The J.C. reached beyond young
people in Catholic organizations to those in fascist movements, declaring
that it harbored no hatred toward the students of the Jeunesses Patriotes
or the white-collar workers of the Volontaires Nationaux. To the contrary,
its mission lay in finding common ground. The manifesto's tenor was such,
the conservative daily *Le Figaro* quipped, that it could have been endorsed
by men of the far right with the alteration of a few words.[6] The J.S. leader
Bernard Chochoy responded bluntly: "Under capitalism, there is no possibility of reconciliation or fraternization with class enemies, whether sworn
or disguised."[7] The J.C. was moving to the right of the J.S. on key issues as it
endeavored to forge the broadest possible antifascist youth coalition.

As surprising as J.C. overtures to fascists was the organization's attention
to young people's thwarted desires to start families. Like many aspects of
the J.C.'s program, this originated with the party. Paul Vaillant-Couturier's
election speech in the spring of 1935, "Rescuing the Family," laid out a dramatically altered communist approach to familial and natalist politics.[8]
Although the party had supported abortion rights since its inception and

opposed the law enacted in 1920 forbidding propaganda on behalf of birth control, Vaillant-Couturier signaled the abandonment of this oppositional stance and the adoption of more mainstream positions. Now, he averred, Communists worried about falling birth rates and a collapsing family. They were also concerned about the future of the country and the French race. Communists would come to the defense of the French family and do so in rather traditional ways, firmly opposing sexual licentiousness, which Vaillant-Couturier termed "a smutty caricature of freedom." Vaillant-Couturier linked young people's inability to exercise their "right to love" to economic difficulties, and he positioned youth and their frustrations at the core of his analysis. Young people's failure to marry and have children doomed the family, while the party's defense of the young underscored its commitment to the family and pro-natalist politics.

The J.C. incorporated the party's emphasis on defending the family into its efforts to appeal broadly. With considerable fanfare and a prominent front-page photograph of an attractive, smiling, and modern-looking young couple, *L'Avant-Garde* announced a major investigation in November 1935 into young people's ability to begin families. As in the previous year during Vaillant-Couturier's investigation into the "malheur d'être jeune," young people were invited to write in to share their difficulties in finding love and starting a family.[9] In the weeks that followed, the prime space at the top right corner of the front page that had long been used to call young male workers to revolutionary action was given over to first-hand accounts and tentative explanations for a decline in marriages from 342,000 in 1932 to 298,000 in 1934. Both young men and young women contributed their frustrations, although the women were more likely to be lyrical about the joys of marriage. As one exclaimed, "Starting a home and family in joy, facing life side by side, feeling sustained by the fire and fervor of a confident love. What a dream!"[10] The reporting in *L'Avant-Garde* made clear that the J.C. identified the desire for family as a powerful aspiration of the young people the movement hoped to rally, with one column beginning, "All young people aspire to create a home and a family, they want to love. Who could deny that the creation of this home, this family is not absolutely indispensable and absolutely necessary?"[11]

To further situate themselves as defenders of young people's right to love and family, the J.C. unveiled new political demands, and communist leaders of all ages stressed the party's role as the protector of young families. In December the J.C. announced that it would campaign for state aid to help

UNE GRANDE ENQUÊTE DE « L'AVANT-GARDE »

# Les jeunes peuvent-ils se créer un foyer ?

Exposez-nous en toute franchise votre cas personnel. Quelles difficultés rencontrez-vous dans la création d'un fover? Quelle est votre conception du « droit à l'amour » ? Nous commencerons prochainement la publication de notre enquête Ecrivez au Docteur TENINE, à l' « Avant-Garde », 149, rue Saint-Denis, Paris (2ᵉ)

**Figure 5** Both the J.O.C. and the J.C. undertook numerous investigations into young workers' lives. In this cover of *L'Avant-Garde* from November 1935, the J.C. uses an attractive, happy young couple to launch its investigation into young people's difficulties in finding love and starting families during the economic crisis of the 1930s. *L'Avant-Garde*, 23 November 1935.

young married couples set up households.[12] Here the J.C. copied the J.O.C., a fact that it only partly conceded.[13] In his major speech on youth at the party congress in the following month, Jacques Duclos, now the party's number two as well as its propaganda chief, returned repeatedly to the theme of family. In Duclos's hands, French young people's inability to begin families highlighted the failings of the capitalist system and the superiority of the socialist homeland. According to Duclos, all Soviet young people had the means to start families and live happily without worrying that their children had enough to eat.[14] The USSR continued to function as the perfect world,

**Figure 6** Hopeful young couples striding into the future under the symbols of the French revolutionary past illustrate the cover of this commemorative issue of *L'Avant-Garde*, 14 July 1936.

the antithesis of a decaying France and the antidote to it, even as calls for the establishment of an analogous regime in France became more muted.

J.C. demands for state aid to young couples became more extensive during the national legislative campaign in April 1936. In addition to financial assistance, the J.C. now called for distributing abandoned housing to needy couples along with an allowance, a layette, a crib, and a car at the birth of the first child.[15] The emphasis on young couples continued past the Popular Front's electoral victory in May, with the front page of a special issue of *L'Avant-Garde* on 14 July dominated by young couples marching arm and arm into the future under the headline "We Are Young France!" The hopeful young couples contrasted sharply with the grim male revolutionaries-in-training whose photos dominated the front page of *L'Avant-Garde* during the 1920s and early 1930s.

The Communists' celebration of family and couples was designed to reap a range of political rewards. As communist leaders were well aware, the politics of family and natality carried tremendous symbolic weight in France.[16] This was especially true for Catholics, whose leaders worked tirelessly to defend the family and who made communist threats to the family a pillar of their anticommunism. By taking up the cause of the family, Communists young and old hoped to inoculate themselves against these kinds of attacks.[17] But the revamped approach also provided fresh ways of appealing to young people in this predominantly Catholic country, where from an early age children from observant homes were drilled in the sanctity of marriage and family, and where economic crisis often delayed young people's transition from youth to adulthood, which marriage symbolized. Raymond Guyot's lengthy speech to the J.C. Congress in March 1936 captured the intent. After briefly surveying the failings of the "old world" toward the young, Guyot read, as Duclos had before him, from a letter written by a sixteen-year-old Catholic woman to the Catholic newspaper *Sept* lamenting her generation's fate. The impossibility of beginning a family was causing "great anguish," and she despaired that no one was responding to youth's cry for help.[18] Guyot reminded his listeners of Duclos's assurance of communist assistance. This was the face of a new party, its leaders promising to aid a young Catholic woman with no discernible connection to the working class.

Communists similarly made altered positions on sport and youth physical fitness part of their move to the center. As we saw in chapter 2, Communists firmly subordinated the practice of sport to revolutionary politics and sharply criticized the militarization of sport by state officials and bourgeois sports organizations during the 1920s and early 1930s. As tactics evolved in 1934 and 1935, however, Communists began to view sport less as training for revolution and more as something that could bring happiness to young people. In the Declaration of the Rights of the Young Generation of October 1934, access to sport emerged as a cultural right that Communists vowed to defend; by the spring of 1935 the recently reunified worker sports movement, the Fédération Sportive et Gymnique du Travail, which was closely aligned to the party, campaigned for the provision of sports grounds, playing fields, and swimming pools for French youth.[19] And for Communists, no sporting activity was more fun or less accessible than flying. Wildly popular yet available only to young people wealthy enough to afford onerous flying club dues, aviation was, according to *L'Avant-Garde*, "a means of emancipation, perfection, beauty and, indeed, poetry."[20] Communists worked to make fly-ing available to all young people, cheering the formation in February 1936 of L'Aile Tendue, which became the nucleus of the Popular Front's popular aviation movement that spring.[21]

But sport could also build strong bodies. When Communists stepped up demands for increased access to sport in late 1935, they made this part of a larger campaign to improve youth physical fitness. As the electoral con-test approached, a party that had previously linked sport to revolution now viewed sport as a way to safeguard the French race. In February 1936 *L'Avant-Garde* illustrated an article on the F.S.G.T.'s program with a photograph of three strapping young men, captioned "We don't want the race to degen-erate. We want a strong and healthy youth."[22] At the same time, the party championed the F.S.G.T.'s call for one billion francs in state spending on sport, making it the centerpiece of proposed legislation that incorporated the organization's demand for mandatory physical education at all levels of the French educational system and the organization of state-sponsored medical surveillance for schools and sporting societies. This proposal, which was deposited in the Chamber soon after the electoral victory of the Popular Front coalition in May, was introduced, explained, and justified by the need to counter the devastating effects of the Depression on youth and promote the race.[23] The last sentence of the preamble left little to the imagination: Communists were proposing their spending program "to insure the defense and improvement of the race through measures allowing our young men and women to develop fully."[24]

The Communists' transformed position on sport and youth fitness again reflected multiple goals and realities. A fight for increased access to sport was consistent with the attempt to "speak the lively language of youth," to defend things that mattered to young people. It was also part of a larger at-tempt to democratize culture, whose broad contemporary meaning included sport.[25] And it doubtless reflected genuine concern over the health of the masses of French youth. In France of the mid-1930s, schools provided almost nothing in the way of physical education, publicly funded facilities such as playing fields and pools were scarce outside of communist and socialist municipalities, and working and housing conditions were often hazardous to the health of young bodies. Young workers succumbed often to serious illness, and studies found a significant proportion of conscripts (sometimes as much as 30 or even 50 percent) to be unfit for military service.[26] All this

led, *L'Avant-Garde* believed, to "a physical degeneration *without precedent in* **179**
*the history of our country.*"[27]

Yet discussions of youth health and fitness were deeply politicized, and the Communists' revamped positions in these domains provided another potent reminder of the party's drastic ideological shift. In the mid-1930s concerns over youth fitness were intimately linked to the larger issue of military preparedness and to concrete worries over the smaller size of the military classes called to military service beginning in 1935. So when the minister of war defended his government's decision to extend the term of military service in March 1935, he did so partly by invoking his government's "anxieties about the physical well-being of the contingent."[28] The physical conditioning of French young men had become an urgent problem in comparison to the situation in France's bellicose and populous neighbor Germany. There, the minister continued, young men benefited physically from National Socialist labor camps. Indeed, by the time these men continued on to the army, they arrived ready, both because they were fitter than their French counterparts and because they had received preliminary military training in the Labor Corps.[29] By coming out so strongly in favor of youth fitness and physical education, therefore, the Communists aligned themselves with military officials whose cause they now supported. More strikingly, they did so in language almost identical to that used by the fascists against whom they struggled. As the celebrated right-wing aviator Jean Mermoz said when he addressed a Croix de Feu meeting in early March, "Today's realities demand that we create a strong and healthy youth to safeguard the race and health of France."[30]

While Communists of all ages moderated their message and used youth-related issues in their race to the center, the J.C. continued to revamp the federation along the lines laid out in Moscow. The beginning of 1936 proved crucial. In early March J.C. leaders instructed local sections to focus heightened attention on a younger segment of the youth population than previously targeted, those between fourteen and sixteen.[31] This was the prime age group targeted by the J.O.C. At the Eighth J.C. Congress in Marseille that month, leaders explained to the 442 delegates the changes entailed by implementing what Guyot termed an "audacious organizational line": cells were to be transformed into clubs, centers, and circles, and the new groups were to operate differently at all levels. Whereas cells had met in dark rooms in cafés and bars and had held meetings that differed little from those of adult

Embracing the Status Quo

cells, circles and clubs would have their own headquarters and radically different gatherings. The youth spaces envisioned by J.C. leaders would be light, attractive places where young people could gather, relax, read, play games, and further their education in the "spirit of Marxism-Leninism."

Since the J.C.'s transformation had begun at the end of 1935, leaders were able to illustrate their points with precise examples. In his lengthy speech "Youth Takes on the Old World," Guyot began his discussion with the changing federation in Vitry, whose J.C. cell had been rebaptized the "Foyer de la Jeunesse." He read from a tract distributed to neighborhood young people and, in another departure, their parents: "In the *foyer*, young people will find many games which are sure to please them, including ping pong, checkers, dominoes, and cards. We also plan to sponsor movie nights which will be free to members. For those comrades who want to read, a library with books appealing to everyone's tastes will be available."[32] Here, Guyot continued, cell meetings were replaced by open houses, during which games only gradually gave way to collective meetings. The story was similar in other locales, even if pool tables sometimes replaced ping-pong tables and radio concerts replaced movie nights. Guyot's emphasis on relations with parents underscored the sea change that was occurring: an organization that had boasted of clashes with police was taking pride in earning the confidence of parents.[33]

The campaign to educate members about the new federation continued once the Congress concluded, with *L'Avant-Garde* providing lengthy stories on vibrant sections such as the "Club de la Jeunesse" in the fourth arrondissement of Paris. The club's brightly decorated room hosted rehearsals for its choir and lectures by experts in the cinema, social issues, literature, and the theater; it also housed a library holding works by Shakespeare, Victor Hugo, and Victor Margueritte, and Michelet's history of France.[34]

As the J.C. remade itself, *L'Avant-Garde* underwent parallel transformations, its pages developing and reflecting themes and approaches visible in other communist publications. With the turn toward a Popular Front strategy, party leaders devoted considerable attention to expanding and revamping communist publishing operations.[35] At the flagship *L'Humanité*, the editor in chief Paul Vaillant-Couturier focused new attention on French history and culture and looked to the mass circulation daily *Paris-Soir* for inspiration in matters of presentation.[36] *L'Avant-Garde* followed suit. The paper ran prominent front-page photographs of better visual quality than in the past, sometimes using movie stills, the stuff of popular youth imagination.[37] *L'Avant-Garde* also gave increased space to sports and the movies, and introduced regular columns for students and young women, the latter featuring sewing patterns for seasonally appropriate, up-to-date attire.[38] Once the Union of French Youth was announced, *L'Avant-Garde* altered its format further. Most noticeable was the change in the newspaper's name. *The Vanguard: Defender of Young Workers* became *The Vanguard: The Newspaper of Young People*.

The revamped approach to youth organizing paid dividends. In clubs such as the one in the fourth arrondissement, membership numbers soared. In only eight days, *L'Avant-Garde* reported proudly, the "Club de la Jeunesse" had gone from forty-one to eighty-three members.[39] Membership increases were similar across the federation: the number of young people joining the new J.C. groups increased sharply in the first months of 1936, with the national federation passing thirty thousand by the March Congress. In a country where political parties were small, these numbers were not insignificant; indeed, the party's own membership stood at 74,400 in late January.[40] *L'Avant-Garde* made similar advances. The paper's readership grew steadily, reaching 44,000 by the time of the 1936 Congress, and the C.Y.I. named it the best youth newspaper in the international communist movement. The J.C. became ever bolder about asserting the preeminent position of *L'Avant-Garde* within the Popular Front youth coalition. On 5 April the J.C. presented the paper's new editorial team to the leaders of its coalition partners, Guyot telling them that Young Communists aimed to make their newspaper the journal of all antifascist and revolutionary youth.[41] Both the J.C. and its paper were on the move; the Popular Front strategy seemed a success.

The transformation was not proceeding as smoothly as J.C. leaders claimed. Many flocked to the circles and clubs, but about one-third of new members departed after only a few weeks.[42] In addition, the reorganization had resulted in serious financial difficulties,[43] and there was confusion about both the J.C.'s goals and the very meaning of engagement in the revamped federation. A key report delivered at the Congress attempted to correct misconceptions surfacing in a number of circles about the balance between leisure, education, and political action. Clubs were not supposed to hide their J.C. flags, as some had been doing, and they were not meant to drop political action altogether.[44] The J.C. was transforming, the report continued, but it remained, its members were to remember, the organization that "concerned itself always and in every instance with the needs and demands of France's laboring youth."[45]

Reports from Paris police suggest that the problems were real. To be sure, certain groups demonstrated robustness in both membership and action, with those in the fourth, nineteenth, and twentieth arrondissements leading the way. But most evidenced "no effective work," while one group, in the eighteenth, devoted most of its attention to what police referred to as "sexual questions."[46] Still another struggled with Trotskyism, whose appeal among Parisian students had created serious problems for the national organization in 1935.[47] There were questions too about the organization's ability to carry out its mandate of education through culture, an undertaking for which militants had neither training nor experience. One young militant entrusted with directing her section's choir later recounted that she had been singing the wrong words at crucial moments in revolutionary hymns. In her hands, *L'Internationale* had become *La terre nationale*, and the partisans of *Partisans* had gone from being those who saved (sauvèrent) the Soviets to being green (sont verts).[48]

The J.C. was also failing completely in its efforts to lure the Young Socialists into a united left youth organization. J.S. leaders and militants continued to oppose the J.C.'s new line, insisting on the importance of class struggle, anticlericalism, and revolutionary pacifism. The J.S. head Chochoy attacked the J.C.'s strategy, and J.S. members refused to sing the expurgated version of "The Young Guard" promoted by J.C. leaders, which removed priests from the groups that should be on guard.[49] The J.S. also rejected J.C. support for "national defense within the capitalist regime," calling for an insurrectionary general strike in the event of war shortly after Hitler moved troops into the Rhineland on 7 March 1936.[50] Police reported at the end of March that negotiations on unity between the two organizations had broken down completely, and that the unity pact between the J.C. and the J.S. was no longer being applied.[51] A month later, delegates to the J.S. National Congress denounced the J.C.'s "abandonment of the principles of class struggle" and its transformation into "an association of leisure and clubs incapable of leading youth to revolutionary combat."[52]

**Contesting the Elections of 1936** The Communists' Popular Front approach was at bottom an electoral strategy whose success or failure would be determined at the polls. During the national legislative campaign of April 1936, Communists reached out vigorously to young people. By this point, though, Communists were hardly alone in their overtures to youth. As the J.C.'s secretary, Léonce Granjon, wrote during the campaign's first week, "Never had there been as many appeals to youth at the beginning of an electoral campaign,"[53] and this was especially true of the Communists' coalition partners. Adult leaders like the Socialist Léon Blum shared the platform with youth leaders at campaign rallies.[54] The eminent Radical politician Paul Reynaud published the small book *Youth, What France Do You Want?*, which was less concerned with consulting the young than with analyzing their political beliefs and lamenting the fact that many "rejected individualism and were tempted by the collective."[55] Communist focus on youth had pushed young people to the front of the Popular Front coalition's electoral preoccupations.

During the short electoral period, the Communists campaigned with more vigor, panache, and discipline than their coalition partners—and they directed more sustained attention to young people in the process. The starting point for the youth electoral effort was the J.C., and militants did their part. They sold communist newspapers; confronted fascists in the streets; handed out invitations to rallies, demonstrations, and meetings; posted J.C. election posters on official electoral bulletin boards across France; and sold pamphlets published by the J.C.'s expanded Éditions de la Jeunesse. By the end of the campaign's first week, the first ten thousand copies of Guyot's *Youth Takes on the Old World* had sold out, and a second printing was under way.[56] Maroussia Naïtchenko, then a thirteen-year-old Young Communist in the seventh arrondissement of Paris, remembered that between selling newspapers, attending demonstrations and meetings, and going on J.C. outings, she no longer had a minute to herself, and certainly no time for her schoolwork.[57]

The electoral message to youth contained many of the themes that had been pioneered during the municipal election campaign the year before, even if this time they came wrapped in the more moderate cloak of 1936. Communists again presented themselves as a young party led by a young leader. *L'Avant-Garde* unveiled the J.C.'s electoral program by positioning it next to a photograph of a smiling, boyish-looking Maurice Thorez, described as "the leader of a young party" and "young himself."[58] The Communists did not simply stress Thorez's relative youth to the youthful, but made this theme part of their broader electoral appeal. In a front-page portrait of Thorez two days before the first round of voting, *L'Humanité* went beyond underscoring his youth to exult that he had retained "the purity and ardor of childhood."[59] Youth was an asset in a political culture dominated by, as the sexagenarian Léon Blum admitted in one of his speeches to youth, the same men who

Embracing the Status Quo

**184**    had been running things for forty years.[60] So too was childhood innocence, which buttressed the party's attempt to portray itself as an unthreatening force. Opponents picked up the theme of party youthfulness. Reporting on the January party congress, the conservative daily *Le Figaro* remarked that the majority of delegates were in their thirties, with many others in their twenties. More telling was the reporter's observation that the congress only came to life during Duclos's speech on youth.[61]

As suggested by the title of Guyot's pamphlet, *Youth Takes on the Old World*, Communists continued to associate their creed with a new world that was needed to replace an old, dying one and to link that idea to young people's ardor and revolutionary élan. Yet Young Communists only fleetingly evoked the socialist state they hoped to build in the future, the French Republic of Soviets, concentrating instead on the effort to improve young lives in the democratic here and now. J.C. materials highlighted the organization's role in combating fascism and leading a strong antifascist youth coalition, and they combined that with an electoral program of concrete, mainstream demands. The J.C. called for public works programs, expanded professional training for young people, a minimum wage, state aid to new families, the extension of mandatory schooling until the age of sixteen, the introduction of physical education throughout the school system, the appropriation of five hundred million francs to build sports facilities and schools, and the restitution of money cut from education by Laval's decree laws in 1935.[62] The main election poster expressed vague, commonly held youth desires, ending:

WE THE YOUNG
We want to live.
We want bread, a trade, work.
We demand the right to culture.
We aspire to starting a family.
We ardently desire peace.
We want to march toward liberty and progress.
United we will be an invincible force, we will lift our generation out of despair, we will be able to face the future with confidence.
LONG LIVE THE UNION OF FRENCH YOUTH!

Nowhere was revolution or the Soviet Union mentioned.

The emphasis on peace represented a further effort to connect with mainstream youth concerns. Historians, especially Eugen Weber, have emphasized the overwhelming desire for peace in France of the mid-1930s. Politicians and trade unions supported it, ordinary citizens supported it, and students supported it, ardently.[63] A lycée student born in 1921 recounted in his memoirs that after February 1934, "War assumed the shape of a many-headed monster that menaced us all." He continued, "Some nights I had trouble falling asleep. What would tomorrow bring?"[64] Youth organizations from across the political spectrum mobilized in support of peace. On 29 February and 1 March 1936 the International Conference of Youth in Support of Peace, whose representatives from 23 countries and 389 youth organizations (including 45 Christian ones) stood resolute against Italy's invasion of Abyssinia and Japanese incursions in the Far East, demanded economic sanctions against Italy and Japan and economic support for the victims of aggression.[65]

Hitler's remilitarization of the Rhineland on 7 March 1936 amplified fears of war in France. With German troops again on the French border, the rumblings of war were more intense than at any time since the close of hostilities in 1918. In movie houses, audiences were subjected to newsreels featuring German troops in the Rhineland, Italian troops fighting in Abyssinia, and French troops massing in Strasbourg or hunkering down in Maginot fortifications before reaching the main fare.[66] The presence of German troops in the Rhineland provided the backdrop against which the elections were fought. Léon Blum devoted much of the early part of his historic national radio address to the issue, explaining what hardly needed to be explained: "When the question of war and peace has to be grappled with, it takes primacy over all other questions."[67] His party, he reassured listeners, was determined to "organize the peace" to avert war.

Communists too attempted to burnish their credentials as defenders of peace, especially in their appeals to the young. This was a delicate task, since the party had always distanced itself from pacifism and had, since the Franco-Soviet Pact of May 1935, thrown its support behind French national defense. Yet the party had also helped to forge a mass movement around the struggle against war and fascism, the logic of which seemed amply confirmed by Hitler's latest maneuvers. In the aftermath of 7 March, who on the center or left could doubt that fascism posed a threat to France or that fascism meant war?

These themes were brought together and highlighted during March and April. The first issue of *L'Avant-Garde* published after German troops moved into the Rhineland devoted its entire front page to the problem of war and peace, presenting the latest events through the dualistic lens of the party's analysis of the mid-1930s. Using photographs, caricatures, and text, the paper deftly juxtaposed fascist, bellicose Germany with a socialist, peace-loving Soviet Union, the latter a longstanding feature of Soviet propaganda.[68] Under a photograph of a heroic Stalin repudiating all designs on foreign territory and a caricature of a snarling Hitler spouting expansionist rhetoric, happy, dancing Soviet couples countered Hitler Youth engaged in military exercises and a solitary Soviet tractor faced off against German tanks. The small feature article in the center of the page rammed home the key points: youth and peace were in grave danger and fascism was the worst scourge possible, the fascists the quintessential warmongers. Only united action could preserve peace.

The J.C. applauded the efforts of the youth peace congress in Brussels, where it had participated in a minor capacity, and called on young people of all views to unite. The Young Communists urged the young to attend the Pilgrimage for Peace to Verdun, sponsored by A.R.A.C.,[69] and used the image of a crazed and menacing Hitler, knife between his teeth,[70] to draw the young to the rally at Buffalo Stadium on 5 April kicking off the electoral campaign.[71] The rally proved a success, drawing, the Communists claimed, eighty thousand people. Party leaders lambasted German and French fascists and detailed Hitler's desire for war, which threatened the Soviet Union. They aligned themselves with the defense of peace and the construction of a strong, free, happy France, unafraid of Germany.[72] The party's claim to be a resolute defender of peace was on the face of it a compelling one, especially since the details of communist positions on war and fascism were buried in lengthy texts. One had to read carefully the joint appeal issued by the central committees of the French and German Young Communist organizations to discover that fighting fascism was a higher priority than fighting war.[73] War would not be welcomed but would be waged if necessary.

Communists innovated by using records and films to disseminate their message to the young. In mid-March police reported that party leaders intended to make "very heavy use" of records of speeches by party leaders, with Duclos's appeal to young people notable among the materials sent to local sections.[74] The most ambitious piece of electoral propaganda was *La vie est à nous*, a sixty-minute film directed by Jean Renoir. Commissioned by the party and shot with a script apparently written partly by Vaillant-Couturier,[75] the film dramatized the main lines of the party's electoral program in the most popular medium of the day. The film was shot quickly in March us-

**Figure 7** Youth is called to rally for peace and combat fascism in April 1936. This caricature of Hitler reverses the usual anticommunist propaganda which depicted Communists clenching knives in their teeth. *L'Avant-Garde*, 4 April 1936, 1.

ing communist militants in lesser roles, and played often at party meetings and festivals starting in early April.[76] Although scholars have outlined the circumstances of the film's production, described its structure and contents, and evaluated it as an example of the *cinéma engagé* of the 1930s, they have had nothing to say about the prominent place that it accords to youth.[77] Yet the film stands as a testament to youth's importance to the party's Popular Front strategy and provides a filmic representation of the new model J.C.

*La vie est à nous* begins with classroom scenes that establish the riches of France—and their inequitable distribution. The fascist threat is then developed and the Communists' antifascist credentials established. Mixing clips from newsreels, footage shot at fascist and antifascist demonstrations in Paris, and front pages from *L'Humanité*, the film illustrates the dangers of fascism, giving special attention to its militaristic bent and warmaking proclivities. The French Communist Party is offered as the antidote, the original and most determined antifascist force in France. The film uses three vignettes to portray Communists as defenders of the principal groups targeted by the party in the election: workers, peasants, and young people.

The youth segment graphically illustrates the manifold frustrations brought on by the Depression and positions Communists as the saviors of youth. The emblematic young person is a recent graduate of the École Supérieure de l'Électricité who is unable to find work and unable to collect unemployment benefits because he has never worked before. With no employment and no job prospects, the disconsolate young man leaves his girlfriend, illustrating Vaillant-Couturier's maxim that economic struggles make love impossible. A menial job ends almost as soon as it begins, and the young man is forced into the street, where he is soon approached by a recruiter for the youth auxiliary of the fascist Croix de Feu, the Volontaires Nationaux. After wiping his shoes with the v.n. membership bulletin he has been given, he joins a long line for a soup kitchen before being turned away without food. Cold and hungry, he collapses against a doorframe, only to be collected by Communists and taken to their local.

At the local the young man is nourished by the food he is given and the fraternity and sense of collective purpose he witnesses around him. He watches appreciatively as a youth choir sings uplifting songs under a banner reading "Long Live the Union of Youth" and listens with rapt attention as a spoken chorus intones, "You are not alone." When the scene changes and short clips are shown of communist leaders addressing the party's newly diverse constituencies, the young man is prominent among the crowd, his girlfriend back by his side. The film's second-to-last speaker, Jacques Duclos, was also the party's second in command. As he had at the January party congress, Duclos speaks directly to youth, at greater length than previous speakers. The speech pays homage to young people's historical revolutionary ardor and élan: as the soul and army of the revolution, he tells them, youth has always been at the forefront of action on behalf of noble causes.

After results from the second round of voting on 3 May were tallied, the Popular Front coalition emerged victorious. Léon Blum, whose party captured more seats in the Chamber than its coalition partners the Radicals and the Communists, would become France's first socialist prime minister. But it was the Communists who recorded the most dramatic gains, increasing their number of seats from ten to seventy-two and their percentage of votes cast to 15. The reversal was stunning, especially when juxtaposed to the Radicals' loss of fifty-one seats since the last legislative elections in 1932. The

**Figure 8.1** The film *La vie est à nous*, made by the French Communist Party for the legislative elections of 1936, showcased the impact of the economic crisis on young people by following the struggles of a recent university graduate who could not find work. In the first still, the youth character lines up for food at a soup kitchen.

**8.2** Turned away by the soup kitchen, the forlorn young man collapses against a door frame.

**8.3** Salvation comes at the communist local, where a communist youth choir practices under a banner reading "Long Live the Union of Youth."

Communists had emerged as a force in national politics, but they announced their intention to wield their influence from outside the government, shunning official participation and forming what Vaillant-Couturier called "a kind of ministry of the masses."[78] The party nevertheless intended to support the government, and to push it forward.

### Youth Politics under Blum's Popular Front Government

Youth's moment in the political spotlight had arrived, with the government seizing the initiative from Communists and moving in directions demanded by the party and its organizations. During its 380 days in power, Blum's government targeted young people in its reform initiatives, met with youth leaders, and put youth at the heart of its efforts to regenerate France and French democracy. In response Young Communists applauded and promoted the government's efforts, all the while expanding their own offerings and membership.

Before the government took office, a powerful strike movement erupted that presented the government with its first challenge. The strikes, which were not Communist-initiated, began in mid-May in isolated aviation factories, spread across the Paris region in late May, and swept across France after 2 June. By early June a wide range of workplaces and industries were affected. Hotel and restaurant workers and young female salesclerks in Parisian department stores joined industrial workers on strike. The number of strikers reached 1,830,938 during June, a figure one-third more than the previous annual record, set in 1920,[79] but the strike movement's power resulted less from the number of strikers than from the form the strikes took. In roughly three-quarters of the strikes, workers occupied their factories and workplaces, sometimes for days and even weeks at a time. France had never witnessed anything like it.

A day after Blum's government took power on 6 June, it convened talks between representatives from government, labor, and employers at the Hôtel Matignon. The Matignon Accords, signed that night, granted workers and their unions important rights and mandated wage increases for French workers.[80] Despite the agreement's historic nature, it failed to end the strikes, and some on the right feared that France might be on the verge of revolution.[81] Thorez stepped in to throw his support behind the government, announcing that it was necessary to know how to stop a strike once gains had been made. The tide began to turn.

The J.C.'s stance during the strikes of May and June reflected the organization's transformed orientation and subservient role in communist politics. *L'Avant-Garde* devoted extensive coverage to the strike movement, sending writers into key occupied factories, including the huge Renault factory, to report on the actions of strikers and strike committees and the involvement of local J.C. clubs. The divide between Young Communists and strikers was wide and telling, as individual Young Communists were rarely singled out as participants, much less as leaders. The one J.C. militant praised by the organization, a fourteen-year-old girl named Simone Priavoux, exemplified the new communist youth.[82] Local J.C. groups restricted their involvement to supporting the strikers. Militants raised money for strike committees; brought youthful strikers cigarettes, coffee, and chocolate; and entertained those camping at idled workplaces. Sections sent choirs and musicians into factories, showed films, and supplied young strikers with games and books. Youth was no longer assigned a vanguard role in trade union activism as it had been in the 1920s; it no longer had much of an active role at all. This was highlighted by *L'Avant-Garde*'s discussion of the positive reception given to J.C. members: "Everywhere they were greeted with the same enthusiasm, because our Young Communists made it clear to the striking male and female workers that they were coming to support a protest movement in which mothers and fathers were fighting for bread for their children."[83] Communist youth now relied on their parents' generation to fight their battles.

Nevertheless, gains won for young workers were impressive. Article 4 of the Matignon Accord mandated across-the-board wage increases, with the highest (15 percent) going to those at the bottom of the wage scale. As *L'Avant-Garde* pointed out, this was tremendously important for young workers whose wages were extremely low. The agreement also called on those negotiating subsequent collective agreements to give priority to readjusting abnormally low wages. Some of the collective agreements that quickly followed, including those in the Paris metalworking and aviation industries, established minimum wages for young workers and apprentices.[84] These gains helped bring new members to left organizations, and the J.C.'s membership approached fifty thousand by mid-June.[85]

June also brought social legislation directly relevant to young people. The government raised the school-leaving age to fourteen, bringing France in line with international conventions and practices in other major European countries. The education minister, Jean Zay, called for creating two thousand teaching positions by 1 October 1936 and a further two thousand by October 1937. Coming after decree laws cutting education spending and the number of teaching positions, these measures were of immense potential importance for students. The government also took steps to improve the living conditions of soldiers and sailors in the military. It sought credits to increase pay and food allowances,[86] and Minister of Defense Édouard Daladier championed troop welfare in a stern letter to regional commanders. He demanded that generals improve the physical and moral health of the troops and lectured them on the negative effects on soldiers of disdainful treatment by superiors, "vulgar paternalism," and pointless exercises and duties.[87]

The most exciting reforms came in the realm of leisure. The government established the forty-hour week and the fifteen-day paid vacation. Young people were the most likely to take advantage of the possibilities thrown up by these initiatives. In fact, facilitating youth access to leisure proved one of the main preoccupations of Léo Lagrange, a socialist lawyer who became France's first undersecretary of state for the organization of sport and leisure. Only thirty-six himself, Lagrange attacked his work with energy and enthusiasm, quickly becoming one of the government's most popular ministers. In his inaugural radio address on 10 June, he followed the Communists' lead in viewing sport as an avenue to health and happiness, telling listeners, "Our simple and humane goal is to allow the masses of French youth to find joy and health in the practice of sport and to organize leisure in such a way that it provides workers with relaxation and a reward for their hard labor."[88] To these ends, Lagrange directed government money toward the construction of playing fields, athletic facilities, stadiums, and swimming pools, always privileging the needs of ordinary young people over those of élite athletes.

Leisure was more than sport, and Lagrange proved himself a champion of youth tourism. As he told *L'Avant-Garde* soon after taking office, he aimed to increase the number of children who went on vacation and facilitate weekends in the country for young people.[89] He negotiated discount train fares in July and vigorously promoted the network of youth hostels that had begun to appear in France in the early 1930s.[90] The self-proclaimed "Minister of Youth Hostels," Lagrange inaugurated, visited, and gave his name to numerous hostels; prodded municipalities to build hostels; directed government money toward both religious and secular hostels; and oversaw the construction of a model youth hostel at the World's Fair of 1937 in Paris.[91] Hostels held a special place for Lagrange: they allowed young people to see France cheaply and provided a microcosm of the fraternity and international cooperation he desired for Europe.[92]

As committed as Lagrange was to helping young people enjoy their new-found leisure time, he always emphasized the larger political significance of his efforts. Lagrange believed that youth possessed regenerative powers, that they could rejuvenate peoples and salvage threatened values.[93] A healthy, enthusiastic youth challenged the widespread notion of a declining France.[94] So too did the successful organization of youth leisure. By the time Lagrange took office, leisure had become deeply politicized across Europe. French politicians realized that fascist governments in Italy and Germany had created successful state-run programs to organize their citizens' free time and some politicians demanded the establishment of similar programs in France.[95] Lagrange was convinced of the importance of showing "that a democracy can organize the physical education of youth as well as a dictatorship."[96] He and his staff worked to organize sport and leisure so that it departed from both fascist and commercial approaches and reflected social democratic ideals.[97]

The popular aviation program became an important plank in the government's effort to strengthen democratic France through youth leisure. Introduced in the summer of 1936 by the youthful air minister Pierre Cot (born in 1895), the regimen aimed to provide a comprehensive program of aeronautical education and training to young men under the age of twenty-one. Students now began their aviation training in school at the age of nine.[98] Once they left primary school at fourteen, they pursued their training in popular aviation sections formed from existing flying clubs and overseen and financed by the government.[99] For only ten francs a month, boys from fourteen to seventeen learned the basics of gliding and collaborated in building a glider. Once they reached eighteen, the young men turned to the study of motorized flying. Successful completion of the program led to a diploma in either civil or military aviation, the latter providing a direct path into the air force.[100]

The aviation program sought to enhance France's military preparedness while simultaneously responding to young men's aspirations to take to the skies. Part of the impetus for the program came from Germany, where efforts to develop flying capabilities were ambitious,[101] but there were domestic origins as well. Right-wing groups sponsored their own flying clubs, and government officials fretted about the political leanings of many Air Force officers.[102] The popular aviation program aimed to create pilots loyal to the

Republic. Consistent with government priorities regarding youth, the program included heavy doses of physical as well as aeronautical training, with officials displaying their successes by marching popular aviation students bare-chested during the Festival of Popular Aviation in September 1937.[103] In combination with the program's clear military goals, officials labored to retain what Jean Moulin, Cot's principal private secretary, described as "son caractère sportif et enthousiaste souhaité par notre jeunesse."[104] For the *Revue populaire de l'aviation*, the official organ of the Fédération Populaire des Sports Aéronautiques (F.P.S.A.), whose clubs were the nucleus of the program, the creation of pilots useful for national defense was a byproduct of their efforts, but not their overriding goal.[105]

Communists greeted the program with enthusiasm during the summer of 1936. According to police, the Communists far surpassed other parties in their efforts to support the initiative and develop a "preponderant influence" within the F.P.S.A. "Almost everywhere," the agent continued, "it was Communists who oversaw propaganda efforts and organized recruitment."[106] For Vaillant-Couturier, a vice-president of the F.P.S.A., "conquering the skies" was not simply a matter of personal liberation but a marker of human progress.[107]

Communists also endeavored to promote youth popular tourism. Since the J.C. had no structures in place to facilitate tourism in 1936, the organization initially provided information and advice about how to make vacations pleasant, affordable, and worthwhile. *L'Avant-Garde* gave its readers details about package tours to the Côte d'Azur sponsored by the recently formed Association Touristique Populaire, and the F.S.G.T. sponsored trips to Barcelona during the alternative Popular Olympics scheduled for July.[108] The newspaper encouraged young people to take advantage of alpine gatherings sponsored by the various youth hostel organizations, to which the Communists had previously paid little attention. (The Communists would affiliate with the Centre Laïque des Auberges de Jeunesse in 1937.) As the summer continued, the J.C. sponsored its own camping trips and joined with the J.S. and the J.L.R. to sponsor a low-cost youth trip to the Côte d'Azur. By staying with local fishermen, young people could visit the beautiful region for only fifteen francs a day.[109]

The J.C. did not simply encourage travel but sought to introduce young people to the new practices and conduct associated with it. *L'Avant-Garde* ran articles about camping that discussed the merits of assorted tents and sleeping bags and advised campers about selecting campsites and preparing

**Figure 9** The vibrant, mixed-sex face of the Communists' Popular Front, featured on this cover of the magazine *Regards* from 1937.

food.[110] When the seasons changed and Lagrange turned his attention to winter sports, the J.C. encouraged young people to try their luck at skiing, traditionally the preserve of a wealthy few. By buying discounted tickets, staying in youth hostels, renting skis, and taking skiing lessons from the F.S.G.T., young people could discover the excitement of racing down the mountain for two hundred francs a weekend.[111]

Communists featured vacationing youth in their publications, using them to symbolize the possibilities created by the Popular Front movement and its government. According to the communist magazine *Regards*, crowds surging through train stations in August 1936 to take advantage of the first paid vacations were mostly young men, young women, and young couples.[112] *Regards* celebrated the joyous young people who availed themselves of this precious gain over and over—on covers, on back covers, and in numerous illustrated stories. The magazine was not alone. As André Chamson wrote in the left-leaning *Vendredi* in August 1936, "If we had to give a face to the Popular Front,

Embracing the Status Quo

as artists have given one to liberty, it would be that of a young man, bronzed by the sun, muscular, used to walking and to the open air, his soul innocent and yet not naive, singing *Allons au devant de la vie*."[113] Yet for Communists, this face was not simply male. The cover of *Regards* on 8 July 1937 featured three young hikers striding happily and confidently down a country road, rucksacks on their back. Two of them were female.

**Organizing Young Women: The Union des Jeunes Filles de France** Mobilizing young women was a prime goal of the Communists' antifascist youth strategy. As Danielle Casanova explained to the J.C. Congress in March 1936 in her report on young women's organizing, the Federation of Young Communists could not call itself a mass organization without having large numbers of female members. Similarly, Young Communists could not speak of a Union of French Youth without attracting the vast majority of young women to their movement. The stakes were high, she insisted, for both the movement and French young women. If the J.C. failed, young women would fall prey to fascist demagoguery; if fascism came to power in France, women would be delivered into even worse slavery than they already faced in capitalist France.[114] Casanova made clear that Communists intended to build a mass organization for young women by pursuing a gender-specific approach to Marxist-Leninist education and political activism.

Young female militants who had distinguished themselves in the masculine world of J.C. politics during the late 1920s and early 1930s were put in charge of the effort. Casanova, a dentist in her late twenties, became secretary general. Tough, intelligent, and experienced in J.C. politics, she had joined the J.C. central committee in 1932 and attended the Sixth C.Y.I. Congress in Moscow in September 1935.[115] Jeannette Vermeersch, appointed education secretary, had made her name as a union organizer and J.C. leader in the early 1930s. She had run afoul of C.Y.I. leaders in 1933 and was, along with Raymond Guyot, hunted by police in 1934 for her role in publishing the antiwar pamphlet *Death in Peacetime*.[116] Claudine Chomat, chosen as organizational secretary, attended the Leninist School in Moscow in 1934–35 with other rising J.C. activists. Yvette Semard, next in the leadership hierarchy, had been active in the J.C. since the late 1920s. The daughter of the early P.C.F. leader Pierre Semard, she participated enthusiastically in street confrontations with fascists and police in the early 1930s.[117] These women belonged to a generation of female communist militants who came of age politically during a period of hard-line revolutionary tactics, state persecution, and tight control by Moscow. They were, to paraphrase the historian Jacqueline Tardivel, determined and devoted to the party, women whose militancy resembled that of their male comrades.[118]

These young women, along with the relatively few female militants in the J.C. rank and file, were given the task of building a single-sex organization that offered models of female activism very different from those previously available. Not surprisingly given the dramatic shift in strategy, many veteran female J.C. militants disagreed initially with the proposed shift. Marie-Claude Vaillant-Couturier, who joined the party in 1934 and became a U.J.F.F. leader in 1938, at first thought the idea absurd.[119] Yvette Semard termed it idiotic.[120] Colette Jobard described the dissatisfaction in her J.C. section: a small group of "very emancipated" young women took the decision so badly that they left the Young Communists, although temporarily as it turned out.[121] Even Maroussia Naïtchenko, then fourteen, wrote later that she rejected the strategy, which transformed a "revolutionary organization into an 'ouvroir,'" by which she meant a space where young women sewed under supervision. She continued, "I had not quit the Girl Scouts to find myself thrown out of the Young Communists and forbidden from hanging out at their local."[122] The decision had been made, however, and female militants accepted their assignment.

Although the first all-female communist youth groups appeared at the end of 1935, the Union des Jeunes Filles de France (U.J.F.F.) was officially unveiled at the J.C.'s congress in March 1936. Delegates from female groups gathered in a preparatory one-day conference to discuss the goals and shape of the organization,[123] whose name pointedly eschewed any mention of communism and highlighted the party's embrace of things French. The congress accorded special attention to the work required to win over young women. In her report, Casanova explained to the assembled the necessity of altered methods. Drawing on discussions with young women, she analyzed the J.C.'s past failure to gain a wide female following.[124] First mentioned were difficulties with parents resulting from the J.C.'s status as a mixed-sex organization, but there were a host of other practices that proved less than welcoming. Young women complained about night meetings and political agendas divorced from their interests and needs. They also objected to their treatment by male comrades: some complained about being spoken to like one of the boys, others about being slotted into menial roles as housekeepers or section treasurers, with no effort to educate or train them.[125] To convert the masses of young women to the antifascist struggle, Casanova continued, Communists had to create a gender-specific approach that educated young women in the spirit of Marxism-Leninism "by taking into account the distinctiveness, the character, and the aspirations and needs of young women." The organization planned to offer activities and formulate demands linked "to the life and even dreams of the young woman."[126] The outlines of a radically different approach to communist femininity and female activism were being traced.

The architects of the U.J.F.F. set out to build an organization that extended the changes implemented in the J.C. to a constituency believed to possess fundamentally different natures, interests, desires, and relationships to parental authority. The organization took the J.C.'s new concern for parents to an extreme, making special efforts to win the approval of parents, especially mothers. Some local circles invited mothers to participate in and even preside over meetings, while others ensured that young women were accompanied home after evening events.[127] The U.J.F.F.'s newspaper, *Jeunes filles de France*, explained that this was part of an effort to show that "the U.J.F.F. is a serious organization" that mothers could trust to educate their daughters.[128] Communists emphasized the U.J.F.F.'s role as a friendship society, even billing the organization's first congress a friendship congress. *Jeunes filles de France* explained, "Friendship and solidarity are our watchwords. We are friends above all, and if animosity sometimes exists, we will get rid of it."[129] Local groups functioned more as sanctuaries from the day's troubles than as centers of political education. According to *Jeunes filles de France*, "What is so pleasant and appealing about the U.J.F.F. is that all of us, young female manual and intellectual workers, have succeeded in forging such tight bonds of friendship that during the difficult hours of the day we long for the arrival of night and the joyful return to . . . our circle."[130]

Political education was not absent from U.J.F.F. circles and the movement's newspaper, but it was carefully crafted for a young female audience. Workplace activism was encouraged, especially in 1936. During the summer's strikes the *Jeunes filles de France* joined *L'Avant-Garde* in applauding the actions of Simone Priavoux, a fourteen-year-old who initiated and helped settle a strike in her predominantly female cardboard factory, and the paper saluted the courage of striking young saleswomen in the great department stores in Paris.[131] For the unnamed reporter, the strikers occupying the Printemps store were all the more inspirational because their frailness, fine

faces, delicate hands, and elegant movements contrasted so sharply with
the features of the rough and powerful metalworkers.[132] Trade unionism, the
article suggested, could look very different from how it had looked in the
past. Jeannette Vermeersch continued the lesson at the December congress,
where she condemned the exploitation of young female workers and roundly
denounced the inadequate enforcement of Labor Code articles pertaining
to women. The U.J.F.F., she announced, would fight for the application of
existing labor laws.[133]

U.J.F.F. leaders affirmed the notion of gender equality, even if they remained silent on the issue of women's rights, and Casanova regularly condemned fascist ideas about women. At the organization's inaugural congress,
she singled out for special ridicule passages in Hitler's *Mein Kampf* stating
that the development of young women's intelligence did not matter.[134] In
the discussion of gender equality, the Soviet Union again functioned as the
model state. As Simone Téry explained in the inaugural issue of *Jeunes filles
de France*, young Soviet women were considered the equals of young men
in every respect: they attended the same schools and universities, and they
aspired to the same jobs when finished. Since unemployment had been abol-
ished in the Soviet Union, young women were dependent on neither parents
nor young men.[135]

The U.J.F.F. took up the J.C.'s emphasis on leisure, introducing its female
members to current activities and practices. The movement and its press
encouraged young women to take up sport and exercise, and sponsored hikes
and camping trips. Like the J.C., the U.J.F.F. helped young women navigate
the codes of behavior associated with popular tourism, with the *Jeunes filles
de France* providing advice on attire for ski trips and weekends in the country.[136] There was never any question that young women should join young
men in exploring the countryside or racing down mountains. Since young
women's access to leisure and especially organized sport had been more
restricted than that of young men, U.J.F.F. positions represented an advance
of sorts.

For *Jeunes filles de France*, conquering the skies became the ultimate emancipatory activity and the female pilot the ultimate modern woman. The paper celebrated the achievements of the period's prominent female pilots,
who tended to be in their twenties and thirties, and applauded them for
overcoming material hardship and surmounting ideas about women's inferiority. The journalist Henriette Nizan explained in a cover story in 1937, "One

of the characteristics shared by female pilots, and which makes them so sympathetic, is their desire to make people forget that they are 'weak women.' They disdain the condescending tenderness that one is inclined to direct toward women. They only want to win the esteem of their peers, their fellow workers."[137] Yet whatever the achievements of celebrated airwomen such as the American Amelia Earhart or the Frenchwoman Maryse Bastié, the paper lamented that female advancement in the male worlds of commercial and military aviation remained impossible. Ending barriers against women in popular aviation sections and in flight schools was imperative.[138]

For all its emancipatory impulses, the U.J.F.F.'s approach to leisure upheld the principle of gender difference. The U.J.F.F. promoted sports thought suitable for young women, such as gymnastics and swimming, and offered night classes in sewing, knitting, cooking, and typing. More tellingly, and unlike the J.C., the U.J.F.F. designed its leisure activities with an eye toward protecting young women from immoral influences. Nodding once again toward parents, the U.J.F.F. promised in its first issue to provide "a rational organization of leisure, one which protects the young woman from immoral literary and cinematic productions which are condemned by parents and which harm the young woman's sensibility."[139] Part of this strategy, Casanova explained, meant developing "the taste for healthy and substantive reading" by making specially selected materials available to young women.[140]

Following a course advocated by Jacques Duclos, the U.J.F.F. adopted the style and idiom of the commercial women's press. In a memorable speech to the party congress in July 1936, the recently elected vice-president of the Chamber of Deputies informed delegates that Communists had not tried hard enough in the past to understand "woman's personality."[141] Love, he explained, had a particularly important place in women's lives, as did popular romances. "Who among us," he continued, "has not heard women, women of the people, become passionate about the hero of a serialized novel and talk about characters with their friends as if they were real people?"[142] For Duclos, valuable organizing lessons could be learned from the women's press. Working his way through two women's magazines, one directed toward women and the other (*La Midinette*) toward young working women, Duclos analyzed appreciatively the magazines' features and complimented them on their ability to engage with the diverse preoccupations of female readers. Those attempting to organize women would benefit, he suggested, from reading the letters to the editor in *La Midinette*. Duclos concluded this part of his speech by urging party members to follow the example set by these magazines. "Yes, women comrades, members of the Communist Party, just because you are Communists doesn't mean you shouldn't concern your-self with fashion and the questions of love and psychology which interest your sisters."[143]

Consistent with this analysis, the U.J.F.F. created a newspaper-cum-magazine that took its inspiration from the women's press, a sector which had evolved and expanded since the late 1920s.[144] In contrast to the weekly *L'Avant-Garde*, which continued to resemble the adult political dailies even as it devoted more space to leisure, sport, and mass culture, the monthly *Jeunes filles de France* resembled magazines aimed toward young women in both form and content. Slightly larger than *Marie Claire*, the hugely successful mass-market weekly introduced in March 1937, *Jeunes filles de France* simu-lated its commercial counterparts by featuring abundant photographs and regular features on the cinema, fashion, and romance. In May 1937 the pub-lication introduced a letters-to-the-editor section, enabling young women to write in with their problems or opinions as they could with other women's magazines.

The U.J.F.F.'s embrace of a youthful femininity promoted within commer-cial culture was especially apparent in the approach that *Jeunes filles de France* took to the young female body. Like the mass circulation women's magazines of the mid-1930s, *Jeunes filles de France* helped young women navigate the new practices associated with the female body and interwar notions of beauty. At a time when the use of cosmetics and sunbathing were becoming more widespread in France, *Jeunes filles de France* instructed its readers in the art of applying makeup and dispensed advice about the proper way to tan.[145] It also encouraged young women to remove hair from their arms and legs. As the paper noted cheerfully in "Always Pretty!," this demonstrated a "desire to be stylish that is not only natural but perfectly commendable."[146] In its pages, *Jeunes filles de France* cultivated the youthful, feminized approach to the body and style promoted within the commercial women's press and an emergent mass consumer culture.

*Jeunes filles de France* devoted considerable attention to affairs of the heart, inviting readers to enter contests sketching the ideal couple or to contribute their ideas about love. A representative letter printed in the regular page-two feature "Song of Love" read in part: "I'm now nineteen years old. For many

**Figure 10** The communist monthly *Jeunes filles de France* projects a new image of the Young Communist woman—modern, feminine, and stylish.

years, I have been dreaming of love. Because for me, love is not simply an accessory but the foundation of my life."[147] In their responses to these letters, the editors rarely editorialized or attempted to move young women away from romantic preoccupations. Casanova even weighed in to defend young women's dreams of perfect love against charges of naïveté: "Naïve illusions, some will say . . . those who do have never been young, have never been stirred by all that is beautiful, just, honorable. No, the young woman's dreams are a weapon in the struggle for happiness she will soon face."[148] To be sure, the occasional commentary by Henriette Nizan might gently chide young women for thinking that they could choose a husband like a commodity, with an eye to superficial characteristics such as hair color or voice.[149] Never, though, did such pieces suggest that an all-encompassing heterosexual love or the search for a husband should be anything other than the young woman's primary concern.

Embracing the Status Quo

The U.J.F.F. joined other communist publications in an effort to ensure that young women conducted their primary emotional and romantic relationships with men.[150] In "My Sighing Heart," *Jeunes filles de France* cautioned young women against forming overly intimate female friendships. They were encouraged to avoid having one close friend and to have instead many female friendships, and were instructed not to expect the impossible from their female friends.[151] As the article concluded, "There are two kinds of people in whom you should confide totally, without fear and without regret: your mother and the man you'll love. But, dear Lucette, that's no longer a question of friendship but one of love."[152]

The U.J.F.F. did not simply promote marriage but defined the dreams and ambitions of young women within the confines of marriage and motherhood. Reminders of the young woman's ultimate task abounded. Photographs of babies and mothers with children dotted the pages of *Jeunes filles de France*, with one capturing Maurice Thorez and Jeannette Vermeersch, the first couple of French communism, gazing warmly down at the cradle, doll, and baby clothes on display at the U.J.F.F.'s "Exhibition of Works by Young Women."[153] Other reminders of the young woman's mission were less subtle. The article "The Joy of Being a Mother" began, "Young women, we all dream of having a family, beautiful children, a home full of light and happiness."[154] The model young woman committed to making revolution was giving way to one who longed to be a mother for France. A similar emphasis on fatherhood was absent within the J.C.

U.J.F.F. members also proved more active campaigners on behalf of family than their male counterparts. The organization pushed the party's proposal to grant interest-free loans of five thousand francs to young married couples, and its petition demanding that the creation of a family be made possible for all left no question about the party's commitment to the French family or young women's role within it. After noting that all young people should have the financial means to start a family, the petition pointed to falling rates of marriage and birth. "Action is necessary," the petition declared. "The Union of Young French Women of France sends out this cry of alarm: the French family must be saved."[155] Adult Communists promoted the maternally inclined and reassuringly feminine *jeune fille communiste*, assigning her a symbolic position in the new strategy. On the occasion of the U.J.F.F.'s first national congress in December 1936, Vaillant-Couturier told delegates, "The young French woman is France's great hope, because she is at once the charm of today and the motherhood of tomorrow."[156] By emphasizing these young women's roles as future mothers of France, Paul Vaillant-Couturier once again affirmed the party's support for family, an issue so important to its repositioning as a mainstream political party.

Yet as Vaillant-Couturier's paean made clear, it was not simply the young communist woman's embrace of maternity that made her a political asset. To be a truly effective symbol of the party's new direction, to help inoculate the party against charges of revolutionary extremism, she had to be attractive and charming as well. During the 1920s and early 1930s, attacks on the supposedly aberrant femininity of female militants were a staple of anticommunist propaganda. For right-wing papers, the figure of the repugnant, unfeminine communist woman symbolized the destructive potential of the party and its ideology.[157] To defuse such attacks and demonstrate the party's commitment to mainstream values, Communists encouraged the young women of the U.J.F.F. to leave behind the androgynous look of the past and cultivate beauty and a "feminine" charm. As Casanova's report of March 1936 made clear, this was a guiding principle of the new organization: the U.J.F.F. had to demonstrate to parents that it would form their daughters into "young educated woman capable of taking on life and struggle but not young women whose emancipation consisted of becoming a bit tomboyish."[158] Years later Marie-Claude Vaillant-Couturier put the matter more directly. She explained that the young women of the U.J.F.F. were expected to be "coquette," or flirtatious and concerned with their appearance; this contrasted with the female J.C. militants before 1936, whom she described as more "garçonne," or cultivating a more androgynous look.[159] The extent to which the movement encouraged and valued physical attractiveness and charm was highlighted by the first verse of the U.J.F.F.'s official song, "Chantons, jeunes filles!" Composed by the eminent communist cultural figure Léon Moussinac, it began: "When we're walking along the paths / Everybody hand in hand / Welcoming the new seasons / We laugh knowing we're pretty."[160]

A style of female political activism consonant with the new emphasis on femininity became imperative. This style was crafted in opposition to that of the young communist woman of the 1920s, who was encouraged to ignore gender difference, and that of the older feminist woman, who was portrayed as difficult and disagreeable. The Popular Front jeune fille communiste would be a subtle blend of charm and determination. As Casanova explained, "In fighting for a happy life, Young Communist women resemble neither harsh and cantankerous women nor tomboys. They are involved in politics and they retain their charm, but their faces express the determination of a youth committed to change."[161] This melding of attractiveness and determination would come first through avoiding political activism that was too closely associated with female disorderliness. One of Casanova's first recommendations was to desist from selling newspapers in the streets.[162] An activity that placed young women in the streets and had the potential to result in arrests or violence violated the organization's ideas of acceptable female political activism and contributed to the notion that Communists were frightening and beyond the pale, and had to be curtailed. No such prohibition was ever implemented in the rival J.O.C.F.

Communists also shaped their Popular Front model of female activism by sponsoring activities and campaigns that resembled those traditionally associated with mainstream women's organizations and the J.O.C.F. The provision of social assistance to the needy quickly became one of the organization's principal activities. In this endeavor the organization concentrated mostly on aiding young people, although it also assisted neighborhood families. U.J.F.F. members collected and distributed gifts to young women confined to sanatoria; knitted and sewed for local families hit by unemployment; and sponsored fund-raising efforts to aid the disadvantaged of all ages. The tone of the work is evident from an announcement of a U.J.F.F. campaign on behalf of unemployed youth: "We will participate with all our heart and all our strength by organizing teas for young women who are out of work, collections of clothes where we'll distribute woolens, and home visits to all those unemployed youth who are ineligible for unemployment insurance and to whom we bring our support and all our friendship."[163] The U.J.F.F. thus rooted its activism in notions of women's distinct natures and special nurturing qualities, their "deep-seated need to soothe the distress and misery of the most unfortunate."[164] Since this approach differed little from that undertaken by the J.O.C.F., the U.J.F.F. had to fend off criticism that its work among the needy was nothing more than philanthropy. The U.J.F.F. defended its actions by asserting that such work was necessary to "bring together all its forces, without losing a single one, in order to move ever more numerous down the path to the complete emancipation of youth."[165]

Since the models of femininity and female political activism being forged within the U.J.F.F. were designed to underscore the party's transformed relationship to French politics and society, they were featured during the massive demonstrations of the summer of 1936. As Julian Jackson and others have shown, the size, mood, and geography of Parisian street demonstrations

**206**   shifted between February 1934 and the summer of 1936.[166] Those immediately following the election victory of 1936 and the strike movement in May–June of the same year tended to be bigger, less combative, more celebratory, and more spatially confident, often extending beyond the traditional confines of working-class neighborhoods to the center of the city. They were the demonstrations of a vast popular movement whose leaders controlled the levers of political power. They were also more broadly representative, with women, children, and young women appearing in larger numbers than before.

Communists used these demonstrations to prove their allegiance to French Republican traditions, their support for mainstream values, and their altered conceptions of youth and young femininity. Indications of the uses to which the refeminized young women of the U.J.F.F. could be put came in the coverage by *L'Humanité* of the march on 24 May 1936 to the Mur des Fédérés at Père Lachaise cemetery in Paris, the first left demonstration since the electoral victory. After remarking on the unbounded enthusiasm, joy, and ardor of the many "revolutionary youth," the reporter singled out the jeunes filles communistes, noting "their magnificent appearance and their determination to fight which did not preclude, to the contrary, their charm and grace." They were "the very image of French youth."[167]

The young women of the U.J.F.F. were assigned a more carefully considered role in the great demonstration of 14 July 1936. During this massive and well-choreographed demonstration, referred to by Jackson as the apotheosis of the Popular Front,[168] communist leaders marched in tricolor sashes while militants often followed in revolutionary or regional costume. In this political pageant of unprecedented proportions, the young women of the U.J.F.F. were dressed and positioned to convey delicacy, even purity. They appeared not in the red, white, and blue of 1789 but in white, the color of purity. To heighten the impression, the U.J.F.F. contingent began with two trucks draped in flowers and filled with young women in three-quarter-length white dresses. The organization's lead groups did not march through the streets but were carried above them. The prominent front-page treatment of les jeunes filles communistes by *L'Avant-Garde* emphasized their elegance and smiling faces, placing them in the context of the Communists' embrace of the nation and the Republican army. When the communist youth contingent passed under a balcony on which an army captain had appeared, the paper wrote, the young women serenaded him with the French revolutionary hymn *La Marseillaise*. This moved the captain to tears and prompted

Le char fleuri des jeunes filles communistes de la Banlieue-Ouest souleva sur tout le parcours des ovations enthousiastes

# Au long du joyeux cortège de la jeunesse

**Figure 11** Members of the Union des Jeunes Filles de France dressed in white and carried through the streets during the giant demonstration of 14 July 1936. *L'Avant-Garde*, 18 July 1936, 1.

him to blow kisses in the young women's direction. Some of the young women clenched their fists in the antifascist salute, but the large front-page photograph in *L'Avant-Garde* made it appear a rather halfhearted gesture.[169] Both the iconography and the reality of Young Communist female militancy had traveled a long way since the 1920s and early 1930s.

Communist antifascist youth politics had evolved considerably since their beginnings in 1933. From an approach that privileged revolutionary political struggle and violence and was resolutely male, Communists adopted one that abandoned revolutionary politics in favor of support for the Third Republic, national defense, the family, and more conventional notions of femininity. The new approach downplayed youth political activism and emphasized the provision of leisure and culture. Popular Front antifascist youth politics was determinedly mixed-sex, its key representations foregrounding young couples striding arm in arm and attractive young women supporting the cause.

The transformation of communist youth politics outlined in this chapter brought a new role for the J.C. and its militants in communist politics. Any possibility of a leading position in French communist politics was quashed once and for all, and communist youth became increasingly important as political symbols, not political actors. In the context of democratic electoral politics, however, the new look proved a winning formula. J.C. membership reached 100,000 in the fall of 1936. The U.J.F.F. also grew quickly, nearing the 11,000 mark by December 1936 and 20,000 a year later. French Communists had demonstrated that they could mobilize large numbers of French youth in the antifascist struggle, their successes among the young both furthering and reflecting the party's transformation into a mass party.

7

**Refusing *la main tendue***

Catholics, the J.O.C., and the Challenge

of Communist Popular Front Politics

The Communists' Popular Front successes greatly intensified Catholic concerns over the communist threat. Anxiety was pronounced in Rome, where Pope Pius XI warned frequently of the dangers of communism. In France, the Holy Father feared, lay Catholics and even clerics were insufficiently vigilant against a force now disavowing revolution, professing support for religion, and multiplying calls for joint action around humanitarian goals.[1] Fears of communist advances increased markedly after the municipal elections of May 1935 and reached new heights in 1936. During the months preceding the legislative elections in the spring of 1936, French clerics denounced the Popular Front coalition repeatedly from pulpits and in the pages of Catholic publications, instructing the faithful to vote against the dangerous bloc. When the left coalition emerged victorious, Catholics exhibited special concern over the surge in communist support, with *La Croix* underlining the need to redouble all aspects of apostolic and propaganda work.[2] The situation deteriorated further with the strike movement of May and June, which Catholic leaders viewed as Communist-led and tending to push workers toward "an attempted Communist political revolution."[3]

Youth was again at the front of clerical anxieties, analyses, and responses. Leading clerics realized that Communists were directing special efforts toward Catholic youth and their organizations.[4] Even worse, socialism, with communism as its most dangerous form, and the Soviet Union were believed to exert "a singular attraction" on youth.[5] Younger members of the clergy were not immune, some worrying their more conservative elders by professing support for communism in public and private. Special attention had to be devoted to young people, especially the young workers most systematically targeted by Communists. As clerics well knew, Young Communists had begun their overtures to J.O.C. militants long before the party leader Maurice

Thorez reached out to Catholics during the electoral campaign of 1936, and they now directed their appeals to young workers of both sexes.

The J.O.C. and its female counterpart, the J.O.C.F., took center stage in Catholic responses to the heightened communist threat of the Popular Front period. For one cleric writing in 1936, the J.O.C. was "the best defense against Communist penetration of working-class circles."[6] Although Pope Pius XI had long been a staunch supporter of the pioneering Catholic Action movement, the majority of French clerics and lay people proved slower to accept it. But the strike movement of May–June 1936 pushed both the J.O.C. and the J.O.C.F. to the forefront of French Catholic consciousness and action. Because Catholic trade unionism had such a weak foothold in industrial France, the youthful militants of the J.O.C. and J.O.C.F. became the main line of Catholic defense at a time when many Catholics were convinced that France teetered on the edge of revolution. When Catholics seized the propaganda opportunities offered by the World's Fair in Paris the following summer, they focused special attention on the J.O.C.'s Tenth Anniversary Congress held over three days in July. Meticulously organized and carefully choreographed, the congress blended strategies from mass politics of the 1930s with variations on more traditional forms of religious pageantry. The largest such gathering of the Fair, it became the symbolic high point of Catholic responses to communism and the Popular Front, demonstrating Catholic skill in placing youth at the service of the church's political goals.

### Forging a Public Role in the Context of Economic Crisis

Those guiding the J.O.C. in the 1930s worked out their organizing strategies against the backdrop of clerical aspirations, economic crisis, and ever-shifting politics. At the beginning of the decade movement leaders experimented with methods to stimulate action by the J.O.C. and create a compelling ideal and public identity. They initially emphasized spiritual and moral efforts, which were cast in revolutionary terms that recalled formulations then current among young intellectuals. As historians have stressed, 1930 marked an important dividing line in interwar French intellectual and cultural history. With the dawn of the new decade, the optimism that marked the 1920s gave way to pessimism about the vitality and even viability of France's economic and political structures.[7] As unemployment rose and industrial output declined, as the Republic faltered, and as international tensions brought fears of war, it was easy to believe that France was entering a period of crisis. Pessimism was particularly pronounced among young intellectuals, who called for radical solutions outside the parameters of mainstream politics. Writing in a range of journals, including *La Revue française*, *Esprit*, *Plans*, and *Ordre nouveau*, they sketched the contours of revolutionary programs promising complete reconstruction of a world that appeared to be crumbling around them.[8] These programs, which were often based on ideas congenial to the political right, aimed to transform not merely economic and political structures but man himself.[9]

The J.O.C.'s revolutionary rhetoric of the early 1930s, doubtless the product of the young clerics animating the movement, reflected these intellectual currents. After the first J.O.C. National Congress in the fall of 1930, *La Jeunesse Ouvrière* announced in a front-page article entitled "Everything Is Possible for Those Who Believe" that five thousand French Jocists had taken a "magnificent oath" to change "this unnatural civilization."[10] They were united in demanding that their dignity as men and as Christians be respected. Using a term often invoked by young intellectuals, the Jocists demanded respect for the human dignity (*personne humaine*) of the young worker, which had been destroyed by materialists and by those who were Christian in name only. The following summer, *La Jeunesse Ouvrière* promised "a magnificent revolution . . . one much more profound than any economic and political transformation."[11] This was to be a peaceful revolution that began with youth and infused Christian moral and spiritual values throughout French society. But the revolution could not be achieved by the thirteen- and fourteen-year-olds first targeted in the 1920s, and J.O.C. leaders increasingly set their sights on young workers between the ages of seventeen and twenty-one.[12] In August 1931 the smiling apprentice disappeared from the top of the front page of *La Jeunesse Ouvrière*.

The revolutionary task assigned to Jocists was an extremely difficult one, not least because of the longstanding suspicion and hostility toward the church among workers. Although some militants embraced their apostolic mission enthusiastically, youth leaders and chaplains voiced concerns over the J.O.C.'s ability to shape its charges into apostles capable of winning over the masses of young workers and refiguring them for Christ and Catholicism. Part of the problem, it was said, stemmed from inadequate education. A report prepared for the National Council meeting of 1931 found that two-thirds of J.O.C. sections and five-sixths of J.O.C. militants had not had a proper Jocist formation.[13] Three years later a chaplain from southeastern France estimated that only three of his section's ten militants had been fundamentally influenced by the J.O.C. and its ideal,[14] a success rate that was a serious impediment to the movement's missionary goals. How could Jocists be asked to "return their brothers to Christianity" if they were not passionate about the Christian life and ideal? Other chaplains were more realistic about the immensity of the challenge they were asking young workers to take on. As one conceded, the work was hard and depressing, and those J.O.C. militants who attempted to bring the J.O.C.'s message and values into the workplace often met with resistance and ridicule.[15] Jocists were mocked when they attempted to spread the organization's message of purity and respect for young female workers, and some were attacked physically for tearing up obscene posters in the workplace.[16]

The economic crisis of the 1930s provided the J.O.C. with an opportunity to undertake social action in a manner that helped recast its position in working-class neighborhoods and French youth politics. The impetus appears to have come from Father Guérin, the movement's founder and effective head. When unemployment took serious hold in France, Guérin identified joblessness as the most important test facing young workers.[17] For Guérin the moral hazards of prolonged unemployment were particularly worrisome. Like any great test, this one would result in either moral victory or defeat.[18] Many unemployed youth, he believed, were already becoming "demoralized," by which he certainly meant that they were sliding toward immoral behavior and becoming discouraged.

Moral concerns were relegated to the background when the J.O.C. began to respond in earnest to youth unemployment in 1932. The most important early initiative was the establishment of the youth unemployment center in Paris, a city where the problem was especially serious. Here the J.O.C. attempted to respond to the diverse needs of unemployed young workers by providing concrete material and moral assistance. The center served free hot meals (an estimated fifteen thousand in 1933),[19] provided unemployed youth with a place to spend their considerable spare time, and offered facilities for doing laundry, washing, showering, and shaving. It even provided temporary lodging for a small number of homeless youth. The J.O.C. combined this assistance, which Communists whose activities predated the Popular Front derided as charity, with basic training in employable skills such as woodworking or electrical work. The J.O.C. also endeavored to find work for unemployed youth, placing six hundred of the five thousand jeunes chômeurs who had come through the center's doors in 1933.[20]

The energy expended at the Paris center in 1932 and 1933 was significant in the context of the J.O.C.'s resources, and the organization shifted more responsibility to sections and federations in 1933.[21] Aiding the young unemployed became an increasingly national effort. In 1933 J.O.C. centers placed 97 young workers in Reims (where the J.O.C. was recognized as an official placement center by the government), 88 in Lille, 60 in Nancy, 127 in Rouen, 150 in Lyon, and 370 in southeast Paris.[22] Providing tangible assistance to young workers remained a cornerstone of J.O.C. activities throughout the 1930s.

The J.O.C. also gave its members a framework for understanding and combating the crisis. If the J.C. drew on economic analyses mapped out in Moscow, the J.O.C. looked to Catholic social doctrine emanating from Rome, especially the papal encyclical *Quadragesimo Anno: Reconstructing the Social Order* (1931). This encyclical, which reaffirmed and updated Leo XIII's *Rerum Novarum* (1891), charted a Catholic path between socialism (including communism) and economic liberalism, the consequences of which Pius XI decried. Writers in *La Jeunesse Ouvrière* condemned the impact of economic liberalism and unregulated competition on workers, explaining that workers paid the price in lost jobs and wages when industrialists attempted to raise output and cut production costs to compete in global markets.[23] To counter the effects of the crisis, the J.O.C. planned to support working-class organizations that sought to implement the pope's goal of placing economic life under the law of a "true and effective guiding principle." At the National Council in 1933, youth leaders for the first time seriously discussed the possibility of collaborating with the Catholic trade union movement, the Confédération Française des Travailleurs Chrétiens (C.F.T.C.).[24]

Demanding government action on youth unemployment became a priority for the J.O.C. As a report of the International Labor Office (I.L.O.) on youth unemployment illustrated in 1935, French authorities were doing little to confront the problem. Unlike most other industrialized countries, France did not collect statistics on the age breakdown of the unemployed, and French officials did not create public works programs geared toward young people.[25] The measures that were taken proved tentative and ineffective. Despite attempts in early 1933 to compel unemployed youth to attend vocational courses, the number of young people doing so actually fell that year.[26] Moreover, the bill to raise the school-leaving age to fourteen introduced in 1932, which would have brought France into compliance with international labor conventions adopted in 1919, was stalled in the Senate.

Beginning in 1933 the J.O.C. endeavored to prod the government toward action, sending a formal list of demands to the ministry of labor. The program, parts of which the J.C. would adopt in 1935, was far-reaching, especially when contrasted with earlier J.O.C. initiatives. It called for an extension of mandatory schooling until the age of sixteen; educational reforms to facilitate professional formation; the safeguarding of apprenticeship; respect for the eight-hour day; free health care for unemployed youth; unemployment benefits for conscripts once they finished their military service; and half-price fares on trains and local urban transport for those looking for work.[27] In line with social Catholic attitudes toward women's work, the J.O.C. protested against replacing young men with cheaper female workers.

The J.O.C. also aimed to raise public awareness of the challenges facing unemployed young workers. In *Le jeune chômeur*, Jocists complained that the French press was paying no attention to the problems of homeless unemployed youth, instead devoting considerable attention to the adventures of young Americans who rode the rails during the Depression. Meanwhile in France, as noted in the short-lived supplement to *La Jeunesse Ouvrière*, police were arresting homeless youth, as they had done in a roundup of two hundred in the second half of May 1933.[28] Twenty-five of those, Jocist writers claimed, were regular visitors to the J.O.C.'s youth unemployment center.

The most sustained effort to draw attention to the lot of unemployed youth was made in the pamphlet *Youth Unemployment* (1934), which began as a study by the Jocist Committee for Mutual Aid for Unemployed Youth of the Paris Region.[29] The pamphlet described the international and national dimensions of the problem and detailed its consequences for youth. Although its authors conceded that France was among the industrialized countries least affected by unemployment, they argued that the situation in the Paris region was roughly equivalent to that in Germany, the United States, and Britain, where the Depression had hit harder. In the capital young workers constituted the "great mass" of the unemployed.[30] Unemployment led to a weakening of intellectual and physical energies, boredom, fear, familial tensions (especially when the young person could no longer contribute a much-needed salary to the family budget), and insufficient professional development. Consistent with the J.O.C.'s earlier emphasis on training, the pamphlet's authors fretted over the long-term consequences of accepting any job on offer, whatever the possibility of acquiring skills. They also fought the notion that the jobless young were lazy and thriftless. As was explained on the pamphlet's opening page, someone who looked like a vagrant might have knocked on the doors of fifty factories in one day looking for work.[31]

Refusing *la main tendue*

The issue of youth unemployment was well suited to the J.O.C.'s attempt to present itself as the movement most strongly dedicated to defending and supporting young workers, for it allowed the J.O.C. to put Christian teachings at the service of worker youth. Memoirs and archival records provide evidence of the unemployment campaign's success in bringing new recruits to the movement and altering perceptions among young workers. Many members spoke of their gratitude for the J.O.C.'s job placement program, with one explaining, "If the J.O.C. had not found me a job, the very day the crisis threw me into the streets, I don't think I would be here among you."[32] As chaplains and youth leaders realized, job placement did not simply lead to individual gratitude but also raised the J.O.C.'s profile. A chaplain explained in 1934 how the section president had gained considerable influence by working tirelessly to find jobs for Jocists in his parish, which had been hit badly by unemployment.[33] The young man had himself been drawn to the J.O.C. because of its job placement, a fact he made sure to point out in his recruiting efforts. Even unsuccessful bids to place young workers led to new appreciation of the J.O.C.[34] The entire undertaking contrasted sharply with earlier religious and moralizing initiatives, which had distanced Jocists from ordinary young workers.

Other out-of-work youth reported that the friendship and activities offered by the J.O.C. exerted a similarly powerful attraction. The experience of André Villette, the son of a worker who voted socialist, was one such case. After completing his certificate of primary studies and receiving his school teaching certificate in 1933, Villette was unable to find work for nine months. During this difficult period he was approached by J.O.C. militants, who told him about the organization and its services. The movement welcomed him into its fold and provided activities that structured his days. It was, he remembered later, a lifesaver.[35] Villette rose through the ranks to become national secretary in 1938. Eugène Descamps, whose father and grandfather both belonged to the C.G.T., likewise spent his days in the mid-1930s learning new skills at the J.O.C. youth center.[36]

The unemployment campaign further allowed the J.O.C. to engage publicly and even politically in a manner acceptable to the church. As a Catholic Action movement firmly under the jurisdiction of church officials, the J.O.C. was commanded to remain outside and above political action and focus its efforts solely on spiritual, moral, and social issues. Individual militants were informed in no uncertain terms that they could not combine membership in the J.O.C. with membership in a political party or organization.[37] But in the Catholic universe, the line separating "social" activism from "political" activism was a fluid one, which varied according to the activists' political sympathies and class positions. While it was acceptable for the Catholic Action men's movement to promote obviously political issues such as family allowances in cooperation with parties on the center and right, cooperation with parties on the far right and especially the far left was forbidden. And although Catholic support for far-right leagues had bedeviled the church since the papal condemnation of Action Française in 1926, there is little doubt that explicit support for the far right was treated much more leniently, especially as fears of communism escalated in the mid-1930s. Within the J.O.C., the real problem, the *gaffe mortelle*, was collaboration with the Marxist left.[38] Given these realities, youth unemployment was an ideal issue: it permitted the J.O.C. to critique the existing economic order and act on behalf of working-class youth in the public and political realms, while still remaining independent from political parties and organizations on the Marxist left.

**The Challenge of Popular Front Politics and the Communist *main tendue*** The prohibition on "political" action within the J.O.C. did not pose particular problems for the movement before 1934, when attempts to effect change outside the channels of established political parties were popular and united action on the working-class left seemed little more than a chimera. But events in February 1934 initiated a process that altered the political landscape and created new pressures on the J.O.C. to justify its refusal to engage in the political battles of the day. After the street violence and demonstrations of February 1934, French political life became increasingly split between the antifascist left and the right, and those who had previously worked outside traditional party structures were pressured to take their place in one camp or the other.[39] Even the tiny groups of left Christians who sought to reconcile Christianity with socialism and communism set aside their differences in the embrace of antifascism and the desire to create a united Christian revolutionary left.[40] A nonaligned stance became more difficult to defend.

The J.O.C. was not immune to these pressures. The first issue of *La Jeunesse Ouvrière* published after the February days ran a front-page editorial beginning with the acknowledgment that after seeing fights, police charges, men being thrown to the ground, and pools of blood, some Jocists wondered

whether the J.O.C. should become involved.[41] The editorial emphatically **217**
rejected such a course of action, proclaiming that the J.O.C. "has nothing
to do with that." The piece went on to explain the J.O.C.'s refusal to engage
politically, introducing themes that would be developed as calls for political
engagement mounted in the coming years. Politics was, above all, inappropriate to the young worker's age and development, since youth was a time
for developing skills as a worker, activist, and Christian citizen. The editorial reminded readers that Jocists had their own task of spreading Christ's
message of purity, justice, and fraternity; this was as important as any political battle. To charges that France was in danger of falling to fascism or
communism, the paper asserted its belief in the essential irrelevance of the
political system. Regardless of the form of government, France would need
courageous men and devoted leaders.

The J.O.C. stepped up its work on behalf of unemployed youth in 1935, in
part to demonstrate the efficacy of its nonaligned stance. At the very moment when French unemployment was reaching its highest levels during the
1930s, the J.O.C. sharpened its rhetoric and calls for reform. In a front-page
article in January, *La Jeunesse Ouvrière* surveyed the damage caused by the
Depression and argued that the lot of the working class was worsening with
each passing day.[42] The need for reform was urgently clear, and J.O.C. writers
reiterated their call for establishing a just and effective guiding principle for
the economy. In the meantime, Jocists redoubled their efforts to represent
les jeunes chômeurs in the public sphere. At the end of January the J.O.C.
brought its case to the government, sending a delegation to meet with officials in the office of the head of government, where they were promised
that the problem would receive serious consideration.[43] And so it did. On 8
February the French minister of labor informed the Chamber of Deputies
that the government would use all its influence to bring about rapid adoption
by the Senate of a bill raising the school-leaving age to fourteen.[44]

The J.O.C.'s most ambitious initiative to represent jeunes chômeurs in the
political arena came in the form of a petition drive to the I.L.O. in Geneva
in June 1935. Working in conjunction with Catholic trade unions, J.O.C. organizations from France, Belgium, Holland, Switzerland, Luxembourg, and
Czechoslovakia would present the grievances of unemployed young workers to the body. The campaign, which marked the J.O.C.'s first significant
international collaboration, absorbed the energies of J.O.C. militants at the
very moment when Communists were intensifying their appeals to youth in
the run-up to the municipal elections. Jocists collected signatures from the

Refusing *la main tendue*

unemployed between the ages of fourteen and twenty-five, taking special care to draw in returning soldiers, whose unconditional right to unemployment benefits the J.O.C. strongly upheld. To publicize their efforts, J.O.C. militants put up an impressive quantity of posters (9,000 in three weeks of February alone), distributed numerous tracts (120,000 were handed out in Paris, Marseille, and Lille by the end of February), and hawked issues of *La Jeunesse Ouvrière* featuring news of the campaign. The issue of the biweekly dated 15 February quickly sold out of its initial print run of 97,000 copies and went to a second printing.[45]

That the campaign found support among French young workers is suggested by the J.C.'s response. In February 1935 the organization announced that it was joining the effort, making clear that it hoped to transform the entire exercise into a communist-led united front campaign that would send a single youth delegation to Geneva. In explaining their decision, J.C. leaders indicated that they held out no hope of substantive results. The I.L.O. was nothing more than "an organism of class collaboration" whose recommendations carried no real weight among governments.[46] Nevertheless, the J.C. called on all French young people to aid the petition drive and ensure that the legitimate demands of unemployed youth were heard in Geneva.[47] The J.O.C. firmly refused the J.C. offers of "assistance."

The Young Communists' attempts to co-opt the J.O.C.'s petition drive and engage J.O.C. sections in joint action with local committees of the unemployed[48] brought the two youth organizations into their sharpest conflict to date. In early March J.O.C. leaders lashed out at the J.C., arguing that the Young Communists' decision to join the Jocist petition drive and adopt the movement's program only confirmed the deficiencies of the J.C.'s vision and the incompetence of its leaders.[49] Only the J.O.C. and its leaders were capable of resolving the problems of wage-earning young people. If the J.C. took its argument to its logical conclusion, *La Jeunesse Ouvrière* continued, it would ask all young workers to join the J.O.C. The movement's leaders also bitterly protested the J.C.'s defacing of their posters. *La Jeunesse Ouvrière* estimated that half had been either torn down completely or had their J.O.C. insignia replaced with an advertisement for a J.C. meeting.[50] As spring continued, J.O.C. leaders ratcheted up their attacks on the Young Communists and on youth involvement in adult party politics. According to J.O.C. leaders writing in March, the J.C. was engaged in nothing more than "empty political agitation," which contrasted with the J.O.C.'s focus on aiding young workers concretely. As the J.O.C. took to saying, "J.O.C. militants are not sterile agitators, they are realizers." Soon there was an even sharper attack: Communists were not trying to help young workers, but simply using them for the adult party's political purposes.[51]

By the time the petition was delivered to the I.L.O. communist successes in the municipal and regional council elections of 1935 had imbued the J.O.C.'s campaign with new significance for influential clerics. Catholics experienced the May elections as a rude awakening, with *La Croix* concluding its front-page editorial on 14 May, "The Communist Advance," by cautioning that the elections had to be taken as "a serious warning." The piece ended on a belligerent note, calling for the formation of a "united anti-revolutionary front" to "repel the fearsome assault that will be carried out with unprecedented fervor and defend our French Christian civilization."[52]

The J.O.C. was assigned a front-line role in the antirevolutionary response. The movement's petition drive received prominent, laudatory coverage in *La Croix*. A centrally positioned front-page photograph captured young male Catholic workers marching through the streets of Geneva beneath banners reading "We are young and already we have no hope!" Articles described Jocists presenting a petition with 85,000 signatures to officials at the I.L.O. and the accompanying address of the French Jocist Alfred Quirin. For what was very likely the first time in a country rigidly stratified along class lines, bourgeois French Catholics heard the voice of an unemployed young worker: "Fear of life overwhelms us. You will never know all the sorrows that break the hearts of young people facing persistent unemployment."[53] *La Croix* deemed the petition campaign "a great spiritual offensive" and "a magnificent effort." With it, the J.O.C. "demonstrated brilliantly the power of its organization and the conquering conviction of its militants."[54]

The petition drive proved a public relations success for the J.O.C. The I.L.O. voted ninety-six to seventeen to study the question of youth unemployment without delay. More importantly, the I.L.O. report *Unemployment among Young Persons*, published later that year, highlighted the significance of the J.O.C.'s efforts in France. Indeed, J.O.C. measures on behalf of unemployed youth received roughly the same amount of coverage as those taken by governments in France. The J.O.C., the report noted, had done "all in its power to assist unemployed youth of both sexes."[55]

By June 1935 the J.O.C. had emerged as a markedly different organization from the one opening the decade. Through its two-pronged strategy of assisting young workers and defending them in the public arena, it had established itself as the largest movement of young workers in France, one whose newspaper had a circulation of ninety thousand and whose campaigns were imitated and appropriated by the Young Communists. Moreover, the focus on social and economic action was altering the balance between clerical and youth responsibilities. The more the J.O.C. defended and assisted young workers, the more religious action and formation receded into the background. One chaplain reported in 1934 that although he used to mention religion at section committee meetings, he no longer did. There was simply too much to do.[56] The relationship between militants and their chaplains was further affected by the aging of J.O.C. leaders. The two militants who led the J.O.C. delegation to Geneva, Paul Bacon and Paul Hibout, were in their late twenties. This made them roughly the same age as a priest such as abbé Godin, who arrived at J.O.C. national headquarters in the eleventh arrondissement of Paris in 1935 and played a powerful part in the movement for the remainder of the decade.[57]

Despite the J.O.C.'s enhanced stature, the movement faced fresh challenges as it tried to steer an independent path. Part of the difficulty stemmed from the Popular Front's heightened dynamism and popular support. After the unveiling of the Popular Front and its youth coalition on 14 July 1935, *La Jeunesse Ouvrière* issued its strongest defense yet of the J.O.C.'s refusal to accept communist offers of united action. The J.O.C. believed that it had nothing to gain from political action, and this was amply demonstrated by J.C. borrowings from its program.[58]

The J.O.C. also contended with new communist appeals to Catholics. In the summer of 1935 *L'Avant-Garde* condemned the persecution of Catholics in Nazi Germany and offered Young Communists as allies in the struggle to defend religious liberties.[59] By the fall and winter of 1935–36 Communists young and old pushed joint action on behalf of the poor. Determined to break the "bourgeois monopoly on charity," communist mayors encouraged cooperation with Catholics in campaigns to aid the needy in Paris suburbs. Despite longstanding tensions between Catholics and Communists, isolated clerics and lay people accepted these offers and joined the committees to aid the unemployed that began to emerge. In Ivry, the electoral seat of Maurice Thorez, the parish priest Father Lorenzo became vice-president of the local committee and encouraged his parishioners to support the effort.[60] Young Communists reached out to their Catholic counterparts by adopting strategies long employed by Jocists. They urged J.O.C. sections to join them in collecting money, food, and overcoats, and illustrated their appeals with a drawing of a young male worker done in the J.O.C.'s graphic style.[61] Young

Communists also embraced the gendered division of labor long evident in Catholic charitable assistance, encouraging young women to knit for children and mend used clothes.[62] Jocists were instructed to have nothing to do with these efforts.

The J.O.C.'s desire to keep its militants away from Popular Front initiatives was complicated by the actions of left Christians associated with the revue *Terre nouvelle* (New Land) and the group Socialist Christian Youth. As we saw, the heightened concern over fascism after February 1934 had compelled the small number of Christians associated with the Union of Christian Socialists and the Union of Spiritualist Communists to put aside their differences in the cause of united antifascism. By mid-1935 these groups were marching in Popular Front demonstrations under the name Socialist Christian Youth and publishing *Terre nouvelle: organe des chrétiens révolutionnaires* monthly.[63] Although the number of Protestants and Catholics involved was small, *Terre nouvelle* moved quickly to print runs of fifteen thousand.

*Terre nouvelle* testified to the group's attempt to meld Christian and socialist ideals into an explicitly political program. Its striking and controversial cover was dominated by a hammer and sickle superimposed over a large red cross, which was in turn set against a map of the northern hemisphere featuring a red France and Soviet Union. The group's manifesto, which appeared in each issue, outlined the publication's principles and beliefs.[64] It staunchly opposed capitalism, assailing it with arguments that resembled those found in social Catholic doctrine and in the J.O.C.'s own literature. *Terre nouvelle* strongly criticized an unregulated economic order which was based on competition and profit and which glorified wealth while disdaining the worker. It called for an economic system that respected the dignity of human beings, permitted them to achieve their spiritual destiny, and organized production and work in relation to the needs of all. But unlike J.O.C. leaders, those writing in *Terre nouvelle* argued passionately for the importance of left political engagement, while also taking the Protestant and Catholic churches to task for supporting capitalism. France was divided into two blocs, the "bourgeois and capitalist oligarchy and its mercenaries and dupes" and "the working classes, worker and peasant," who had to be joined by the middle class; it was necessary to take a side.[65] Those at *Terre nouvelle* joined forces with the second bloc, whose ultimate goal was socialist revolution.

*Terre nouvelle*, whose contributors included abbé Boulier, the author of the J.O.C.'s first major pamphlet *Call of the J.O.C.*, targeted Jocists specifically, and its youth page was run by two former Jocists, Camille Val and François

Houllé. In May 1935 it urged Jocists to take a stand in favor of socialism and the Popular Front. Dismissing the J.O.C.'s claim to be "on neither the right nor the left," *Terre nouvelle* argued that "Jocists are citizens and must act as such; they must, for example, vote according to their consciences, their ideal, and their interests as workers."[66] Although it is impossible to know how many Jocists followed Val and Houllé to the Young Socialist Christians, the J.O.C. took the threat seriously enough to issue a front-page warning against *Terre nouvelle* in the issue of *La Jeunesse Ouvrière* of 15 May.[67]

By 1936 J.O.C. militants thus faced considerable pressure to abandon the movement's stance of political independence and take their place in the Popular Front youth coalition alongside Young Communists, Young Socialists, and Young Socialist Christians. The hotly contested legislative elections in the spring only intensified the allure of political engagement. An incident described by the J.O.C. secretary general Fernand Bouxom suggested the seriousness of the challenge. In Bouxom's local section in Moulins-Lille, seven Jocists had asked his permission to leave the J.O.C. to work for a political organization popular at the time. Although Bouxom persuaded them to stay, others deserted the J.O.C. to participate in the election campaign and the political struggles of the moment.[68] J.O.C. leaders intensified their attacks on politics and insisted on the superiority of the movement's program of assisting, defending, and educating young workers. Political action was sterile, the J.O.C. argued, providing nothing of value to young workers. The contrast between the J.O.C.'s and the J.C.'s approaches was captured by the J.O.C. banner: "An overcoat is much warmer than a speech."[69]

The J.O.C. also intensified its own public activism, which was deeply politicized even if disconnected from party politics. In March 1936, as their communist youth counterparts geared up for the national legislative campaign, the J.O.C. launched a massive propaganda campaign on behalf of wage-earning youth. In an effort to push government officials to action on the problems of working youth, the J.O.C. sent its militants into the streets to put up 10,000 posters, distribute 200,000 tracts, and sell as many copies of *La Jeunesse Ouvrière* as possible. Officials had to realize, as Bouxom proclaimed in a front-page editorial, that "the most pressing duty of the day" was to come to the aid of the young worker who "seems to no longer have a right to a normal life." The article ended: "Youth must be saved if a better future is to be built."[70]

As much as J.O.C. leaders touted the virtues of political independence, they realized that adult allies were necessary. For the J.O.C. the logical and permissible ally was the Catholic trade union movement, the C.F.T.C. Ties between the J.O.C. and the C.F.T.C. had expanded as the youth movement embraced social and economic action, with J.O.C. leaders seriously discussing the role the J.O.C. might play in Catholic trade unionism at the National Council meeting of 1933. Father Guérin was again prominent, intervening to argue that each J.O.C. federation should have a youth leader responsible for trade union work; indeed, Jocists should become trade union leaders.[71] In the following year J.O.C. federations endeavored to establish contacts with local Catholic trade unions.[72] Cooperation increased further in 1935, when the C.F.T.C. and the J.O.C. combined forces on the petition drive to Geneva and J.O.C. militants were active in trade union protests at Saint-Chamond in the fall.[73] Collaboration continued in the first half of 1936. By early that year some Jocists had moved over to full-time work in the C.F.T.C.; in April the regional congress of the Catholic labor federation in the heavily Catholic department of the Nord made a special point of saluting the increased number of militants among former Jocists.[74] The influx of Jocists to the C.F.T.C. was significant because it helped dilute the labor federation's strength among white-collar workers.[75] As the J.O.C. pursued its campaign to highlight the plight of working youth in March 1936, its leaders drew attention to the C.F.T.C.'s recently released plan as evidence that they had both a larger program for reconstructing the social order and concrete ideas about immediate reforms.[76]

The election results of May 1936 intensified Catholic concerns over communism and focused new attention on youth. For *La Croix*, the strong communist advances proved the most worrisome outcome of the two rounds of voting. As the paper complained early in its front-page story on the first round of voting, the communist peril seemed "more and more threatening." Communists might camouflage it, but the party remained bent on "violent revolution and intolerable dictatorship."[77] After communist advances were confirmed in the second round of voting, *La Croix* called for redoubled apostolic and propaganda efforts. Communists had patiently and methodically prepared their successes in a way Catholics had not; the trend had to be reversed.[78]

Yet communist overtures to Catholics did not end once the elections were over. Days after the second round of voting, Thorez proposed joint action against poverty along lines already under way in his own suburb of Ivry. This latest tactic exacerbated the pope's worries over the communist threat in France. Meeting with Pius XI privately in Rome on 8 May, the recently reelected deputy abbé Desgranges found the pope "haunted" by communist plans for antireligious propaganda.[79] For Pius XI, Father Desgranges recorded in his diary, communism presented a world danger that the complacency of certain French Catholics and even certain priests was making more agonizing.[80] Father Desgranges was much less worried, but he decided to act on the Holy Father's concerns. Doing so, he wrote, required finding apostles among young Catholics.[81]

**The J.O.C., the J.O.C.F., and the Strikes of 1936** The strike movement that began in May and spread rapidly across the country after 2 June brought further challenges. Paris was hit particularly hard. By 4 June transportation in the capital was paralyzed, and *La Croix* spoke of the possibility of widespread food shortages.[82] The shape and scale of the movement surprised and worried observers, especially clerics convinced of communist strike leadership and frightened of revolution. Both branches of the J.O.C. were thrust to the fore of social conflict in ways that enhanced the young militants' roles in the struggle against communism.

The first clerical response struck a circumspect note. On 5 June the socially active Cardinal Verdier, archbishop of Paris, issued a call for peace and cooperation that demonstrated unusual sympathy for working-class suffering and the need to reorder society. His manifesto, released to foreign and domestic newspapers and read to French Catholic congregations, acknowledged the horrible situation facing the working class and reminded listeners of earlier papal pronouncements decrying deficiencies in the social order. Verdier called on everyone to pursue "peace, harmony, and real fraternity" and to help bring about "this new order that everyone demands."[83] Communists applauded the speech, prompting *La Croix* to clarify the archbishop's meaning. "To speak of a new social order," the paper's director Father Merklen explained on page one, "was not to accept the chimeras of Communist theories."[84] There was no possibility of doctrinal accord between Catholicism and communism, which was termed "an illusion, an error, a terrible danger for civil society even more so than for the Church."

Between Verdier's pronouncement and the correction published in *La Croix*, the historic labor agreement negotiated at the Hôtel Matignon was signed. Yet the agreement did not end or even slow the strike movement. Instead the situation deteriorated in the ensuing days, prompting fears that revolution was close at hand. These developments intensified Catholic concern over communism's appeal to the young, including youthful members

Refusing *la main tendue*

of the clergy. On 9 June the staunchly anticommunist Monsignor Calvet had a remarkable exchange with a thirty-three-year-old priest that proved the point. The priest informed Calvet that revolution was brewing and that it might be necessary to take to the streets. If this happened, the priest continued, he would stand with the Communists, "because they were right and the future was on their side."[85] Tensions in the capital reached their worst point two days later, when the socialist interior minister Roger Salengro moved mobile guards into the capital and Thorez intervened to instruct workers about the importance of knowing when to end a strike.[86] Abbé Desgranges provided further details of what seemed like a pre-revolutionary situation: service workers at the Catholic Bon-Secours Hospital were threatening to walk off the job, strikers had managed to fly a red flag from scaffolding outside the Quai d'Orsay, and foreigners were leaving Paris out of fear of revolution.[87]

The J.O.C., the J.O.C.F., and their militants found themselves on the front lines of a social explosion, and they scrambled to respond. Much of the youth militants' significance resulted from the C.F.T.C.'s weakness vis-à-vis the recently reunified C.G.T., which had long held a dominant position in French trade unionism. When the strikes broke out, the C.F.T.C. counted approximately 150,000 members, who were spread unevenly across the country and the economy. Close to a third were white-collar workers, although miners and textile workers were numerous in areas of traditional Catholic strength such as the Nord and Alsace.[88] With the C.F.T.C. weak in many sectors, the young men of the J.O.C. stood as important—and sometimes solitary—representatives of Catholic trade unionism in affected workplaces. Young women were also at the fore, a fact consistent with the longstanding emphasis on women's activism in the C.F.T.C.,[89] where women had their own unions and federations and positions were reserved for them at every level of the administrative structure.[90] By contrast, the C.G.T., whose pre-strike membership was close to ten times that of the C.F.T.C., had no need to rely on the young as it worked to gain control of the strike movement.

It must have been a shock for militants of the J.O.C. and J.O.C.F. to find themselves in occupied workplaces, where men and women of all ages often lived together and strike committees dominated by the C.G.T. controlled daily life. Some Jocists simply went home,[91] but others stood their ground. Although the exact number of Jocists who participated in the strikes is not known, the major inquiry into the strikes of 1936 done subsequently by the J.O.C., which resulted in the lengthy *Documentation sur les grèves de 1936*, makes clear that a large number of Jocists of both sexes lived the strikes intensely.[92] This report, drawn mainly from answers to an extensive questionnaire interrogating Jocists on diverse aspects of the strikes, paints a picture of Jocist strikers as young, ignorant of trade unionism, and vastly outnumbered.

When the strikes began, militants wrote to J.O.C. national headquarters to describe their situations and ask for direction. A letter from a female Jocist was typical. She began by regretting that she knew absolutely nothing about trade unionism, and went on to ask for detailed instructions about how she should proceed.[93] Despite the inexperience of both J.O.C. and J.O.C.F. militants, they generally received little support from adult Catholic trade union leaders, who were themselves overwhelmed by events. A regional J.O.C. leader described the situation his members faced: "The C.F.T.C. local is appalling. All the strikes were handled by one paid staffer. For many strikes, the C.F.T.C. sent no one. Our militants, who have recruited new members (like the one who brought in forty), do not have the union's support and risk having the new recruits turn against them. Some wonder whether they should even recruit for the C.F.T.C."[94] The difficulties faced by J.O.C. militants were compounded by C.G.T. pressures to join the recently reunified union. From across France J.O.C. militants reported that workers were being threatened with dismissal if they did not join the C.G.T.; from Nanterre one reported simply, "70 members of the C.G.T. before the strike; 900 after threats of dismissal."[95] In these circumstances Jocists often found themselves in the C.G.T. Indeed, the J.O.C. regional leader quoted above reported that many of his members had joined the C.G.T., with one having been elevated to the strike committee. He ended by asking the national leadership for immediate direction as to the correct J.O.C. position on *les grèves d'occupation*.

That stance was complicated since Catholic clerics viewed the strikes as illegitimate, illegal, and potentially revolutionary. Clerics generally believed that Communists were the driving force behind the strike movement and were attempting to push the strikes beyond professional concerns toward political revolution. This position was outlined forcefully and systematically by the Jesuits of Action Populaire, who were closely linked to Father Guérin, the national chaplain for both the J.O.C. and the J.O.C.F. In the J.O.C.'s declaration on the strikes, published initially in *La Croix* and reprinted in *Dossiers de l'Action Populaire*, the Jesuits mixed a perfunctory admission of the legitimacy of workers' demands with a vivid denunciation of the strikes themselves. The strikes were judged illegitimate because they had been called before all other means of conflict resolution had been exhausted; were contrary to the social order and violated property rights; exposed the country to economic danger; and, finally, were political and revolutionary. In the Jesuits' estimation, Communists sought not only to use "illegal and even anarchic methods to solve an economic conflict but to bring workers toward an attempted Communist political revolution."[96]

The J.O.C.'s official declarations, issued by the National Council and published in *La Jeunesse Ouvrière*, followed the outlines established by Action Populaire: they recognized the legitimacy of the strikers' demands but refused to support the strikers' tactic of occupying the workplace.[97] Although it is not known how the leadership arrived at this position, Pierre Pierrard suggests in his biography of Father Guérin that Guérin intervened to alter the J.O.C. leaders' stand.[98] Certainly Guérin considered this a moment that demanded extra vigilance and unity on the part of movement chaplains.[99] Chaplains were instructed to ensure that J.O.C. federations helped Jocists to understand why they should try to push others "toward the most acceptable solution," which favored arbitration over work stoppages and sought to depoliticize the strikes.[100]

Jocists caught up in strike action in early June did not have the luxury of waiting for official declarations from either Action Populaire or the J.O.C. leadership. Instead they followed the guidelines laid out in J.O.C. circulars, like that from Paul Hibout dated 6 June. These instructions urged militants of the J.O.C. and J.O.C.F. to do their best to shape the strikes according to J.O.C. principles and goals. Strikes were to be "depoliticized" whenever possible. This meant moderating demands that seemed excessive or too political and removing emblems of political affiliation, such as the red flags that sometimes hung from workplace windows. Militants were also encouraged to struggle against any unnecessary prolongation of the strikes. Moderation was in the best interest of workers, since excess might result in backlash against them.[101]

J.O.C. and J.O.C.F. militants were also entrusted with safeguarding moral standards, since, as Hibout explained, morality had been further compromised by the promiscuity resulting from the occupations of the workplace. Although many of the accounts excerpted in the section on morality in *Documentation sur les grèves de 1936* complimented workers' behavior, others made clear that militants were appalled by instances of heavy drinking, salacious stories, bawdy songs, and "dirty" literature passed hand to hand.[102] In Roanne one Jocist was horrified that a woman had taken off her clothes and danced naked in front of her co-workers, and that workers of both sexes had cross-dressed. Consistent with earlier J.O.C. analysis, women were held particularly responsible for these instances of moral corruption. The report's subsection "More immorality among women than men" quoted one militant in Paris: "Among female workers, the level of morality was very low and more depressing than among male workers." Others told of women sneaking down to the men's sleeping quarters, dancing in their pajamas with men, or hiding in closets so they would not be sent home by strike committees anxious to avoid charges of immorality. Another Jocist was sure that "after the strikes, France will have more children." To counter these abuses, Jocists of both sexes were instructed to be constantly vigilant against immorality, to demand that women and young workers of both sexes be sent home at night, and to protest energetically against all attacks on "the moral dignity of the worker."[103]

Jocists were also directed to fight on behalf of the C.F.T.C., by either recruiting members, representing the trade union during the strikes, or defending the very right of the union to participate—and sometimes exist—during the momentous events. As we saw, unions affiliated with the C.G.T. attempted to monopolize trade union activism. At the national level the C.F.T.C. was excluded from negotiations leading to the Matignon Agreement and prohibited from acting as a signatory to the accord. At the local level C.G.T. members pressured workers to join the union in a variety of ways. *La Croix* reported that a Jocist was put before a mock revolutionary tribunal where he was forced to defend Christ, the C.F.T.C., and the J.O.C.[104] The J.O.C. and J.O.C.F. called upon their militants to defend the C.F.T.C. and the larger principle of trade union freedom and to do their utmost to represent young workers during strike deliberations and negotiations, primarily by ensuring that the problems of apprentices and young workers were considered in the formulation of demands.

It is impossible to measure the militants' success in defending the Jocist version of the Catholic agenda, or even to know the real extent of their efforts. As we saw in chapter 3, J.O.C. workplace moralizing had met considerable resistance in tamer times; now the atmosphere sometimes verged on the carnivalesque. In these circumstances it is unlikely that militants made much progress on moral issues, except when the demands of the J.O.C. and J.O.C.F. converged with the desires of strike committees, as they did on the question of sending female strikers home. J.O.C. militants probably had the most success in ensuring that youth concerns were considered, especially since the C.G.T.'s record in this area was poor. From Strasbourg came a report of a meeting where all went according to plan: "The president of the local J.O.C. section spoke up to call attention to a huge omission: the question of young workers. In front of his workmates, he pleaded the cause of young workers and laid out their demands in accordance with the circular provided by the J.O.C. national headquarters. These were accepted immediately by the committee. The Jocist was applauded warmly. In this workshop the following days, all the apprentices came to shake his hand and thank him for his intervention."[105] How often these kinds of triumphs occurred is less clear. In a memo the following year, the J.O.C. noted only that Jocists had succeeded "in some places" in inserting clauses into collective agreements protecting the interests of young workers.[106]

When it came to recruiting new members for the C.F.T.C., some Jocists clearly achieved results. There was a limit, however, to what even the most effective or respected J.O.C. militants could accomplish. For Pierre Trimouille, who studied Catholic unions in the metalworking industry between 1935 and 1939, the J.O.C.'s most important contribution was to help ensure the C.F.T.C.'s very survival. He asserts that the union "would have been wiped out" were it not for "the existence of a few trade union militants ready to stand up in the face of popular opinion." Although not all these militants were Jocists, he adds, they "played a decisive role in these events."[107]

Trimouille refers, without saying so, to male Jocists. What can be said of their female counterparts? Evidence suggests that young women, who often worked in workplaces dominated by women and without a strong C.G.T. presence, could meet with a very different reception during the strikes. Two J.O.C.F. strikers later recalled their experience in almost identical terms: "There wasn't a union but, spontaneously, the workers came to find me to be a delegate and launch the union."[108] It is hard to imagine young male Jocists *ever* being in this position. Communists appreciated the important role that young female Jocists could play as strikers. According to an article in *Jeunes filles de France*, when local Young Communist women heard that the 130 female and 70 male workers of Maison Dinou had gone on strike, they immediately dropped their evening course in stenography and rushed to the factory to see if they could offer assistance. Returning the next day with a phonograph, the Young Communist women asked to speak with a Jocist striker, who had presented the young women's demands to the employer and was taking her turn standing guard at the factory gate. The Jocist questioned the Young Communist women on their attitudes toward religion and family life and on their ultimate goals. She concluded that Jocists fought alongside their communist and socialist comrades for the same demands—and sometimes even for the same ideal—without, however, taking the same path.[109] Although an obvious effort to illustrate the possibility of solidarity between Communists and Catholics, the article underscored that the strikes had altered the position of J.O.C.F. militants at the workplace, while also serving as a powerful reminder of the Communists' own altered approach to young women's activism. In the new communist narrative, Catholic young women occupied workplaces while communist young women entertained and interviewed them.

Despite such glimpses of meaningful strike action by J.O.C.F. militants, other accounts suggest that the majority of young women struggled mightily alongside their male counterparts. One female militant recalled: "There were only two of us who belonged to the C.F.T.C. out of 400! I was unprepared for this workers' struggle. It was very hard for me. The factory occupation lasted two months. I was subjected to pressure—even blows—in an effort to make me join the C.G.T. There was a hateful atmosphere that made me very uncomfortable."[110] A second striker described how she put her name forward as a delegate on the C.F.T.C. list after the strikes, prompting C.G.T. leaders to prohibit the union's members from speaking to her.[111] A third was resigned about what could be accomplished, noting that results were "very thin" for the C.F.T.C. "We were," she recalled, "girls, young, too young. But we did everything we could, even if we didn't measure up."[112]

Catholic leaders put on the defensive by the events of May and June 1936 took a more celebratory view of J.O.C. and J.O.C.F. achievements. In a lengthy front-page article, the *La Croix* director Father Merklen praised the militants for their "admirable courage" and significant achievements.[113] According to Merklen, they had calmed the situation, ensured proper respect for people and factory materials, and defended trade union freedom. In the course of the lengthy article, Merklen provided numerous examples of J.O.C. and J.O.C.F. heroics—of male and female Jocists preventing strikes, providing "healthy" leisure, standing firm against C.G.T. intimidation, and bringing older workers to the C.F.T.C. These young, outnumbered militants had struggled heroically to defend Catholic interests; as such, they became potent symbols of Catholic resistance to the revolutionary threat and evidence that Catholic efforts within the working class were bearing fruit, and would continue to do so.

Refusing *la main tendue*

Not all French Catholics were as enthusiastic about the strike participation of the J.O.C. and J.O.C.F., and Father Merklen's celebration also functioned as a defense of a movement that many now considered too radical.
As tame as the strike actions might have been, they were sometimes cast as
revolutionary by Catholic journalists and employers. Individual militants
were denounced as "red Christians" by employers,[114] and a J.O.C. section
was accused in the provincial press of instigating a strike in Montrouge.[115]
To counter these views, leading clerics came out strongly in favor of the
movement and its actions. Cardinal Verdier issued his own communiqué in
support of the J.O.C. in late June.[116]

For those in the J.O.C., the strikes of 1936 demonstrated the necessity
of enhanced engagement with trade unionism. As the J.O.C. leadership explained in a memorandum in 1937, the strikes had resulted in a new stature
for unions and convinced many previously skeptical workers of the need for
strong professional organizations.[117] The J.O.C. needed therefore to increase
its participation in trade union matters by establishing liaison positions
at the local and federal levels.[118] The movement also encouraged leading
militants to became trade unionists once they were too old for the J.O.C.
By February 1938 forty-five former Jocists were employed by the C.F.T.C. as
full-time staffers.[119]

**Celebrating the J.O.C. at the World's Fair of 1937**  As French
Catholics attempted to regain the initiative after the shocks of 1936, they
paid special attention to the possibilities offered in 1937 by the Exposition
Internationale in Paris. The dominant event of the year in France,[120] the
fair is remembered as an ideological battleground where rival governments
used national pavilions to tout the superiority of their approaches to political, social, and cultural issues.[121] The physical opposition between the National Socialist and Soviet pavilions at one of the major entrances became
the fair's iconic image, one still reproduced in textbooks. Yet the ideological
battles played out at the fair extended well beyond this symbolic confrontation between fascism and communism. Those seeking to mobilize youth
for political advantage in France also viewed the fair as an opportunity to
demonstrate their accomplishments.

Blum's Popular Front government, which had much to prove to its foreign rivals and domestic critics, made youth part of the effort to highlight
French achievements at the fair. After coming to power in June 1936, the

government added pavilions and reshaped exhibitions to reflect government priorities—and to prove, as Shanny Peer has argued, that democratic France was as attentive as its ideological rivals to crucial social questions.[122] The status of youth was one of these social questions, and demonstrating that France, like other nations, was making youth "one of its most urgent preoccupations" provided the rationale for the last-minute addition of the section on youth, "Oeuvre de la Jeunesse."[123] With time of the essence, the government's fair plans for youth concentrated on leisure, the key component of its youth politics. The government built a scouting pavilion and a youth hostel, the latter nestled between the Tourism Pavilion and the Wood Pavilion. The biggest youth-related undertaking was the youth center known as Centre Kellerman, constructed far from the central fairgrounds at the Porte d'Italie in southeastern Paris. This vast, modern complex included a hostel which provided low-cost lodging to young visitors to Paris and spaces for youth to gather and pursue leisure interests, such as scouting and the theater. *L'Illustration*, which noted that France had been the last country to grapple with youth leisure, conceded that the delay had been beneficial in the case of the Centre Kellerman. According to the magazine, the government had succeeded in creating a specifically French hostel out of an institution with German origins.[124]

Sport figured prominently in the fair plans of Léo Lagrange, who continued as undersecretary of state for the organization of sport and leisure after Blum resigned and the Radical Camille Chautemps succeeded him as prime minister in June 1937.[125] For Lagrange the 610 sports days initially scheduled for the fair would simultaneously showcase the vitality of French sport and celebrate youth and the joy of sport.[126] Communists helped organize the competitions and exhibitions held by the worker sport movement, the F.S.G.T., which took place throughout the Paris region during the course of the fair and especially between 4 and 8 August. The August events featured top Soviet athletes, who traveled to France as part of the largest delegation of athletes ever to leave the Soviet Union.[127] Popular aviation, the government-sponsored and Communist-supported program that combined military preparedness with youth adventure, was shown off at the Festival of Popular Aviation on 5 September. The festival brought three thousand young male fliers to Vincennes from across France to demonstrate the vitality of the program, and by extension the government's national defense program. The festival's high point came when the fliers, clad either in uniform or matching pants and bare chests, filed past the air minister to the sound of military music and planes flying overhead.[128]

Besides participating in sporting events sponsored by the F.S.G.T. and government-supported leisure exhibitions, the Communists sought to showcase their youth movement at the J.C.'s Ninth Congress in July 1937. An official event of the fair, the congress linked sport and outdoor spectacle to more traditional political oratory in an illustration of the Communists' transformed approach to youth organizing. Advertisements for the "National Rally of French Youth," inaugurating the proceedings, stressed the entertainment possibilities offered by an event that mixed bicycle and motorcycle races with regional folkloric dances and political speeches. "Sport. . . . Dance . . . Joy . . . Laughter!," promised the prominent front-page advertisement in *L'Humanité*.[129] The rally, which Communists claimed brought fifty thousand young people to Buffalo Stadium, led off with a parade whose costumed marchers represented different regions of France and episodes in French and Soviet revolutionary history. The presence of U.J.F.F. members, who marched in white dresses and regional costumes, was singled out in advertisements and in the coverage provided by *L'Humanité*. These young women, as Vaillant-Couturier argued, not for the first time, represented the grace, beauty, courtesy, and even courage of France.[130]

The J.C. Congress displayed the Communists' firm subordination of youth to the party and their thematic emphases in the waning days of the Popular Front coalition. Jacques Duclos, the party's number two, opened the congress before three thousand delegates from France and Algeria and presided over the proceedings as chairman. The main speeches, however, were delivered by Young Communist leaders, who themselves had well-established roles in communist politics. Raymond Guyot, now at the helm of the Communist Youth International, delivered the keynote address.[131] Surveying the conditions facing French youth, his message revolved around two themes: the movement's inclusiveness and the Popular Front's achievements on behalf of youth. All French young people except fascists and Trotskyists were welcome in the movement, which now included organizations for young women and peasants. The Popular Front government, moreover, was to be applauded for what it had achieved for the young. Even though, Guyot went on to concede, the government had not established a public works program or provided much in the way of training, the tide had turned for youth. As Guyot and the communist press emphasized, youth was no longer a sacrificed group thanks to the Popular Front government and the Matignon Accords.[132] According to Vaillant-Couturier, writing on the front page of *L'Humanité*, youth had emerged from the long night of the "curse of being young" to find the dawn of a new period of youth happiness.[133]

From across the political spectrum, Catholics similarly appreciated and exploited the propagandistic opportunities offered by the Paris world's fair. Visits to the imposing Pontifical Pavilion started with extensive exhibits on children, youth, and adolescents situated on the main floor.[134] And despite the government's attention to sport, it was Catholics who organized the largest sporting event during the fair, the festival of the Fédération Gymnastique et Sportive des Patronages de France (F.G.S.P.F.). At the very moment when Young Communists were gathering in Paris, an estimated 25,000 uniformed French male athletes plus 3,000 more from elsewhere in Europe descended on the capital for two days of competitions and demonstrations of force, including a nocturnal gymnastic pageant at the Parc des Princes stadium and an open-air Mass.[135] Yet Catholics were not content to mount displays of male strength, seeking as well to claim territory in government-sponsored youth settings. Much to their satisfaction, they succeeded in obtaining half the space at both the scouting installation and the Centre Kellerman's youth hostel.[136] These were impressive achievements at a fair long derided as "the Popular Front's expo" by the conservative press.[137]

The J.O.C.'s Tenth Anniversary Congress was designed as the cynosure of Catholic participation at the world's fair. Clerics maneuvered to ensure that the congress received official status at the Expo, and that status was granted by the government in March.[138] From his sickbed Pius XI reminded French bishops of the importance he assigned to the J.O.C. Extending and further intensifying "the providential movement" was "of the utmost importance in stopping the spread of evil."[139] Coming four months after his lengthy encyclical *Divini Redemptoris: On Atheistic Communism*, the July Congress became a weapon in the church's anticommunist crusade. The J.O.C. World Congress, as it was officially known, was to project the image of a powerful, disciplined, international movement of Catholic young workers able to counter the international communist youth movement. Consistent with the Communists' new mixed-sex approach to youth and youth organizing, the J.O.C. congress brought together both branches of the movement in their first major collaborative effort. The expected seventy thousand male and female delegates included ten thousand representing J.O.C. sections in Belgium, Portugal, Holland, Switzerland, Spain, Luxembourg, England,

Czechoslovakia, Canada, the United States, Colombia, and China, as well as the French colonies of Algeria, Morocco, and Indochina. Opening just days after the Young Communists dispersed, the congress became the largest gathering of its kind during the fair—one that signaled the church's intention to use young workers and strategies from the mass politics of the 1930s in the service of its political goals.

Congress preparations were extensive and meticulous. Clerics played central roles, with abbé Rodhain, the thirty-seven-year-old chaplain of the J.O.C.F. federation of Paris-Sud, writing and rehearsing Saturday night's Festival of Labor. At the local level chaplains guided Jocists as they readied themselves for an event more ambitious than any previous J.O.C. undertaking. Militants were encouraged to view the congress as a public affirmation of the movement's successes as well as an opportunity for recruitment, and they were to devote all their energies to its preparation between the fall of 1936 and July 1937. The congress thus provided an absorbing, alternative focus for much of the life of Blum's short-lived Popular Front government, a period when politics continued to tempt male Jocists. By July 1937, in fact, J.O.C. attacks on politics had reached a new pitch. No longer simply inappropriate for young people, politics was denounced as an unnatural, corrupting force that left young workers spent, disappointed, and morally compromised.[140]

Spiritual matters were primordial in the run-up to the congress, returning both the church's agenda and movement chaplains to the center of action in the J.O.C. and J.O.C.F. after their marginalization in the summer of 1936. Young people gathered in retreats to contemplate the main congress themes of family and work. Some rehearsed with abbé Rodhain, who traveled the country to ready militants for their role in Saturday night's Festival of Labor.[141] Militants studied the key documents of social Catholic doctrine under the guidance of chaplains, paying special attention to the encyclical *Divini Redemptoris: On Atheistic Communism* of 19 March 1937.[142] The lengthy teaching examined the enemy doctrine, analyzed its dissemination, bemoaned its consequences, and laid out the Catholic response, which pivoted around doctrinal refutation and concrete action. Catholic workers received special and affectionate mention in the encyclical. For Pius XI, workers "doing battle" in Catholic Action organizations, of which the J.O.C. was the successful prototype, provided "the means best calculated to save these, Our beloved children, from the snares of Communism."[143] An attempt to energize the faithful in the struggle against communism, the encyclical had the desired effect among J.O.C. militants, at least officially. A J.O.C. report expressed leaders' pride over the pope's "solemn endorsement" and gratitude for the "enlightened weapons" it gave them to defend their faith and "to unmask the insidious maneuvers of the agents of atheistic Communism."[144]

To ready themselves for the congress, militants were called upon to modify their behavior in ways that reflected the J.O.C.'s ideology and enhanced the movement's smooth operation. Both male and female militants were expected to make specific sacrifices or stipulate areas to which they would apply renewed attention; these pledges were written down or announced publicly to enhance their importance.[145] Sometimes pleasures were forgone, such as dancing or smoking or, in the case of young women, reading novels. Sometimes the duties of membership in the J.O.C. or J.O.C.F. were to be executed more diligently. Members of the J.O.C.F. Federation of Pau thus vowed to attend meetings regularly, to be more attentive at study circles, and to perform faithfully their religious obligations. One J.O.C.F. member pledged to "do all that was asked of her by the J.O.C. without argument"; another promised she would be "faithful to all" of her Jocist duties.[146]

Militants also prepared collectively. Section members put up red, black, and yellow congress posters featuring a male and female worker wearing berets against the background of a factory. Below ran the congress slogan, "For a New Era / A New Worker Youth," superimposed over J.O.C. insignia.[147] Militants sold special editions of *La Jeunesse Ouvrière Féminine* (200,000 copies) and *La Jeunesse Ouvrière* (180,000 copies) in May and April.[148]

Most crucially, section members planned for and attended the roughly four hundred regional congresses held across France in the year preceding the congress. The largest and most prominent of these, which drew thousands to large indoor arenas, demonstrated that the J.O.C. was developing forms of mass demonstration and religious pageantry to counter those employed by the Popular Front coalition. In Lille in September 1936 fifteen thousand uniformed militants of both sexes moved through the streets for two hours, singing J.O.C. songs and shouting memorized cheers.[149] One of the cheers, in which Jocists repeatedly chanted "Justice," "Freedom," and "Peace" in answer to the question "What do we want?," would not have been out of place at a Popular Front demonstration. In this and other ways, the congresses adapted the forms of the mass politics of the 1930s to Catholic youth politics. Delegates watched as brightly colored banners were paraded into large arenas, belted out J.O.C. songs (including the movement's rewritten version of the "International," "Worker Be Proud"), swore collective loyalty oaths to the movement, and followed large, highly choreographed spoken choruses. A technique pioneered on the left and used the previous year in the youth segment of the communist film *La vie est à nous* was now being used to dramatize Catholic messages.

Despite the new techniques, mainstream Catholic themes, notably the church's brand of familial politics, predominated at the J.O.C. congresses of 1936 and 1937. In Lille militants marched under banners demanding a special wage for fathers and the return of mothers to the home. The J.O.C.F. spoken chorus performed at the Lille congress illustrated both the moral dangers facing young women and the salvatory powers of the J.O.C.F. and its gender-specific ideal through the fall and eventual moral rescue of the young worker Jeannette.[150] Initially happy and proud to enter the workforce, Jeannette quickly lost her innocence and betrayed her ideals in the morally corrupt atmosphere of the workplace. Resisting help from the J.O.C.F., she preferred to pursue pleasure and the company of young men, behavior which led straight to serious illness and a stay in a sanatorium. J.O.C.F. members came to her rescue: they helped her when she was sick and after her release from the sanatorium. The climax was Jeannette's engagement to be married, which only occurred, the audience was told, because her intended was impressed by her status as a Jocist. The members of the chorus intoned: "JOC / you rescue / young female workers / by making them understand / you alone / the beauty / the grandeur / the nobility of love / of their splendid destiny / as working-class mothers."[151] The young working woman's ideal adult role could not have been presented more pointedly.

The Tenth Anniversary Congress was carefully planned to convey a particular image of the J.O.C. in a way that generated enthusiasm and enhanced young people's commitment to their movement. Simply attending the congress was an exciting opportunity for tourism, travel, and adventure, and the J.O.C.F. attempted to maximize the number of provincial delegates by charging a uniform rate regardless of proximity to Paris. Delegates chose between various congress packages, which included round-trip travel to Paris, a ticket to the fair, admission to the congress, and meals and lodging for a specified number of days. Once at the congress, militants of both sexes stayed in the vast halls constructed by fair organizers to provide low-cost accommodation for visitors to Paris. Hotel industry protests ensured that only members of youth-related movements used these facilities,[152] and the J.O.C.F. appears to have been the sole organization of young women to house its members in this way. The government report on housing at the fair is

**238**    accompanied by a photograph of smiling, uniformed female Jocists.¹⁵³ To encourage and facilitate explorations of the capital city, which few of the provincial delegates had visited previously, J.O.C.F. leaders included in the joint *Congress Manual* a section on touring in Paris, which gave tips on taking public transport and using public telephones.¹⁵⁴ The manual also reminded J.O.C.F. militants that their preordered fair souvenirs would be waiting for them at their lodgings in Paris.¹⁵⁵

The congress combined indoor sessions with outdoor religious pageantry over three days that built to a Sunday climax. The first session, which took place on Friday morning before 25,000 male and female Jocists in the Vélodrome d'Hiver, introduced the congress's principal theme: the J.O.C.'s determination to defend the family. Jean Quercy set the tone in the first presentation: "We appeal to everyone, to employers, public authorities, our friends, wage-earning youth, so that together we will build this young workers' movement which will give the family its grandeur and dignity."¹⁵⁶ Through a combination of carefully prepared reports, a rousing rendition of the song "Nuptials," a modest spoken chorus, and the reading of a special resolution by the J.O.C.F. secretary general Jeanne Aubert, the Jocists affirmed their commitment to the church's vision of family politics. Once again belying the movement's claim to operate outside the realm of adult politics, the J.O.C.'s resolution called on the state to intervene on behalf of the family and demanded economic reforms to allow mothers to leave the workforce and return to the home.¹⁵⁷ The J.O.C. also insisted on decent wages, clean and adequate housing, and moral standards in entertainment, printed materials, and public spaces. That opening evening, leading Jocists and select clerics attended a reception in their honor at the Hôtel de Ville, the seat of municipal government in Paris. René Berthier, the municipal council's secretary, welcomed the youth delegates and their clerical minders by paying homage to the movement, terming it "a great force." Berthier told the Jocists: "Those who think about the destiny of our country have their eyes fixed on you."¹⁵⁸

The next day's proceedings spotlighted the congress's second principal theme, the recasting of attitudes toward labor; as we have seen, this was an important component of the Catholic effort to remake the working class. Jocists were encouraged to take pride in their work and to see it as a noble endeavor imbued with deep religious meaning. They were to become exemplary workers who labored diligently, protected machinery, and avoided strike action. These ideas had special resonance for church leaders after the labor disruptions of the previous summer, and they were illustrated in multiple ways on Saturday. During the morning's study session, attended by forty thousand persons, the J.O.C. secretary general Fernand Bouxom reminded militants that work was both a sacred duty and a permanent right; it was through his labor that man collaborated with God.[159] Yet the tragic conditions of work and apprenticeship made it impossible for young workers to "fulfill their duties" and "exercise their rights." The J.O.C. demanded reforms to make this possible.

The Festival of Labor that night provided a more original dramatization of Catholic approaches to work.[160] Conceived and carefully prepared by the young abbé Rodhain, this event was a highly choreographed nocturnal pageant performed at the huge Parc des Princes stadium. The festival's first part celebrated the joy of work through a symphony of labor featuring skits, dances, and processions. Grouped by region, attired in regional costume or work garb, and carrying large replicas of the products and tools characteristic of their region, participants paraded solemnly around the field of the packed stadium to the accompaniment of regional airs and traditional work songs. Thus female textile workers from Alsace and the Nord marched with a loom and giant spools of thread; northern miners had a large slab of coal; and young workers from St. Nazaire carried a model of the ocean liner *Normandie* on their shoulders.[161] The young workers acted out skits, performed songs, and danced in an homage to the joy of work. By binding the J.O.C.'s celebration of work to a celebration of France's regional diversity, the pageant's creators effectively subordinated the working class to the nation. They also highlighted Catholic commitment to a notion of work that was overwhelmingly artisanal.[162]

The evening's second part was devoted to the construction of a new Christian city. The Jocists had a central role to play in this endeavor, which they illustrated by depositing the products of their labor on the central podium. As Jean-Pierre Coco and Joseph Debès point out, however, the young workers could not build the new city by themselves but would need the help of mothers and employers. Cooperation and cross-class collaboration were essential to constructing the new world.[163] So too was Christ, whose symbolic entrance onto the scene provided the evening's dramatic high point. At 10:30, in total darkness, an immense white cross more than thirteen meters long was carried into the stadium between fifty uniformed nurses and a group of torch bearers. Once the cross was placed upright on the podium, the torch bearers fanned out and lit the stadium, symbolizing the light that only Christ could bring to the world. After the festival concluded, a hundred Jocists watched over the altar through the night, their torches burning continuously.[164]

More religious pageantry awaited the Jocists. On Sunday morning delegates returned to the Parc des Princes for an open-air Mass marking the first decade of the French movement. The service incorporated the pomp and circumstance associated with the princes of the church, adding distinctive J.O.C. touches to create an imposing spectacle for the estimated seventy to eighty thousand Jocists and Catholic dignitaries in attendance. The Mass began with a procession of leading Catholic clerics, including all four French cardinals and forty-nine bishops, and hundreds of brightly colored flags from J.O.C. sections across the globe and other Catholic Action youth movements. An interactive service, conducted wholly in French as opposed to the customary Latin of the time, was performed by Gustave Laugeois, a Jocist metalworker turned priest. In yet another reminder of young working women's adult role, he was accompanied to the altar by his mother.

If the young Father Laugeois said Mass, it was left to more powerful figures to whip up Jocist enthusiasm for their mission. A letter from Pius XI and an address by Cardinal Verdier praised the movement and urged its members onward. According to the Holy Father, the J.O.C. was "an impressive legion of militants who, when faced with pagan Communism and atheistic nationalism, have sworn to spread their Christian ideal of justice and charity." That God's grace was with them was clear from their "large and fervent phalanxes." Their apostolic work, performed with such generosity and ardor, gave them a supernatural nobility far exceeding any earthly honor. They were "Christ's glory."[165] Verdier informed Jocists that their congress was as "beautiful, moving and full of promise" as the recent triumphal visit to France of the pope's secretary of state, Cardinal Pacelli, soon to be pope himself.[166] Going further, Verdier proclaimed: "Not since the Crusades has such Christian ardor lifted so many hearts and aroused such enthusiasm." The Mass culminated in a collective loyalty oath and a spoken chorus involving two thousand persons. Together the crowd roared, "We promise!" Then, taking turns, different groups shouted out pledges to give themselves entirely to the J.O.C., to observe its rules and discipline, and to defend its principles.[167]

The congress had the desired effect. Years later participants called the experience of attending the congress unforgettable, a high point of their lives.[168] A female militant from Alsace described how important it had been to meet young people from across France with the same ideals and goals; for her the congress was not an end point but the beginning of total engagement.[169] So important were memories of the congress to another militant that he recalled relying on his congress souvenir album for sustenance during his darkest moments of captivity in Germany during the Second World War.[170]

But if the congress was designed to heighten the Jocists' devotion to their movement, it was also designed to project the image of a powerful and disciplined movement of working-class Catholics firmly subordinate to the church. Youth organizers stressed discipline and uniformity as they readied their troops. Participants were to dress uniformly—white blouses, navy skirts, and blue berets for J.O.C.F. militants, white shirts, navy pants and the red-and-blue congress tie for young men—and to learn their songs and parts by heart. The J.O.C.F. section of the *Congress Manual* even counseled militants to refrain from yelling in order to preserve their voices for official demonstrations.[171] In its lavish coverage of the festivities, which included front-page reports and full-page photo spreads, *La Croix* emphasized the presence of leading French clerics and the strength and discipline, even docility, of the congress. As the paper noted in one article, "A movement which is capable of mobilizing 100,000 young people is a great power . . . And this great force is disciplined . . . Orders are applied rigorously, joyfully. Difficulties are resolved quickly thanks to everyone's docility."[172] Coming a year after some Catholics worried that the J.O.C. was too radical, there could be no doubt that the church hierarchy backed the movement completely—and controlled it completely.

The J.O.C. Congress succeeded at the symbolic level, receiving prominent, illustrated coverage in leading Parisian dailies. Articles commented on the size of the undertaking, the enthusiasm of the militants, and the discipline and strength of the movement, with many citing the almost talismanic number of 100,000 J.O.C. militants,[173] the same number of youth militants claimed by Communists. For the mass- circulation daily *Paris-Soir*, "The Congress which took place in Paris surprised Parisians by the virtue of the astronomical number of those present";[174] not even during the arrival of the Tour de France had the Parc des Princes stadium been so full.[175] For its part, the far-right *L'Intransigeant* commented, "Make no mistake, a great movement is coming into being."[176] Writing in *Le Figaro*, the vice-president of the National Federation of Catholics approvingly contrasted the Jocists' conquering spirit to that of earlier, more timid Catholic youth movements.[177]

*Refusing la main tendue*

For *Le Matin*, the J.O.C. was a "vast and peaceful army of young men and women."[178]

The events of the summer of 1937 testified to the Catholics' renewed vigor after the shocks of the previous two years. Clerics were pleased by the presence they had been able to establish at the Centre Kellerman, and astonished by the reception accorded to Cardinal Pacelli, the Vatican's secretary of state, by Republican authorities.[179] But the J.O.C. congress was seen as the greatest triumph. Never before had the church been able to rally so many workers, and the congress displayed the Catholics' success in creating a style of religious pageantry suitable to an era of mass politics. As the Catholic intellectual Henry Daniel-Rops wrote later, "It was clear to everyone that with this public demonstration of intense faith, the Church had begun a new era."[180] The congress also had positive consequences for the J.O.C., moving the movement into the Catholic mainstream and increasing its popularity among young workers. By the spring of 1938 national leaders reported that 1,203 J.O.C. sections in France and French North Africa were progressing toward official affiliation, a figure that exceeded the number of existing sections. J.O.C. leaders were convinced that the congress had made the organization fashionable in many quarters, and they pondered the best ways to integrate the influx of members without losing the movement's dynamism and unity.[181] Perhaps everything was possible for those who believed.

## Conclusion

By the time of the World's Fair in 1937, youth occupied a place in French public life very different from that which it had occupied two decades earlier. Political and religious leaders competed for their allegiance and featured young supporters in mass demonstrations, rallies, and pageants. At this time of ideological tension and fear of war, the ability to rally large numbers of young people demonstrated strength and was assigned symbolic significance. The young themselves engaged more fully, joining youth movements in unprecedented numbers. These activists were now female as well as male, for youth had become a mixed-sex political category and constituency. Strategies of mobilization too had mutated, with movements according greater importance to leisure, tourism, and culture in their efforts to rally the young.

This book has argued that Communists and Catholics played critical roles in these developments. They targeted youth with vigor, devised fresh strategies of mobilization and display, and incorporated young women centrally into their initiatives. These French representatives of two of the twentieth century's leading ideologies shared an acute appreciation of the possibilities presented by the young in disseminating belief and forging long-term support. Convinced that youth could be counted on to defend extreme positions or accept missionary responsibilities refused by adults, Communists and Catholics created dynamic, competing movements that incited imitation and propelled youth to the center of political life. By putting youth at the service of antifascism during the mid-1930s, Communists pushed young people to the heart of the Popular Front coalition's electoral promises and governing aims. For their part, Catholics made Jocists the agents and symbols of a new era in worker-church relations, and their determination to enlist young women was taken up by Popular Front Communists. In the Union des Jeunes Filles de France, Communists made appeals to young women in fresh ways

**244**  and remade Young Communist femininity so that it resembled conventional approaches to women and female political activism. It was Communists, not Catholics, who discouraged young women from selling newspapers in the streets and celebrated their female militants' grace and charm. The new model Young Communist woman played a symbolically important role in the party's Popular Front strategies.

One of the striking characteristics of interwar communist and Catholic youth politics, especially when viewed through the lens of the activism of the 1960s, was the extent of adult involvement. Adults were initiators and over-seers, prompting efforts to disguise their role and promote cross-generational alliances. This was most evident in the Jeunesse Ouvrière Chrétienne, in which chaplains, who were usually young and marked by the generational upheavals of the First World War, founded J.O.C. sections, chose youth lead-ers, developed the movement's distinctive spirituality, and oversaw forma-tion and education. The chaplains remained discreetly out of sight during most public events, but when it counted, they stepped in and exerted influ-ence. The relationship between adults and youth took different forms within communism. Although adult Communists had no day-to-day roles in the Jeunesse Communiste, Comintern and party officials had the final word on youth policy and strategy.

The story of these youth movements was far from a simple tale of adult manipulation. Young people engaged fully, creating new styles of youth ac-tivism in the process. They wrote, published, and distributed movement literature, ran meetings and congresses, and devised and implemented cam-paigns, often risking arrest or the scorn of those around them. They also resisted adult directives and advanced their own agendas. During the 1920s Young Communists viewed themselves as an age-based vanguard that would lead the party to revolution, and they clashed with adults as they pursued their goal. In the following decade male Jocists took to the streets to defend unemployed youth and the J.O.C.'s brand of public activism, pushing chap-lains and their spiritual and moral concerns to the background. When strikes shut down workplaces across France in 1936, male and female Jocists stepped forward as defenders of Catholic trade unionism, their actions suggesting ways of reconciling the apparently irreconcilable identities of worker and Christian.

Yet the movements were more than a locus of activism. They offered di-verse opportunities to young people whose childhoods had been scarred by war or economic crisis, whose formal educations had been curtailed at

Conclusion

primary school, and whose lives were dominated by work. The movements
allowed members, especially the most dedicated, to continue their educations. Militants learned public speaking and improved their reading and writing, skills which often had special significance for young female workers. The movements also promised a rare age-specific sociability in a setting where young workers were thrown in with adults at the workplace, few young people attended high school or university (the incubators of youth culture in interwar North America), and most lived in cramped apartments. Meetings and congresses combined socializing with more serious work, and both movements sponsored outings and trips that were exciting and fun. Discovering the French countryside or journeying to Paris or Italy could be the highlight of a young working-class life, especially when seen through the retrospective lens of the Second World War.

The outbreak of war in September 1939 brought this vibrant period of youth organizing to a close. Once war began, normal political, economic, and social life was suspended. Young men were most strongly affected, with those over twenty mobilized and sent to the front. When French forces gave way in the face of the German onslaught of May–June 1940, an estimated 1.58 million soldiers were taken prisoner and sent to Germany; of these most were in their twenties and thirties.[1] Defeat brought partition and the direct military occupation of two-thirds of the country, including Paris. In occupied France the Germans controlled all aspects of life. A southern zone was left under nominal French control. In the spa town of Vichy, legislators ended the Third Republic, handing to an old man, eighty-four-year-old Marshal Philippe Pétain, the authority to create a new state.

The Vichy regime adapted and extended interwar approaches to youth. More than any Republican government and in imitation of authoritarian regimes elsewhere in Europe, the men of Vichy put the reeducation and retraining of youth at the heart of their programs and goals. Youth would provide the shock troops for the regime's National Revolution. For this government, regenerating youth was a masculine affair privileging young men and relegating young women to supporting roles. Young men were to be molded into strong, healthy, virile, and obedient new men for a new France. To this end the government set out to revamp the educational system, promote sport and physical fitness, coordinate the activities of existing youth movements, and establish state-run youth organizations.[2] Prominent among Vichy's innovations were the Chantiers de la jeunesse, which shipped all twenty-year-old young men to the countryside for eight months of physical training and communal life. Yet the recreation of French youth was considered incomplete without the simultaneous retraining of young women. In Vichy schools, girls and young women prepared for future roles as mothers, taking compulsory courses in domestic science beginning in March 1942.[3] With young men leading the way, the young would remake the French family and the French nation.

Vichy efforts were only part of the story of wartime youth politics. During the dark, complicated years between 1939 and 1945, youth movements and their members past and present faced complex choices, the responses to which can only be suggested here. For Communists the war's beginnings brought disarray and dishonor. Hostilities began soon after the conclusion in August 1939 of a nonaggression pact between Nazi Germany and the Soviet Union. French Communists were instructed to abandon the struggle against Hitler, news which the longtime J.C. leader and staunch Comintern supporter Raymond Guyot delivered from Moscow.[4] The French government, which had already suspended communist publications, outlawed the party and its affiliated organizations in late September. What remained of the once strong party moved underground, its leaders and remaining militants hunted by French officials. Young communist militants, especially women who escaped military mobilization, helped reconstitute the party, both immediately and after Vichy arrested communist leaders in the spring of 1941.[5]

Hitler's attack on the Soviet Union on 22 June 1941 altered the Communists' relationship to the Resistance dramatically, creating the conditions for French Communists to embrace Resistance efforts. Communists threw themselves into armed struggle, and the young were prominent among those who took up arms. Young men who had been active in the interwar J.C. moved into groups affiliated with the Francs-Tireurs et Partisans (F.T.P.), the communist arm of the Resistance. Many were arrested, while some, including Gabriel Péri, whom we met in chapter 1, were executed by the Germans. Young women from the U.J.F.F. also did their part. A select few joined armed Resistance groups, with Fanny Ladsky commanding a youth detachment within the F.T.P.[6] Other young communist women participated in ways reminiscent of the female political activism of the mid- to late 1930s.[7] They served as liaison agents, edited the clandestine press, and organized women's protests.[8] Young women were vital to the survival and success of Resistance networks, and they too incurred the wrath of German authorities. Ladsky died after being arrested and deported to a concentration camp, as did Danielle Casanova, the U.J.F.F.'s founding head.

Conclusion

The wartime situation of the J.O.C. diverged sharply from that of the J.C., its members pursuing more diverse courses of action during the war. Unlike its banned communist counterpart, the J.O.C. was allowed to exist in both occupied and unoccupied France after 1940. Operating separately on both sides of the demarcation line, the male and female branches continued their pre-war work of youth training and aid to the unemployed. J.O.C. approaches adapted easily to the problems thrown up by the war, and Jocists offered war-related social assistance, especially to refugees. For those male Jocists sent to Germany as prisoners of war, captivity often intensified their spiritual life by bringing them closer to the figure of the suffering Christ.[9] Prisoner-of-war camps fueled a transformed apostolic mission that gave meaning to the difficult circumstances of their lives. As a Jocist wrote from Stargard in July 1942, "I was a half-hearted section member and now, strengthened by my faith, I'm going to bring Christ to my mates. What a beautiful life."[10]

Archival evidence suggests that like church leaders, J.O.C. leaders in the southern zone were initially sympathetic to Vichy efforts to remake youth. The report from the seventeenth National Council meeting in November 1940 noted, "The change in government and the assumption of power by Marshal Pétain, which have as their goal the reconstruction of France, must not leave the J.O.C. indifferent and uninvolved. Hasn't the J.O.C. program arrived at its moment?"[11] Similarities between the J.O.C.'s pre-war program and Vichy's National Revolution were indeed pronounced.[12] The movement's celebration of work and family at its Anniversary Congress in 1937 anticipated Vichy's triple emphasis on work, family, and fatherland. The J.O.C.'s steadfast promotion of Catholic moral values, which has been underplayed by French scholars, resembled Vichy's own. At the end of December 1940, a J.O.C. section in Montpellier wrote to the Vichy youth minister to enlist his support in closing down a neighborhood house of prostitution, telling him, "Finally someone is taking an interest in us and wants to help us build a new France that is healthy and decent."[13] Some Jocists supported Vichy's youth agenda by participating in its training programs and agencies. Paul Hibout, who led the youth delegation to Geneva in 1935 and helped direct J.O.C. strikers in 1936, became regional commissioner of youth work for the Vichy government.[14] Fifteen Jocists belonged to the second cohort of students at the Vichy training school for youth élites at La Faulconnière.[15]

As recent historical scholarship has demonstrated, attitudes toward Vichy evolved as the war ground on and circumstances changed. The government's policies on youth labor in 1942 and 1943 moved many Jocists to oppositional stances of one sort or another. After a voluntary but coercive effort to put young people to work on behalf of the German war effort failed to produce enough workers to satisfy German authorities, the Vichy government instituted a compulsory labor program on 16 February 1943. Under the Service du Travail Obligatoire (s.t.o.), young workers from the military classes of 1940, 1941, and 1942 were required to labor for two years on behalf of the German war effort in either Germany or occupied France; students faced only a one-year term.[16] This program, which sent young men to Germany to live and work in prison-like conditions, was widely resented across France.[17] Even Cardinal Liénart, the head of the Assembly of Cardinals and Archbishops that had previously supported Vichy, held out the possibility of clerical approval if young men refused to depart. Liénart announced in March 1943 that they could evade their s.t.o. duties without committing a sin.[18] He was not, he confirmed, advising them to depart.[19] Yet there was much that a young Christian could accomplish if he went to Germany. Cardinal Liénart had seen young workers leave with "conquering souls," and he knew how they served their brothers upon arriving in Germany. In this way they were "contributing to the extension of God's reign."[20]

Members of the j.o.c. followed both courses of action laid out by Cardinal Liénart, one of the movement's first episcopal champions. Officially the j.o.c. viewed the s.t.o. as an opportunity for apostolic mission.[21] Those Jocists who left for Germany were encouraged to spread their faith, to work on behalf of the material, moral, and spiritual well-being of those around them. Once in the work camps, Jocists cooperated with other Christians to found clandestine groups, such as "Youth Who Reacts." A year after its foundation, this group was thought to have a thousand members spread across seventy federations.[22] The young men's actions constituted a form of spiritual resistance that German authorities discovered and sought to repress starting in June 1944. Leaders were arrested and deported to concentration camps, where some, including Lucien Croci, perished. Not all Jocists chose this path. Some refused to report for the s.t.o., while others refused to reenlist. These actions moved the young workers outside the law and into the underground, where they relied on networks of assistance to survive and elude capture by authorities. From here certain Jocists moved into the Resistance. Some, like the longtime editor of *La Jeunesse Ouvrière* Paul Bacon, distributed *Témoignage chrétien*, while others joined armed combat groups, including the Jeunes Chrétiens Combattants.[23]

Conclusion

By war's end activists formed in the J.C. and J.O.C. resisted German occupiers and the Vichy government. Through their actions they helped remove
the stain of earlier wartime inaction by communist and Catholic leaders, and
helped position both the party and progressive Catholics to assume influential roles in postwar French politics. As the historian W. D. Halls comments
about the J.O.C., "The activities of these young 'social Catholics,' not least
of which was the 'mission' they saw as having to fulfill in Germany, were
one influential factor in determining French attitudes to the Church after
the War."[24] Youth action was equally important for a Communist Party that
cloaked itself in the mantle of Resistance to assert legitimacy in the postwar
era.[25] Those who had passed through the Young Communists and died at the
hands of the Germans figured prominently among Communists celebrated
as Resistance martyrs. They included Felix Cadras, who was said to have
met his death while singing "La Marseillaise," and Danielle Casanova, who
became *the* female communist Resistance heroine. The generation of young
people forged in the communist and Catholic youth organizations of the
1920s and 1930s served adult aims well, although not always in ways envisioned by their founders.

Conclusion

# Notes

### Introduction

1    The historical literature on youth and interwar Soviet communism, Italian fascism, and German National Socialism is extensive. See for example Anne E. Gorsuch, *Youth in Revolutionary Russia: Enthusiasts, Bohemians, Delinquents* (Bloomington: Indiana University Press, 2000); Tracy H. Koon, *Believe, Obey, Fight: Political Socialization of Youth in Fascist Italy, 1922–1943* (Chapel Hill: University of North Carolina Press, 1985); Victoria de Grazia, *How Fascism Ruled Women: Italy, 1922–1943* (Berkeley: University of California Press, 1992), chapter 5; Michael H. Kater, *Hitler Youth* (Cambridge: Harvard University Press, 2004); and Detlev K. Peukart, *Inside Nazi Germany: Conformity, Opposition, and Racism in Everyday Life* (New Haven: Yale University Press, 1987), chapter 8.

2    For an examination of the life and legend of Pavlik Morozov, who became a Soviet boy hero after being murdered by relatives for denouncing his father to Soviet authorities during the collectivization drive, see Catriona Kelly, *Comrade Pavlik: The Rise and Fall of a Soviet Boy Hero* (London: Granta Books, 2005).

3    Hitler said in 1933, for example, "I am beginning with the young. We older ones are used up. . . . But my magnificent youngsters! Are there finer ones anywhere in the world? Look at these young men and boys! What material! With them I can make a new world." Cited in Gerhard Rempel, *Hitler's Children: The Hitler Youth and the S.S.* (Chapel Hill: University of North Carolina Press, 1989), 1–2.

4    Julian Jackson first made this point in his important study *The Popular Front in France: Defending Democracy, 1934–1938* (Cambridge: Cambridge University Press, 1988), 134.

5    On the school-leaving age as an international issue see International Labour Conference, 19th session, *Unemployment among Young Persons* (Geneva: International Labour Office, 1935), chapter 2.

6    See Shanny Peer, *France on Display: Peasants, Provincials, and Folklore in the 1937 World's Fair* (Albany: State University of New York Press, 1998), chapter 1, for a good introduction to the fair and its politicization.

7    Edmond Labbé, *Exposition internationale des arts et techniques dans la vie moderne, Paris 1937, rapport général*, vol. 5, *La section française*, 144.

**252**  **8**  Archives Nationales (hereafter AN) F12 12139, folder "Hébergement," Service de l'Hébergement: Rapport Général.

**9**  Labbé, *Exposition internationale*, vol. 5, *La section française*, 145.

**10**  See *Vie catholique*, 28 May 1937, for a discussion of the Catholic youth presence at the exposition. The Catholic gymnastic demonstration is described in AN F12 12218, "Communiqué officiel."

**11**  For an overview of the vast literature see Rémi Fabre, "Les mouvements de jeunesse dans la France de l'entre-deux-guerres," *Mouvement social*, no. 168, July–September 1994, 9–30.

**12**  Blum, *La jeunesse et le socialisme*, 3.

**13**  Cachin, *Jeunesse, progrès et avenir*, 3.

**14**  This small book was written by the Radical politician Paul Reynaud and published by Gallimard in 1936.

**15**  "La Jeunesse et les Élections," *L'Avant-Garde ouvrière et communiste: organe officiel du Comité de l'Internationale Communiste des Jeunes* (hereafter *L'Avant-Garde*), 11 April 1936, 4.

**16**  On young intellectuals and their relationship to politics see the following classic studies: Jean Touchard, "L'Esprit des années 1930: une tentative de renouvellement de la pensée politique française," *Tendances politiques dans la vie française depuis 1789* (Paris: Hachette, 1960), 189–220; J. L. Loubet del Bayle, *Les non-conformistes des années 30: une tentative de renouvellement de la pensée politique française* (Paris: Le Seuil, 1969); Michel Winock, *Histoire politique de la Revue "Esprit," 1930–1950* (Paris: Le Seuil, 1975); and Jean-François Sirinelli, *Génération intellectuelle: khâgneux et normaliens dans l'entre-deux-guerres* (Paris: Fayard, 1988). Although the literature on youth movements focuses on individual movements, the historian Aline Coutrot, who died in 1987, attempted to take a broader view in her articles. However, she was less interested in youth movements associated with political parties. See for example Aline Coutrot, "Le Mouvement de jeunesse, un phénomène au singulier?," *Mouvements de jeunesse chrétiens et juifs: sociabilité juvénile dans un cadre européen 1799–1968*, ed. Gérard Cholvy (Paris: Le Cerf, 1985), 109–23.

**17**  V. I. Lenin, *On Youth* (Moscow: Progress, 1967), 229.

**18**  Gorsuch, *Youth in Revolutionary Russia*, 1.

**19**  For an excellent analysis of youth politics and culture during the first decade of Soviet communism see Gorsuch, *Youth in Revolutionary Russia*.

**20**  On primary education see for example Sarah Curtis, *Educating the Faithful: Religion, Schooling and Society in Nineteenth-Century France* (DeKalb: Northern Illinois University Press, 2000). For a good discussion of political battles over girls' secondary education in the second half of the nineteenth century, see Rebecca Rogers, *From the Salon to the Schoolroom: Educating Bourgeois Girls in Nineteenth-Century France* (University Park: Pennsylvania State University Press, 2005), chapter 7.

**21**  For a good introduction to turn-of-the-century Catholic efforts see Agnès Thiercé, *Histoire de l'adolescence, 1850–1914* (Paris: Belin, 1999), chapter 7. For a first-class discussion of Catholics' relationship to summer camps see Laura Lee Downs,

*Childhood in the Promised Land: Working-Class Movements and the Colonies de Va-cances in France, 1880–1960* (Durham: Duke University Press, 2002), chapter 2.

22 For more on new approaches to adolescence in France see Thiercé, *Histoire de l'adolescence.*

23 For recent statements on youth as a social and cultural construct see the intro-duction to Giovanni Levi and Jean-Claude Schmitt, eds., *A History of Young People in the West,* trans. Carol Volk (Cambridge: Harvard University Press, 1997), vol. 1, *Ancient and Medieval Rites of Passage,* and the prologue to Richard I. Jobs, *Riding the New Wave: Youth and the Rejuvenation of France after the Second World War* (Stanford: Stanford University Press, 2007). See also John R. Gillis's pioneering *Youth and History: Tradition and Change in European Age Relations, 1770–Present,* expanded student edn (New York: Academic, 1981).

24 In early modern Europe, for instance, youth (read "young men") played impor-tant cultural roles as guardians of local morality, especially during festivals. See for example Norbert Schindler, "Guardians of Disorder: Rituals of Youthful Culture at the Dawn of the Modern Age," *A History of Young People in the West,* ed. Levi and Schmitt, vol. 1, *Ancient and Medieval Rites of Passage,* esp. 249–55. See also Natalie Z. Davis's "The Reasons of Misrule," *Society and Culture in Early Modern France* (Stanford: Stanford University Press, 1975).

25 For Scott's now classic statement on gender see Joan W. Scott, "Gender: A Use-ful Category of Analysis," *Gender and the Politics of History* (New York: Columbia University Press, 1988), 28–52. For a good analysis of both the emergence of gender history and the forms it has taken since the 1980s see Laura Lee Downs, *Writing Gender History* (London: Hodder Arnold, 2004).

26 As Caroline Ford points out in the introduction to her *Divided Houses: Religion and Gender in Modern France* (Ithaca: Cornell University Press, 2005), the "femi-nization of religion" in nineteenth-century France has been used variously to denote the increased importance of women among the faithful and among reli-gious personnel, and the shifts in religious devotion that corresponded to these developments.

27 The historical literature on women and religion is vast. Important works include Clarissa W. Atkinson, Constance H. Buchanan, and Margaret R. Miles, eds., *Immaculate and Powerful: the Female in Sacred Image and Social Reality* (Boston: Beacon, 1985); Caroline Walker Bynum's many books and articles on medieval religion; and Robert Orsi, *Thank You, St. Jude: Women's Devotion to the Patron Saint of Hopeless Causes* (New Haven: Yale University Press, 1996).

28 See for example the following important studies of women's relationship to Catholicism in nineteenth-century France: Bonnie G. Smith, *Ladies of the Lei-sure Class: The Bourgeoises of Northern France in the Nineteenth Century* (Princeton: Princeton University Press, 1985); Claude Langlois, *Le catholicisme au féminin: les congrégations françaises à supérieures générales au XIXᵉ siècle* (Paris: Le Cerf, 1984); Ruth Harris, *Lourdes: Body and Spirit in the Secular Age* (London: Allen Lane / Penguin, 1999); Ford, *Divided Houses*; and Hazel Mills, "Negotiating the Divide: Women, Philanthropy and the 'Public Sphere' in Nineteenth-Century France,"

**254**    *Religion, Society and Politics in France since 1789*, ed. Frank Tallett and Nicholas Atkin (London: Hambledon, 1991), 29–54.

**29**    See the works cited in n. 16.

**30**    The first figure is taken from Statistique Générale de la France, *Annuaire Statistique*, vol. 56, *1940–1945* (Paris: Imprimerie Nationale, 1946); that for 1939 is cited in Siân Reynolds, *France between the Wars: Gender and Politics* (London: Routledge, 1996), 47.

**31**    For a good examination of the lives of working-class youth in the nineteenth century, see Michelle Perrot, "Worker Youth: From the Workshop to the Factory," *A History of Young People in the West*, ed. Levi and Schmitt, vol. 2, 66–116.

**32**    Michaud, *J'avais vingt ans*, 83.

**33**    E. Delesalle, *Le travail de la femme dans l'industrie textile et du vêtement de l'arrondissement de Lille* (diss., Lille, 1951), cited in Annie Fourcaut, *Femmes à l'usine: ouvrières et surintendantes dans les entreprises françaises de l'entre-deux-guerres* (Paris: François Maspero, 1982), 160.

**34**    See for example Annie Kriegel, *Les communistes français: essai d'ethnographie politique* (Paris: Le Seuil, 1968), chapter 5. See also Philippe Buton, "Les générations communistes," *Vingtième siècle: revue d'histoire*, special issue, 1989 ("Les générations"), 81–91.

**35**    See Buton, "Les générations communistes."

**36**    This is most evident in Philippe Robrieux, *Histoire intérieure du Parti Communiste*, vol. 1, *1920–1945* (Paris: Fayard, 1980).

**37**    Jacques Varin, *Jeunes comme JC: sur la jeunesse communiste*, vol. 1, *1920 à 1939* (Paris: Éditions Sociales, 1975).

**38**    Recent works on Soviet and German communism have not simply integrated women into the story but have also mapped how communist political categories and practices were often deeply masculinized. On German communism see Eric D. Weitz, *Creating German Communism, 1890–1990: From Popular Protests to Socialist State* (Princeton: Princeton University Press, 1997). For a good synthetic discussion of women and gender in the first decade of Soviet communism see Barbara Alpern Engel, *Women in Russia, 1700–2000* (Cambridge: Cambridge University Press, 2004), chapter 8. Anne Gorsuch also makes gender analysis central in her previously cited book on Russian youth in the 1920s.

**39**    See Joseph Debès and Émile Poulat, *L'appel de la J.O.C., 1926–1928* (Paris: Le Cerf, 1986); Jean-Pierre Coco and Joseph Debès, *L'élan jociste: le dixième anniversaire de la J.O.C., Paris, juillet 1937* (Paris: Éditions Ouvrières, 1989); and Pierre Pierrard, Michel Launay, and Rolande Trempé, eds., *La J.O.C.: regards d'historiens* (Paris: Éditions Ouvrières, 1984).

**40**    Aubert, *J.O.C., qu'as-tu fait de nos vies?*

**Chapter 1** Age and Generation in French Communism

**1**    On the party's formative years see Robert Wohl, *French Communism in the Making, 1914–1924* (Stanford: Stanford University Press, 1966); Philippe Robrieux, *Histoire intérieure du Parti Communiste*, vol. 1, *1920–1945* (Paris: Fayard, 1980); and

Stéphane Courtois and Marc Lazar, *Histoire du Parti Communiste Français* (Paris: Presses Universitaires de France, 1995), chapters 1–2.

2   For example, the median age of participants at the Bolshevik congress in 1917 was twenty-nine, and the average age of those in leadership positions in that year was thirty-nine. Anne E. Gorsuch, *Youth in Revolutionary Russia: Enthusiasts, Bohemians, Delinquents* (Bloomington: Indiana University Press, 2000), 16.

3   Wohl, *French Communism in the Making*, 216.

4   Jacques Dupâquier et al., *Histoire de la population française*, vol. 4, *De 1914 à nos jours* (Paris: Presses Universitaires de France, 1988), 52.

5   Ibid.

6   The damage to men's bodies by this unprecedentedly violent warfare has been discussed perceptively by Stéphane Audoin-Rouzeau and Annette Becker in *14–18: Understanding the Great War*, trans. Catherine Temerson (New York: Hill and Wang, 2003), chapter 1, and in Leonard V. Smith, Stéphane Audoin-Rouzeau, and Annette Becker, *France and the Great War, 1914–1918* (Cambridge University Press, 2003), esp. 92–93 (the phrase "mass corporeal destruction" is used on p. 92).

7   Smith, Audoin-Rouzeau, and Becker, *France and the Great War*, 69.

8   This is based on a statistic for 1922 cited in Guy Pedroncini, *Histoire militaire de la France*, vol. 3, *De 1871 à 1940* (Paris: Presses Universitaires de France, 1992), 323.

9   Ibid., 69.

10  See Robert Wohl, *The Generation of 1914* (Cambridge: Harvard University Press, 1979), chapter 1, for a good discussion of this survey.

11  *Journal officiel de la République Française, Débats parlementaires, Chambre des Députés*, Session Ordinaire, 1ère séance du 8 avril 1919, 1757.

12  See Wohl, *The Generation of 1914*, chapter 1 ("France: The Young Men of To-day").

13  For more on soldiers' attitudes toward the home front see Stéphane Audoin-Rouzeau, *Men at War, 1914–1918: National Sentiment and Trench Journalism in France during the First World War*, trans. Helen McPhail (Providence: Berg, 1992), chapter 4. For a good discussion of soldiers' attitudes toward women and their gendering of the division between the front and the home front, see Mary Louise Roberts, *Civilization without Sexes: Reconstructing Gender in Postwar France, 1917–1927* (Chicago: University of Chicago Press, 1994), chapter 1.

14  According to Modris Eksteins, the book's sales were "unprecedented in the entire history of publishing." Modris Eksteins, *Rites of Spring: The Great War and the Birth of the Modern Age* (New York: Doubleday, 1989), 276.

15  Erich Maria Remarque, *All Quiet on the Western Front*, trans. A. W. Whelan (New York: Fawcett Crest, 1982), 294.

16  *Clarté (bulletin français de l'Internationale de la Pensée)*, 11 October 1919, 2. To render the phrase "les mots glorieux" I use "big words"—the phrase employed by Jay Winter at various points in his *Sites of Memory, Sites of Mourning: The Great War in European Cultural History* (Cambridge: Cambridge University Press, 1995).

17   For good biographical essays on Lefebvre and Vaillant-Couturier see the entries by Nicole Racine and Annie Burger in *Dictionnaire biographique du mouvement ouvrier français: le Maitron*, ed. Claude Pennetier (Paris: l'Atelier, 1997 [CD-ROM]). The CD-ROM version of the dictionary is particularly useful for scholars of working-class politics, since it updates the bound volumes of "Le Maitron" in a number of significant ways. For example, it includes more entries on women and on Catholic militants. It also includes revised entries on communist militants which incorporate material from Comintern archival collections that became accessible to scholars after the collapse of the Soviet Union. Among records mined were autobiographical questionnaires completed by French militants upon their arrival in Moscow in the 1930s.

18   Quoted in Racine, "Raymond Lefebvre," *Dictionnaire biographique du mouvement ouvrier français*, ed. Pennetier.

19   Henri Barbusse, "Nous voulons faire la révolution dans les esprits," *Clarté*, 11 October 1919, 1.

20   Collection Bergeret, box 10, folder 185, Vassar College, 72 (in English in the original). I am grateful to Annie Burger-Roussennac for generously sharing this quotation with me.

21   Robrieux, *Histoire intérieure du Parti Communiste*, vol. 1, *1920–1945*, 25.

22   Wohl, *The Making of French Communism*, 25.

23   For more on the wartime organization of the workplace see for example Patrick Fridenson, ed., *The French Home Front, 1914–1918* (Providence: Berg, 1992).

24   Doriot's relationship to the war was slightly different from that of most other leading J.C. figures of the early 1920s. Born in 1898, this young metalworker from the socialist stronghold of Saint-Denis worked in a variety of wartime munitions factories and joined the J.S. in 1916. Unlike the slightly younger members of this first J.C. cohort, he was mobilized in 1917 with the military class of 1918. His unit saw intense fighting in the fall of 1918 and he was kept under arms until May 1920. For more on Doriot's life see Jean-Paul Brunet, *Jacques Doriot: du communisme au fascisme* (Paris: Balland, 1986).

25   Henri Barbé, "Souvenirs de militant et de dirigeant communiste," Hoover Institution Archives, 3–4 [typescript, n.d.].

26   These membership figures are from Christian Delporte, "Les jeunesses socialistes dans l'entre-deux-guerres," *Mouvement social*, no. 157 (October–December 1991), 34–35.

27   Barbé, "Souvenirs de militant et de dirigeant communiste," 5–6.

28   "Maurice Laporte," *Dictionnaire biographique du mouvement ouvrier français*, ed. Pennetier.

29   See Jean-Jacques Becker, *The Great War and the French People*, trans. Arnold Pomerans (Providence: Berg, 1993), 206, for a discussion of prices.

30   Jean-Jacques Becker makes this point regarding Paris and Toulouse in ibid., 210. Robert Wohl also makes this point in his history of the early years of French communism.

31   See Wohl, *French Communism in the Making*, 83.

Notes

**32** Ibid., 84–86. Interestingly, this view was shared by leaders of the Provisional
Government, who according to Orlando Figes "saw themselves as re-enacting
the French Revolution on Russian soil." Orlando Figes, *A People's Tragedy: The
Russian Revolution, 1891–1924* (London: Pimlico, 1997), 357–58.

**33** Becker, *The Great War and the French People*, 220.

**34** Ibid., 221.

**35** "Rosa Michel," *Dictionnaire biographique du mouvement ouvrier français*, ed. Pennetier. Born Marie Wacziarg in Poland, "Rosa Michel" spent little time in the
J.C., although she did represent it at the renegade Communist Youth International conference in Berlin in the spring of 1921, no doubt because she spoke
more languages than most members of Jeunesse Communiste. She went on to
have a rather remarkable life in international communism, joining the German
Communist Party (KPD) in 1922, spending considerable time in the USSR in the
1920s and 1930s, and marrying Walter Ulbricht, the future leader of the German
Democratic Republic, in 1925. After the Second World War, no longer married
to Ulbricht, she worked for *L'Humanité* as its correspondent from the GDR.

**36** Barbé, "Souvenirs de militant et de dirigeant communiste," 6.

**37** Wohl, *French Communism in the Making*, 97.

**38** Jean-Louis Robert, *Les ouvriers, la patrie et la révolution: Paris 1914–1919* (Paris:
Annales Littéraires, 1995), 279–80.

**39** Michaud, *J'avais vingt ans*, 79.

**40** Nicholas Papayanis, "Masses révolutionnaires et directions réformistes: les tensions au cours des grèves métallurgistes français en 1919," *Mouvement social*,
October–December 1975, 52.

**41** Cited in Robert, *Les ouvriers, la patrie et la révolution*, 320.

**42** Ibid., 323–24.

**43** Ibid., 328.

**44** Barbé, "Souvenirs de militant et de dirigeant communiste," 12.

**45** Ibid., 12.

**46** Ibid., 17.

**47** Bruhat, *Il n'est jamais trop tard*, 21.

**48** In their biographical entry on Péri, A. Olivesi and Claude Pennetier quote from
his biography. *Dictionnaire biographique du mouvement ouvrier français*, ed. Pennetier.

**49** Gabriel Péri, *Toward Singing Tomorrows: The Last Testament of Gabriel Péri*, quoted
in Richard Cornell, *Revolutionary Vanguard: The Early Years of the Communist Youth
International, 1914–1924* (Toronto: University of Toronto Press, 1982), 50.

**50** The entry on Billoux in the *Dictionnaire biographique* contains both these explanations. The one regarding Brion comes from Billoux's autobiographical questionnaire of 1932 for the Comintern.

**51** Stéphane Audoin-Rouzeau, *La guerre des enfants, 1914–1918: essai d'histoire culturelle* (Paris: Armand Colin, 1993), 18.

**52** Archives de la Guerre, E.M.A./3, 7N4033, dossier 2–9.

**53** Congar, *Journal de guerre*, 25.

.. 

**54** They first developed these ideas in *14–18* and have also made them an important part of Smith, Audoin-Rouzeau, and Becker, *France and the Great War*.

**55** Thorez-Vermeersch, *La vie en rouge*, 9.

**56** Their involvement will be discussed in chapter 5.

**57** Michaud, *J'avais vingt ans*, 67.

**58** In her study of young working women in interwar Paris, Catherine Rhein supplemented her sample of retirement dossiers with nine life histories. All of the nine women whose life histories were done remembered wartime restrictions and their families' sharp drop in living standards. They also remembered getting little to eat. Catherine Rhein, "Jeunes femmes au travail dans le Paris de l'entre-deux-guerres" (diss., Université de Paris VII, 1977), 97.

**59** Susan R. Grayzel, " 'The Souls of Soldiers': Civilians under Fire in First World War France," *Journal of Modern History* 78 (September 2006), 608–9.

**60** Ibid., 610.

**61** Jean-Jacques Becker argues that separation allowances created more difficulties for families of skilled workers, who were accustomed to higher male wages, than they did for day laborers and agricultural laborers. Becker, *The Great War and the French People*, 17.

**62** Pascale Quincy-Lefebvre, *Familles, institutions et déviances: une histoire de l'enfance difficile (1880–fin des années trente)* (Paris: Economica, 1997), 37.

**63** They first developed these ideas in *14–18*, especially part 3 ("Mourning").

**64** Olivier Faron, *Les enfants du deuil: orphelins et pupilles de la nation de la première guerre mondiale (1914–1941)* (Paris: La Découverte, 2001), 33.

**65** Audoin-Rouzeau and Becker, *14–18*, 222.

**66** Jacqueline Tardivel, "Des pacifistes aux résistantes, les militantes communistes, en France, dans l'entre-deux-guerres" (diss., Université de Paris VII, 1993), letter of 25 May 1990, annexe, 60. I am very grateful to Dr. Tardivel for making a copy of her thesis available to me.

**67** This discussion draws heavily on Faron's interesting analysis in chapter 6 ("Vivre le deuil").

**68** Tardivel, "Des pacifistes aux résistantes, les militantes communistes, en France, dans l'entre-deux-guerres," letter of 22 April 1990, annexe, 61.

**69** Quincy-Lefebvre, *Familles, institutions et déviances*, 38.

**70** See Wohl, *French Communism in the Making*, for an extended discussion of the debate over the future of French socialism.

**71** See Varin, *Jeunes comme JC*, vol. 1, *1920 à 1939*, chapter 4, for an account of the socialist youth conferences occurring during the first ten months of 1920.

**72** See the "Résolution et programme d'action présentés au Congrès National par le Comité de l'Internationale Communiste des Jeunes," *L'Avant-Garde*, 9 October 1920, 3.

**73** See for example Wohl, *French Communism in the Making*, 159–60.

**74** "À L'AVANT-GARDE!," *L'Avant-Garde*, 25 September 1920, 1.

**75** See for example "Résolution," *L'Avant-Garde*, 11 November 1920, 6.

Notes

**76** "Le Mouvement International des Jeunesses," *L'Avant-Garde*, 9 October 1920, 7.

**77** See Cornell, *Revolutionary Vanguard*, esp. chapter 3.

**78** Ibid., 88.

**79** Isabel A. Tirado, *Young Guard! The Communist Youth League, Petrograd 1917–1920* (New York: Greenwood, 1988), 17.

**80** Diane P. Koenker, "Urban Families, Working-Class Youth Groups and the 1917 Revolution in Moscow," *The Family in Imperial Russia: New Lines of Historical Research*, ed. David L. Ransel (Urbana: University of Illinois Press, 1978), 300.

**81** Diane P. Koenker, "Urbanization and Deurbanization in the Russian Revolution and Civil War," *Party, State, and Society in the Russian Civil War*, ed. Diane Koenker, William Rosenberg, and Ronald G. Suny (Bloomington: Indiana University Press, 1989), 88–89.

**82** For an overview of this process see Ralph T. Fisher Jr., *Pattern for Soviet Youth: A Study of the Congresses of the Komsomol, 1918–1954* (New York: Columbia University Press, 1959).

**83** Gorsuch, *Youth in Revolutionary Russia*, 15 22.

**84** "The Communist International and the Communist Youth Movement," *Theses, Resolutions and Manifestoes of the First Four Congresses of the Third International*, ed. Alan Adler (London: Inks Links, 1980), 231.

**85** For an account of the impact of the Third Comintern Congress on the Communist Youth International, see Cornell, *Revolutionary Vanguard*, chapter 7.

**86** *L'Avant-Garde*, 15 January 1921, 3.

**87** *L'Avant-Garde*, 15–30 May 1921, 3.

**88** "Les Assemblées de Moscou," *L'Humanité*, 9 July 1921, 3.

**89** For a discussion of the J.C. campaign see for example "À bas la mobilisation: la classe ou l'Armée Rouge," *L'Avant-Garde*, 15–31 May 1921, 1.

**90** I am basing this discussion on the account contained in Leon Trotsky, *Le mouvement communiste en France (1919–1939): textes choisis et présentés par Pierre Broué* (Paris: Éditions de Minuit, 1967), "Nouvelle étape (après le IIIᵉ Congrès)," 106–8.

**91** "Lettre de l'Exécutif du C.D. au P.C.F.," ibid., 129.

**92** Maurice Laporte, "Dernier jour du Congrès: vive la Troisième Internationale," *L'Avant-Garde*, 1–15 January 1922.

**93** Maurice Laporte, "Les Jeunesses Russes," *L'Avant-Garde*, special issue, 1921, 2.

**94** Maurice Honel, "Adaptation," *L'Avant-Garde*, 15–31 December 1921, 2.

**95** That this occurred is suggested by a letter written by the Jeunesses Syndicalistes and published in *L'Avant-Garde*, 15 August 1922, 4.

**96** Yolande Cohen, *Les jeunes, le socialisme et la guerre: histoire des mouvements de jeunesse en France* (Paris: L'Harmattan, 1989), 165.

**97** See for example Commissaire de Nantes, 7 May 1927, AN F7 13183.

**98** Barbé, "Souvenirs de militant et de dirigeant communiste," 20.

**99** Bruhat, *Il n'est jamais trop tard*, 44.

Notes

**100** Communist histories by Robert Wohl and by Stéphane Courtois and Marc Lazar both make this point.

**101** There are many indications of close involvement on the part of Comintern officials. For example, French military officials had already discovered in May 1922 that Comintern officials were giving German and French Communists "precise and formal" instructions regarding their response to a French invasion of the Ruhr. Archives de la Guerre, E.M.A./2 SCR, 7N7570, note no. 10830/2 S.C.R. 2. Courtois and Lazar also discuss Comintern involvement in this campaign on p. 78.

**102** Archives de la Guerre, E.M.A./2 S.C.R., 7N2570, "Renseignement: a/s d'un congrès de l'internationale des J.C. [sic] à Moscou," 10 January 1923 ("[sic]" in original).

**103** This statistic comes from Wohl, *French Communism in the Making*, 323.

**104** Barbé's participation in the Ruhr occupation is discussed both in his typescript memoirs (26–29) and in the biographical entry on him in the *Dictionnaire biographique du mouvement ouvrier français*, ed. Pennetier.

**105** Archives de la Guerre, E.M.A./3, 7N4044 dossier 2/3, le général Degoutte, "Rapport sur le moral," 20 August 1923.

**106** Ibid.

**107** That party officials had been rebuked for their insufficient commitment to the anticolonialist struggle is pointed out in the police summary of communist action in Morocco contained in "La campagne communiste contre les opérations du Maroc" (1925), AN F7 13172. Barbé discusses the transfer of money from Moscow directly to the J.C. on p. 36 of his typescript memoirs. David Slavin has argued that the J.C. was more radical when it came to Morocco because its leaders were less racist than party leaders. See David H. Slavin, "The French Left and the Rif War, 1924–1925: Racism and the Limits of Internationalism," *Journal of Contemporary History* 26 (1991), 5–32. Whether or not this is true, there is no question that the J.C. was out front on this issue.

**108** The telegram is reprinted in Brunet, *Jacques Doriot*, 54. For more on political responses to the war in Morocco see Slavin, "The French Left and the Rif War."

**109** This is the conclusion reached by Brunet.

**110** This story is recounted by Brunet, *Jacques Doriot*, 61–62.

**111** "Assemblée générale de la 4ᵉ Entente des J.C.," AN F7 13171.

**112** AN F7 13172.

**113** "La Campagne communiste contre les opérations du Maroc."

**114** Ibid.

**115** Barbé, "Souvenirs de militant et de dirigeant communiste," 84.

**116** Slavin, "The French Left and the Rif War," 15.

**117** Ferrat's comments on his work against the Rif War are quoted in "André Ferrat," *Dictionnaire biographique du mouvement ouvrier français*, ed. Pennetier.

**118** Brunet, *Jacques Doriot*, 70.

**119** Cited in ibid.

Notes

120 For a discussion of anticommunism within the French army see Paul-Marie de la Gorce, *The French Army: A Military-Political History*, trans. Kenneth Douglas (New York: George Braziller, 1963), chapter 10 ("The Army against Communism").

121 For example, the leading Young Communist Pierre Célor was put in solitary confinement after his mail was opened. Upon his release from solitary confinement he was discharged from the army and sent back to France for security reasons. "Pierre Célor," *Dictionnaire biographique du mouvement ouvrier français*, ed. Pennetier.

122 Jean-Paul Brunet, "Jacques Doriot," *Dictionnaire biographique du mouvement ouvrier français*, ed. Pennetier.

123 "Henri Barbé," *Dictionnaire biographique du mouvement ouvrier français*, ed. Pennetier.

124 "La répression," *L'Avant-Garde*, 25–30 April 1921, 4.

125 "Un beau Congrès National des Jeunesses Communistes," *L'Avant-Garde*, 6–15 June 1923, 3.

126 "La répression continue," *L'Avant-Garde*, 16–30 October 1923, 4.

127 "Action anti-militariste et questions militaires," *L'Humanité*, 16 February 1921, 5.

128 "Contre le crime: guerre capitaliste et guerre prolétarienne," *L'Avant-Garde*, 15–31 January 1923, 1.

129 Cited in Brunet, "Jacques Doriot," 65.

130 See Laird Boswell, *Rural Communism in France, 1920–1939* (Ithaca: Cornell University Press, 1998), for a study of the party's relationship to the peasantry during the interwar period.

131 Albert Vassart, "Memoirs," Hoover Institution Archives, n.d., part 1, 38.

132 See "Organisons la propagande à l'usine," *L'Avant-Garde*, 1–15 October 1922, 3.

133 Courtois and Lazar, *Histoire du Parti Communiste Français*, 88.

134 Ibid.

135 Doriot's fellow Young Communists in Saint-Denis worked extremely hard on behalf of his campaign in part because they wanted to use his victory—and consequent parliamentary immunity—to get him released from prison. It worked. For more on this see Barbé, "Souvenirs de militant et de dirigeant communiste," 40–42.

136 For more on the role that class played in interwar Soviet Russia see for example Sheila Fitzpatrick, *Everyday Stalinism: Ordinary Life in Extraordinary Times: Soviet Russia in the 1930s* (Oxford: Oxford University Press, 1999), 11–13 ("A Note on Class").

137 *L'Avant-Garde*, 15–31 January 1925, 4.

138 This was articulated clearly at the Sixth Comintern Congress in the summer of 1928. Courtois and Lazar, *Histoire du Parti Communiste Français*, 100.

139 Ibid.

140 For more on this see ibid., 96–99.

**262** **141** The best account of this confrontation can be found in Robrieux, *Histoire inté-rieure du Parti Communiste*, vol. 1, *1920–1945*, 290–91. My description is drawn from this account.

**142** "La Jeunesse Communiste à la tête de la Jeunesse Ouvrière," *L'Avant-Garde*, 27 August 1927, 1.

**143** "Un appel des Jeunesses Communistes aux jeunes travailleurs," *L'Avant-Garde*, 2 September 1927, 4.

**144** Barbé, "Souvenirs de militant et de dirigeant communiste," 134.

**145** "Une lettre des camarades Barbé et Ferrat aux membres du Comité Central de la Fédération," *L'Avant-Garde*, 29 December 1928, 3.

**146** Courtois and Lazar, *Histoire du Parti Communiste Français*, 101.

**147** Robrieux, *Histoire intérieure du Parti Communiste*, vol. 1, *1920–1945*, 300.

**148** See for example "Pour la formation d'un véritable parti bolchévik en France," *L'Avant-Garde*, 6 April 1929, 1.

**149** Robrieux, *Histoire intérieure du Parti Communiste*, vol. 1, *1920–1945*, 343.

**150** "Courage et en avant!," *L'Avant-Garde*, 27 July 1929, 1.

**151** Robrieux, *Histoire intérieure du Parti Communiste*, vol. 1, *1920–1945*, 345.

**152** Chapters 10 and 11 of Annie Kriegel and Stéphane Courtois, *Eugen Fried: le grand secret du* PCF (Paris: Le Seuil, 1997), provide the best and most recent examina-tion of the Barbé-Célor affair. My brief discussion of the affair relies very heavily on it. For the best earlier account see Jean-Paul Brunet, "Une crise du Parti Com-muniste Français: l'affaire Barbé-Célor," *Revue d'histoire moderne et contemporaine* 16 (July–September 1969), 439–61. Henri Barbé also discusses the events in his unpublished memoirs.

**153** Kriegel and Courtois, *Eugen Fried*, 159.

**154** Ibid., 169.

**155** Brunet, "Une crise du Parti Communiste Français," 461.

**156** See for example "La Région Parisienne à la tête des luttes de la jeunesse la-borieuse," *L'Avant-Garde*, 7 May 1932, 6.

**Chapter 2** Building a Communist Youth Organization

**1** "The Communist International and the Communist Youth Movement," *Theses, Resolutions and Manifestoes of the First Four Congresses of the Third International*, ed. Alan Adler (London: Inks Links, 1980), 231.

**2** Jacques Doriot, "Dans l'Internationale Communiste des Jeunes: au deuxième congrès," *L'Avant-Garde*, 15–31 December 1921, 3.

**3** The position of the Communist Youth International was first published in *L'Avant-Garde* as "Appel de l'Internationale des Jeunes," *L'Avant-Garde*, 31 July 1922, 1.

**4** See for example *L'Avant-Garde*, 1–15 February 1922, 3.

**5** *L'Avant-Garde*, 28 May 1922, 3.

**6** *L'Avant-Garde*, 1 May 1924, 4.

**7** See Robert Soucy, *French Fascism: The First Wave, 1924–1933* (New Haven: Yale University Press, 1986), for a discussion of these movements' establishment, ideology, and constituencies. Although there has been considerable scholarly discussion over whether these movements were fascist, the Young Communists certainly treated them as such.

**8** Cited in ibid., 39.

**9** Ibid., 27.

**10** Taittinger, *Les cahiers de la Jeune France*, 87–88.

**11** Ibid., 80.

**12** Soucy, *French Fascism: The First Wave*, 29.

**13** See Samuel Kalman, "Faisceau Visions of Physical and Moral Transformation and the Cult of Youth in Inter-war France," *European History Quarterly* 33, no. 3 (2003), 348–50.

**14** This comes from a police analysis from 1925 of Jeunesses Patriotes membership, quoted in Soucy, *French Fascism: The First Wave*, 50.

**15** Ibid., xi.

**16** *L'Avant-Garde*, 15–31 January 1925, 4.

**17** See for example Jacques Doriot writing in *L'Avant-Garde*, 1–15 January 1925, 1.

**18** See Soucy, *French Fascism: The First Wave*, 55–56, for an account of the evening from the perspective of the Jeunesses Patriotes.

**19** *L'Avant-Garde*, 1–15 May 1925, 1.

**20** "Le congrès du parti: il a consacré la défaite de la droite et la marche vers la bolchévisation," *L'Avant-Garde*, 1–15 February 1925, 1.

**21** Both of Doriot's biographers describe how Doriot was a new kind of Bolshevik deputy, one faithful to Comintern directives regarding communist parliamentary behavior. Jean-Paul Brunet argues for the distinctiveness of this particular speech in Jean-Paul Brunet, *Jacques Doriot: du communisme au fascisme* (Paris: Balland, 1986), 50–51.

**22** *Journal officiel de la République Française, Débats Parlementaires, Chambre des Députés*, 19 December 1924, 4609.

**23** Ibid., 4611.

**24** Ibid., 4614.

**25** This representation of the Soviet Union and its leaders often had deep resonance for French Communists during the 1920s. Lise London described her Spanish-born father's reaction to Lenin's death in the following way: "Pour papa, pour nous, Lénine avait prouvé qu'il n'était pas besoin d'attendre au-delà de la mort un paradis problématique où les derniers seraient les premiers, mais qu'il était possible de le construire sur terre, de notre vivant." London, *Le printemps des camarades*, 47.

**26** *L'Avant-Garde*, 9 January 1926, 1.

**27** See for example *L'Avant-Garde*, 15 January 1927, 4.

**28** See for example "Rapport moral des JC," St-Étienne, 24 February 1927, AN F7 13183.

**29** *L'Avant-Garde*, 26 December 1925, 1.

**30** See Anne E. Gorsuch, *Youth in Revolutionary Russia: Enthusiasts, Bohemians, Delinquents* (Bloomington: Indiana University Press, 2000), 36–37.

31   Ibid., 36.

32   Thorez-Vermeersch, *La vie en rouge*, 37.

33   Anne Gorsuch points out that the Komsomol paid special attention to political pageantry during the NEP period in the 1920s. Gorsuch, *Youth in Revolutionary Russia*, 59.

34   In his interesting collection of first-hand accounts by French travelers to the Soviet Union between 1917 and 1939, for instance, Fred Kupferman includes a description of the congress of the Internationale Syndicale Rouge in 1921 which illustrates how Lenin's very appearance was carefully managed to create the most powerful effect among delegates. According to Gaston Leval, Lenin only appeared at the congress on the sixth day, and his long-awaited appearance was greeted with an explosion of "Long Live Lenin!" in all the languages. He noted further that Lenin turned his head to demonstrate his simplicity. Leval remembers, "On aurait dit une danseuse, refusant les applaudissements pour en provoquer davantage." Fred Kupferman, ed., *Au pays des soviets: le voyage français en Union Soviétique, 1917–1939* (Paris: Gallimard, 1979), 42.

35   *L'Avant-Garde*, 1–15 September 1924, 2.

36   Barbé, "Souvenirs de militant et de dirigeant communiste," 57.

37   "Si tu songeais un peu . . . ," *L'Avant-Garde*, 25 December 1923, 1.

38   See for example Michelle Perrot, "Worker Youth: From the Workshop to the Factory," *A History of Young People in the West*, ed. Levi and Schmitt, vol. 2, 88–93.

39   "Une grande enquête de *L'Avant-Garde* sur la crise de l'apprentissage," *L'Avant-Garde*, 8 January 1927, 1.

40   Stéphane Courtois and Marc Lazar, *Histoire du Parti Communiste Français* (Paris: Presses Universitaires de France, 1995), 97.

41   Philippe Robrieux, *Histoire intérieure du Parti Communiste*, vol. 1, *1920–1945* (Paris: Fayard, 1980), 227.

42   Danielle Tartakowsky, "Un instrument de culture politique: les premières écoles centrales du P.C.F.," *Mouvement social*, no. 91 (April–June 1975), 102.

43   Ferrat, *Faisons vivre nos cellules!*, 11.

44   Ibid., 44.

45   The "No Soviets!" example comes from Herrick Chapman, *State Capitalism and Working-Class Radicalism in the French Aircraft Industry* (Berkeley: University of California Press, 1991), 51.

46   Robrieux, *Histoire intérieure du Parti Communiste*, vol. 1, *1920–1945*, 228.

47   As Jean-Paul Brunet points out, many communist workers in Saint-Denis were reluctant to risk their jobs to join factory cells. Jean-Paul Brunet, *Saint-Denis, la ville rouge: socialisme et communisme en banlieue ouvrière, 1890–1939* (Paris: Hachette, 1980), 264.

48   "Lettre du Cussat à Raymond Berger," 13 April 1927, AN F7 13183.

49   Jean Paul Depretto and Sylvie V. Schweitzer, *Le communisme à l'usine: vie ouvrière et mouvement ouvrier chez Renault, 1920–1939* (Paris: EDIRES, 1984), 92–93.

50   Chapman, *State Capitalism and Working-Class Radicalism in the French Aircraft Industry*, 57.

Notes

**51**   *L'Avant-Garde*, 15–31 January 1925, 4.

**52**   *L'Avant-Garde*, 1 November 1924, 1.

**53**   Robrieux, *Histoire intérieure du Parti Communiste*, vol. 1, *1920–1945*, 234. It should be noted, however, that Robrieux does not define "young worker" in terms of age.

**54**   His activities in this sphere are described in his memoir as well as in Jean-Paul Brunet's study of Saint-Denis.

**55**   AN F7 13185.

**56**   *Bulletin d'organisation*, April 1931, AN F7 13185.

**57**   12 March 1931, AN F7 13185.

**58**   "Rapport de Billoux au congrès du parti sur le travail réalisé par la Jeunesse Communiste," *La vie de la Fédération*, suppl. to *Bulletin de la Fédération*, no. 10 (April 1929), 10.

**59**   "Notre Comité Central," *L'Avant-Garde*, 7 April 1928, 4.

**60**   *L'Avant-Garde*, 17 March 1928, 3.

**61**   AN F7 13184.

**62**   "Rapport sur les grèves du Nord et sur l'activité de la J.C. pendant les grèves," October 1930, AN F7 13184.

**63**   *L'Avant-Garde*, 7 April 1928, 4.

**64**   See for example "Matériaux pour la résolution antimilitariste," *La vie de la Fédération*, no. 12 (1929), 28, in AN F7 13181.

**65**   For more on the establishment of the eight-hour workday in France and challenges to it, see Gary Cross, *A Quest for Time: The Reduction of Work in Britain and France, 1840–1940* (Berkeley: University of California Press, 1989), esp. chapter 6.

**66**   "Nos enquêtes: amusons-nous," *L'Avant-Garde*, 16–31 May 1924, 1.

**67**   See Richard Holt, *Sport and Society in Modern France* (London: Macmillan, 1981), chapter 10, for a good discussion of the political uses of organized sport in turn-of-the-century France. Robert A. Nye also discusses fin-de-siècle sport in the concluding chapter of his *Masculinity and Male Codes of Honor in Modern France* (Oxford: Oxford University Press, 1993).

**68**   Holt, *Sport and Society in Modern France*, 196.

**69**   For more on employers' attitudes toward sport see for example Patrick Fridenson, "Les ouvriers de l'automobile et le sport," *Actes de la Recherche en Sciences Sociales*, September 1989, 50–62.

**70**   Charles Rearick, *The French in Love and War: Popular Culture in the Era of the World Wars* (New Haven: Yale University Press, 1997), 49.

**71**   "Désagrégons les sociétés sportives bourgeoises! Développons nos clubs ouvriers!," *L'Avant-Garde*, 3 November 1928, 1.

**72**   "Sport et communisme," *L'Avant-Garde*, special issue, 1921, 4.

**73**   Ibid.

**74**   *L'Avant-Garde*, 1–15 December 1922, 4.

**75**   See for example "Sport et communisme."

**76**   See Christopher S. Thompson, *The Tour de France: A Cultural History* (Berkeley: University of California Press, 2006), esp. chapter 4, for an interesting discussion of Tour racers' class backgrounds and their treatment by race sponsors. As Thompson makes clear, Tour de France racers came overwhelmingly from the working class and lower middle class.

**77**  For information on racers' occupations see Thompson, *The Tour de France*, 267–68 ("Appendix: Racers' Occupations").

**78**  For more on adult Communists' critiques of the Tour see Thompson, *The Tour de France*, 195–97.

**79**  "Le Tour de France cycliste: sous le signe du chronomètre," *L'Avant-Garde*, 25 June 1927, 2.

**80**  *L'Avant-Garde*, 15–30 February 1922, 4.

**81**  "Dans la F.S.T.," *L'Avant-Garde*, 1–15 July 1924, 4.

**82**  "Les travailleurs sportifs russes à Pershing et à Saint-Denis," *L'Avant-Garde*, 9 January 1926, 1.

**83**  "Notes. . . . années 1925–1932," AN F7 13137.

**84**  For a discussion of the development of these festivals in the Soviet Union see Robert Edelman, *Serious Fun: A History of Spectator Sports in the U.S.S.R.* (New York: Oxford University Press, 1993), chapter 2.

**85**  W. J. Murray, "The French Workers' Sports Movement and the Victory of the Popular Front in 1936," *International Journal of the History of Sport* 4, no. 2 (1987), 205.

**86**  "En marge des sports: jeunesses-communistes de la F.S.T.," *L'Avant-Garde*, 1–15 April 1924, 2.

**87**  "Notes. . . . années 1925–1932," AN F7 13137.

**88**  "Le triomphe de la ligne révolutionnaire s'est affirmé au Congrès de la F.S.T.," *L'Avant-Garde*, 1 February 1930, 1.

**89**  29 July 1931, AN F7 13185.

**90**  "Rapport de Billoux au congrès du parti sur le travail réalisé par la Jeunesse Communiste," 9.

**91**  21 July 1932, AN F7 13137.

**92**  London, *Le printemps des camarades*, 85–86.

**93**  London includes this photograph in ibid.

**94**  The "red suburbs" have been studied extensively. See for example Annie Fourcaut, *Bobigny, banlieue rouge* (Paris: Éditions Ouvrières / Fondation Nationale des Sciences Politiques, 1986); Annie Fourcaut, ed., *Banlieue rouge, 1920–1960: années Thorez, années Gabin: archétype du populaire, banc d'essai des modernités* (Paris: Autrement, 1992); Tyler Stovall, *The Rise of the Paris Red Belt* (Berkeley: University of California Press, 1990); Michel Hastings, *Halluin la rouge, 1919–1939: aspects d'un communisme identitaire* (Lille: Presses Universitaires de Lille, 1991); and Laura Lee Downs, *Childhood in the Promised Land: Working-Class Movements and the Colonies de Vacances in France, 1880–1960* (Durham: Duke University Press, 2002), chapter 6.

**95**  Annie Fourcaut, *Bobigny, banlieue rouge*, 143.

**96**  Michel Hastings, "Identité culturelle locale et politique festive communiste: Halluin la rouge, 1920–1934," *Mouvement social*, no. 139 (April–June 1987), 13.

97  *L'Avant-Garde*, 5 November 1927, 2.

98  AN F7 13184.

99  "Rapport de Billoux au congrès du parti sur le travail réalisé par la Jeunesse Communiste," 9.

100  "La diffusion de *L'Avant-Garde*," *L'Avant-Garde*, 19 March 1928, 4.

101  "Les jeunes travailleurs doivent rediger eux-mêmes leur journal," *L'Avant-Garde*, 7 July 1928, 1.

102  "Comment la J.C. de Roubaix a su distraire et éduquer les jeunes travailleurs," *L'Avant-Garde*, 22 September 1928, 1.

103  *L'Avant-Garde*, 15 June 1929, 1.

104  In 1922 she went to work for the publishing arm of the Communist Youth International and joined the German Communist Party. She subsequently spent considerable time in the Soviet Union in the 1920s and 1930s. "Rosa Michel," *Dictionnnaire biographique du mouvement ouvrier français*. See also n. 35 to chapter 1.

105  AN F7 13183; C.C. de Bordeaux, 6 July 1932, AN F7 13185.

106  For an analysis of the Bolsheviks' complicated and often conflicted efforts to mobilize women in revolutionary Russia see Elizabeth A. Wood, *The Baba and the Comrade: Gender and Politics in Revolutionary Russia* (Bloomington: Indiana University Press, 1997).

107  Ibid., 55. According to Wood, those targeted included young female members of the party, Komsomol, and trade unions, students in primary and secondary schools, and the unemployed.

108  Anne Gorsuch argues that young women's greater responsibilities at home and more restricted opportunities within society combined with parental prohibitions and concerns and a masculine culture within the Komsomol to limit young women's participation in the Komsomol. See Gorsuch, *Youth in Revolutionary Russia*, esp. chapter 5 ("Gender and Generation").

109  "Une visite d'usine à Moscou," *L'Avant-Garde*, 16–31 August 1924, 3.

110  "Nos jeunes filles: une tribune nouvelle," *L'Avant-Garde*, 1–18 January 1922, 3–4.

111  Gilberte Lesage ran this, and wrote the occasional article in *L'Avant-Garde*.

112  In her essay on the woman worker of the nineteenth century, for example, Joan W. Scott notes how male workers often treated the woman worker as a threat to male wages who must be excluded from both the workplace and trade unions. Joan W. Scott, "The Woman Worker," *A History of Women in the West*, vol. 4, *Emerging Feminism from Revolution to World Wars*, ed. Geneviève Fraisse and Michelle Perrot (Cambridge: Harvard University Press, 1993), 417–20. See also Charles Sowerwine, *Sisters or Citizens? Women and Socialism in France since 1876* (Cambridge: Cambridge University Press, 1982), 22–23, for examples of male concern over the presence of female workers in the workplace voiced at the first worker congresses of the 1870s.

113  Gaston Monmousseau made this clear at the C.G.T.U.'s fourth congress in 1927. See the proceedings from the Congrès National Ordinaire (4ᵉ Congrès de la C.G.T.U.), Bordeaux, 19–24 September 1927, 13.

**268**  114  "La Semaine internationale des femmes," *L'Avant-Garde*, 3 March 1928, 2.

115  See for example "L'exploitation des femmes à la fabrique des chaussures Ple," *L'Avant-Garde*, 30 March 1929, 3, and "Jeunes ouvriers, manifestez le 8 mars!," *L'Avant-Garde*, 5 March 1932, 3.

116  For discussions of the party's relationship to women in the 1920s see Christine Bard and Jean-Louis Robert, "The French Communist Party and Women, 1920–1939," *Women and Socialism, Socialism and Women: Europe between the Two World Wars*, ed. Helmut Gruber and Pamela Graves (New York: Berghahn, 1998), 321–47, and Jacqueline Tardivel, "Des pacifistes aux résistantes, les militantes communistes, en France, dans l'entre-deux-guerres" (diss., Université de Paris VII, 1993).

117  See for example *L'Avant-Garde*, 5 February 1927, 5.

118  For example, Jeanne Curninier, who was from a family of working-class militants, kept in contact with working-class organizations through her membership in sports clubs when she worked as a domestic in the early 1930s. Claudine Chomat's first involvement in a working-class organization was in the theater organization the F.T.O.F. *Dictionnnaire biographique du mouvement ouvrier français*, ed. Pennetier.

119  Semard described her activities in an interview with the author, Paris, 9 December 1990.

120  "Jeannette Vermeersch," *Dictionnaire biographique du mouvement ouvrier français*, ed. Pennetier.

121  Interview with author, Paris, 4 December 1990.

122  "Juliette Nédelec," *L'Avant-Garde*, 20 May 1933, 1–2.

123  For an excellent discussion of the ways women's new behaviors and fashions were debated as gender relations were recast in the 1920s, see Mary Louise Roberts, *Civilization without Sexes: Reconstructing Gender in Postwar France, 1917–1927* (Chicago: University of Chicago Press, 1994).

124  Many commented on this phenomenon. See for example Ouzoulias-Romagon, *J'étais agent de liaison des F.T.P.F.*, 44, who commented that the majority of parents did not accept the idea of young women in mixed-sex groups.

125  6 July 1932, AN F7 13185.

126  Ouzoulias-Romagon, *J'étais agent de liaison des F.T.P.F.*, 46.

127  During the 1920s only primary schools in small rural communities educated both girls and boys, and the two sexes were carefully separated inside classrooms. French secondary education only became coeducational with laws passed in 1976. For more on relations between the sexes in French education see Rebecca Rogers, ed., *La mixité dans l'éducation: enjeux passés et présents* (Paris: ENS, 2004).

128  Thorez-Vermeersch, *La vie en rouge*, 32–33. As Gorsuch points out, involvement in the Komsomol was similarly seen as morally suspect. Gorsuch, *Youth in Revolutionary Russia*, 99.

129  London, *Le printemps des camarades*, 78.

130  *L'Avant-Garde*, 1–15 January 1923, 4.

Notes

131  Quoted in Renée Rousseau, *Les femmes rouges: chronique des années Vermeersch* (Paris: Albin Michel, 1983), 14.

132  Interview with author, Nanterre, 10 December 1990.

133  Significantly, the first article on young women in *L'Avant-Garde* remarked on the innumerable yet unknown typists within the organization. *L'Avant-Garde*, 1–18 January 1922, 3.

134  London, *Le printemps des camarades*, 85.

135  AN F7 13181, folder: Internationale Semaine de Jeunes.

136  AN F7 13181, folder: Renseignements.

**Chapter 3**  Age, Generation, and Catholic Anticommunism

1  Lhande, *Le Christ dans la banlieue*, 34.

2  Joseph Debès and Émile Poulat, *L'appel de la J.O.C., 1926–1928* (Paris; Le Cerf, 1986), delineates the role played by clerics in the J.O.C.'s establishment but does not analyze the movement itself.

3  Michel Launay, "La J.O.C. dans son premier développement," *La J.O.C.: regards d'historiens*, ed. Pierre Pierrard, Michel Launay, and Rolande Trempé (Paris: Éditions Ouvrières, 1984), 30.

4  See *Jocisme français: 1927–1939*, part 1, Bibliothèque Historique 46, Archives Centrales de la J.O.C.

5  For an introduction to nineteenth-century social Catholicism see Gérard Cholvy and Yves-Marie Hilaire, *Histoire religieuse de la France contemporaine, 1880/1930* (Paris: Bibliothèque Historique Privat, 1986), esp. 73–83. For more sustained analysis see Jean-Marie Mayeur, *Catholicisme social et démocratie chrétienne: principes romains, expériences français* (Le Cerf, 1986), esp. part 1.

6  Stéphane Courtois and Marc Lazar, *Histoire du Parti Communiste Français* (Paris: Presses Universitaires de France, 1995), 81.

7  See Édouard Blanc, *La ceinture rouge: enquête sur la situation politique et sociale de la banlieue de Paris* (Paris: Spes, 1927). For a general discussion of the emergence of the idea of the red belt see Annie Fourcaut, *Bobigny, banlieue rouge* (Paris: Éditions Ouvrières / Fondation Nationale des Sciences Politiques, 1986), esp. chapters 1–2.

8  For more on Action Populaire see Paul Droulers, *Politique sociale et christianisme: le père Desbuquois et l'Action Populaire* (Paris: Éditions Ouvrières, 1969, 1981).

9  Jeanne Moret, *Le Père Lhande, pionnier du Christ dans la banlieue et à la radio* (Paris: Beauchesne, 1964), 101.

10  Lhande, *Le Christ dans la banlieue*, 8.

11  Ibid., 11.

12  Ibid., 34.

13  Ibid., 34–35.

14  On nineteenth-century Catholic schools see Sarah Curtis, *Educating the Faithful: Religion, Schooling and Society in Nineteenth-Century France* (DeKalb: Northern Illinois University Press, 2000).

**270**  15  For a sympathetic analysis of the turn-of-the-century *patronage* see Laura Lee
Downs, *Childhood in the Promised Land: Working-Class Movements and the Colonies de Vacances in France, 1880–1960* (Durham: Duke University Press, 2002),
chapter 2.

16  Agnès Thiercé, *Histoire de l'adolescence, 1850–1914* (Paris: Belin, 1999), 193.

17  On Catholic efforts to create summer camps see Downs, *Childhood in the Promised Land*, esp. chapter 2.

18  Although this was an international development, its contours varied across
national boundaries. On the French case see Thiercé, *Histoire de l'adolescence*.
Catholic approaches are examined in chapter 7.

19  Ibid., 195.

20  Gérard Cholvy, "Patronages et oeuvres de jeunesse dans la France contemporaine," *Revue d'histoire de l'Église de France* 68, no. 181 (July–December 1982), 246.

21  Jacques Leurent, *La jeunesse ouvrière*, extrait du *Messager du Coeur de Jésus* (Toulouse: Apostolat de la Prière, 1926), 9.

22  Annette Becker, *La guerre et la foi: de la mort à la mémoire, 1914–1930* (Paris:
Armand Colin, 1994), 50.

23  Pierre Pierrard, *Le prêtre français* (Paris: Bloud et Gay, 1969), 153–54.

24  Becker, *La guerre et la foi*, 36.

25  For an interesting account of one military chaplain's wartime experiences see
Catherine Masson, *Le cardinal Liénart, évêque de Lille, 1928–1968* (Paris: Le Cerf,
2001), chapter 2.

26  The Légion d'Honneur was bestowed by General Pétain in 1917. Ibid.

27  Ibid., 72, 80.

28  Quoted in Pierrard, *Le prêtre français*, 156.

29  Béjot, *Un évêque à l'école de la J.O.C.*, 22.

30  Béjot remembered that his cohort at Issy consisted mostly of adults in the professions. Ibid., 18.

31  Masson, *Le cardinal Liénart, évêque de Lille*, 75–76.

32  Cited in Pierre Pierrard, *Georges Guérin: une vie pour la J.O.C.* (Paris: L'Atelier /
Éditions Ouvrières, 1997), 90.

33  According to Michel Launay, the crusade against "Bolshevik barbarism" formed
a central part of the organization's mission. Michel Launay, *La C.F.T.C.: origines
et développement, 1919–1940* (Paris: La Sorbonne, 1986), 71.

34  Véret, *J'ai vu grandir la J.O.C.*, 22.

35  My discussion of Guérin's life relies almost entirely on information provided in
Pierrard, *Georges Guérin*.

36  Ibid., 105.

37  Quoted in ibid., 106.

38  This account first appeared in Droulers's book on Action Populaire (p. 274) and
has been accepted by scholars who have written on the J.O.C.'s birth.

39  Pierrard, *Georges Guérin*, 107–8.

40  For a thorough treatment of the circumstances surrounding the J.O.C.'s beginnings in 1926 and 1927 see Debès and Poulat, *L'appel de la J.O.C.*

Notes

41  Droulers, *Politique sociale et christianisme*, 276.

42  Pierrard, *Georges Guérin*, 137.

43  In fact there was considerable tension with the A.C.J.F. during the J.O.C.'s first years. For more on the tensions and the negotiations that followed see Debès and Poulat, *L'appel de la J.O.C.*

44  Ibid., 62–63.

45  See for example Cheryl Koos, "Fascism, Fatherhood and the Family in Interwar France: The Case of Antoine Rédier and the Légion," *Journal of Family History* 24 (1999), 317–29.

46  Cardinal Baudrillart noted in March 1936, "On a été si content depuis la guerre de les voir remplies d'hommes, de voir tant de brave gens, anciens combattants et autres demander des messes, des sermons." Baudrillart, *Les carnets du cardinal Baudrillart*, 147–48.

47  For more on Catholic sporting exhibitions see AN F12 12218.

48  The following account of male mobilization draws heavily on Cholvy and Hilaire, *Histoire religieuse de la France contemporaine*, 282–87.

49  Ibid., 285.

50  Ibid.

51  See for example *L'essentiel pour commencer la J.O.C.*

52  Georges Guérin, "La préservation de la Jeunesse contre le Communisme et les autres erreurs," Intention générale, approuvée et bénie par le pape, *Messager du coeur de Jésus*, October 1928, 513–20, repr. as annexe VII in Debès and Poulat, *L'appel de la J.O.C.*, 262–69 (citation from p. 263).

53  Ibid., 263.

54  Ibid., 264.

55  Leurent, *La jeunesse ouvrière*, 6–7.

56  Joseph Cardyn, "Conférences à des prêtres sur leur rôle dans la J.O.C." (1933), Bibliothèque Historique 424, Archives de la J.O.C., 4–5.

57  See for example Leurent, *La jeunesse ouvrière*, 4–5.

58  *L'essentiel pour commencer la J.O.C.*, 3 [recte 1].

59  Leurent, *La jeunesse ouvrière*, 12.

60  Ibid., 15.

61  For historical approaches to leisure among young workers see for example Kathy Peiss, *Cheap Amusements: Working Women and Leisure in Turn-of-the-Century New York* (Philadelphia: Temple University Press, 1986); Nan Enstad, *Ladies of Labor, Girls of Adventure: Working Women, Popular Culture, and Labor Politics at the Turn of the Twentieth Century* (New York: Columbia University Press, 1999); and W. Scott Haine, "The Development of Leisure and the Transformation of Working-Class Adolescence, Paris 1830–1940," *Journal of Family History* 17, no. 4 (1992), 451–76.

62  On the popularity of dance in the 1920s see Jeffrey H. Jackson, *Making Jazz French: Music and Modern Life in Interwar Paris* (Durham: Duke University Press, 2003), 40–46.

63  Quoted in ibid., 40.

64 *Jeunesse Ouvrière*, 1 December 1931, 1.

65 Rearick, *The French in Love and War*, 91.

66 Jacques Valdour, *Ouvriers parisiens d'après-guerre* (Paris: Arthur Rousseau, 1921), 175.

67 "Compagnes de travail," *Jeunesse Ouvrière*, 1 August 1931, 1.

68 Joseph Cardyn, "Les jeunes travailleurs en face du mariage: leçons données par M. le chanoine Cardyn à la semaine d'études de Godinne, 1–5 avril 1932" (Paris: J.O.C, 1938), 21.

69 Le père Ranson, *Le problème de la jeunesse ouvrière: une formule de solution, la J.O.C.*, Conférence donnée par le P. Ranson, S.J., à un groupe d'industriels du Nord (Lille: H. Morel, 1929), 9.

70 Ibid., 12.

71 *Jeunesse Ouvrière*, November 1931, 1.

72 *La collaboration jociste: le carnet du semainier*, 2ᵉ Semaine Nationale d'Études de la J.O.C., September 1929 (Paris: Jeunesse Ouvrière), Bibliothèque Historique 122, Archives de la J.O.C., 16.

73 Ranson, *Le problème de la jeunesse ouvrière*, 21.

74 For a more extensive discussion of J.O.C. spirituality see Launay, "La J.O.C. dans son premier développement," 42–46.

75 *L'équipe ouvrière*, 1 February 1930, 27. The material cited also appears verbatim in Charles Bordet, *Regards jocistes sur l'Évangile* (Paris: Éditions Jocistes, 1933), 11.

76 See for example *L'équipe ouvrière*, 1 April 1930, 9, 52.

77 See for example Alphonse de Parvillez, "Le beau départ de la J.O.C.," Extrait des *Études* du 20 novembre 1928 (Paris: Secrétariat de la J.O.C.), Bibliothèque Historique 426, Archives de la J.O.C., 25.

78 "Extrait de l'allocution de Mgr. Herbigny," *Souvenirs du premier pèlerinage de la J.O.C. française à Rome (19–27 septembre 1931)*, Bibliothèque Historique 419, Archives de la J.O.C., 39.

79 "Discours de Monsieur l'abbé Bordet," *Souvenirs du premier pèlerinage de la J.O.C. française à Rome*.

80 Ibid., 46.

81 *Jocistes dans la tourmente: histoire des jocistes (JOC-JOCF) de la région parisienne, 1937–1947* (Paris: Témoignage Chrétien / Éditions Ouvrières, n.d.), 26.

82 See for example *Pour être jociste* (Paris: Jeunesse Ouvrière, n.d.), Bibliothèque Historique 449, Archives de la J.O.C.

83 Ibid., 4–6.

84 Joseph Cardyn, "Conférences à des prêtres sur leur rôle dans la J.O.C.," 11.

85 Letter from J. Boulier to J. Cardijn, 30 June 1927, published in full in Debès and Poulat, *L'appel de la J.O.C.*, 143–45 (quotation from p. 143).

86 Émile Mithout, editor of *Jeunesse ouvrière* from 1935 to 1939, explained in recollections deposited in the J.O.C. archives: "Jusqu'en 1939, un élément peu connu existait: il y avait une censure. Aucun papier ne pouvait pas [*sic*] sur J.O. sans

qu'il passe par la censure (une commission menée par un Jésuite, le père Robinot **273**
Mercy)." Cited in Françoise Richou, "La J.O.C./F. dans l'ouest" (diss., Université
de Nantes, 1986), 516.

87  Cardijn, "Conférences à des prêtres sur leur rôle dans la J.O.C.," 8.
88  *L'appel de la J.O.C.*, 45–46.
89  Ibid., 37.
90  This will be analyzed in detail in chapter 7.
91  *L'appel de la J.O.C.*, 55.
92  Ibid., 55.
93  *Comment débuter dans un cercle d'études jociste: programme d'étude et d'action pour les sections débutantes* (Paris: Jeunesse Ouvrière, n.d.), 18–19.
94  Ibid., 21.
95  "Les jeunes travailleurs en face du mariage," 12. Although this speech was originally given in Belgium, it was reprinted many times in France.
96  *Jocistes dans la tourmente*, 31.
97  Cited in Émile Poulat, *Naissance des prêtres-ouvriers* (Paris: Casterman, 1965), 89.
98  Speaking to seminarians at Issy in 1929, for example, Cardijn described the importance of maintaining a low profile during J.O.C. study sessions, even if this sometimes meant letting incorrect ideas go uncorrected. Cardijn, "L'apostolat de la Jeunesse Ouvrière: conférence donnée au Séminaire d'Issy, le 4 décembre 1929," Bibliothèque Historique, Archives de la J.O.C.
99  Ibid.
100 Philippe Rocher, "Valeurs du sport catholique, valeurs catholiques du sport: L'église catholique et le vélo," *Mouvement social*, no. 192 (July–September 2000), 87.
101 Béjot, *Un évêque à l'école de la J.O.C.*, 30.
102 Ibid.
103 *Mémoires de monseigneur Jean Calvet* (Lyon: Le Chalet, 1967), 107.
104 Berthe, ed., *J.O.C., je te dois tout*, 27.
105 In *Jocisme français*, for example, the authors described the importance of teaching Jocists to take good notes.
106 One of the themes that emerges in interviews with former J.O.C. militants was bitterness that family circumstances had not permitted them to continue their formal educations past the age of twelve or thirteen. See especially the interviews in Bard, ed., *Paroles de militants*. In his biography of Eugène Descamps, who joined the J.O.C. in the mid-1930s and later became the first leader of the C.F.D.T., Franck Georgi argues that Descamps always viewed the fact that he could not continue his education after receiving his certificate of primary studies at twelve as a profound injustice, one that was both personal and social. Franck Georgi, *Eugène Descamps, chrétien et syndicaliste* (Paris: L'Atelier / Éditions Ouvrières, 1997), 27.
107 Michaud, *J'avais vingt ans*, 83.

**108** Cited in Bard, ed., *Paroles de militants*, 15.

**109** Debès and Poulat, *L'appel de la J.O.C.*

**110** *Jocistes dans la tourmente*, 24.

**111** Cardijn, "L'apostolat de la jeunesse ouvrière."

**112** The historian Eric Hobsbawm, an avid adolescent cyclist during this period, wrote passionately in his memoirs about the freedom afforded by the bicycle. See Eric Hobsbawm, *Interesting Times: A Twentieth-Century Life* (London: Abacus, 2003), 88.

**113** Descamps, *Militer*, 18.

**114** Cliquet, *Sillons*, 18–19.

**115** Few police reports of J.O.C. meetings exist, presumably because the police did not consider the J.O.C. a serious threat. For isolated police reports on J.O.C. assemblies see M 154/121, folder: 1930, Archives Départementales du Nord.

**116** *Jeunesse Ouvrière*, 1 October 1930, 1.

**117** "Rapport de Billoux au congrès du parti sur le travail réalisé par la J.C.," *La vie de la Fédération*, suppl. to Bulletin de la Fédération (April 1929), AN F7 13184, 9.

**118** P.P. 8, January 1931, AN F7 13185.

**119** Béjot, *Un évêque à l'école de la J.O.C.*, 28.

**120** Véret, *J'ai vu grandir la J.O.C.*, 38–39.

**121** Béjot, *Un évêque à l'école de la J.O.C.*, 16.

**122** L'abbé Godin, *Carnets manuscrits*, cited in Poulat, *Naissance des prêtres-ouvriers*, 60.

**123** *J.O.C., je te dois tout*, 41–42.

**124** *Jocistes dans la tourmente*, 28.

## **Chapter 4** Rereading the J.O.C.

**1** See for example Joseph Cardyn, "Les jeunes travailleurs en face du mariage: leçons données par M. le chanoine Cardyn à la semaine d'études de Godinne, 1–5 avril 1932" (Paris: J.O.C., 1938), 2. This talk was reprinted in *Jeunesse Ouvrière Féminine*, January 1933, 1.

**2** *Jocisme français: 1927–1939*, Archives de la J.O.C.

**3** Pierre Pierrard, Michel Launay, and Rolande Trempé, eds., *La J.O.C.: regards d'historiens* (Paris: Éditions Ouvrières, 1984), 53–56.

**4** See for example the studies mentioned in notes 27 and 28 to the Introduction.

**5** *Jocisme français: 1927–1939*, GII, 3.

**6** See "Quelques notes sur la J.O.C.F.," ADHS 45J6. A similar account can be found in Aubert, *J.O.C., qu'as-tu fait de nos vies?*, 197–203.

**7** Aubert, *J.O.C., qu'as-tu fait de nos vies?*, 198.

**8** The feminization of Catholicism during the nineteenth century has been studied from a number of angles. For more on the split between religious women and irreligious men within the nineteenth-century bourgeoisie see Bonnie G. Smith, *Ladies of the Leisure Class: The Bourgeoises of Northern France in the Nineteenth Century* (Princeton: Princeton University Press, 1985). For a study of female congregations and the femininization of the French clergy during the nineteenth century see Claude Langlois, *Le catholicisme au féminin: les congrégations françaises à supérieures générales au XIX<sup>e</sup> siècle* (Paris: Le Cerf, 1984). For an exploration of the central role played by women in the emergence of the pilgrimage movement to Lourdes and in late-nineteenth-century Catholicism see Ruth Harris, *Lourdes: Body and Spirit in the Secular Age* (London: Allen Lane / Penguin, 1999). For an analysis of the ways Catholic discussions of women legitimated certain types of female activism in nineteenth-century France see Hazel Mills, "Negotiating the Divide: Women, Philanthropy and the 'Public Sphere' in Nineteenth-Century France," *Religion, Society and Politics in France since 1789,* ed. Frank Tallett and Nicholas Atkin (London: Hambledon, 1991). For a recent discussion of the larger phenomenon see the Introduction to Caroline Ford's *Divided Houses: Religion and Gender in Modern France* (Ithaca: Cornell University Press, 2005).

9   See for example Judith F. Stone, "Gender Identities and Anti-clerical Conflict," Paper delivered to the Society for French Historical Studies, 50<sup>e</sup> Congrès Annuel, Paris, 17–20 June 2004.

10  For an early overview of these organizations and their activities see Sylvie Fayet-Scribe, *Associations féminines et catholicisme XIX<sup>e</sup>–XX<sup>e</sup> siècle* (Paris: Éditions Ouvrières, 1990). For more recent analyses see Anne Cova, "Au service de l'Église, de la patrie et de la famille," *Femmes catholiques et maternité sous la III<sup>e</sup> République* (Paris: L'Harmattan, 2000), and Bruno Dumons, "Mobilisation politique et ligues féminines dans la France catholique: la Ligue des Femmes Françaises et la Ligue Patriotique des Françaises (1901–1914)," *Vingtième siècle,* no. 73 (January–March 2002), 39–50.

11  For more on the Ligue see the works by Cova and Dumons cited above and Odile Sarti, *The Ligue Patriotique des Françaises (1902–1933): A Feminine Response to the Secularization of France* (New York: Garland, 1992).

12  See Marie-Thérèse Chéroutre, *Le scoutisme au féminin: les Guides de France, 1923–1998* (Paris: Le Cerf, 2002), chapter 1, for a history of the Guides' founding and early years.

13  Ibid., 44.

14  "Quelques notes sur la J.O.C.F."

15  Aubert, *J.O.C., qu'as-tu fait de nos vies?,* 199.

16  Ibid.

17  Declaration of Jeanne Bajeux-Labbé, ADHS 45J442.

18  Aubert, *J.O.C., qu'as-tu fait de nos vies?,* 219.

19  Ibid.

20  Pierre Pierrard, *Georges Guérin: une vie pour la J.O.C.* (Paris: L'Atelier / Éditions Ouvrières, 1997), 142.

21  Ibid.

22  Father Aubry recalled that a nun played the crucial role in beginning the J.O.C.F. in Le Mans. Declaration of Jean Aubry, S.J., ADHS 45J443.

23  Aubert, *J.O.C., qu'as-tu fait de nos vies?,* 262. She notes that after 1930 the movement had to remove around a hundred of these "conseillères."

24  See for example *L'équipe ouvrière féminine,* May 1931, 3.

**25** *L'équipe ouvrière féminine*, October 1930, 3.

**26** "Quelques notes sur la J.O.C.F."

**27** *L'équipe ouvrière féminine*, August 1931.

**28** *L'équipe ouvrière féminine*, June 1931.

**29** Cited in Aubert, *J.O.C., qu'as-tu fait de nos vies?*, 215.

**30** See for example the taped memoirs of the postal worker Marcelle Boutot deposited in the Archives Municipales d'Ivry.

**31** Declaration of Raymonde Tourbier, ADHS 45J442.

**32** In one local area studied closely, an estimated 52.6 percent of Jocists were industrial workers, 14.2 percent came from the ranks of "petites professions," 23.8 percent were white-collar workers, and 9.3 percent were employed as domestic workers. Cited in Aubert, *J.O.C., qu'as-tu fait de nos vies?*, 100.

**33** For a discussion of Catholic promotion of family allowances in interwar France see Susan Pedersen, *Family, Dependence, and the Origins of the Welfare State* (Cambridge: Cambridge University Press, 1993), chapter 4.

**34** Lhande, *Le Christ dans la banlieue*, 11.

**35** *Jeunesse Ouvrière*, 1 August 1930, 1.

**36** See Mary Louise Roberts, *Civilization without Sexes: Reconstructing Gender in Postwar France, 1917–1927* (Chicago: University of Chicago Press, 1994), esp. part 1.

**37** Ibid., 46.

**38** Joseph Cardyn, "Les jeunes travailleurs en face du mariage," 31–32.

**39** *L'équipe ouvrière féminine*, September 1928, 3.

**40** *L'équipe ouvrière féminine*, September 1930, 7.

**41** Ibid., 2.

**42** *L'équipe ouvrière féminine*, September 1928, 2.

**43** *L'equipe ouvrière féminine*, January 1937, 10–11. The results of this *enquête* became the basis of another book by Lhotte and Dupeyrat, *Préparations du futur foyer* (Courbevoie: J.O.C.F., 1937).

**44** *L'équipe ouvrière féminine*, February 1931, 8.

**45** According to the 1931 census, 60.9 percent of women between fifteen and twenty-four were considered economically active; this proportion dropped to 41.5 percent for women between twenty-five and thirty-nine. Siân Reynolds, *France between the Wars: Gender and Politics* (London: Routledge, 1996), 86. Catherine Omnès found that women between the ages of twenty and twenty-nine had the highest rate of labor force participation. Catherine Omnès, *Ouvrières parisiennes: marchés du travail et trajectoires professionnelles au 20ᵉ siècle* (Paris: École des Hautes Études en Sciences Sociales, 1997), 13.

**46** Occupational diversity in the Paris region is highlighted by Omnès in *Ouvrières parisiennes*.

**47** This contrasted with one white-collar worker for every three female industrial workers in 1906. Madeleine Rebérioux, "Les femmes et la révolution industrielle," in *Le féminisme et ses enjeux*, cited in Reynolds, *France between the Wars*, 93.

Notes

**48** Catherine Rhein found that working as a "bonne à tout faire" was often transitional employment in the 1920s and 1930s. Catherine Rhein, "Jeunes femmes au travail dans le Paris de l'entre-deux-guerres (diss., Universitéde Paris VII, 1977)," 175.

**49** See for example the recollections in Aubert, *J.O.C., qu'as-tu fait de nos vies?*, 63–64.

**50** Ibid., 62.

**51** Ibid.

**52** Of the forty-six women in Catherine Rhein's sample group of two hundred interwar Parisian young working women who apprenticed, thirty-nine did so in the fashion industry. Rhein, "Jeunes femmes au travail dans le Paris de l'entre-deux-guerres," 112.

**53** Omnès, *Ouvrières parisiennes*, 45, 28.

**54** For an analysis of discussions of women's work by nineteenth-century political economists see Joan W. Scott, "'L'ouvrière! Mot impie, sordide': Women Workers in the Discourse of French Political Economy, 1840–1860," *Gender and the Politics of History* (New York: Columbia University Press, 1988), 139–63. For a very brief discussion of interwar social Catholic women's analysis of women's work and its effects on female bodies see Mary Lynn Stewart, *For Health and Beauty: Physical Culture for Frenchwomen, 1880s–1930s* (Baltimore: Johns Hopkins University Press, 2001), 182.

**55** *L'équipe ouvrière féminine*, June 1931 and September 1931.

**56** *L'équipe ouvrière féminine*, January 1930.

**57** See for example "À la recherche d'un métier féminin," *Jeunesse Ouvrière Féminine*, October 1933, 1.

**58** See for example "Métiers féminins," *Jeunesse Ouvrière Féminine*, August 1928, 4.

**59** *Jeunesse Ouvrière Féminine*, October 1932, 3.

**60** "C'est Honteux, Honteux! . . . ," *Jeunesse Ouvrière Féminine*, November 1928, 2.

**61** *Jeunesse Ouvrière Féminine*, November 1932, 3.

**62** "C'est Honteux, Honteux! . . . ," *Jeunesse Ouvrière Féminine*, November 1928, 2.

**63** Aubert, *J.O.C., qu'as-tu fait de nos vies?*, 79.

**64** Lhotte and Dupeyrat, *Révélations sur la santé des jeunes travailleuses*.

**65** Ibid., 54.

**66** Ibid., 111–12.

**67** Ibid.

**68** Aubert, *J.O.C., qu'as-tu fait de nos vies?*, 53.

**69** Lhotte and Dupeyrat, *Révélations sur la santé des jeunes travailleuses*, 34.

**70** Declaration of Ruffet, ADHS 45J443.

**71** *Jeunesse Ouvrière Féminine*, November 1928, 1.

**72** Lhotte and Dupeyrat, *Révélations sur la santé des jeunes travailleuses*, 113.

**73** See for example "Une 'star' jugée par elle-même," *Jeunesse Ouvrière Féminine*, May 1932, 3.

**74** "À l'écran," *Jeunesse Ouvrière Féminine*, January 1932, 3.

**75** "Il y avait une fois une petite fille," *Jeunesse Ouvrière Féminine*, December 1932, 1.

76 "Méditations sur l'évangile: il est ressuscité," *L'équipe ouvrière féminine*, May 1931, 2.

77 Ibid.

78 *L'équipe ouvrière féminine*, March 1931, 6.

79 Ibid.

80 For an interesting discussion of images of Christ in nineteenth-century French Catholic devotional literature see Thomas A. Kselman, *Miracles and Prophecies in Nineteenth-Century France* (New Brunswick: Rutgers University Press, 1983), 95–99.

81 Ibid., 98.

82 A good introduction to Mary's place in nineteenth-century French Catholicism is Barbara Corrado Pope, "Immaculate and Powerful: The Marian Revival in the Nineteenth Century," *Immaculate and Powerful: the Female in Sacred Image and Social Reality*, ed. Clarissa W. Atkinson, Constance H. Buchanan, and Margaret R. Miles (Boston: Beacon, 1985), 173–200. For more on the rise of Lourdes as a new kind of pilgrimage site see Harris, *Lourdes*, and Suzanne Kaufman, *Consuming Visions: Mass Culture and the Lourdes Shrine* (Ithaca: Cornell University Press, 2005). Kselman also analyzes the place of Mary in nineteenth-century piety.

83 See for example *L'équipe ouvrière féminine*, June 1932, 8.

84 "Méditations sur l'évangile: dans le sillage des parfums de la Vierge," *L'équipe ouvrière féminine*, February 1930.

85 "Coeur de Marie," *Bulletin des dirigeantes fédérales*, no. 2 (April 1932), 1.

86 See for example *L'équipe ouvrière féminine* of March 1930 (p. 2) and April 1929 (p. 2).

87 *Rome* (Les Moulineaux: Saint-Paul, 1935), 42, in ADHS 45J518, 2K1.

88 Ibid., 78–79.

89 Ibid., 101–2.

90 *Guide du pèlerinage de la J.O.C.F. à Rome* (1933), ADHS 45J518 2K1.

91 These efforts were not new, as Catholics had used the railway, the mass press, and modern advertising techniques to shape Lourdes into a new kind of pilgrimage site. See Suzanne Kaufman, "Selling Lourdes: Pilgrimage, Tourism and the Mass-Marketing of the Sacred in Nineteenth-Century France," *Being Elsewhere: Tourism, Consumer Culture, and Identity in Modern Europe and North America*, ed. Shelley Baranowski and Ellen Furlough (Ann Arbor: University of Michigan Press, 2001), 63–88.

92 *Rome*, 47.

93 Ibid., 120.

94 *L'équipe ouvrière féminine*, March 1932, 8.

95 Worry over "excessively pious" women had also been a concern for those running female *patronages* before the war. Laura Lee Downs, *Childhood in the Promised Land: Working-Class Movements and the Colonies de Vacances in France, 1880–1960* (Durham: Duke University Press, 2002), 79.

96 *L'équipe ouvrière féminine*, October 1930, 2.

97 "Le zèle des âmes," *Bulletin des dirigeantes fédérales*, no. 1 (March 1932), 1.

Notes

**98** *Bulletin des dirigeantes fédérales*, October 1932.

**99** *L'équipe ouvrière féminine*, March 1930, 6.

**100** *L'équipe ouvrière féminine*, November 1930, 5.

**101** Aubert, *J.O.C., qu'as-tu fait de nos vies?*, 364.

**102** Ibid., 363.

**103** Ibid., 365.

**104** Declaration of Yvonne Ruffet, ADHS 44J443.

**105** E. Delasalle, *Le travail de la femme dans l'industrie textile et du vêtement de l'arrondissement de Lille*, cited in Annie Fourcaut, *Femmes à l'usine: ouvrières et surintendantes dans les entreprises françaises de l'entre-deux-guerres* (Paris: François Maspero, 1982), 160.

**106** Aubert, *J.O.C., qu'as-tu fait de nos vies?*, 51.

**107** Ibid.

**108** Aubert, *J.O.C., qu'as-tu fait de nos vies?*, 80.

**109** "L'élite," *Bulletin des dirigeantes fédérales*, July 1932.

**110** "Un exemple de cran, de ténacité et d'audace," *Jeunesse Ouvrière Féminine*, July 1932, 2.

**111** "Pour le suffrage féminin," *L'équipe ouvrière féminine*, September 1933, 6.

**112** *Bulletin des dirigeantes fédérales*, March 1934, 8.

**113** Declaration of Yvonne Sommeille, ADHS 45J443.

**114** Aubert, *J.O.C., qu'as-tu fait de nos vies?*, 250.

**115** Ibid.

**116** "La petite vendeuse de journaux de la J.O.C.F.," *Jociste, chante! Recueil de chants de la J.O.C.F.* (Paris: Jeunesse Ouvrière, 1934).

**117** The Communists' approach to young women and female activism is explored in chapter 6.

**118** ADHS 45J443, declaration of Yvonne Ruffet.

**119** *L'équipe ouvrière féminine*, March 1937.

**120** *L'équipe ouvrière féminine*, May 1931, 4.

**121** Aubert, *J.O.C., qu'as-tu fait de nos vies?*, 228.

**122** Ibid., 268.

**123** Ibid., 376.

**124** Declaration of Jeanne Bajeux-Labbé, ADHS 45J442.

**125** Response by the Millau section to a questionnaire entitled "La jeune travailleuse et sa famille" (1938). From the personal collection of Jeanne Aubert.

**126** *Bulletin des dirigeantes fédérales*, March 1932, 5.

**127** *L'équipe ouvrière féminine* mentioned this problem in April 1931.

**128** *Jeunesse Ouvrière Féminine*, January 1934, 2.

**129** Declaration of Raymonde Tourbier, ADHS 45J442.

**130** Declaration of Yvonne Ruffet, ADHS 45J443.

**131** Declaration of Paulette Beaudor, ADHS 45J443.

**132** *L'équipe ouvrière féminine*, November 1930, 5.

**133** Jean Nizey, "Les militants de la J.O.C. dans la Maitron," *La part des militants: biographie et mouvement ouvrier autour du Maitron*, ed. Michel Dreyfus, Claude

Pennetier and Nathalie Viet-Depaule (Paris: L'Atelier / Éditions Ouvrières, 1996), 320.

134 Declaration of Jeanne Bajeux-Labbé, ADHS 45J442.
135 Jeanne Rolland, "Les Débuts de la J.O.C. en Berry," ADHS 44J442.
136 Aubert, *J.O.C., qu'as-tu fait de nos vies?*, 383.
137 Declaration of Yvonne Ruffet, ADHS 45J443.
138 Aubert, *J.O.C., qu'as-tu fait de nos vies?*, 456.

## **Chapter 5** Youth and Communist Antifascist Politics

1 "L'offensive du fascisme et les tâches de l'Internationale Communiste . . . ," Résolution sur le rapport du comrade Dimitrov, VII<sup>e</sup> Congrès Mondial de l'I. C., *Contre la guerre et le fascisme: l'unité, résolutions et décisions* (Paris: Bureau d'Éditions, 1935), 19.
2 See Julian Jackson, *The Popular Front in France: Defending Democracy, 1934–1938* (Cambridge: Cambridge University Press, 1988), 25–27, for a discussion of changes in communist tactics in 1931–32.
3 As we saw in chapter 1, the early 1930s marked the last step in the imposition of Comintern control over the party. For a discussion of the processes by which this occurred see Stéphane Courtois and Marc Lazar, *Histoire du Parti Communiste Français* (Paris: Presses Universitaires de France, 1995), 104–6.
4 Ibid., 109.
5 AN F7 13185.
6 Fédération des J.C. de France, "À tous les membres de C.C. et aux secrétaires régionaux," August 1932, AN F7 13185.
7 Ibid.
8 The speech is described in *L'Avant-Garde*, 18 June 1932, 1, 4.
9 August 13, 1932, AN F7 13185.
10 "Pour une J.C. vraiment 'jeune,'" *L'Avant-Garde*, 19 November 1932, 2.
11 This was the title of the article outlining the Central Committee's resolution on the new orientation. *L'Avant-Garde*, 26 November 1932, 2.
12 2 November 1932, AN F7 13185.
13 Ibid.
14 See for example *L'Avant-Garde*, 15 and 22 October 1932.
15 Circular, December 1932, AN F7 13185.
16 "Comment doit travailler la cellule d'entreprise," AN F7 13185.
17 Julian Jackson, *The Politics of Depression in France, 1932–1936* (Cambridge: Cambridge University Press, 1985), 29.
18 Ibid., 29, 27.
19 Ibid., 30, 24.
20 Ibid., 29.
21 For a study of the history of unemployment assistance in France see Christine Daniel and Carole Tuchszirer, *L'état face aux chômeurs: l'indemnisation du chômage de 1884 à nos jours* (Paris: Flammarion, 1999).

22 By 1933, for example, fewer than 20 percent of those receiving unemployment assistance did so from union funds. Ibid., 120.

23 As Daniel and Tuchszirer point out, cities in northern France followed the national government's regulations to the letter, but Paris and Lyon created their own modifications, with Paris imposing a means test and creating a central registry of *chômeurs secourus*. Ibid., 109–11.

24 At the end of December 1931 the state raised its contribution to local funds to between 60 and 90 percent of operating costs. Ibid., 120.

25 Ibid., 351 n. 6, 123, 126.

26 Jackson, *The Politics of Depression in France*, 29. As Jackson points out, the proportion of those who received aid increased as the crisis worsened and more unemployment funds were established. Nonetheless, the proportion of *chômeurs secourus* did not reach 60 percent according to the official figures from 1936.

27 Daniel and Tuchszirer, *L'état face aux chômeurs*, 105.

28 Ibid., 349 n. 35.

29 This was the case in the Lyon region. London, *Le printemps des camarades*, 84.

30 This was the case for both Lise London (ibid., 83) and the Jocist Eugène Descamps. See Descamps, *Militer*, 17.

31 His story was told in two successive issues: *L'Avant-Garde*, 31 December 1932 and 7 January 1933, 1.

32 *L'Avant-Garde*, 13 December 1932, 1.

33 "L'example de Dmitrousenko," *L'Avant-Garde*, 22 October 1932, 3.

34 "Les jeunes communistes de l'usine Kharkow réalisent un 'travail d'assaut,'" *L'Avant-Garde*, 2 July 1932, 3.

35 This was stated very explicitly in "Vive le VII$^e$ Congrès des J.C. de l'U.R.S.S.!," *L'Avant-Garde*, 9 July 1932, 3, and more implicitly in other articles.

36 See for example "Comment on étudie en U.R.S.S.," *L'Avant-Garde*, 2 July 1932, 3.

37 See for example "Elle sera ingénieur," *L'Avant-Garde*, 5 November 1932.

38 For a discussion of the Komsomol's responsibilities during the First Five-Year Plan see Ralph T. Fisher Jr., *Pattern for Soviet Youth: A Study of the Congresses of the Komsomol, 1918–1954* (New York: Columbia University Press, 1959), 157–62.

39 Communist Youth workers are front and center in two important contemporary accounts: Valentine Kataev's novel *Time, Forward!* (1932) and John Scott's *Behind the Urals: An American Worker in Russia's City of Steel* (1942). The experience of Komsomol members during industrialization is also dealt with in the autobiographical accounts in Nikolai K. Novak-Deker, ed., *Soviet Youth: Twelve Komsomol Histories*, trans. Oliver J. Frederiksen (Munich: Institute for the Study of the U.S.S.R.), series 1, no. 51 (July 1959).

40 Fisher, *Pattern for Soviet Youth*, 160.

41 W. I. Hryshko in Novak-Deker, ed., *Soviet Youth*, 98.

42 Fred Kupferman, ed., *Au pays des soviets: le voyage français en Union Soviétique, 1917–1939* (Paris: Gallimard, 1979), 65, 68.

**43** N. Prokofiev, "Le tourisme soviétique au service du plan quinquennal," *L'Avant-Garde*, 19 November 1932, 3.

**44** John Scott, *Behind the Urals: An American Worker in Russia's City of Steel*, enlarged edn prepared by Stephen Kotkin (Bloomington: Indiana University Press, 1989), 3.

**45** Ibid., 19–20.

**46** Figuères, *Jeunesse militante*, 21.

**47** "Deux mois de compte rendu de mon voyage: moi aussi, je veux aller en Union Soviétique," *L'Avant-Garde*, 1 August 1933, 1.

**48** Sheila Fitzpatrick is particularly good on the creation of outcasts and enemies in Stalinist Russia in *Everyday Stalinism: Ordinary Life in Extraordinary Times: Soviet Russia in the 1930s* (Oxford: Oxford University Press, 1999).

**49** See "La Jeunesse Communiste de France à un poste international de combat," *L'Avant-Garde*, 25 June 1932, 4.

**50** Both Thorez and c.y.i. officials stressed this. For Thorez's comments on this subject see the Congress coverage in *L'Avant-Garde*, 18 June 1932, 1, 4.

**51** *L'Avant-Garde*, 1 October 1932, 1.

**52** *L'Avant-Garde*, 8 October 1932, 1.

**53** For more on the j.s. in the interwar period see Christian Delporte, "Les jeunesses socialistes dans l'entre-deux-guerres," *Mouvement Social*, no. 157 (October–December 1991), 33–66.

**54** "Unité d'Action," *L'Avant-Garde*, 19 November 1932, 1.

**55** For more on this see Mona L. Siegel, *The Moral Disarmament of France: Education, Pacifism, and Patriotism, 1914–1940* (Cambridge: Cambridge University Press, 2004), esp. chapter 4.

**56** Alix, *La nouvelle jeunesse*, 145.

**57** See the reports contained in Archives de la Guerre, E.M.A./3 7N4033 dossier 2.

**58** See Norman Ingram, *The Politics of Dissent: Pacifism in France, 1919–1939* (Oxford: Clarendon, 1991), 161.

**59** Ibid.

**60** *L'Avant-Garde*, 18 March 1933, 1.

**61** *L'Avant-Garde*, 18 March 1933, 2.

**62** See Ingram, *The Politics of Dissent*, 127, for a discussion of the fear of war in France of the early 1930s.

**63** One report in 1932 listed fifty pacifist organizations and seventeen more which "sympathized with pacifism." See ibid., 1.

**64** "Le manifeste du Congrès Mondial contre la Guerre Impérialiste," AN F7 13148.

**65** Ibid. Interestingly, Rolland, who missed the founding Congress because of illness, threatened to resign from the committee unless it described pacifism more respectfully; in December 1932 the leadership issued a declaration clarifying somewhat the committee's position on pacifism. David James Fisher, *Romain Rolland and the Politics of Intellectual Engagement* (Berkeley: University of California Press, 1988), 167–68.

Notes

66 "Rapport général du Congrès Régional de Lutte contre la Guerre" (February
1933), AN F7 13148.

67 P.P. 6 May 1933, AN F7 13148.

68 "Lettre à la jeunesse française," *L'unité contre la guerre impérialiste*, 12 March 1933,
AN F7 13148.

69 Richard J. Evans provides these numbers in his book *The Third Reich in Power,
1933–1939* (New York: Penguin, 2005), 11.

70 Ibid.

71 As Vicki Caron points out, France received more refugees (25,000) in the spring
of 1933 than any other country. Vicki Caron, *Uneasy Asylum: France and the Jewish
Refugee Crisis, 1933–1942* (Stanford: Stanford University Press, 1999), 1–2.

72 P.P. 9 April 1933, AN F7 13148.

73 *L'Humanité*, 7 June 1933, 1.

74 "Manifeste à la jeunesse travailleuse d'Europe," *L'Avant-Garde*, 1 July 1933, 2.

75 Ibid.

76 "Une conférence internationale des jeunes," *L'Humanité*, 3 June 1933, 2.

77 P.P. 9 May 1933, AN F7 13148.

78 See for example *L'Humanité*, 2 June 1933, 1.

79 C.C. de Bordeaux, 18 May 1933, AN F7 13148.

80 P.P. 20 September 1933, AN F7 13148.

81 AN F7 13148.

82 *L'Avant-Garde*, 23 December 1933, 1.

83 "1917 . . . Enfant, j'ai souffert de la guerre," *L'Avant-Garde*, July 1933.

84 *L'Avant-Garde*, 1 July 1933, 1.

85 *L'Avant-Garde*, 24 June and 1 August 1933.

86 *L'Avant-Garde*, 12 August 1933, 1.

87 The best coverage of the congress can be found in *L'Humanité*. This citation
comes from "'Nous voulons combattre! Nous voulons vaincre!,' cri d'espérance
du Congrès Mondial des Jeunes," *L'Humanité*, 23 September 1933, 2.

88 Discussion of the morning's events (including the oath) can be found in both
*L'Humanité* (26 September 1933, 2) and *L'Avant-Garde* (30 September 1933, 4).

89 "Les jeunesses dans la lutte," *L'Humanité*, 17 September 1933, 1.

90 Ibid., 2.

91 "Salut au Congrès des Jeunes!," *L'Humanité*, 22 September 1933, 2.

92 *L'Humanité*, 23 September 1933, 2.

93 This analysis was laid out in a number of places. See for example Raymond
Guyot, "Congrès extraordinaire de la J.C.," *L'Avant-Garde*, 13 January 1934, 1, and
"Les tâches pour la préparation et la tenue du Congrès Extraordinaire des J.C.,"
Brb 4835, Bibliothèque Marxiste de Paris.

94 By early December police reported that the Comité des Jeunes possessed few resources and was engaged in almost no work. P.P. 4 December 1933, AN F7 13148.

95 This problem surfaced most clearly in "La J.C. en lutte: pour la conquête des
masses: Résolution . . . Congrès Extraordinaire de la J.C." (February 1934), Brb
4169, Bibliothèque Marxiste, 12.

**284** 96 Ibid.

97 "Les tâches pour la préparation et la tenue du Congrès Extraordinaire des J.C.," Brb 4835, Bibliothèque Marxiste de Paris.

98 Ibid.

99 For his editorial see Marcel Cachin, "À la conquête de la Jeunesse Ouvrière," *L'Humanité*, 2 February 1934, 1.

100 "Le Congrès de la J.C.," *L'Humanité*, 6 February 1934, 4.

101 "Le délégué de l'I.C.J. trace les directives pour la conquête des masses des jeunes travailleurs," *L'Humanité*, 9 February 1934, 4.

102 For a good account of the events of this night see Robert Soucy, *French Fascism: The Second Wave, 1933–1939* (New Haven: Yale University Press, 1995), 30–33.

103 I am basing my account of the J.C.'s involvement in the night's events on the autobiographical account provided by Lise London. Although it is only one person's account, the details that she gives correspond to analyses of the night's events by historians such as Robert Soucy and Julian Jackson. London, *Le printemps des camarades*, 113–15.

104 "En avant contre le gouvernement des fusilleurs," Archives de la Police de Paris, BA 1860.

105 See for example *L'Avant-Garde*, 17 February 1934, 1.

106 Archives de la Police de Paris, BA 1860.

107 Ibid.

108 Delporte, "Les jeunesses socialistes dans l'entre-deux-guerres," 52.

109 "Note, June 1934," 3, Archives de la Police de Paris, BA 1860.

110 "Le Maréchal de France Ministre de la Guerre à M. le Général Commandant la Région de Paris," 14 May 1934, Archives de la Guerre, 5N601–4.

111 Raymond Guyot, "Nous terrasserons le fascisme!," *L'Avant-Garde*, 17 March 1934, 1.

112 "La Jeunesse Communiste affirme sa fidelité au parti et à son comité central," *L'Avant-Garde*, 1 May 1934, 2.

113 Ibid. For a quick synopsis of the "Doriot affair" see Jackson, *The Popular Front in France*, 29–30.

114 Fred Zeller, *Trois points c'est tout* (Paris: Robert Laffont, 1976), 55.

115 Eric Hobsbawm, *Interesting Times: A Twentieth-Century Life* (London: Abacus, 2003), 73.

116 Ibid., 73–74.

117 Jamet, *Notre Front Populaire*, 21–22.

118 This dynamic was on display at the conference of the Tarn federation of the J.S. in spring 1934. "Avant la Conférence Nationale des J.S.: les congrès fédéraux," *Le Populaire*, 1 April 1934, 6.

119 *L'Avant-Garde*, 19 May 1934, 1.

120 "L'appel des jeunes socialistes," *L'Avant-Garde*, 26 May 1934, 1.

121 *L'Avant-Garde*, 26 May 1934, 1.

122 *L'Avant-Garde*, 26 May 1934, 2. Delporte confirms the numbers lost by the J.S.

Notes

**123**  *Le Populaire*, 24 May 1934, 1.

**124**  See Courtois and Lazar, *Histoire du Parti Communiste Français*, 121–23, for a good account of Thorez's move, aided by the Comintern, away from the class-against-class strategy at the June party congress.

**125**  *L'Avant-Garde*, 30 June 1934, 1.

**126**  "Paris montre la voie," *L'Avant-Garde*, 14 July 1934, 1.

**127**  "4,000 jeunes travailleurs acclament le front unique," *L'Humanité*, 27 July 1934, 2.

**128**  Ibid.

**129**  *L'Avant-Garde*, 7 July 1934, 1.

**130**  *L'Avant-Garde*, 28 July 1934, 2.

**131**  The text of the pact proposed by the Communists can be found in *L'Humanité*, 27 July 1934, 1.

**132**  *L'Humanité*, 30 July 1934, 1.

**133**  *Le Populaire*, 29 July 1934, 1.

**134**  *L'Avant-Garde*, 8 September 1934, 1–2.

**135**  "Le Congrès National de la J.O.C.," *L'Avant-Garde*, 22 September 1934, 2.

**136**  Pierre Cot, "Les jeunes radicaux et le Front Populaire," *L'Avant-Garde*, 13 July 1935, 1.

**137**  For the text of the "Proclamation des droits des jeunes générations" see *L'Avant-Garde*, 27 October 1934, 4.

**138**  Soucy, *French Fascism: The Second Wave*, 109.

**139**  Ibid.

**140**  Indeed, *L'Humanité* devoted its usual front-page editorial to Dimitrov's words to the Congress on 29 December 1934. Dimitrov began: "L'apparition d'un mouvement grandissant contre la guerre et le fascisme parmi les étudiants de grands pays capitalistes appartient aux phénomènes les plus remarquables de cette époque riche en grands évènements."

**141**  The information on J.E.U.N.E.S. comes from the report "Conférence organisée par les 2ᵉ, 3ᵉ, 10ᵉ et 11ᵉ équipes des J.E.U.N.E.S.," 19 March 1936, AN F7 12965.

**142**  "Le Bloc des jeunes générations," *L'Avant-Garde*, 3 November 1934, 1.

**143**  See Jackson, *The Popular Front in France*, 38, for a discussion of the Comitern's position on the new strategy.

**144**  Much of the letter is reprinted in Jacques Varin, *Jeunes comme JC: sur la jeunesse communiste*, vol. 1, *1920 à 1939* (Paris: Éditions Sociales, 1975), 198.

**145**  "Conférence National 1935: rapport politique, agit-prop," 23–24 March 1935, Parti Communiste, Région Paris-Ville, Fonds de l'Institut Marxiste-Leniniste, Bibliothèque Marxiste de Paris.

**146**  *L'Humanité*, 31 January 1935, 1.

**147**  See for example "Le malheur d'être jeune: jeunes filles qui travaillent," *L'Humanité*, 15 February 1935, 1–2.

**148**  *Élections municipales de mai 1935: directives et conseils aux régions, rayons et cellules*, Fonds Institut Marxiste-Leniniste at the Bibliothèque Marxiste, 8.

Notes

**286** 149 *L'Humanité*, 24 February 1935, 6.

150 These themes, which Vaillant-Couturier returns to again and again during the investigation, are first clearly laid out in the article announcing the *enquête*: "Jeunes, écrivez-nous!," *L'Humanité*, 4 February 1935, 4.

151 Paul Vaillant-Couturier, "u.r.s.s., jeunesse du monde . . . ," *L'Humanité*, 15 March 1935, 1, 4.

152 See for example W. I. Hryshko, "An Interloper in the Komsomol," *Soviet Youth*, ed. Novak-Deker, 91.

153 Sophie Coeuré makes this point in her interesting study of the Soviet effort to elaborate a positive image of the Soviet Union in France (and the West). Sophie Coeuré, *La grande lueur à l'est: les Français et l'Union Soviétique, 1917–1939* (Paris: Le Seuil, 1999), 215–16.

154 These ideas were developed most extensively in Paul Vaillant-Couturier, "Génération de la crise et génération du feu," *L'Humanité*, 11 February 1935, 2.

155 This is stated in the very first "Le malheur d'être jeune," *L'Humanité*, 10 February 1935, 1–2.

156 See for example "Documents de la Conférence Internationale Permanente de la Jeunesse pour la Paix, la Liberté, et le Progrès" (April 1935), Bibliothèque Marxiste, 6.

157 Cachin, *Jeunesse, progrès et avenir*, 3.

158 Ibid., 4.

159 These directions can be found in the brochure *Élections municipales de mai 1935: directives et conseils aux régions, rayons et cellules*, Fonds Institut Marxiste-Leniniste at the Bibliothèque Marxiste, 10.

160 The text of his speech can be found in the *Journal Officiel*, *Débats Parlementaires*, *Chambre des Députés*, Second Session, 15 March 1935, 1021–22.

161 "L'Acte d'Accusation," *L'Avant-Garde*, special issue, April 1935, 1.

162 Maurice Thorez, "Les 2 ans et la guerre," Discours prononcé à la Chambre des Députés, 15 March 1935, Bibliothèque Marxiste, 21.

163 See for example "Tempêtes sur les casernes," *L'Avant-Garde*, 13 April 1935, 1, and "Libération immédiate des 'libérables,' " *L'Avant-Garde*, special issue, April 1935, 2.

164 "Soldats et conscrits," *L'Avant-Garde*, 13 April 1935, 1.

165 *L'Avant-Garde*, 13 April 1935, 6.

166 This point is made by both Jackson, *The Popular Front in France*, 39, and Yves Santamaria, *L'enfant du malheur: le Parti Communiste Français dans la lutte pour la paix (1914–1947)* (Paris: Seli Arslan, 2002), 208.

167 Zeller, *Trois points c'est tout*, 72–73.

168 Figuères, *Jeunesse militante*, 38.

169 Courtois and Lazar, *Histoire du Parti Communiste Français*, 126.

170 Delporte, "Les jeunesses socialistes dans l'entre-deux-guerres," 55.

171 Archives de la Guerre, 5N601–4, "Note: 14 janvier 1936."

172 "Le discours de Jacques Duclos à Buffalo," *L'Humanité*, 15 July 1935, 4.

173 "Ordre du cortège: la jeunesse," *L'Avant-Garde*, 13 July 1935, 1.

Notes

174  Delporte, "Les jeunesses socialistes dans l'entre-deux-guerres," 55.

175  Ibid.

176  Figuères, *Jeunesse militante*, 48.

177  The short speech is printed in its entirety in *Le Populaire*, 15 July 1935, 4.

178  Courtois and Lazar, *Histoire du Parti Communiste Français*, 129.

179  See Peschanski, ed., *Marcel Cachin, carnets 1906–1947*, vol. 4, *1935–1947*, 110–11.

180  Ibid., 118–19.

181  "Discours du Camarade Dimitrov," *L'Avant-Garde*, 12 October 1935, 8.

**Chapter 6** Embracing the Status Quo

1  For a text of the speech see "Discours d'ouverture prononcé par notre camarade Raymond Guyot," *L'Avant-Garde*, 12 October 1935, 7–8.

2  On the vital interests of youth see "Discours de camarade Dimitrov," *L'Avant-Garde*, 12 October 1935, 8. For the language of youth see Michal Wolf, *Unifions les forces de la jeune génération*, Rapport du camarade Michal Wolf au VIᵉ Congrès de l'Internationale Communiste des Jeunes (September 1935) (Paris: Jeunesse Communiste), 34.

3  Maurice Thorez, "L'indépendance de la jeunesse," *L'Avant-Garde*, 23 November 1935, 1.

4  Victor Michaut explained the efforts toward achieving unity between the J.C. and the J.S. in "Unité avec les Jeunesses Socialistes," *L'Avant-Garde*, 1 February 1936, 3.

5  See *L'Avant-Garde*, 14 December 1935, 1, for a text of the manifesto.

6  "Clôture du congrès communiste: les jeunes," *Le Figaro*, 26 January 1936, 4.

7  Quoted in Victor Michaut, "Union possible et nécessaire," *L'Avant-Garde*, 22 February 1936, 1.

8  An original recording of Vaillant-Couturier delivering the speech can be found on the cassette "1936–1986: discours et chants du Front Populaire," which was available at the Bibliothèque Marxiste de Paris.

9  *L'Avant-Garde*, 23 November 1935, 1.

10  *L'Avant-Garde*, 7 December 1935, 1.

11  *L'Avant-Garde*, 21 December 1935, 1.

12  Ibid.

13  Although the J.C. admitted that this demand had already been put forward by the delegation of unemployed youth that had visited the International Labor Organization six months earlier, it did not explain that the J.O.C. had been the driving force behind this delegation—or this demand.

14  Jacques Duclos, *L'avenir de la Jeunesse Française*, Rapport présenté au VIIIᵉ Congrès National du Parti Communiste S.F.I.C.," Villeurbanne, 22–25 January 1936 (Paris: Publications Révolutionnaires, 1936), 29.

15  "La jeunesse réclame . . . ," *L'Avant-Garde*, 18 April 1936, 4.

16  See Siân Reynolds, *France between the Wars: Gender and Politics* (London: Routledge, 1996), chapter 1, for a good introduction to the politics of population in interwar France.

288   **17**  In the article laying out its call for state aid to young households, *L'Avant-Garde* noted, for instance: "Voici la réponse à ceux qui représentent les communistes comme des destructeurs de la famille." *L'Avant-Garde*, 21 December 1935, 1.

**18**  Guyot, *La jeunesse à l'assaut du vieux monde*, 5 (speech begins on p. 4).

**19**  W. J. Murray, "The French Workers' Sports Movement and the Victory of the Popular Front in 1936," *International Journal of the History of Sport* 4, no. 2 (1987), 219.

**20**  "Voler pour 10 francs par mois," *L'Avant-Garde*, 7 March 1936, 6.

**21**  Ibid.

**22**  *L'Avant-Garde*, 22 February 1936, 6.

**23**  See the preamble to the "Proposition de résolution invitant le gouvernement à déposer un projet de loi tendant à octroyer une somme de 1 milliard de crédits pour le développement de sport," *La Jeune France: projets de lois et propositions du Groupe Parlementaire Communiste* (Paris: Comité Populaire de Propagande, 1936), 13–14.

**24**  Ibid., 14.

**25**  For more on the relationship of sport to culture see Pascal Ory, *La belle illusion: culture et politique sous le signe du Front Populaire, 1935–1938* (Paris: Plon, 1994).

**26**  "Oui, sauvons la race française," *L'Avant-Garde*, 1 May 1936, 6, mentions two studies, one claiming 30 percent to be unfit, the other 50 percent.

**27**  Ibid.

**28**  *Journal Officiel, Débats parlementaires, Chambre des Députés*, Second Session, 15 March 1935, 1046.

**29**  Ibid.

**30**  P.P. 8 March 1936, AN F7 12964.

**31**  5 March 1936, AN F7 12964.

**32**  Guyot, *La jeunesse à l'assaut du vieux monde*, 12.

**33**  Ibid., 19.

**34**  "Une visite au Club de la Jeunesse au IVème arrondissement," *L'Avant-Garde*, 4 April 1936, 2.

**35**  For more on communist publishing in the Popular Front era see Ory, *La belle illusion*, 75–78.

**36**  For the attention to cultural issues in *L'Humanité* after 1935 see Ory, *La belle illusion*, 76–77. For the reference to *Paris-Soir* see Annie Burger-Roussennac, "Les intellectuels du PCF: le cas des journalistes de *L'Humanité* (1921–1939)," *Cahiers de l'Institut d'Histoire du Temps Présent* 26 (1994), 178.

**37**  See for example *L'Avant-Garde*, 30 November 1935.

**38**  See for example "Pour la jeune fille," *L'Avant-Garde*, 26 October 1935, 5.

**39**  "Une visite au Club de la Jeunesse au IVème arrondissement," *L'Avant-Garde*, 4 April 1936, 2.

**40**  Party membership numbers come from Philippe Robrieux, *Histoire intérieure du Parti Communiste*, vol. 1, *1920–1945* (Paris: Fayard, 1980), 463.

**41**  *L'Avant-Garde*, 11 April 1936, 2.

42 Archives de la Police de Paris, BA 1937, 25 April 1936.

43 P.P. 9 March 1936, AN F7 12964.

44 Fédération des Jeunesses Communistes de France, *En avant pour unir la jeunesse de France* (VIII^e Congrès National, 19–22 March 1936), 29.

45 Ibid., 30.

46 Archives de la Police de Paris BA 1937, 17 April 1936.

47 The lure of the Fourth International proved particularly troublesome for the J.C. in the second half of 1935. Some members were expelled, while others left voluntarily to join the rival International. Such was the perception of the threat that the J.C. published 60,000 anti-Trotskyist tracts in 1935. This figure comes from *Quatre années de luttes pour l'unité: le pain, la paix, la liberté*, VIII^e Congrès National du PCF, 22–25 January 1936, 96.

48 Naïtchenko, *Une jeune fille en guerre*, 99–100.

49 P.P. 16 March 1936, AN F7 12965; Henri Noguères, *La vie quotidienne en France au temps du Front Populaire, 1935–1938* (Paris: Hachette, 1976), 25–26.

50 P.P. 24 March 1936, AN F7 12965.

51 23 March 1936, AN F7 12965.

52 "Le coin des jeunes: les résolutions de la Conférence Nationale des Jeunesses Socialistes," *Le Populaire*, 22 April 1936, 6.

53 "La jeunesse et les élections," *L'Avant-Garde*, 11 April 1936, 4.

54 See for example "La grande manifestation de Toulouse," *Le Populaire*, 12 April 1936, 2.

55 Reynaud, *Jeunesse, quelle France veux-tu?*, 8.

56 *L'Avant-Garde*, 11 April 1936, 4.

57 Naïtchenko, *Une jeune fille en guerre*, 98.

58 *L'Avant-Garde*, 18 April 1936, 4.

59 *L'Humanité*, 24 April 1936, 1–2.

60 Blum, *La jeunesse et le socialisme*, 8.

61 *Le Figaro*, 25 January 1936, 4; *Le Figaro*, 26 January 1936, 4.

62 The J.C.'s set of demands is published as "Élections Législatives 1936: La jeunesse réclame . . . ," *L'Avant-Garde*, 18 April 1936, 4.

63 Although the theme of French support for pacifism runs throughout Eugen Weber's *The Hollow Years: France in the 1930s* (New York: W. W. Norton, 1994), the chapter "A Wilderness Called Peace" deals with it most extensively.

64 Desailly, *Prêtre-ouvrier*, 57.

65 The resolutions from the congress are printed in *L'Avant-Garde*, 7 March 1936, 1.

66 P.P. 19 March 1936, AN 12965.

67 His radio address is printed in full in *Le Populaire*, 22 April 1936, 4.

68 *L'Avant-Garde*, 14 March 1936, 1. See Yves Santamaria, *L'enfant du malheur: le Parti Communiste Français dans la lutte pour la paix (1914–1947)* (Paris: Seli Arslan, 2002), for a historical analysis of the Soviet Union's peace campaign.

69 For more on the origins of this communist-affiliated veterans' association see chapter 1.

**70**  By portraying Hitler with a knife between his teeth, the J.C. inverted the stereo-typical anticommunist image of a menacing Bolshevik.

**71**  *L'Avant-Garde*, 4 April 1936, 1.

**72**  See *L'Humanité*, 6 April 1936, 1–2, for the speeches of Cachin and Thorez.

**73**  The appeal was printed in *L'Avant-Garde*, 28 March 1936, 1.

**74**  11 March 1936, AN F7 12964.

**75**  Ory, *La belle illusion*, 565.

**76**  Ibid., 566. Police reported that one shoot was transformed into a communist rally. P.P. 9 March 1936, AN F7 12964.

**77**  For a discussion of the film's production and distribution see Ory, *La belle illusion*, 564–66. For a discussion of the film in relation to Renoir's oeuvre and French cinema of the 1930s see Dudley Andrew and Steven Ungar, *Popular Front Paris and the Poetics of Culture* (Cambridge: Harvard University Press, 2005), 148–52. Julian Jackson also gives a brief description of the film in *The Popular Front in France: Defending Democracy, 1934–38* (Cambridge: Cambridge University Press, 1988), 140–41.

**78**  Stéphane Courtois and Marc Lazar, *Histoire du Parti Communiste Français* (Paris: Presses Universitaires de France, 1995), 147.

**79**  Ibid., 85.

**80**  For a text of the agreement see Jackson, *The Popular Front in France*, appendix 3.

**81**  See for example Desgranges, *Journal d'un prêtre député*, 34.

**82**  She was first mentioned by *L'Avant-Garde* on 6 June 1936, 2, and subsequently mentioned by Michaut at the victory rally on 14 June 1936 (*L'Avant-Garde*, 20 June 1936, 1).

**83**  *L'Avant-Garde*, 6 June 1936, 1.

**84**  "Victoire!," *L'Avant-Garde*, 6 June 1936, 1.

**85**  *L'Avant-Garde*, 13 June 1936, 2.

**86**  This was reported in *L'Avant-Garde*, 4 July 1936, 1.

**87**  The letter is printed in full in *L'Avant-Garde*, 25 July 1936, 4.

**88**  "Discours: la voix de Paris" (10 June 1936), *1936: Léo Lagrange*, ed. Benigno Cacérès (Paris: Temps Libres, 1980), 8.

**89**  *L'Avant-Garde*, 20 June 1936, 1.

**90**  The first French youth hostel was founded by the progressive Catholic Marc Sangnier in 1930. Soon thereafter Sangnier founded the Ligue Française pour les Auberges de la Jeunesse (LFAJ). In 1933 a secular hostel association, the Centre Laïque des Auberges de la Jeunesse (CLAJ), was established, which was closely associated with the Socialists. Ory, *La belle illusion*, 776–78.

**91**  Ibid., 778–79.

**92**  For more on Lagrange's attitudes toward hostels see Jean-Louis Chappat, *Les chemins de l'espoir ou combats de Léo Lagrange* (Lille: Fédération Léo Lagrange, 1983), chapter 8 ("Jeune Ministre-Ministre des Jeunes").

**93**  Ibid., 277.

**94**  Ibid., 272.

**95** In 1936 the Conseil Général du Bas-Rhin passed a motion demanding that the state assume the organization of the new leisure time, with the debate making specific reference to the Italian and German experiences. Jean-Claude Richez and Léon Strauss, "Revendication et conquête des congés payés en Alsace et en Moselle," *Mouvement social*, no. 150 (January–March 1990), 94.

**96** Quoted in *L'Avant-Garde*, 20 June 1936, 1.

**97** Ellen Furlough points out that the Popular Front's leisure and vacation initiatives were designed to express social democratic ideals in her "Making Mass Vacations: Tourism and Consumer Culture in France, 1930s to 1970s," *Comparative Studies in Society and History* 40, no. 2 (April 1998), 253.

**98** For a good introduction to the program see "Jeunesse de France, l'aviation t'appelle," *L'Avant-Garde*, 27 February 1937, 1.

**99** According to Ory, the sections received between 10,000 and 15,000 francs annually to cover the costs of insurance, material, fuel and mechanics. Ory, *La belle illusion*, 744.

**100** Ibid.

**101** *Revue populaire de l'aviation*, no. 1 (November 1936), 5.

**102** Henri Noguères quotes Laure Moulin saying that Croix de Feu and Cagoulard propaganda had contaminated too large a number of Air Force officers. Noguères, *La vie quotidienne en France au temps du Front Populaire, 1935–1938* (Paris: Hachette, 1976), 168.

**103** *Revue populaire de l'aviation*, October 1937, 6.

**104** Quoted in Noguères, *La vie quotidienne en France au temps du Front Populaire*, 167.

**105** *Revue populaire de l'aviation*, November 1936, 7.

**106** 17 February 1937, AN F7 12966.

**107** *Revue populaire de l'aviation*, December 1936, 9.

**108** See the "Vivent les vacances!" columns in *L'Avant-Garde* on 14 July and 27 July 1936.

**109** "La Côte d'Azur pour 15 Fr. par jour," *L'Avant-Garde*, 15 August 1936, 5.

**110** "Camping," *L'Avant-Garde*, 29 August 1936, 6.

**111** See for example "J'ai fait du ski," *L'Avant-Garde*, 30 January 1937, 5.

**112** "Des vacances qui ne sont pas volées," *Regards*, 13 August 1936, 23.

**113** André Chamson, " . . . Au devant de la vie," *Vendredi*, 21 August 1936, cited in Louis Bodin and Jean Touchard, *Front Populaire: 1936* (Paris: Armand Colin, 1961), 167.

**114** "Rapport sur le travail parmi les jeunes filles communistes," P.P. 30 mars 1936, AN F7 12965.

**115** For more on Casanova's life see the *Dictionnaire biographique du mouvement ouvrier français: le Maitron*, ed. Claude Pennetier (Paris: l'Atelier, 1997 [CD-ROM]), and the hagiographic biography by Pierre Durand, *Danielle Casanova, l'indomptable* (Paris: Messidor, 1991).

**116** She was also, by this point, pregnant by Thorez. For more on Vermeersch's life see the *Dictionnaire biographique du mouvement ouvrier français*, ed. Pennetier, and her interesting if highly selective autobiography *La vie en rouge*.

117 She described her enthusiastic participation in these events in an interview with the author, Paris, 4 December 1990.

118 Jacqueline Tardivel, "Des pacifistes aux résistantes, les militantes communistes, en France, dans l'entre-deux-guerres" (diss., Université de Paris VII, 1993), 54.

119 Interview with author, Paris, 27 November 1990.

120 Interview with author, Paris, 4 December 1990.

121 Interview cited in Jacques Varin, *Jeunes comme JC: sur la jeunesse communiste*, vol. 1, *1920 à 1939* (Paris: Éditions Sociales, 1975), 239.

122 Naïtchenko, *Une jeune fille en guerre*, 105.

123 P.P. 30 mars 1936, AN F7 12965.

124 "Rapport sur le travail parmi les jeunes filles communistes."

125 Juliette Plissonnier explained in an interview that young women were made treasurers because of their habitual role as managers of tight working-class household budgets. Interview with author, Nanterre, 10 December 1990.

126 "Rapport sur le travail parmi les jeunes filles communistes."

127 Yvette Semard recalled that in her U.J.F.F. circle in Paris, mothers supported the organization because it made sure that young women were accompanied as they made their way home from night meetings. Interview with author, Paris, 4 December 1990.

128 *Jeunes filles de France*, December 1937, 14.

129 *Jeunes filles de France*, February 1937, 6.

130 Ibid.

131 See the coverage in *Jeunes filles de France*, July 1936, 4–5.

132 "En visitant les grands magasins en grève à la veille de la victoire," *Jeunes filles de France*, July 1936, 5.

133 "Animées d'une foi inébranlable . . . ," *L'Humanité*, 27 December 1936, 2.

134 Ibid.

135 "Il y a des jeunes filles heureuses . . . ," *Jeunes filles de France*, June 1936, 6.

136 See for example "Aux sports d'hiver," *Jeunes filles de France*, December 1937, 7, and "Pour la promenade aux champs," *Jeunes filles de France*, April 1937, 9. This was not unique to *Jeunes filles de France*. Other communist publications provided similar advice for women. See for example "Mode et costume: costumes d'été et de sport," *Regards*, 2 July 1936, 19.

137 *Jeunes filles de France*, February 1937, 8. The wife of the intellectual Paul Nizan, Henriette Nizan was a journalist who created the women's page at *Vendredi*, an independent literary and political weekly with left leanings. At the behest of Danielle Casanova, who apparently liked Nizan's women's page, she was an occasional contributor to *Jeunes filles de France*. Nizan and Jaubert, *Libres mémoires*, 228–30.

138 "Filles du Ciel," *Jeunes filles de France*, January 1938, 13, 17. In chapter 3 of *France between the Wars*, Siân Reynolds makes provocative comments about the military consequences of this gendered approach to aviation.

139 *Jeunes filles de France*, November 1936, 1.

140 "Jeunes filles de France voici votre Congrès," *L'Avant-Garde*, 26 September 1936, 4.

Notes

141 Duclos, *Pour l'Union des Femmes de France*, 15.

142 Ibid.

143 Ibid., 20.

144 For an introduction to the women's press in interwar France see Evelyne Sullerot, *La presse féminine* (Paris: Armand Colin, 1963), 45–61.

145 See for example "Comment se maquiller," *Jeunes filles de France*, November 1936, 8, and "Sportives et coquettes," *Jeunes filles de France*, July 1937, 5.

146 *Jeunes filles de France*, June 1938, 5.

147 *Jeunes filles de France*, August 1937, 2.

148 "La Chanson de l'Amour," *Jeunes filles de France*, June 1937, 2.

149 "Catherinettes," *Jeunes filles de France*, November 1937, 1.

150 The U.J.F.F. support for heterosexuality was consistent with party approaches to sexuality. As François Delpla has shown, the communist illustrated magazine *Regards* was unambiguous in its condemnation of homosexuality. François Delpla, "Les communistes français et la sexualité (1932–1939)," *Mouvement social*, 1975, 128–29.

151 *Jeunes filles de France*, March 1938, 4.

152 Ibid.

153 *Jeunes filles de France*, May 1938, 6.

154 *Jeunes filles de France*, August 1936, 6.

155 *Jeunes filles de France*, March 1938, 10.

156 Paul Vaillant-Couturier, "Jeunes filles de France!," repr. in *Jeunes filles de France*, November 1937, 4.

157 This was Juliette Plissonier's recollection and explanation for the shift in approaches to femininity signaled by the U.J.F.F. Interview with author, Nanterre, 10 December 1990. The interwar right's depiction of the revolutionary threat in gendered terms was not new. As Gay Gullickson has demonstrated, the dangerous, unruly woman became an international symbol of the Commune and the evils of revolution in nineteenth-century France. Gay Gullickson, "La Pétroleuse: Representing Revolution," *Feminist Studies* 17 (1991), 241–62.

158 "Rapport sur le travail parmi les jeunes filles communistes."

159 Interview with author, Paris, 27 November 1990.

160 See *L'Avant-Garde*, 8 May 1937, for the entire song.

161 *L'Avant-Garde*, 28 March 1936, 1.

162 "Rapport sur le travail parmi les jeunes filles communistes."

163 *Jeunes filles de France*, February 1938, 2.

164 *Jeunes filles de France*, April 1937, 11.

165 Ibid.

166 Although Jackson discusses the demonstrations at various points in his book, he makes this point clearly in appendix 4: Popular Front Paris. Jackson, *The Popular Front in France*, 307–11.

167 *L'Humanité*, 25 May 1936, 7.

168 Jackson, *The Popular Front in France*, 10.

169 *L'Avant-Garde*, 18 July 1936, 1.

1 The pope's concerns about France and French Catholic attitudes are discussed in many sources, including Paul Christophe, *1936: Les Catholiques et le Front Populaire* (Paris: Éditions Ouvrières, 1986) and Catherine Masson, *Le cardinal Liénart, évêque de Lille, 1928–1968* (Paris: Le Cerf, 2001), 203. See as well Desgranges, *Journal d'un prêtre député*, esp. 24.

2 "Le scrutin de ballottage a aggravé la poussée communiste," *La Croix*, 5 May 1936, 1.

3 *Dossiers de l'Action Populaire*, 25 June 1936, 1458.

4 See Christophe, *1936*, 43, for a confidential letter dated 4 March 1936 from Cardinal Maglione to Monsignor Chollet, describing the pope's preoccupation with communist propaganda that had a tendency to "insinuate itself among the ranks of Catholics *and especially among youth*."

5 See for example R. P. Jouet, "Le mirage du socialisme," *Dossiers de l'Action Populaire*, 10 January 1936, 117.

6 "Circulaires diverses aux aumôniers fédéraux 1932 à 1939," ADHS, 44J718C.

7 See for example J. L. Loubet del Bayle, *Les non-conformistes des années 30: une tentative de renouvellement de la pensée politique française* (Paris: Le Seuil, 1969), introduction.

8 See for example the special issue of April 1933 of *La revue française*, "Témoignages sur la jeunesse française."

9 Loubet del Bayle, *Les non-conformistes des années 30*, 59.

10 "Tout est possible à celui qui croit," *Jeunesse Ouvrière*, 1 October 1930, 1.

11 "Les sauveurs que nous voulons être," *Jeunesse Ouvrière*, 1 July 1931, 1.

12 In late 1930 J.O.C. leaders announced that they now aimed to recruit at least 50 percent of the organization's members from young workers between the ages of seventeen and twenty-one. "Recrutement!," *L'équipe ouvrière*, November 1930, 89.

13 "Le problème de la conquête," ADHS 44J251, folder: Conseils Nationaux.

14 "Questionnaire sur les contacts de nos militants," ADHS 44J976 G.

15 Ibid.

16 Berthe, ed., *J.O.C., je te dois tout*, 29, and L. Berne, *Dossiers de l'Action Populaire*, 10 May 1936, 1058.

17 Pierre Pierrard, *Georges Guérin: une vie pour la J.O.C.* (Paris: L'Atelier / Éditions Ouvrières, 1997), 181.

18 Ibid.

19 *Le chômage des jeunes* (Paris: Secrétariat Général de la J.O.C., 1934), ADHS 46J150, 20.

20 Ibid., 20.

21 Ibid., 21–22.

22 ADHS 44J251, folder: 1933.

23 *Jeunesse Ouvrière*, 15 July 1933, 1.

24 ADHS 44J251, Conseils Nationaux: 1933.

Notes

25  See International Labor Conference, 19th Session, *Unemployment among Young Persons* (Geneva: International Labor Office, 1935).

26  Ibid., 72.

27  The program is printed in full in *Jeunesse Ouvrière*, 15 February 1935, 2.

28  *Le jeune chômeur*, June 1933. This supplement was published from the summer of 1932 to the summer of 1933.

29  *Le chômage des jeunes.*

30  Ibid., 8.

31  Ibid., 5 (first page of text).

32  *Jeunesse Ouvrière*, 15 January 1935, 2.

33  ADHS 44J76 G.

34  See for example *Jeunesse Ouvrière*, 15 January 1935, 2.

35  "Témoignage d'André Villette," ADHS 45J7.

36  Descamps, *Militer*, 23.

37  See "La J.O.C. et les mouvements politiques," *L'équipe ouvrière*, 15 July 1928, 8.

38  In one J.O.C. section in traditionally conservative western France, for example, a Jocist later reported being suspended from section meetings in 1936 for complaining that half a dozen of the section's militants were violating J.O.C. statutes by belonging to the far-right Volontaires Nationaux. This incident is described in 1984 in a letter from M. R. Briant, printed in full in Françoise Richou, "La JOC/F dans l'ouest" (diss., Université de Nantes, 1986), 491–92.

39  See for example Loubet del Bayle, *Les non-conformistes des années 30*, 73.

40  Agnès Rochefort-Turquin, *Front Populaire: socialistes parce que Chrétiens* (Paris: Le Cerf, 1986), 32.

41  "À la J.O.C. . . . pas de politique!," *Jeunesse Ouvrière*, 15 February 1934, 1.

42  *Jeunesse Ouvrière*, 16 January 1935, 1–2.

43  *Jeunesse Ouvrière*, 1 March 1935, 2.

44  International Labor Conference, 19th Session, *Unemployment among Young Persons*, supplementary report, 5.

45  Reported in *Jeunesse Ouvrière*, 1 March 1935, 2.

46  See for example "Quand le Bureau International du Travail s'occupe des jeunes chômeurs . . . ," *L'Avant-Garde*, 13 April 1935, 2.

47  Ibid.

48  *Jeunesse Ouvrière*, 1 April 1935, 1.

49  "Nous porterons au BIT les revendications des jeunes chômeurs," *Jeunesse Ouvrière*, 1 March 1935, 1–2.

50  Ibid., 2.

51  Ibid.

52  "La poussée communiste," *La Croix*, 14 May 1935, 1.

53  "La Jeunesse ouvrière chrétienne à Genève," *La Croix*, 9–10 June 1935, 1.

54  "La J.O.C. et le chômage des jeunes: la délégation jociste à Genève," *La Croix*, 31 May 1935, 2.

55  *Unemployment among Young Persons*, 72. France is discussed on pp. 71–73.

**56** "Questionnaires sur les contacts de nos militants," ADHS 44J976 G.

**57** For an interesting discussion of abbé Godin and his experience with the J.O.C. see Émile Poulat, *Naissance des prêtres-ouvriers* (Paris: Casterman, 1965), part 1, chapter 1.

**58** *Jeunesse Ouvrière*, 15 July 1935, 1.

**59** See for example "À toi Jociste, compagnon de misère," *L'Avant-Garde*, 27 July 1935, 3.

**60** See the Ivry parish bulletin from March 1936 extracted in Martine Langignon, "Relations entre communistes et Chrétiens à Ivry entre les deux guerres," unpublished MS, Archives Municipales d'Ivry-sur-Seine, 70.

**61** See for example *L'Avant-Garde*, 1 February 1936, 1.

**62** Ibid.

**63** My discussion of *Terre Nouvelle* draws heavily on Rochefort-Turquin, *Front Populaire*.

**64** A copy of the "Manifeste de 'Terre Nouvelle'" can be found in AN F7 13186.

**65** Ibid.

**66** Quoted in Rochefort-Turquin, *Front Populaire*, 140.

**67** *Jeunesse Ouvrière*, 15 May 1935, 1.

**68** Fernand Bouxom, "Les jeunes et la politique," *Face au nouveau paganisme: journées d'aumôniers jocistes du 19 et 20 juillet 1937* (Paris: Jeunesse Ouvrière), Bibliothèque Historique 435, Archives de la J.O.C., 86–87.

**69** *Jeunesse Ouvrière*, 1 January 1936, 1.

**70** *Jeunesse Ouvrière*, 15 February 1936, 1.

**71** ADHS 44J251, folder: 1933.

**72** ADHS 44J251, folder: 1934

**73** For more on Saint-Chamond see Pierre Pierrard, Michel Launay, and Rolande Trempé, eds., *La J.O.C.: regards d'historiens* (Paris: Éditions Ouvrières, 1984), 63–66.

**74** *La Croix*, 10 April 1936, 4.

**75** Pierrard, Launay, and Trempé, *La J.O.C.: regards d'historiens*, 63.

**76** See for example "Le plan de la C.F.T.C.," *Jeunesse Ouvrière*, 15 February 1936, 1–2.

**77** *La Croix*, 28 April 1936, 1.

**78** "Le scrutin de ballottage a aggravé la poussée communiste," *La Croix*, 5 May 1936, 1.

**79** Desgranges, *Journal d'un prêtre député*, 24.

**80** Ibid.

**81** Ibid., 25.

**82** See for example the coverage in *La Croix* on 5 June 1936, 1.

**83** The text of Verdier's appeal was reprinted in *La Croix*, 9 June 1936, 2, and in Christophe, *1936*, 366–67.

**84** "Vers un ordre nouveau," *La Croix*, 9 June 1936, 1.

**85** Calvet, *Mémoires de Monseigneur Jean Calvet*, 107.

**86** See Julian Jackson, *The Popular Front in France: Defending Democracy, 1934–1938*

Notes

(Cambridge: Cambridge University Press, 1988), 88, for material on the mobile guards.

87 Desgranges, *Journal d'un prêtre député*, 33–34.

88 For a snapshot of the C.F.T.C. in 1936 see Michel Launay, *La C.F.T.C.: origines et développement, 1919–1940* (Paris: La Sorbonne, 1986), 302–3.

89 See Joceline Chabot, *Les débuts du syndicalisme féminin chrétien en France (1899–1944)* (Lyon: Presses Universitaires de Lyon, 2003), for an examination of the Catholic female trade union movement.

90 Launay, *La C.F.T.C.*, 305.

91 Jean-Pierre Coco and Joseph Debès, *L'élan jociste: le dixième anniversaire de la J.O.C., Paris, juillet 1937* (Paris: Éditions Ouvrières, 1989), 20.

92 *Documentation sur les grèves de 1936*, Archives de la J.O.C. I am extremely grateful to Father Jean-Pierre Coco for sharing his copy of this lengthy report with me.

93 Ibid., part 2 ("L'apport de la J.O.C., préliminaire à l'action des jocistes").

94 Ibid.

95 Ibid., part 2 ("Les grèves"), section 14 ("Liberté syndicale").

96 "Une note de l'Action Populaire sur la grève généralisée avec occupation des usines," *Dossiers de l'Action Populaire*, 25 June 1936, 1458.

97 See "Les grèves: un ordre du jour du Conseil National de la J.O.C.," *Jeunesse Ouvrière*, 15 June 1936, 1.

98 Pierrard notes that the "social events" of 1936 marked the first time Guérin intervened "in a significant way" in J.O.C. publications. Pierrard, *Georges Guérin*, 175.

99 See *Documentation sur les grèves de 1936*, part 2 ("Directives aux aumôniers").

100 Ibid.

101 See for example the directive of 6 June sent by Paul Hibout to local leaders in *Documentation sur les grèves de 1936*, part 2 ("Préliminaire à l'action des Jocistes").

102 *Documentation sur les grèves de 1936*, part 1, section 9 ("Moralité").

103 Hibout directive, *Documentation sur les grèves de 1936*, part 2 ("Préliminaire à l'action des jocistes").

104 *La Croix*, 2 July 1936, 1.

105 *Documentation sur les grèves de 1936*, part 2 ("Revendications des jeunes").

106 ADHS 44J252, folder 1937, "La J.O.C. et l'action professionnelle."

107 Pierre Trimouille, "Les syndicats chrétiens dans la métallurgie française de 1935 à 1939," *La France en mouvement, 1934–1938*, ed. Jean Bouvier (Champ Vallon, 1986), 200.

108 Berthe, ed., *J.O.C., je te dois tout*, 123. Jeanne Bayeux-Labbé remembered the situation in almost identical terms: "Il n'y avait pas de syndicat mais spontanément les ouvriers sont venus me chercher pour être déléguée et lancer le syndicat." ADHS 45J442.

109 "Jeunes Chrétiennes," *Jeunes filles de France*, no. 3 (August 1936), ADHS 45J583.

110 Cited in Aubert, *J.O.C., qu'as-tu fait de nos vies?*, 88.

111 Ibid., 89.

**112** Ibid., 87.

**113** "L'Action des militants jocistes," *La Croix*, 2 July 1936, 1.

**114** See for example the story of Émile Leduc in Bard, ed., *Paroles de militants*, 38.

**115** See the foreword to *Documentation sur les grèves de 1936*.

**116** "Le cardinal Verdier publie un communiqué au sujet de la J.O.C.," *La Croix*, 28–29 June 1936, 2.

**117** ADHS 44J252, folder 1937, "La J.O.C. et l'action professionnelle."

**118** Ibid.

**119** ADHS 44J362 B, "Notes documentaires pour les permanents du S.G.: J.O.C. et syndicalisme chrétien."

**120** This is how Bertrand Lemoine describes the fair in Bertrand Lemoine, ed., *Paris 1937: cinquantenaire de l'Exposition Internationale des Arts et des Techniques dans la Vie Moderne* (Paris: Institut Français d'Architecture, 1987), 13.

**121** See Shanny Peer, *France on Display: Peasants, Provincials, and Folklore in the 1937 World's Fair* (Albany: State University of New York Press, 1998), chapter 1, for a good introduction to the fair as an ideological battleground.

**122** Peer, *France on Display*, 50.

**123** Edmond Labbé, *Exposition internationale des arts et techniques dans la vie moderne, Paris 1937, rapport général*, vol. 5, *La section française*, 143–44.

**124** "Pour une jeunesse heureuse: le Centre Kellerman à Paris," *L'Illustration*, 7 May 1938.

**125** See the undated memorandum from Lagrange in AN F12 12219, folder: Brochure sur les Sports à l'Exposition.

**126** Ibid.

**127** AN F12 12218 (5).

**128** "Fête de l'Aviation Populaire," *Revue populaire de l'aviation*, October 1937, 6.

**129** *L'Humanité*, 11 July 1937, 1.

**130** *L'Humanité*, 12 July 1937, 1.

**131** See *L'Humanité*, 13 July 1937, 4, for a description de Guyot's speech.

**132** *L'Avant-Garde*, 26 June 1937, 1.

**133** *L'Humanité*, 13 July 1937, 1.

**134** Paul Tournon, "États pontificaux," *Paris 1937*, ed. Lemoine, 152.

**135** For more on this see stories in *La Croix* on 1 July 1937, 6, and 13 July 1937, 6.

**136** "Le centre principal de la jeunesse," *Vie catholique*, 28 May 1937, AN F12 12140.

**137** See Peer, *France on Display*, 33–40, on "the Popular Front expo."

**138** See Desgranges, *Journal d'un prêtre député*, 95, 100.

**139** Quoted in "Révolutionnaires?," *La Croix*, 7 July 1937, 2.

**140** Bouxom, "Les jeunes et la politique," 86–89.

**141** These preparations are discussed in a letter dated 17 August 1986 from Alice Walter to Father Coco. Private collection of Father Coco.

**142** *Atheistic Communism: Encyclical Letter (Divini Redemptoris) of His Holiness, Pope Pius XI* (Vatican Press translation), issued 19 March 1937 (Washington: National Catholic Welfare Conference, 1937).

**143** Ibid, 46.

Notes

144 "Avant le Congrès du X^e anniversaire de la J.O.C.," Archives Centrales de la   **299**
J.O.C.

145 According to Father Berne, "Chaque jociste en vue de Congrès a dû faire une promesse précise." Louis Berne, *Études*, August 1937, 747, cited in Coco and Debès, *L'élan jociste*, 57 n. 5.

146 "Promesses pour le Congrès Jubilaire de 1937," ADHS 45J430.

147 See the cover of Coco and Debès, *L'élan jociste*, for a facsimile of the Congress poster.

148 *Vie Catholique*, "Numéro Spécial pour le X^e anniversaire de la J.O.C.," 5, ADHS 45J430.

149 See the extract from *Jeunesse Ouvrière* published in Coco and Debès, *L'élan jociste*, 58.

150 See the account provided in *Congrès Régional de la J.O.C.*, Lille: 20 septembre 1936.

151 Ibid., 46.

152 Peer, *France on Display*, 37.

153 AN F12 12139, folder: Hébergement.

154 *Manuel du Congressiste*, 42, ADHS 45J430.

155 Ibid., 25.

156 "Le Congrès jubilaire de la J.O.C.," *La Croix*, 17 July 1937, 2.

157 The resolution is printed in full in Coco and Debès, *L'élan jociste*, 66–67.

158 "Le Congrès jubilaire de la J.O.C.," *La Croix*, 17 July 1937, 2.

159 "Le Congrès jubilaire de la J.O.C.," *La Croix*, 18 July 1937, 2.

160 My discussion of the night's events draws heavily on the analysis in Coco and Debès, *L'élan jociste*, 88–97. Ordained priests, both Coco and Debès were involved with Catholic Action movements in the Paris suburb of Saint-Denis in the 1980s.

161 Photographs of these can be found in the Congress's Souvenir Album.

162 Catholics were not alone in celebrating artisans at the fair. As Peer points out, artisans had their own center at the fair, which included displays of artisanal products and twenty-two model home workshops. See Peer, *France on Display*, 44. Artisanal products also figured prominently in regional pavilions.

163 Coco and Debès, *L'élan jociste*, 92.

164 *Jocistes dans la tourmente: histoire des jocistes (JOC-JOCF) de la région parisienne, 1937–1947* (Paris: Témoignage Chrétien / Éditions Ouvrières, n.d.), 36.

165 See *La Croix*, 11–12 July 1937, 1, for a text of the pope's letter.

166 Verdier's speech is printed in *La Croix*, 20 July 1937, 1.

167 See Coco and Debès, *L'élan jociste*, for a more extensive description.

168 See for example the recollections collected in ADHS 45J443.

169 "Propositions de texte" prepared by Marie Grasser for abbé Coco. Private collection of Father Coco.

170 Berthe, ed., *J.O.C., je te dois tout*, 78.

171 *Manuel du Congressiste*, ADHS 45J430.

172 "Le Congrès Jociste," *La Croix*, 22 July 1937, 4.

**300**

173 For a selection of Congress press coverage see ADHS 45J430, folder: Coupures de presse.

174 *Paris-Soir*, 20 July 1937, cited in Coco and Debès, *L'élan jociste*, 169.

175 "Le 10ᵉ anniversaire de la J.O.C.," *Paris-Soir*, 19 July 1937, 5.

176 *L'Intransigeant*, 19 July 1937, cited in Coco and Debès, *L'élan jociste*, 169.

177 Cited in *La Croix*, 20 July 1937, 5.

178 *Le Matin*, 19 July 1937, in ADHS 45J430, folder: Coupures de presse.

179 See Baudrillart, *Les carnets du cardinal Baudrillart*, 551, for a discussion of Catholic responses to the honors that the government was planning to accord to Cardinal Pacelli.

180 Henry Daniel-Rops, *L'église des révolutions: un combat pour Dieu, 1870–1939* (Paris: Fayard, 1963), 488–89.

181 ADHS 44J251, folder: 1938.

### Conclusion

1 For these figures see Sarah Fishman, *We Will Wait: Wives of French Prisoners of War, 1940–1945* (New Haven: Yale University Press, 1991), xii.

2 Vichy policies toward youth have received considerable attention from historians. See, most prominently, W. D. Halls, *The Youth of Vichy France* (Oxford: Clarendon, 1981); Pierre Giolitto, *Histoire de la jeunesse sous Vichy* (Paris: Perrin, 1991); and John Hellman, *The Knight-Monks of Vichy France: Uriage, 1940–1945* (Montreal: McGill-Queen's University Press, 1993).

3 For a discussion of Vichy approaches to girls' education see Miranda Pollard, *Reign of Virtue: Mobilizing Gender in Vichy France* (Chicago: University of Chicago Press, 1998), chapter 3.

4 Stéphane Courtois and Marc Lazar, *Histoire du Parti Communiste Français* (Paris: Presses Universitaires de France, 1995), 168.

5 The point about 1941 is made in Jean-Pierre Azéma, Antoine Prost, and Jean-Pierre Rioux, eds., *Le Parti Communiste Français des années sombres, 1938–1941* (Paris: Le Seuil, 1986), 110.

6 "Fanny Ladsky," *Dictionnaire biographique du mouvement ouvrier français: le Maitron*, ed. Claude Pennetier (Paris: l'Atelier, 1997 [CD-ROM]).

7 Paula Schwartz has argued that many women engaged in Resistance activities in ways that were an extension of traditional feminine roles in the home and workplace. See Paula Schwartz, "Redefining Resistance: Women's Activism in Wartime France," *Behind the Lines: Gender and the Two World Wars*, ed. Margaret Higonnet et al. (New Haven: Yale University Press, 1987), 147.

8 For more on the activities of leading U.J.F.F. militants during the Second World War see Jacqueline Tardivel, "Des pacifistes aux résistantes, les militantes communistes, en France, dans l'entre-deux-guerres" (diss., Université de Paris VII, 1993); Josette Cothias-Dumeix, "La participation des femmes à la vie sociale et politique (1935–1945)" (thesis, Université de Paris VII, 1987), 11–15; and entries in the CD-ROM version of *Dictionnaire biographique du mouvement ouvrier français*, ed. Pennetier.

Notes

9 See for example the letter of 1 July 1943 contained in ADHS 44J155, folder: "Témoignages d'équipes, 1943–44."

10 Letter of 5 July 1942, ADHS 44J155, folder: "Témoignages d'équipes, 1943–44."

11 ADHS 44J251, Conseils Nationaux, folder: 1940, zone sud.

12 As John Hellman argues, however, the J.O.C. was not alone among prewar Catholic youth movements in having thematic similarities with Vichy's National Revolution. See Hellman, *The Knight-Monks of Vichy France*, 5–6.

13 AHDS 44J18C.

14 "Paul Hibout," *Dictionnaire biographique du mouvement ouvrier français*, ed. Pennetier.

15 Hellman, *The Knight-Monks of Vichy France*, 25.

16 For more on the S.T.O. see Halls, *The Youth of Vichy France*, chapter 14 ("Youth and Forced Labour in Germany"), and H. R. Kedward, *In Search of the Maquis: Rural Resistance in Southern France 1942–1944* (Oxford: Clarendon, 1993), esp. chapter 2.

17 See for example John F. Sweets, *Choices in Vichy France: The French under Nazi Occupation* (New York: Oxford University Press, 1986, 1994), 24–25.

18 This is quoted in "La vrai pensée de S. Em. le cardinal Liénart au sujet du travail obligatoire," ADHS 44J155, folder: "Lettres des évêques, 1943."

19 Ibid.

20 Ibid.

21 See "Résolutions prises aux récollections de militants," ADHS 44J155, folder: "Organiser les départs."

22 E. Belouet, "Lucien Croci," *Dictionnaire biographique du mouvement ouvrier français*, ed. Pennetier.

23 Pierre Pierrard, Michelle Launay, and Rolande Trempé, eds., *La J.O.C.: regards d'historiens* (Paris: Éditions Ouvrières, 1984), 87.

24 Halls, *The Youth of Vichy France*, 379.

25 Henry Rousso comments briefly on the Communists' postwar use of their Resistance past in his *The Vichy Syndrome: History and Memory in France since 1944*, trans. Arthur Goldhammer (Cambridge: Harvard University Press, 1991), 299.

# Bibliography of Primary Sources

## Archives
*Archives Nationales*
Series F1 13983
Series F7 12964–66, 13028, 13137, 13148, 13156, 13181–86, 13935
Series F12 12135, 12139–40, 12147, 12211, 12218 19, 12223, 12325

*Institut Français d'Histoire Sociale*
14AS175, 14ASAM231, 14ASAM 249

*Archives Départementales des Hauts-de-Seine*
Series J: Fonds de la Jeunesse Ouvrière Chrétienne et de la Jeunesse Ouvrière
    Chrétienne Féminine 44J155, 44J976, 45J6, 45J251, 45J278, 45J367, 45J430, 45J442
    (témoignages), 45J443 (témoignages), 45J518, 45J583–4, 46J150

*Archives de la Guerre, Vincennes*
5N 601–4, 5N 602 (dossier 1), 7N 4033 (dossier 2), 7N 4034 (dossier 1)

*Archives Centrales de la J.O.C., J.O.C. / F. Headquarters, Courbevoie*
Speeches, pamphlets, bulletins, and directives contained in the Bibliothèque His-
    torique. This material has since been transferred to the Archives Départemen-
    tales des Hauts-de-Seine and reclassified.

*Archives de la Préfecture de Police, Paris*
BA 1860, BA 1862, BA 1867, BA 1937

*Archives Départementales du Nord*
M 154/121, M 154/223–24

*Bibliothèque Marxiste de Paris*
Brb 1441, Brb 4824, Brb 2738, Brb 4600
Fonds de l'Institut Marxiste-Léniniste 744, 745, 746, 747, 749

*Hoover Institution Archives*
Henri Barbé, "Souvenirs de militant et de dirigeant communiste" [typescript]
Albert Vassart, "Memoirs" [typescript]

*Archives Municipales d'Ivry-sur-Seine*
Marcelle Boutot, "Témoignage enregistré"
Martine Langignan, "Relations entre communistes et Chrétiens à Ivry entre les
  deux guerres" [unpublished manuscript]

## Official Publications

International Labour Conference, 19th session, *Unemployment among Young Persons*
  (Geneva: International Labour Office, 1935).
*Journal officiel de la République Française, Débats parlementaires, Chambre des Députés*,
  1919, 1924, 1934–39.
Edmond Labbé, *Exposition internationale des arts et techniques dans la vie
  moderne, Paris 1937, rapport général* (Paris: Imprimerie Nationale, 1938–40), vols.
  4, 5, 7, 11.

## Newspapers and Periodicals

*L'Avant-Garde* (1920–38)
*Bulletin des dirigeantes fédérales de la J.O.C.F.* (September 1934 to 1938)
*Clarté* (1919–22)
*La Croix* (1935–37)
*Dossiers de l'Action Populaire* (1936–37)
*L'équipe ouvrière: bulletin mensuel des militants de la J.O.C.* (1927–32)
*L'équipe ouvrière féminine* (1928–39)
*Le Figaro* (1936)
*L'Humanité* (1919–24, 1929, 1933–37)
*Jeunes filles de France* (June 1936 to 1938)
*La Jeunesse Ouvrière* (1927–39)
*La Jeunesse Ouvrière Féminine* (1928–36)
*L'Illustration* (1937–38)
*Le Populaire* (1934–36)
*Regards* (1936–37)
*Revue de la paroisse et des oeuvres d'Ivry-sur-Seine* (September–October 1936 to January 1938)
*La revue française*, April 1933 [special issue: "Témoignages sur la jeunesse française"]
*Revue populaire de l'aviation* (November 1936 to 1937)
*Le Temps* (1936)

## Interviews

Jeanne Aubert. Paris, 23 November 1990.
Juliette Plissonier. Nanterre, 10 December 1990.

Bibliography of Primary Sources

Yvette Semard. Paris, 4 December 1990.
Marie-Claude Vaillant-Couturier. Paris, 27 November 1990.

## Selected Books and Pamphlets

Alix, Roland. *La nouvelle jeunesse: enquête auprès des jeunes gens d'aujourd'hui*. Paris: Valois, 1930.

*L'appel de la J.O.C.* Paris: Jeunesse Ouvrière, 1931.

Blum, Léon. *La jeunesse et le socialisme*. Conférence prononcée le 30 juin 1934 à la Maison de la Mutualité. Paris: Librairie Populaire, 1936.

Cachin, Marcel. *Jeunesse, progrès et avenir*. Discours prononcé au Comité Central des J.C. de France, 1ᵉʳ mars 1935. Paris: Jeunesse Communiste.

Duclos, Jacques. *Pour l'Union des Femmes de France*. Rapport prononcé le 11 juillet à la Conférence Nationale du Parti Communiste Français. Paris: Comité Populaire du Propagande, 1936.

*L'essentiel pour commencer la J.O.C.* Paris: Éditions Jocistes, n.d.

Ferrat, André. *Faisons vivre nos cellules! Petit guide pratique pour les adhérents de la J.C.* Paris: L'Humanité, 1925.

Guyot, Raymond. *La jeunesse à l'assaut du vieux monde*. Rapport présenté au VIIIᵉ Congrès de la Fédération des J.C. de France, Marseille, 18–22 mars 1936. Marseille: Imprimerie Spéciale du P.C.

Lhande, Pierre. *Le Christ dans la banlieue: enquête sur la vie religieuse dans les milieux ouvriers de la banlieue de Paris*. Paris: Plon, 1927.

Lhotte, Céline, and Elisabeth Dupeyrat. *Révélations sur la santé des jeunes travailleuses*. Paris: Spes, 1936.

Reynaud, Paul. *Jeunesse, quelle France veux-tu?* Paris: Gallimard, 1936.

Taittinger, Paul. *Les cahiers de la Jeune France*. Paris: Le National, 1926.

## Autobiographies, Journals, and Published Recollections

Aubert, Jeanne. *J.O.C., qu'as-tu fait des nos vies? La jeunesse ouvrière chrétienne féminine, 1928–1945*. Paris: Éditions Ouvrières, 1990.

Bard, Christine, ed. *Paroles de militants: témoignages de syndicalistes C.F.T.C./C.F.D.T. du Nord–Pas-de-Calais, 1925–1985*. Lille: Association 1884–1984, 1990.

Baudrillart, Alfred. *Les carnets du cardinal Baudrillart (20 novembre 1935–11 avril 1939)*. Paris: Le Cerf, 1996.

Bêjot, Georges. *Un évêque à l'école de la J.O.C. (entretiens avec Étienne Gau)*. Paris: Éditions Ouvrières, 1978.

Berthe, Léon-Noël, ed. *J.O.C., je te dois tout*. Paris: Éditions Ouvrières, 1978.

Bruhat, Jean. *Il n'est jamais trop tard*. Paris: Albin Michel, 1983.

Calvet, Jean. *Mémoires de Monseigneur Jean Calvet*. Lyon: Le Chalet, 1967.

Cliquet, Maurice. *Sillons: 50 ans d'action pour la justice sociale*. Paris: Témoignage Chrétien, 1984.

Congar, L'Enfant Yves. *Journal de guerre, 1914–1918*. Présenté par Stéphane Audoin-Rouzeau et Dominique Congar. Paris: Le Cerf, 1997.

Desailly, Jean. *Prêtre-ouvrier: mission de Paris, 1946–1954*. Paris: L'Harmattan, 1997.

Descamps, Eugène. *Militer: une vie pour un engagement collectif*. Paris: Fayard, 1971.

Desgranges, Jean-Marie. *Journal d'un prêtre député, 1936–1940*. Paris: La Palatine, 1960.

Figuères, Léo. *Jeunesse militante: chronique d'un jeune communiste des années 30–50*. Paris: Éditions Sociales, 1971.

Jamet, Claude. *Notre Front Populaire: journal d'un militant (1934–1939)*. Paris: Table Ronde, 1977.

London, Lise. *Le printemps des camarades*. Paris: Le Seuil, 1996.

Michaud, René. *J'avais vingt ans: un jeune ouvrier au début du siècle*. Paris: Éditions Syndicalistes, 1967.

Naïtchenko, Maroussia. *Une jeune fille en guerre: la lutte antifasciste d'une génération*. Paris: Imago, 2003.

Nizan, Henriette, and Marie-José Jaubert. *Libres mémoires*. Paris: Robert Laffont, 1989.

Ouzoulias-Romagon, Cécile. *J'étais agent de liaison des F.T.P.F.* Paris: Messidor, 1988.

Peschanski, Denis, ed. *Marcel Cachin, carnets 1906–1947*, vol. 4, *1935–1947*. Paris: CNRS, 1997.

Thorez-Vermeersch, Jeannette. *La vie en rouge: mémoires*. Paris: Belfond, 1998.

Véret, Charles. *J'ai vu grandir la J.O.C.: témoignage d'un aumônier jociste*. Paris: Éditions Ouvrières, 1977.

# Index

Page numbers in *italics* refer to illustrations.

Susan B. Whitney  is associate professor of history and associate dean of the Faculty of Arts and Social Sciences at Carleton University.

*Library of Congress Cataloging-in-Publication Data*
Whitney, Susan B., 1962–
Mobilizing youth : communists and Catholics in
interwar France / Susan B. Whitney.
p. cm.   Includes bibliographical references and index.
ISBN 978-0-8223-4595-4 (cloth : alk. paper)
ISBN 978-0-8223-4613-5 (pbk. : alk. paper)
1. Jeunesse ouvrière chrétienne (France). 2. Jeunesse ouvrière chrétienne féminine (France).
3. Front populaire. 4. Communism and Christianity—Catholic Church—
History—20th century. 5. Communism and Christianity—France—History—
20th century. 6. Church work with youth—Catholic Church—History—20th century.
7. Church work with youth—France—History—20th century.
I. Title. BX1396.4.W46 2009   323'.04208350944—dc22
2009012704